WOMEN'S ROMANTIC THEATRE AND DRAMA

In Memory of Olga English and Lucie English Zivengwa

Women's Romantic Theatre and Drama

History, Agency, and Performativity

Edited by

LILLA MARIA CRISAFULLI
University of Bologna, Italy

and

KEIR ELAM
University of Bologna, Italy

Routledge
Taylor & Francis Group

LONDON AND NEW YORK

First published 2010 by Ashgate Publishing

2 Park Square, Milton Park, Abingdon, Oxon OX14 4RN
711 Third Avenue, New York, NY 10017, USA

Routledge is an imprint of the Taylor & Francis Group, an informa business

First issued in paperback 2016

British Library Cataloguing in Publication Data
Women's Romantic Theatre and Drama: History, Agency, and Performativity.
1. Romanticism – Great Britain. 2. English drama – 18th century – History and criticism. 3. English drama – 19th century – History and criticism. 4. English drama – Women authors – History and criticism. 5. Women in the theater – Great Britain – History – 18th century. 6. Women in the theater – Great Britain – History – 19th century. 7. Theater – Great Britain – History – 18th century. 8. Theater – Great Britain – History – 19th century. I. Crisafulli, Lilla Maria. II. Elam, Keir.
792'.082'09033–dc22

Library of Congress Cataloging-in-Publication Data
Women's Romantic Theatre and Drama: History, Agency, and Performativity / [edited by] Lilla Maria Crisafulli and Keir Elam.
    p.   cm.
Includes bibliographical references and index.
1. English drama – Women authors – History and criticism. 2. Women and literature – Great Britain – History – 18th century. 3. Women and literature – Great Britain – History – 19th century. 4. Women in the theater – Great Britain – History – 18th century. 5. Women in the theater – Great Britain – History – 19th century. 6. English drama – 18th century – History and criticism. 7. English drama – 19th century – History and criticism. 8. Theater – Great Britain – History – 18th century. 9. Theater – Great Britain – History – 19th century. 10. Romanticism – Great Britain. I. Crisafulli, Lilla Maria. II. Elam, Keir.
PR719.W66W66 2010
822'.8099282–dc22   2009035476

ISBN 978-0-7546-5577-0 (hbk)
ISBN 978-1-138-26513-4 (pbk)

Contents

List of Figures

Notes on Contributors

Gioia Angeletti teaches English and Anglophone Literatures at the University of Parma. She is the author of the volumes *Eccentric Scotland: Three Victorian Poets. James Thomson ('B. V.'), John Davidson and James Young Geddes* and *Teorie target-oriented della traduzione poetica: trans-creazione e riscrittura dell'alterità*, as well as numerous essays on British poetry and theatre in the Romantic and Victorian periods. She has an interest in contemporary Scottish women playwrights, and has just completed a co-authored volume on Joan Ure. She is presently editing a collection of essays under the title of *Liberation and Freedom: Romantic Drama and Theatre in Britain*, and completing a book with the provisional title *The Discourse of Otherness: Essays on Byron*.

Serena Baiesi is research fellow in English Literature at the University of Bologna. She holds a PhD in Literatures and Cultures of the English Speaking Countries. She has published a volume on colonial women writers in Australia (*Pioniere in Australia: diari, lettere e memoriali del periodo coloniale, 1770-1850*), and articles on colonial and postcolonial literature. She has edited a special issue of the interdisciplinary journal *La Questione Romantica* on colonialism and imperialism (2008). Her research in the field of English Romantic literature has particular reference to Letitia Elizabeth Landon, Jane Austen and Maria Edeworth, together with historical drama by women playwrights.

Catherine Burroughs is Ruth and Albert Koch Professor of English at Wells College and Visiting Professor of English at Cornell University. In addition to her many articles on British Romantic theatre and drama, her publications include: *Reading the Social Body*; *Closet Stages: Joanna Baillie and the Theater Theory of British Romantic Women Writers*; and *Women in British Romantic Theatre: Drama, Performance and Society, 1790–1840*. Her co-edited book for MLA's Options for Teaching Series –*Approaches to Teaching Early British Women Playwrights* – is forthcoming. She is also a member of the Actors' Equity Association.

Claudia Corti is Professor of English Literature and History of the English Theatre at the University of Florence. Her research fields include relations between literature and the visual arts, aesthetic theories, and sixteenth- to twentieth-century drama. She has written extensively on Romantic poetry and art, Shakespeare and his contemporaries, Modernism, and fantasy literature. Her publications include the volumes *Prospettive joyciane*; *Sul discorso fantastico: La narrazione nel romanzo gotico*; *Shakespeare illustrato*; *Silenos: Erasmus in Elizabethan Literature*; *Rivoluzione e Rivelazione*; *William Blake tra profeti,* *radicali e giacobini*; *Stupende fantasie: Saggi su William Blake*; *Shakespeare e gli emblemi*; *Poesia come pittura nel Romanticismo inglese*; and *'Esuli': dramma, psicodramma, metadramma*. She is co-editor of the journal *Rivista di Letterature Moderne e Comparate*, and a member of the Accademia di Scienze e Lettere 'La Colombaria'.

Lilla Maria Crisafulli is Professor of English Literature in the Faculty of Modern Languages and Literatures, University of Bologna. She is the director of the Interuniversity Centre for the Study of Romanticism, editor of the interdisciplinary journal *La Questione Romantica* [*The Romantic Question*], and member of the editorial board of international literary journals. She has written extensively on English Romanticism and on cultural relations between Italy and Great Britain. Her volumes include *La realtà del desiderio: saggi morali, teoria estetica e prosa politica di P. B. Shelley*; *La rivoluzione francese in Inghilterra*; *Shelley e l'Italia*; and *Antologia delle poetesse romantiche inglesi* (an anthology in two volumes). With Cecilia Pietropoli she has edited *The Languages of Performance in British Romanticism*, and with Keir Elam the translation into Italian and critical edition of Mary Shelley's *Valperga*.

Franca Dellarosa teaches English Literature at the University of Bari. Her publications include *Drama on the Air* (a monograph on British 006), and the newly completed monograph study *Slavery on Stage: Representations of Slavery in British Theatre, 1760s–1830s*, as well as articles on eighteenth-century and Romantic studies, contemporary literature and cultural mediation. She is presently editing a collection of international essays entitled *Slavery: Histories, Fictions, Memory, 1760–2007*, and preparing a volume on Liverpool abolitionist poet Edward Rushton. She is also working on an edition, with translation, of George Eliot's selected non-fiction prose.

Keir Elam is Professor of English Literature in the Faculty of Arts and Head of the Department of Modern Languages of the University of Bologna. Educated at University College London, UCLA and Yale, he has published several volumes, including *Semiotics of Theatre and Drama*, *Shakespeare's Universe of Discourse*, and the Arden *Twelfth Night* (3rd series), as well as numerous articles on Shakespeare and early modern drama, Beckett and contemporary European theatre. He is also general editor of the bilingual Shakespeare series for Rizzoli, and with Lilla Maria Crisafulli he published the translation into Italian and critical edition of Mary Shelley's *Valperga*.

Isabella Imperiali teaches English Literature at the University of Rome 'La Sapienza'. Her research is centred primarily on the history of British theatre. Her publications include *La lezione shakespeariana di Peter Brook*, *Shakespeare al cinema*, and, together with Agostino Lombardo, *Storia del teatro inglese – Dal Medioevo al rinascimento*. In the field of romantic drama, she has published the volume *Le passioni della mente nel teatro di Joanna Baillie*. She has also directed a stage production of Baillie's *De Monfort*.

Gary Kelly is Distinguished University Professor in the Comparative Literature Program and the Department of English and Film Studies, University of Alberta, Canada. He has published books and essays on British Romantic fiction and on British women writers of Revolution and Romanticism, and has edited poetry and fiction by women writers in addition to documents and fiction of crime and punishment from the 1780s to the 1830s. He is general editor of the forthcoming Oxford History of Popular Print Culture; directs the Streetprint database program; and is presently researching topics in popular Romanticism, Romantic apocalyptic literature, and women's learning in Romantic Britain.

Greg Kucich is Professor of English, University of Notre Dame. His areas of research include British Romanticism, historiography, theatre studies, and women's writing. His publications include *Keats, Shelley and Romantic Spenserianism*. He has co-edited (with Jeffrey Cox) two volumes of the Pickering and Chatto *Selected Writings of Leigh Hunt*, and he has co-edited (with Keith Hanley) a collection of articles, *Nineteenth-Century Worlds: Global Formations Past and Present* (2008). His recent publications include articles on the Keats–Hunt Circle, Romanticism and historiography, and Romantic era theatre. He is currently writing a monograph on Romanticism and the politics of women's historical writing. He is co-editor of *Nineteenth-Century Contexts: An Interdisciplinary Journal*.

Stefania Magnoni graduated in English Language and Literature at the University of Pisa, where she also took her PhD with a dissertation on the eighteenth- and nineteenth-century adaptations of Shakespeare's *A Midsummer Night's Dream*. Her publications include an article on John Philip Kemble's adaptation of *Antony and Cleopatra*, a book chapter on John Philip Kemble's *Coriolanus*, and a book chapter on Joseph Swetnam and the identity of Early Modern Woman.

Vita Mastrosilvestri received her PhD in Translation Studies in 2009. Her current research interests include Legal Translation in the field of International Law. She has recently worked on the creation of a database on the influence of Italian theatre in Britain from 1771 to 1800, as part of the National Research Project *An Italian in London: The presence of Italian authors, actors and characters on the British stage*.

Jane Moody is Professor in the Department of English and Related Literature at the University of York. She is the author of *Illegitimate Theatre in London, 1770–1840* and has co-edited *Celebrity and British Theatre, 1660–2000* and *The Cambridge Companion to British Theatre, 1730-1830*. Her essays include 'Illusions of Authorship', in Tracy C. Davis and Ellen Donkin (eds), *Nineteenth Century British Women Playwrights*; 'Dictating to the Empire: Performance and Theatrical

Geography in Eighteenth Century Britain', in the *Cambridge Companion*; 'Stolen Identities: Character, Mimicry and the Invention of Samuel Foote', in *Theatre and Celebrity*; and 'The Drama of Capital: Risk, Belief and Liability on the Victorian Stage', in Francis O'Gorman (ed.), *Victorian Literature and Finance*. She is currently completing a book on censorship in the Romantic period.

Cecilia Pietropoli is a former associate professor of English Literature at the University of Bologna. She is the author of the volumes *I tipi del comico nel teatro ciclico inglese*, *Havelok il Danese*, and *Il teatro dei Miracoli e delle Moralità*. She has published extensively on the Romantic reception of the Middle Ages, in particular on Scott's historical fiction and on Romantic poetry, and has edited a special issue of *La questione Romantica* dedicated to *Romanticismo/Medievalismo*. She has also worked on and published Romantic theatre and drama. She is co-editor, with Lilla Maria Crisafulli, of *Romantic Women Poets: Genre and Gender* and *The Languages of Performance in British Romanticism*.

Diego Saglia teaches British literature and culture at the University of Parma (Italy). His research focuses mainly on the Romantic period. He is the author of *Poetic Castles in Spain: British Romanticism and Figurations of Iberia* and *Lord Byron e le maschere della scrittura*, and is co-editor of *British Romanticism and Italian Literature: Translating, Reviewing, Rewriting* (with Laura Bandiera). His essays have appeared in *Textual Practice*, *Studies in Romanticism*, *La questione romantica*, The *Keats–Shelley Journal*, *Nineteenth-Century Contexts*, *ELH*, *Studies in the Novel*, *Philological Quarterly*, *ELN*, and other international journals. He is currently working on the first critical edition of Robert Southey's *Roderick, the Last of the Goths*.

Introduction

Lilla Maria Crisafulli and Keir Elam

1. 'A blank': From Shakespeare's Sister to Byron's Half-sister

In her celebrated reflections on that historical oxymoron, the woman dramatist, Virginia Woolf gives Shakespeare a fictional younger sister, Judith,[1] whom she imagines as an aspiring playwright, endowed with the same gifts as her brother and determined to follow in his footsteps. Like William, Judith sets off full of great expectations for London, only to encounter not the fame and success she had aspired to (and that William had emphatically achieved) but merely – owing to her sex – hostility, madness and probable death:

> This [story] may be true or it may be false – who can say? – but what is true in it, so it seemed to me, reviewing the story of Shakespeare's sister as I had made it, is that any woman born with a great gift in the sixteenth century would certainly have gone crazed, shot herself, or ended her days in some lonely cottage outside the village, half witch, half wizard, feared and mocked at. … No girl could have walked to London and stood at a stage door and forced her way into the presence of actor-managers without doing herself a violence ….[2]

Woolf's tragical history of the Elizabethan female dramatist in *A Room of One's Own* thus turns out to be a tragical non-history – a history that never came about – and as such recalls Viola's story of her fictional sister in *Twelfth Night*, similarly doomed to misery and possible death:

> ORSINO: And what's her history?
> VIOLA: A blank, my lord. …
>   She pined in thought,
> And with a green and yellow melancholy
> She sat like Patience on a monument,
> Smiling at grief. (2.4.109–15)[3]

---

[1]   It is not a fiction that Shakespeare had a younger sister who survived infancy, but her name was Joan; Judith was instead the name of his daughter. As far as we know, neither wrote plays.

[2]   Virginia Woolf, *A Room of One's Own* (1929), in *A Room of One's Own and Three Guineas* (London, 1984), pp. 46–7.

[3]   William Shakespeare, *Twelfth Night*, ed. Keir Elam (London, 2008).

Judith's history, like that of Viola's sister, is a 'blank', partly because it remains a mere fiction, never actually taking place, but also because, unlike its male equivalent, the putative early modern female drama produces no copy,[4] only blank pages and empty shelves. In any case, observes Woolf, a hypothetical Elizabethan woman's play would have been destined for anonymity or pseudonymity, thereby blanking out the author's identity and agency:

> And undoubtedly, I thought, looking at the shelf where there are no plays by women, her work would have gone unsigned. That refuge she would have sought certainly. It was the relic of the sense of chastity that dictated anonymity to women even so late as the nineteenth century. Currer Bell, George Eliot, George Sand, all the victims of inner strife as their writings prove, sought ineffectively to veil themselves by using the name of a man. Thus they did homage to the convention, which if not implanted by the other sex was liberally encouraged by them (the chief glory of a woman is not to be talked of, said Pericles, himself a much talked-of man), that publicity in women is detestable. Anonymity runs in their blood. The desire to be veiled still possesses them.[5]

Had Virginia Woolf set her biographical fiction two centuries later, at the beginning of the nineteenth century, the plot would have been a good deal less tragic, although perhaps still not blessed with a resoundingly happy ending. If, instead of Shakespeare's fictional younger sister Judith, the story had regarded, say, Byron's real-life elder half-sister Augusta, the circumstances would have been quite different (and not merely because, as far as we know, Shakespeare did not entertain incestuous relations with his siblings). First, Byron's own success with plays like *The Two Foscari* was quite un-Shakespearian in its modest dimensions and in its literary rather than theatrical character. More significantly, had Augusta chosen to follow her half-brother in publishing plays, or even submitting them for performance, she would not have been alone: she could have appealed to important precedents in Hannah Cowley, Joanna Baillie, Elizabeth Inchbald and others (not to mention earlier pioneers such as Aphra Behn). Although Augusta chose not to try her luck on the stage, other women of the period chose differently: indeed, a female playwright literally followed Byron in writing a Foscari play – in this case, not Augusta Leigh but Mary Russell Mitford (*Foscari*, 1826).[6] If Augusta Leigh's

---

4　　Compare Viola again, upbraiding Olivia: 'Lady, you are the cruell'st she alive / If you will lead these graces to the grave / And leave the world no copy' (1.5.233–5).

5　　Woolf, *A Room of One's Own*, p. 47.

6　　Mitford actually composed her *Foscari* prior to the publication of Byron's play and therefore quite independently of it: indeed, by an unfortunate coincidence, as her biographer Vera Watson notes, 'on the day it was sent to the management of Covent Garden, Lord Byron published his tragedy on the same subject' – Vera Watson, *Mary Russell Mitford* (London, 1949), p. 147; see Cecilia Pietropoli, 'The Story of the Foscaris, a Drama for Two

dramatic career is a fiction, it is no longer a historically necessary or socially imposed fiction.

The history of Romantic drama by women is by no means a 'blank', therefore. Byron himself testifies to the sheer number of playscripts by women brought to his attention in his capacity as member of the management subcommittee and reader of scripts for the Drury Lane theatre:

> Then the Scenes I had to go through! – the authors – and the authoresses – the Milliners – the wild Irishmen –[7]

Nor could Romantic period women's drama – as Byron's complaint about 'the authoresses' suggests – be dismissed as a minor or marginal phenomenon. According to the data gathered by David D. Mann and Susan Garland Mann, between 1789 and 1823 a total of ninety women wrote for the theatre.[8] Of these women dramatists, as Jeffrey Cox notes, a third saw their works both published and performed, a third only published and another third only performed.[9]

Of the many authoresses who happened under Byron's severe critical gaze, Joanna Baillie in particular earned his somewhat grudging admiration, leading the poet to grant her – in an attempt to come to terms with the paradox of a talented woman dramatist – some unsuspected anatomical attributes:

> When Voltaire was asked why no woman has ever written even a tolerable tragedy? 'Ah (said the Patriarch) the composition of a tragedy requires testicles'. If this be true Lord knows what Joanna Baillie does – I suppose she borrows them.[10]

Indeed, to be fair to Byron, it was he who in 1820 prompted Kean to read Baillie's exemplary 'testicular' tragedy *De Montfort* in the belief that the actor

---

Playwrights: Mary Mitford and Lord Byron', in Lilla Maria Crisafulli and Cecilia Pietropoli (eds), *The Languages of British Romanticism* (Berne and Oxford, 2008), pp. 115–26.

[7] George Gordon, Lord Byron, *Letters and Journals*, ed. Leslie Alexis Marchand, 12 vols (London, 1973–80), vol. 1, p. 35. On Byron and the subcommittee, see Richard Lansdown, *Byron's Historical Drama* (Oxford, 1992), pp. 28–38.

[8] David D. Mann and Susan Garland Mann with Camille Garnier (eds), *Women Playwrights in England, Ireland, and Scotland 1660–1823* (Bloomington and Indianapolis, 1996), pp. 403–17. This statistic does not, moreover, take into account the number of plays written by each woman dramatist: Elizabeth Inchbald, for example, wrote twenty, Joanna Baillie twenty-six, and Jane Scott at least fifty. The number of dramatic texts composed by women in this period thus becomes exponentially higher than the quoted statistic might suggest.

[9] Jeffrey N. Cox, 'Baillie, Siddons, Larpent: Gender, power, and politics', in Catherine B. Burroughs (ed.), *Women in British Romantic Theatre, Drama, Performance, and Society, 1790–1840* (Cambridge, 2000), pp. 23–47, at p. 25.

[10] Byron, *Letters and Journals*, vol. 4, p. 290.

might discern performance potential in the script; he was right, so much so that Kean took the play first on an American tour and then, after revision, onto the Drury Lane stage on 27 November 1821, even if the performances turned out not to be a great critical or commercial success. The most public sign of Byron's admiration for Baillie is his coming out in print in her praise, in the preface to *Marino Faliero* (1821), where he includes the Scottish dramatist in a short list of authors who – unlike him – have attempted with some degree of success to compose tragedies for the contemporary stage (even if Byron's view of success on stage is to say the least ambivalent):

> Were I capable of writing a play which could be deemed stage-worthy, success would give me no pleasure, and failure great pain.[11] It is for this reason that, even during the time of being one of the committee of one of the theatres, I never made the attempt, and never will. But surely there is dramatic power somewhere, where Joanna Baillie, and Milman,[12] and John Wilson[13] exist. The 'City of the Plague' and the 'Fall of Jerusalem' are full of the best '*matériel*' for tragedy that has been seen since Horace Walpole, except passages of Ethwald[14] and De Montfort.[15]

Baillie received further public praise from other male authors and managers, notably Richard Brinsley Sheridan in a speech to the House of Commons,[16] although in actual (theatrical) practice Sheridan was hostile to her work and obstructed its success.

Baillie's 'testicular' talent, together with Byron's praise, was shared by other women playwrights, in particular Elizabeth Inchbald, whose skill and professionalism were undeniable even to male poets, critics and theatre managers of the period. As a sixteen-year-old Harrow schoolboy Byron responded powerfully to *Lover's Vows*, Mrs Inchbald's adaptation of August von Kotzebue's *Das Kind*

---

[11]　In a letter to John Murray of 14 May 1821, Byron notes that, 'A Milan paper states that the play has been represented and universally condemned. As remonstrance has been vain, complaint would be useless'; see Thomas Moore, *Life of Lord Byron: With his Letters and Journals. In Six Volumes*, vol. V (London, 1854), p. 176. The report was false.

[12]　Henry Hart Milman, author of tragedies such as *Fazio* (1818), *Belshazzar* (1822) and *Anne Boleyn* (1826), and of the dramatic poem *The Fall of Jerusalem* (1820).

[13]　John Wilson, otherwise known as Christopher North, author of the dramatic poem *The City of the Plague* (1816).

[14]　Joanna Baillie's tragedy *Ethwald* was published in 1800.

[15]　George Gordon Byron, 'Preface', *Marino Faliero, Doge of Venice* (1821), in *The Works of Lord Byron*, ed. E.H. Coleridge, vol. IV (London, 1901), p. 408.

[16]　Ellen Donkin, *Getting into the Act: Women Playwrights in London, 1776–1829* (London, 1995), p. 168.

der Liebe, which he saw in London in 1804.[17] Nine years later, in his journal entry for 7 December 1813, he writes enthusiastically of Inchbald as novelist and as critic (especially of Byron himself):

> Talking of vanity – whose praise do I prefer? Why, Mrs Inchbald's, and that of the Americans. The first, because her 'Simple Story' and 'Nature and Art are, to me, *true* to their *titles*; and consequently, her short note to Rogers about the 'Gaiour' delighted me more than any thing, except the Edinburgh Review.[18]

Inchbald had other male admirers. Her playwriting was patronized first by Thomas Harris at Covent Garden, even if this patronage involved possible attempted rape and financial skulduggery,[19] and then by George Colman, instrumental in getting her first play performed at the Haymarket. When, in her 'Remarks on Everyone Has His Fault' (1793) Inchbald observes that '[t]he English Theatres never flourished as they do at present',[20] she is in part alluding to her own professional success as dramatist and actress.

Nevertheless, even in these improved historical conditions some of Woolf's observations regarding women's drama still held good. Even now it was not considered entirely proper for a woman to write and publish plays under her own name, hence Baillie's initial decision to publish her plays of the passions anonymously. Frances Burney had likewise published her play 'Eveline' anonymously in 1778. Elizabeth Inchbald's début similarly went 'unsigned', in Woolf's terms: George Colman's condition for the Haymarket performance of *The Mogul Tale* in 1784 was the author's anonymity, although since she acted in her own play her identity was rapidly revealed.[21]

---

[17]   See Paul Elledge, *Lord Byron at Harrow School: Speaking Out, Talking Back, Acting Up, Bowing Out* (Baltimore, 2000), pp. 110–15. Here Byron's half-sister re-enters into the picture, together with his mother, since Byron's reaction to the play was probably due in part to its plot regarding the relationships between a bastard son, Frederick, his mother Agatha and his half-sister Amelia. Elledge observes, 'No child in so vexed a maternal relationship as Byron's could have witnessed without pangs (and perhaps disbelief) the mutually doting, compassionate, sacrificing (Byron might have said "treacly"), at times almost spousal attentiveness of Agatha and Frederick' (p. 113). See also Paul Douglass, 'Lord Byron's Feminist Canon: Notes toward Its Construction', *Romanticism on the Net*, 43 (August 2006): 1–47.

[18]   Byron, *Letters and Journals*, vol. 2, p. 236.

[19]   Donkin, *Getting into the Act*, pp. 112 and 115.

[20]   Quoted in Catherine B. Burroughs, *Closet Stages: Joanna Baillie and the Theater Theory of British Romantic Women Writers* (Philadelphia, 1997), p. 14.

[21]   Donkin, *Getting into the Act*, p. 119.

2. Empty Shelves and Girlish Dolls

The situation was destined, however, to worsen drastically during the following decades. The patronage that women playwrights had received from male theatre managers from the Restoration[22] through the eighteenth century[23] up to the early years of the nineteenth gradually diminished in the following decades, beginning with the aftermath of Waterloo. Women playwrights were among the many victims of a new conservative spirit that, from the time of the Napoleonic wars onwards, began to look with suspicion at the slightest form of social unrest or the vindication of individual rights. It was during the wars that voice was definitively given to the male patriot who upheld the supremacy of the three great patriarchal institutions – family, church and state – over any other individual or collective aspirations. Such values entailed the imposition of a private and domestic role for women, in silent support of the new patriotism. For a woman, writing professionally implied, on the contrary, assuming a public voice.

The moral as well as the political climate of the late Romantic period proved decidedly unfavourable to women's involvement in theatrical endeavour. The moral legislators unleashed explicit anathemas against the presence of women in playhouses even as mere spectators. Thomas Gisborne, a well-known compiler of 'conduct books' for young ladies, had decreed, in the last years of the eighteenth century, that

> Among the usual causes by which female modesty is worn away, I know not one more efficacious, than the indelicate scenes and language to which women are familiarised in the [public] theatre.[24]

As for writing for the stage, it was designed, warned Gisborne, 'to encourage vanity; to excite a thirst of applause and admiration',[25] i.e. to offer oneself indecorously to the public gaze. The tone of such admonitions became more virulent in the post-Napoleonic years. The theatre came to be seen by contemporary moralists – in a vigorous revival of puritanical antitheatrical prejudice – as 'an unmixed evil or a school of immorality and vice'[26] and as a social phenomenon 'subversive of religion, the rule of law and parental control'. The so-called 'penny gaffs' – that is to say, the small popular theatres – were defined 'hotbeds of vice and prostitution', while even the 'licenced theatres', Drury Lane and Covent Garden, earned an

---

[22]   In particular, Thomas Betterton's promotion of the plays of Aphra Behn.

[23]   David Garrick hosted and supervised over fifteen productions by female dramatists, among whom Frances Sheridan, Charlotte Lennox, Susanna Cibber, Catherine Clive, Hannah Cowley, Elizabeth Griffith and Hannah More.

[24]   Thomas Gisborne, *An Enquiry into the Duties of the Female Sex* (London, 1797), p. 172.

[25]   Ibid., p. 15.

[26]   Ibid.

equally damning judgement from, among others, the Reverend T. Thirlwall: 'They are calculated to corrupt the morals, and instil the most dangerous and criminal maxims'.[27]

The woman/theatre association thus became doubly dangerous. Not only was writing for the stage a questionable 'public' activity in itself, but, worse, it also required the frequentation of the worst of public places or spaces. Unlike the writing of poetry or fiction, which could be decorously exercised at home, playwriting, if it was to leave the confines of the closet, required experience of and contact with playhouses, actors, managers and audiences, as Byron discovered to his distaste. This involved not only exposure to public attention but also submittal to the often troublesome constraints of collaboration. Even the professional woman of the theatre par excellence, Elizabeth Inchbald – a highly experienced actress, and critic as well as playwright – complained, at the height of her success, of the often mortifying moral, commercial and political conditioning and censorship to which the dramatist (and above all the woman dramatist) was subjected:

> The Novelist [by comparison] is a free agent. He lives in a land of liberty, whilst the Dramatic Writer exists but under a despotic government. Passing over the subjection in which an author of plays is held by the Lord Chamberlain's office, and the degree of dependence which he has on his actors – he is the very slave of the audience. He must have their tastes and prejudices in view, not to correct, but to humour them ... the will of such critics is the law, and execution instantly follows judgement.[28]

Such difficulties, as well as the moral issues attending women's association with the playhouse, came to be resolved a priori, in the sense that the privileged, albeit problematic, position of an Elizabeth Inchbald at the very centre of the public theatre was unthinkable only two decades later. Women's drama took its effective curtain call in the 1820s, and virtually disappeared from the scene for over a century.

---

27   These quotations are taken from Maria Rosaria Cocco's interesting study *Arlecchino, Shakespeare e il Marinaio. Teatro Popolare e melodramma in Inghilterra (1800–1850)* (Napoli, 1990), p. 41. The sources quoted are, in particular, A. Thomson's *Sermons on Theatricals Amusements* (London, 1817) and T. Thirlwall's *Against the Revival of Scenic Exibitions and Interludes at the Royality: Containing Remarks on Pizarro, the Stranger and John Bull* (London, 1803). On the antitheatrical prejudice in general, see Jonas Barish, *The Antitheatrical Prejudice* (Berkeley, CA, 1981).

28   Elizabeth Inchbald, 'To the Artist', *The Artist*, 1, n. 14 (13 June 1807): 16, quoted in Donkin, *Getting into the Act*, p. 5. Elizabeth Inchbald mentions the Lord Chamberlain – that is to say, the man responsible in the government for censorship –, whose post had been created under the Licensing Act of 1737; censorship had become even tighter in the years following the French Revolution. See also Elizabeth Inchbald, *Remarks for the British Theatre 1806–9* (Delmar, NY, 1990).

Such silencing of the female dramatic voice was accompanied by the erasing of female dramatic history. Perhaps the most enduring problem regarding women dramatists has been their entry or otherwise into the literary and dramatic canons of Romanticism. Here Virginia Woolf's empty-shelf trope comes back into play. It is not that women did not continue to compose drama; it is that Romantic and post-Romantic drama by women was – until very recently – silently but systematically excluded from collections (even specialized anthologies of Romantic plays) and from critical histories. Unlike the novels of their women contemporaries, the plays went missing from the shelves – not stolen (an enviable fate reserved for Jane Austen), but removed to make space for texts deemed more significant.

To some extent, the progressive disappearance of women playwrights was an epiphenomenon of the broader erasure of Romantic-period plays at large. On the whole, 'Romantic drama' has generally been treated, until recently, as a paradoxical entity or nonentity, on a par, say, with the modern epic poem or the postmodern sermon. Even Byron's – not to mention Coleridge's or Keats's – dramatic efforts were relegated to appendices and footnotes, saved from total oblivion as titles, rather than as scripts, by their sheer metonymic association with their author's eminent names. In the case of Baillie or Inchbald there was no august (male) name to save the metonym, and hence even the titles. After the 1820s, women's drama ceased, by and large, to be performed, published, anthologized or even mentioned in histories of the drama.

Those canon-makers who might have acknowledged women's literary and dramatic talent failed conspicuously, and indeed strategically, to do so. One exemplary case of the censorship of female Romantic dramatists is the critic par excellence of Romanticism, namely William Hazlitt. In his celebrated essay *The Spirit of the Age* (1825), which characterizes an entire epoch and its revolutionary *ethos*, Hazlitt operates a decisive if silent gender censorship, omitting altogether the contribution of those women who had played as significant a role as that of the men he elects as protagonists of his account. Such silence is particularly indicative in a work intended to express the Romantic *Zeitgeist*, as if to signify that women did not appear on the cultural scene of the age at all. It would be pointless to search in the authoritative preliminary notes for *The Spirit of the Age* for any reference – even negative – to female Romantic authors, let alone women playwrights. It would be similarly vain to enquire into an earlier text containing Hazlitt's canonical judgements regarding more specifically contemporary theatre and drama, *A View of the English Stage*, where very little is said about women and virtually nothing about female playwrights.

We might instead linger a while over the *Lectures on the English Poets* (1818), especially the chapter 'On the Living Poets' in Lecture VIII.[29] In these pages the critic expresses few, but quite incisive, opinions concerning the female writers of his time, opinions that, coming from the major British theorist of Romanticism,

---

[29]   William Hazlitt, 'On the Living Poets', in *The Selected Writings of William Hazlitt*, ed. Duncan Wu, 9 vols (London, 1998), vol. 2, pp. 298–320.

might be taken as indicative of a more widespread view, and which in any case assume the aura of authoritative if not definitive decrees. Early in the chapter, Hazlitt claims: 'I am a great admirer of the female writers of the present day; they appear to me like so many modern Muses'.[30] This opening *captatio benevolentiae* sets the tone for the chapter as a whole: women writers are objects rather than subjects of the contemporary scene, modern *Muses* who, as such, inspire rather than being inspired. They remain dumb icons in the male realm of art. This is all to the good, adds Hazlitt, paraphrasing *As You Like It*: 'Thank the Gods / For not having made them poetical'.[31]

If Hazlitt accords somewhat grudging acknowledgement of Mrs Inchbald and Mrs Radcliffe as novelists (but then for him the novel was a minor literary genre, inferior to poetry and drama), Inchbald's contribution to the theatre is altogether ignored despite the fact that she had just edited the first great anthology of English dramatic texts, from the origins to her time, complete with introduction and illuminating commentaries, in *The British Theatre*. One female dramatist and poet briefly mentioned by Hazlitt is Hannah More, erstwhile protégée of David Garrick,[32] whose work is dismissed – probably on account of her increasingly conservative politics – with a sarcastic quip: 'Mrs. Hannah More is another celebrated modern poetess, and I believe still living. She has written a great deal which I have never read'.[33]

Hazlitt's essay next turns to the work of the most celebrated of contemporary women dramatists, Joanna Baillie. With a passing stab at Baillie's religious affiliations,[34] and an ungenerous comparison with the Bard, Hazlitt pours scorn on her project for a series of plays respectively dramatizing the various passions:

> Miss Baillie['s] … tragedies and comedies, one of each to illustrate each of the passions, separately from the rest, are heresies in the dramatic art. She is Unitarian in poetry. With her the passions are, like the French republic, one and indivisible: they are not so in nature, or in Shakespeare.[35]

---

[30]   Ibid., vol. 2, p. 300.

[31]   Ibid.

[32]   In 1773 More wrote her first play, *The Inflexible Captive*, an adaptation of Metastasio's *Attilio Regolo*. The work was represented in Bath and was so successful that Garrick, a member of the audience, asked the author for her permission to stage it himself at his Drury Lane theatre. Although this project was not carried out, there soon arose a close understanding among Garrick, his wife, Eva, and Hannah More, which led More to produce one of the most well received tragedies of the time, *Percy*. This was so successful that it would then be staged at Covent Garden, in the winter of 1774/75.

[33]   Hazlitt, 'On the Living Poets', vol. 2, p. 301.

[34]   See Isabella Imperiali's essay in this volume, pp. 215–30.

[35]   Hazlitt, 'On the Living Poets', vol. 2, p. 301.

Hazlitt goes on to accuse Baillie of an equally un-Shakespearean and especially un-masculine infantilism, comparing her manipulation of both male and female characters with young girls at play: 'She treats her grown men and women as little girls treat their dolls – makes moral puppets of them, pulls the wires, and they talk virtue and act vice'.[36] Despite such patronization, Hazlitt concludes his few and sarcastic comments on female playwrights with a single instance of (albeit reluctant) praise, noting that despite Baillie's girlish ingenuity her *De Monfort* was decidedly superior to Coleridge's *Remorse* in its 'continued unity of interest' and its 'precision of outline'.[37] One is left wondering whether Coleridge had likewise spent too much time playing with dolls.

Hazlitt's judgement of Baillie's achievement finds many echoes among male reviewers of the period, from Francis Jeffrey's plea to the dramatist to keep her plays 'in her portfolio' to 'Z''s fear that her example might encourage other 'superannuated governesses to follow her lead into the marketplace' (see Greg Kucich's essay in this volume, p. 25). The legacy of this contemporary male reception – especially the views of the great Romantic canon-maker Hazlitt – was not only the silencing of later potential dramatists among the superannuated governesses of England but above all a collective amnesia regarding the women's drama that did manage to appear in print or on stage, a strategic critical–historical erasure that endured until quite recent times. Thus there is little or no trace of Joanna Baillie and Elizabeth Inchbald in the most authoritative histories of literature and drama until the last ten years or so, even in those works that, unusually, dedicate space to Romantic drama at all. In her groundbreaking *Closet Stages*, Catherine Burroughs expresses the well-founded suspicion that the causes of such omissions are primarily (and by definition undeclaredly) ideological:

> When a writer like Joanna Baillie is dropped from anthologies of *British Romantic Literature* and collections of plays, we should suspect the canonizers' motives … Terry Eagleton has argued that aesthetic judgements mask ideology.[38]

3. Back on the Shelves, Back on the Stage: Recent Critical Studies and the Present Volume

Happily, this situation of strategic forgetfulness has changed radically over the past ten to fifteen years. Whereas in 1986 a volume such as *The Romantic Theatre: An International Symposium*, edited by Richard Allen Cave, while laudably bringing Romantic drama back onto the critical scene, could still fail to dedicate any space to women writers (being unquestioningly limited to the 'great' male

---

[36]   Ibid.
[37]   Ibid.
[38]   Burroughs, *Closet Stages*, p. 14.

poets), the following decade saw an emphatic change of attitude within the critical community. If the 1790s decreed the definitive affirmation of female dramatists on the Romantic stage, the 1990s saw their decisive readmission into the canons of dramatic and theatrical history. The first studies to take a degree of interest in women's Romantic drama were wide-ranging surveys such as the one edited in 1991 by Mary Anne Schofield and Cecilia Macheski, *Curtain Calls: British and American Women and the Theater, 1660–1820*, which includes chapters on Inchbald, Cowley and More (see also later historical overviews such as Margarete Rubik's *Early Women Dramatists 1550–1800* [1998]). Likewise, studies devoted to women Romantic writers in general began in the 1990s to pay attention to the drama; the first of these was Carol Shiner Wilson and Joel Haefner's collection *Re-visioning Romanticism: British Women Writers 1776–1837* (1994), which includes a discussion by Catherine B. Burroughs of Baillie as theatre theorist. Marjean D. Purinton's *Romantic Ideology Unmasked* (1994) devotes a chapter to 'mentally constructed tyranny' in the drama of Joanna Baillie.

A breakthrough volume, already referenced more than once in this introduction, is Ellen Donkin's *Getting into the Act: Women Playwrights in London, 1776–1829* (1995), which recounts the difficulties and successes of women playwrights in getting their work read, performed and published in the context of the necessarily collaborative character of all theatrical enterprises. Donkin's volume examines the cases of a wide range of women dramatists over a fifty-year period, from Frances Brooke to Frances Burney.

The first significant study of a single woman dramatist is Catherine B. Burroughs's influential *Closet Stages: Joanna Baillie and the Theater Theory of British Romantic Women Writers* (1997), which centres on the tensions between the private and public dimensions of Baillie's work – between the closet and the stage – within the framework of her own and other women writers' theories of drama. A more recent volume dedicated to the same author is the collection edited by T.C. Crochunis, *Joanna Baillie, Romantic Dramatist* (2004), which discusses such topics as Baillie and medical science, her theory of the passions, her treatment of history and gender, and her staging of Scotland.[39]

The innovative collection edited by Tracy C. Davis and Ellen Donkin, *Women and Playwrights in Nineteenth-Century Britain* (1999), addresses above all the social position of women dramatists – the relationship between private and public spheres, critical reception, questions of authorship, the conflict between 'properness' and public voice, etc. – and has chapters dedicated in particular to Sara Lane, Joanna Baillie, Elizabeth Polack, and the writer–manager Jane Scott.

---

[39] Other recent studies of Baillie include Michael Gamer's chapter 'National Supernaturalism: Joanna Baillie, Germany, and the Gothic Drama', in his *Romanticism and the Gothic: Genre, Reception, and Canon Formation* (Cambridge, 2000), pp. 127–62. In Italy, Isabella Imperiali's *Le passioni della mente nel teatro di Joanna Baillie* (Rome, 2007) presents, together with a critical introduction, the first translations into Italian of *De Montfort*, the 'Introductory Discourse', and the epistle 'To the Reader'.

The collection edited by Catherine B. Burroughs, *Women in British Romantic Theatre: Drama, Performance and Society, 1790–1840* (Cambridge, 2000), takes up a wide range of topics, from national identity to domesticity, from closet drama to criticism and theory, and from dramatic genres to translation, adaptation and revision. It includes specific discussions of the work of More, Yearsley, Burney, Mitford, Baillie, Inchbald, Scott, and Anne Plumptre. The question of national identity is likewise the central theme of Betsy Bolton's monograph *Women, Nationalism and the Romantic Stage: Theatre and Politics in Britain, 1780–1800* (2001), which places women's drama in the context of the contemporary political debate on nationalism, addressing such issues as the staging of the nation, the public roles of men and women, and the development of such critical and satirical genres as imperial farce. The writers discussed include Cowley, Inchbald and the poet–actress Mary Robinson.

Another sign of the re-canonization of women's drama – besides the numerous journal articles on the subject (see Bibliography) – has been its inclusion in recent anthologies, not only those dedicated specifically to the subject, such as Adrienne Scullion's edition of *Female Playwrights of the Nineteenth Century* (1996), which includes plays by Baillie and Fanny Kemble, among others, but also – perhaps more significantly – collections of Romantic plays in general, such as Paul Baines's and Edward Burns's World's Classics anthology *Five Romantic Plays* (2000), which includes texts by Baillie and Inchbald, and Jeffery Cox's and Michael Gamer's *Broadview Anthology of Romantic Drama* (2003), which has three plays by women (out of a total of ten): Cowley's *A Bold Stroke for a Husband*, Inchbald's *Every One Has His Fault*, and Baillie's *Orra*.

The present volume is thus situated within a recent but already significant critical tradition. What it adds to the existing literature on the subject is, first, a range of topics that have not been fully explored in earlier studies. These include such issues as eroticism in women's drama, the cultural politics of the drama, processes of indirect theatrical censorship towards which women contributed, the network of women's friendships that lay behind some of the texts, and the plays by Scottish women other than Baillie. Considerable attention is paid here, moreover, to a vital but little-discussed genre with regard to women playwrights, namely the history play, especially in its relations with contemporary feminist historiography. Other relatively little-investigated genres and subgenres examined here include the Romantic siege play. Furthermore, the territory explored in this volume extends beyond dramatists to include actresses (Sarah Siddons) and theatre managers (Madame Vestris).

Another novelty of the present collection is that it represents a productive meeting between leading British and American experts on the one hand, and Italian scholars on the other. In Italy a good deal of attention has been paid to English women's Romantic drama in recent years, including a major national research project of which this volume is in part the result.[40] One of the emphases of this Italian critical tradition has been precisely English women's historical drama, some of it indeed set in Italy itself (Mitford's *Foscari*, Hemans's *Vespers of Palermo*).

This volume is also unusual for the sheer number of writers discussed. If the most recurrent points of reference here are Baillie and Inchbald, both as dramatists and as theorists or critics, ample space is given to dramatists such as Hannah More, Felicia Hemans, Ann Yearsley, Mary Russell Mitford, Frances Kemble and Frances Brooke, as well as such Scottish playwrights as Eglantine Wallace and Mary Diana Dods.

The collection is divided into three sections. The first section, 'Historical Drama and Romantic Historiography', considers the importance of this rediscovered genre on the Romantic stage and the specific uses to which women playwrights put it within the framework of the contemporary debate on the role of women in history. Thus Greg Kucich sets the historical dramas of Baillie and Mitford in the context of the efforts of Romantic-era women writers to intervene in national politics through historical revisionism. The comparison between women's history plays and the new feminist historiography of Elizabeth Macauley and others sheds light on the commitment of the dramatists to the promotion of social transformation, but also on their reservations regarding the limits of such change. Kucich singles out the use of stage pictures and tableaux vivants by both playwrights as modes of introducing affective exchange into the representation of history.

Lilla Maria Crisafulli's reflections on historical agency in women's drama – with reference to a number of writers, from More to Hemans to Baillie – argue that, through the genre of historical tragicomedy, women dramatists entered into a traditionally male field and challenged it, in order to gain authority themselves within the public sphere. Such a conquest of the highly gendered arena of historical drama allowed women playwrights to affirm a new subjectivity or agency.

Cecilia Pietropoli's discussion of Hannah More's and Ann Yearsley's Anglo-Saxon history plays, while acknowledging the nostalgic social and political conservatism of Romantic medievalism, argues that these playwrights reinvented historical drama from a gendered perspective, giving voice and form to a feminine historical poetics. Serena Baiesi turns her attention to a particular genre in vogue particularly among women dramatists, namely siege drama. In the siege plays of Frances Brooke, Joanna Baillie and Felicia Hemans, the central event dramatizes the violent clash not only between opposing political factions but also between different cultures, religions and genders. The plays also show how private family affection is strictly connected with public political reality, thereby deconstructing received notions regarding the separate spheres of action for women and men respectively.

---

[40] 'British Romantic Theatre and Drama (1760/1830): Text, Theory and Dramatic Practice', directed by Lilla Maria Crisafulli and financed by the Italian Ministry of Higher Education and Research, with the collaboration of the Universities of Bologna, Bari, Florence, Rome, Parma and Pavia.

Gary Kelly examines Felicia Hemans's adaptation of Schillerian drama in order to influence the cultural politics of the English-speaking world. In historical plays such as *The Vespers of Palermo* and *The Siege of Valencia*, Hemans's representation of both liberalism and feminism made a vital contribution to the formation of the modern liberal state, arguably greater than that of Schiller himself.

The second section, 'Dramaturgical and Cultural Processes', is concerned with some of the modes whereby women dramatists participated in the representation of social, political and familial values, as well as with their own reflections on the dramatic forms of such representation. Catherine Burroughs investigates the connections between eighteenth-century British erotica and the dramas written by Romantic-period women. In particular, she places Joanna Baillie's *The Bride* (1828) in relation to the recurrent defloration fantasies of the time and examines Frances Anne Kemble's *An English Tragedy* with reference to contemporary representations of incest. The dramatization of such themes enabled the playwrights to express resistance to the passivity and restrictions of woman's sexual role, while at the same time keeping the sphere of *eros* firmly within the confines of the home.

With reference to the socio-cultural framework within which the drama was composed, Diego Saglia explores the personal and intellectual friendship that arose between Joanna Baillie and Nancy Russell Mitford following their meeting in 1836, within the broader context of a veritable network of female playwrights in the late Romantic period, a phenomenon that conditioned and consolidated the expression of a female dramatic poetics. Still within the context of relations among fellow dramatists, Franca Dellarosa focuses on Inchbald as critic, with particular reference to her critique of Baillie's *De Monfort*. Within the Romantic dialectic between performance and reading of the playtext, Inchbald identifies a middle ground, namely reading aloud, subject to its own performative rules and capable of modifying the mode of reception of the play.

Vita Mastrosilvestri, in discussing the cultural mediation operated by Inchbald with regard to Kotzebue's *Lover's Vows*, notes, instead, how the necessary adaptation of the original to an English context, including the processes of re-territorialization and normalization, also bespeaks a resistance to the German author's female stereotypes and patriarchal values of domesticity. Gioia Angeletti's chapter dedicated to Scottish women playwrights examines how writers such as Jean Marshall, Eglantine Wallace and Mary Diana Dods negotiated a 'double marginalization effect', namely as women dramatists and as members of a 'minority' regional theatrical community.

The final section, 'Women Staging, Women Staged', moves beyond the sphere of the dramatic text to examine women's involvement in the practical and political machinery of the Romantic and post-Romantic stage, as performed (and censored) playwrights, as actresses, and even, in one isolated but conspicuous case, as theatre managers.

Jane Moody's essay explores the undeclared politics of women's drama, showing how unofficial modes of censorship conditioned the 'Jacobin' plays of

Elizabeth Inchbald and Thomas Holcroft respectively. Moody, following Inchbald herself, redefines theatrical censorship as a collaborative phenomenon including the more or less conscious complicity of playwrights. While Holcroft expresses his radical views quite openly through his characters, Inchbald participates in theatrical self-censorship by treating similar themes and characters with far more caution and guile. The quite different destinies of the two dramatists testifies to the effects of their respective strategies.

Still with reference to the political and ideological context of the performance of women's plays, Isabella Imperiali enquires, from a performative perspective, into the importance of science and religion in the work of Joanna Baillie. At the centre of the Hampstead Dissenting community, Baillie participated actively, in and outside her plays, in the Protestant campaign for religious freedom. At the same time, as part of a prominent medical family, she had access to the scientific discourses of the day. Baillie's 'scientific' and ethical attempt to represent the emotions of the modern subject, however, called for an intimate theatrical space that was not available at the time, but that has since made it possible to recuperate the theatrical dimensions of her drama.

Outside the domain of playwrighting, but still within the territory of women's performativity, Claudia Corti's discussion of the theatrical portrait centres on the figure of the Romantic actress par excellence Sarah Siddons, at the core of the interchange between poetry, theatre and painting characterizing British culture at the turn of the century. Corti considers theatrical portraiture as a performative mode in its own right, whereby, for example, Thomas Lawrence's celebrated portrait of Siddons, while endeavouring to show forth the actress's character, also competes in its pictorial flair with the histrionic skills of its subject. The final essay regards the leading woman stage manager of her day, Madame Vestris. Stefania Magnoni considers in particular Vestris's celebrated production of *A Midsummer Night's Dream* both on a textual level and on the performance plane. Vestris's restitution of Shakespeare's text went hand in hand with her spectacular scenic inventions, whereby she succeeded in the arduous enterprise of reconciling page and stage.

Inevitably, such a division into sections is somewhat arbitrary, and there are numerous recurrent thematic interests that cross these notional boundaries, and that can be summarized under the two key words contained, together with 'history', in the title of this volume, namely 'agency' and 'performativity'. In Chapter 23 of the *Biographia Literaria* (the so-called 'Critique of Bertram' in the 1817 edition), Coleridge poses for the first time the question of agency in drama, with reference to a male, not to say macho, protagonist; writing of Shadwell's version of the old Spanish play *Don Juan, or Atheista Fulminato*, Coleridge refers admiringly to 'the super-human entireness of Don Juan's agency', which 'prevents [his] wickedness from shocking our minds to any painful degree'.[41] Coleridge, unsurprisingly, is not troubled with female agents, superhuman or merely human. This volume, instead,

---

[41] Samuel Taylor Coleridge, *Biographia Literaria*, ed. James Engell and W. Jackson Bate, 2 vols (Princeton and London, 1983), vol. II, p. 218.

addresses his women contemporaries' explorations precisely of the possibility of an 'entireness' of female agency both in the drama (as protagonists) and through the drama (as active participants in social transformation). This is especially the case with the modes of historical agency that are represented in the plays. If, as Carlyle affirms (still with reference to male agents) in his 'Thoughts on History', 'we do nothing but enact History',[42] the question that Romantic women playwrights pose is whether subjects enact history according to fixed canons of behaviour, or whether these canons are themselves historically determined and thus subject to change. Women dramatists devoted their energies to composing scripts that, in William Jewett's words, 'complicate, contest, disrupt, anatomize, and otherwise render strange and unacceptable the routines by which people stake their conceptions of self upon their capacities to act'.[43]

As for the second key term, performativity, one of the strengths of this collection is its exploration of the manifold modes of dramatic, theatrical and cultural performance through which the new female agency expressed itself. At one level, such performativity is entrusted primarily to language – for example by Baillie in the verbal expression of the passions, or by Hemans in the attempt to found a persuasive liberal rhetoric – and as such is close to J.L. Austin's original formulation of the 'performative' as a direct 'doing things' with words.[44] For other playwrights, such as Inchbald, performativity is invested in the social habitus of the characters and the semiotics of the actors' 'doing things' on stage.

One of the old critical bugbears that long haunted Romantic drama was the question of the performability, or rather the supposed non-performability, of plays of the period, leading to the oft-repeated accusation that they were written merely to be read. Apart from the fact that recent studies of Romantic 'closet drama' have revealed the unsuspected and sometimes transgressive social and political force of the plays in question (see Burroughs's *Closet Stages*, and her essay in this volume) – not to mention the performance potential of reading aloud (see Dellarosa's essay) –, the sheer theatricality of plays by such successful professional playwrights as Cowley and Inchbald demonstrate that the page/stage dichotomy cannot in any case be applied to Romantic period drama at large, at least women's drama. The largely unhelpful notion of performability has given way in recent critical discourse to the more versatile and fruitful category of performativity in its extended sense whereby all cultural expression can be viewed as a mode of performance or of social action. This move has opened up the discussion of Romantic theatre and

---

[42]   Thomas Carlyle, 'Thoughts on History', *Fraser's Magazine*, II (November 1830): 413. See Richard W. Schoch, '"We Do Nothing but Enact History"': Thomas Carlyle Stages the Past', *Nineteenth-Century Literature*, 54/1 (June 1999): 27–52.

[43]   Even if Jewett is in fact alluding to male poets; *Fatal Autonomy: Romantic Drama and the Rhetoric of Agency* (New York, 1997), p. 5.

[44]   See J.L. Austin, *How to Do Things with Words* (Oxford, 1962). On performative language in the drama, see Keir Elam, *Semiotics of Theatre and Drama*, 2nd edn (London, 2001), pp. 142–54

drama not only to non-canonical forms of spectacle (see Jane Moody's *Illegitimate Theatre*), and to non-dramatic forms of performativity such as posing for portraits (see Corti in this volume), but also to a less scholastic conception of the interaction between drama and society, allowing us to recover, for example, the extraordinary political force of writers (from More to Hemans to Dods) long relegated to the dusty archives of 'poetic' drama.

PART I
Historical Drama and Romantic Historiography

Chapter 1

Baillie, Mitford, and the 'Different Track' of Women's Historical Drama on the Romantic Stage

Greg Kucich

London's recent theatrical sensation, Alan Bennett's *The History Boys*, features a feminist critique of history tantalizingly applicable to women's historical drama of the romantic era. During a practice interview for sixth-form English boys at a middling northern school trying to make the improbable leap to 1950s Cambridge, the school's one female historian scornfully derides the marginalization of women in world history. 'Can you for a moment', she asks the room of male auditors, 'imagine how dispiriting it is to teach five centuries of masculine ineptitude? ... History's not such a frolic for women as it is for men ... They never got round the conference table. In 1919, for instance, they just arranged the flowers then gracefully retired ... History is a commentary on the various and continuing incapabilities of men ... History is women following behind with the bucket'.[1] Lady Morgan anticipated the point in *Woman and Her Master* (1840) with similarly caustic irony: 'From the earliest aggregations of society, man, in his shallow pride, has laboured to perpetuate the memory of his own imperfection, the story of his selfishness and his errors ...'.[2] If female writers of the romantic era anticipated current theatrical denunciations of women's historical elision, they also initiated a wide range of discursive historical innovations and exerted great political energy in seeking, particularly through historical drama, to write women back into the story of the past.

Although Thomas Lovell Beddoes's complaint about the creative impoverishment of the British stage – a 'haunted ruin' of its Elizabethan grandeur – found much contemporary assent,[3] many dramatists, particularly women playwrights, advocated the public theatre's unique educational possibilities for the improvement of morals, national politics, and gender relations. Thus Hannah Cowley envisions the theatre as a 'great National School' where 'a mother can ... lead her daughters [to] ... UNDERSTANDING, DISCERNMENT, and

---

[1] Alan Bennett, *The History Boys* (London, 2004), p. 85.

[2] Lady Morgan, *Woman and Her Master*, 2 vols (Westport, CT, 1976), vol. 1, p. 13.

[3] Thomas Lovell Beddoes, *The Letters of Thomas Lovell Beddoes* (London, 1894), p. 51.

EDUCATION'.[4] For Cowley's female contemporaries in theatre circles, the special appeal of that schooling through the medium of historical drama registers in their avid inclination to the past for the setting of so many of their plays, such as: Hannah More's *Percy* (1778); Frances Burney's *Edwy and Elgiva* (1788/89); Ann Yearsley's *Earl Goodwin* (1791); Jane West's *Edmund Ironisde* (1791); Mary Devrell's *Mary, Queen of Scots* (1792); Hannah Brand's *Huniades, A Tragedy* (1792); Joanna Baillie's *Count Basil* (1798), *Ethwald Part First* and *Second* (1802), *Constantine Paleologus* (1804), and *The Family Legend* (1810); Felicia Hemans's *The Siege of Valencia* (1823); Mary Russell Mitford's *Foscari: A Tragedy* (1826), *Rienzi* (1828), and *Charles the First* (1834); Francis Ann Kemble's *Francis the First* (1832). If women's general reclamation of history during the romantic era produced numerous discursive avenues for joining Mary Hays in 'the generous contention between the sexes for intellectual equality',[5] the historical drama proved unusually fit for a literary mother wishing to 'lead her daughters' into that liberating fray.

Despite the vibrant outpouring of critical studies over the last decade on romantic-era women's writing across the genres and its important political work, the teeming variety of this historical revisionism and its keen political significance are just beginning to gain attention from such critics as Devoney Looser, Mark Salber Phillips, and Miriam Burstein.[6] Amid the particular upsurge of recent critical work on the political impact of female playwrights of the romantic era, their massive investment in historical drama for the national lessons of a feminized theatrical school, as Katherine Newey and Betsy Bolton have shown, still awaits comprehensive examination.[7] My general aim here is to suggest why historical drama so appealed to the period's women writers. More particularly, I will highlight their transformative approach to the form – taking a 'different track', as Mary Russell Mitford put it[8] – by examining the political functions <u>and</u> limitations of a specific type of performance innovation utilized by Mitford and Joanna Baillie:

---

[4]   Hannah Cowley, 'Preface', in *The Town Before You, a Comedy* (London, 1795), p. xi.

[5]   Mary Hays, *Female Biography; or, Memoirs of Illustrious and Celebrated Women, of All Ages and Countries*, 6 vols (London, 1803), vol. 1, p. iv.

[6]   See Devoney Looser, *British Women Writers and the Writing of History: 1670–1820* (Baltimore, 2000); Mark Salber Phillips, *Society and Sentiment: Genres of Historical Writing in Britain* (Princeton, NJ, 2000); Miriam Burstein, *Narrating Women's History in Britain, 1770–1902* (Aldershot, 2004).

[7]   Katherine Newey, 'Women and History on the Romantic Stage: More, Yearsley, Burney Mitford', in Catherine Burroughs (ed.), *Women in British Romantic Theatre: Drama, Performance, and Society, 1790–1840* (Cambridge, 2000), pp. 79–101; Betsy Bolton, *Women, Nationalism and the Romantic Stage: Theatre and Politics in Britain, 1780–1800* (Cambridge, 2001).

[8]   Mary Russell Mitford, *Foscari: A Tragedy* (London, 1826), p. 2. All subsequent references to this text are cited hereafter parenthetically by page number.

staging pictures of a re-imagined past that strategically revise male precedents in historiography and historical drama so as to display social models for infusing what Mitford calls 'human sympathies' (p. 19), gendered as an empowering female force, into the dynamics of justice and mercy in the national politics of the present. This analysis specifically addresses one of the most vigorously debated issues in the ongoing project of recovering and assessing women dramatists of the romantic era: that is, the actual degrees – the possibilities and boundaries – of political intervention they exercised in the public theatre of their time.[9]

For women writers of the romantic era, the appealing concept of historical drama as a 'National School' emerged out of a wider, intensive cultural dispute about the present epoch's relation to Britain's illustrious literary traditions and the attendant question of any remaining creative opportunities following the exhaustive accomplishments of the past, particularly those seemingly inimitable triumphs of Britain's golden age in the Renaissance. This charged debate made the future of literature seem dependent on its ability to rival that monumental past, a daunting prospect that consumed the imaginations of so many romantic-era writers and inspired the rise of influence theory in the later twentieth century.[10] The challenge tended to focus on what was widely perceived as the glorious apex of Renaissance creativity, the brilliant fecundity of its drama. Hence the urgent question of creative life for the present – did a 'second' Renaissance beckon forth or was the 'scroll' of 'mighty Poets', as Keats once apprehended, 'folded by the Muses'[11] – turned squarely on the state of the national drama. Not surprisingly, Keats's greatest creative ambition, for which the 1819 odes seemed to him but a preliminary nerving himself up to the challenge, centered on 'the writing of a few fine Plays'.[12] Echoes of Beddoes's gloomy warning against any such hope proliferated, such as Leigh Hunt's lament about 'the degraded conditions of the modern drama'.[13] Yet more than a few critics, some quite prominent, found

---

[9]   For a range of divided responses to this questions, see Anne K. Mellor, 'Joanna Baillie and the Counter-Public Sphere', *Studies in Romanticism*, 33 (1994): 560–67, and *Mothers of the Nation: Women's Political Writing in England, 1780–1830* (Bloomington, IN, 2000); Catherine Burroughs, *Closet Stages: Joanna Baillie and the Theater Theory of British Romantic Women Writers* (Philadelphia, 1997); Ellen Donkin, *Getting into the Act: The Performance of Power: Women Playwrights in London, 1776–1829* (London, 1995); Terence Hoagwood, 'Elizabeth Inchbald, Joanna Baillie, and Revolutionary Representation in the "Romantic" Period', in Adriana Craciun and Kari E. Lokke (eds), *Rebellious Hearts: British Women Writers and the French Revolution* (Albany, NY, 2001), pp. 293–316.

[10]   See, in particular, Harold Bloom's study of Keats in *Poetry and Repression: Revisionism from Blake to Stevens* (New Haven, 1976), pp. 112–42.

[11]   Keats, *Endymion*, Book II, ll. 724–5, in *The Poems of John Keats*, ed. Jack Stillinger (London, 1978).

[12]   *The Letters of John Keats*, ed. Hyder Edward Rollins, 2 vols (Cambridge, MA, 1958), vol. 2, p. 234.

[13]   *Leigh Hunt's Dramatic Criticism*, eds Lawrence Huston Houtchens and Carolyn Washburn Houtchens (New York, 1949), p. 52.

a resurgent force of cultural renewal pouring into staged and written drama. Elizabeth Inchbald, whose prefaces to the 25-volume *British Theatre* (1808) made her a leading voice in early nineteenth century theatre criticism, admonishes those who deplore the creative poverty of the drama to take a closer look at the teeming theatres: 'It is said that modern dramas are the worst that ever appeared on the English stage – yet it is well known, that English theatres never flourished as they do at present …'.[14] Elaborating on this sentiment a decade later, Hazlitt reacts against 'that general complaint of the degeneracy of the stage' and insists that 'our times … [are] not unfruitful in theatrical genius.' He detects no falling-off from the drama's illustrious past 'either in the written or the acted performances'.[15] Still more sanguine, a *Blackwood's* theatre critic pronounces in a major 1825 survey of 'Modern English Drama' that 'dramatic genius' is 'kindling over the whole land' with a buoyancy surpassing even the prodigious energies of 'our best dramatic writers' of the Elizabethan age.[16]

Mobilizing their strongest case against 'that general complaint' of a crippled stage, those proponents of the drama's new vigor applied the classic argument of theatre's social virtues – famously articulated in P.B. Shelley's equation of 'the highest perfection of human society' with 'the highest dramatic excellence'[17] – to its revitalized social role in the present. 'The stage', Hazlitt declares, 'is one great source of public amusement, not to say instruction'.[18] A rejuvenated theatre, Walter Scott concludes, has 'enriched' national life.[19] The evidence of this cultural rehabilitation came from a wide variety of texts, performances, and authors, but many writers on the drama, including Scott, based their optimism about a linked renewal of stage and society on the recent influx of women dramatists onto Britain's literary scene.

Indeed, a substantial portion of the state of the drama controversy focused on the strength of women writers' specific contributions, inspiriting or disabling, to theatrical life. Although the tradition of eminent female dramatists in Britain stretches back at least to the time of Behn and Centlivre, the exponential increase of women writers in the late eighteenth century gave them an unprecedented prominence in drama, as well as in the other major literary genres, and the new creative energies they brought to both written and acted plays struck many drama

---

[14]   Elizabeth Inchbald, *The British Theatre*, vol. 23 (London, 1808), p. 3.

[15]   William Hazlitt, *A View of the English Stage; or a Series of Dramatic Criticisms* (London, 1818), p. ix, and 'The Drama. No.1', *The London Magazine*, 1 (January–June 1820): 64–70, at p. 64.

[16]   'Analytical Essays on the Modern English Drama', *Blackwood's Edinburgh Magazine*, 18 (July 1825): 119–36, at p. 119.

[17]   *Shelley's Poetry and Prose*, eds Donald H. Reiman and Neil Fraistat (New York, 2002), p. 521.

[18]   Hazlitt, *A View of the English Stage; or a Series of Dramatic Criticisms*, p. v.

[19]   Walter Scott, *Essays on the Drama. Essays in Chivalry, Romance, and the Drama* (London, 1868), p. 223.

critics as the breadth of renewed life for a moribund theatre and possibly the key ingredient, even, to that deeply desired overall renewal of the national literary scene. *The European Magazine*, for instance, invokes the plays of Hannah Cowley as 'the Works of one highly gifted' who has stopped the flow of dramatic genius from 'desert[ing] the realm'.[20] Hannah More's 'soundness of judgment' in *Percy*, according to *The Theatrical Inquisitor*, brings 'pure and enlightened piety' back to the stage.[21] Both *The Monthly Mirror* and *The Lady's Magazine* agree that Harriet Lee's *The Mysterious Marriage* and Elizabeth Inchbald's many 'dramatic pieces' establish new models of emulation for the renewal of dramatic achievement.[22] A chorus of reviewers declares with remarkable enthusiasm that Joanna Baillie, rising foremost among all dramatists of the present, brings back the glories of the Elizabethan stage and leads the charge to reinvigorate not only theatrical life but the entire national literature. Her 'genius' stands out as 'a matter of peculiar triumph', proclaims *The Annual Review*, because of its power to refresh the 'dispirit[ed] drama'. It is her originality, in particular, that makes Scott sanguine about the growing movement to 'enrich' the 'national tragedy'. And *Blackwood's* declares that Baillie's 'strong influence' has sparked a 'reformation' in all of 'our poetic literature', which transforms the current epoch into 'another Age of Genius, only second to that of Elizabeth'.[23]

To be sure, not everyone felt so thrilled about Baillie and the new surge of women dramatists. *The Imperial Review*, taking Baillie as representative of aspiring female playwrights, loathes the 'insult[ing] ... effusions of female sentiment ... and inferiority of genius' in women's drama. Francis Jeffrey, relentless in his critical antipathy to Baillie, expresses disgust at the 'voluntary perversity' of women who employ their 'delicate hand[s]' in the task of writing serious tragedy, and he 'earnestly exhort[s] Miss Baillie' to put her plays back 'in her portfolio' well out of public view. Z.'s infamous Cockney School reviews associate the intrusive effrontery of 'vulgar' writers like Keats and Hunt with Baillie's 'melancholy effect' of inciting 'we know not how many ... unmarried ladies ... [and] superannuated governesses' to follow her lead into the literary marketplace'.[24] Even these dismissive reactions betray, however, through their

---

   [20]   'Mrs. Cowley's Works', *The European Magazine*, 66 (August–September, 1814): 234.

   [21]   'Dialogue on the Drama', *The Theatrical Inquisitor* (February 1820): 74–6, at p. 75.

   [22]   Review of *The Mysterious Marriage, or the Hermit of Roselva*, by Harriet Lee, *The Monthly Mirror*, 5 (March 1798): 166; 'Account of Mrs. Inchbald's New Comedy [*Wives as They Were*]', *The Lady's Magazine*, 28 (1797): 120.

   [23]   'Baillie's *Series of Plays*', *The Annual Review; and History of Literature*, 1 (1802): 680; Scott, *Essays on the Drama*, p. 223; 'Celebrated Female Writers. No. I. Joanna Baillie', *Blackwood's Edinburgh Magazine*, 16 (August 1824): 165, 162.

   [24]   'Plays, by Joanna Baillie', *The Imperial Review; or London and Dublin Literary Journal*, 1 (1804): 338; Jeffrey, 'Miss Baillie's *Plays on the Passions*', *The Edinburgh*

anxious hyperbole, reminiscent of Richard Polwhele's diatribe against those Wollstonecraftian hordes in *The Unsex'd Females* (1798), a troubled recognition of the substantial literary and social impact of women's dramatic writing. For good or ill, depending as much on the gender politics as the aesthetic values of cultural observers, the drama potentially offered women writers of the romantic era a distinctive presence in the social sphere.

Those women actively engaged in dramatic writing faced such an opportunity with some trepidation about overstepping the bounds of female decorum – Baillie cautions women not to 'neglect' domestic 'occupations' in their pursuit of learning[25] –, but also with an enthusiasm that registers in their confident, frequently innovative theorizing about the drama's ameliorative social functions. Elizabeth Macauley, proposing in her *Mary Stuart* of 1823 a new mode of historical performance art through dramatic recitations on stage (what she characterizes as *A Histrionic Delineation of Historical Character*), justifies her invention by emphasizing its 'value' and 'utility' for promoting 'information and improvement' on the 'national' level.[26] Women dramatists and theatre theorists of the romantic era found many urgent political applications for this model of staging national 'improvement'. During the 'momentous ... period' of Napoleon's threatened invasion, for instance, Jane West urges her audiences to turn their eyes and hopes to the renovated drama, whose 'consecrated ... purpose' aims to 'nerve our courage and elevate our minds' in the noble defense of 'religious principle ... social order' and the patriotic 'interests of [our] country'. 'Instruction' is the true purpose of the theatre, according to Inchbald, and she finds the political lessons of the stage in anti-slavery plays contributing directly to the 'alleviation' of the 'hardships of slavery' with abolition in 1807.[27] Hannah Cowley's feminist concept of 'THE THEATRE' as a 'great National School' for women as well as men receives an even more sophisticated formulation in Baillie's *Introductory Discourse*, which represents the theatre as 'a school' for teaching the values of mercy, kindness, and compassion in the performance of public duties (pp. 454, 442).

It is no coincidence that many of these women dramatists focus their theorizing about the drama's social impact on the specific possibilities for such civic influence in the writing and staging of historical drama. That genre had acquired considerable popularity during the romantic era, according to Richard Altick and

---

Review, 2 (July 1803): 277, 280; Jeffrey, 'Miss Baillie's Miscellaneous Plays', *The Edinburgh Review*, 5 (1805): 421; Z., 'Cockney School of Poetry. No IV', *Blackwood's Edinburgh Magazine*, 3 (August 1818): 519–20.

[25] Joanna Baillie, *The Dramatic and Poetical Works of Joanna Baillie: Complete in One Volume* (London, 1851), second edn, repr., *The Dramatic and Poetical Works of Joanna Baillie* (Hildesheim and New York, 1976), p. 709. All Baillie quotations refer to this edition and will be cited parenthetically hereafter by page number.

[26] Elizabeth Macauley, *Mary Stuart* (London, 1823), pp. iv–v.

[27] Jane West, 'Preface to the Plays', in *Poems and Plays*, 4 vols (London, 1799), vol. 4, p. viii; Inchbald, *The British Theatre*, vol. 19, p. 3 and vol. 20, p. 3.

Michael Wilson,[28] because of Britain's protracted wars with America and France and the related public craving for scenic representation – in painting, plays, stage spectacles – of recent and more distant historical events. Shelley's *The Cenci*, Keats's *Otho the Great*, and Byron's *Marino Faliero* and *The Two Foscari* all grew out of a burgeoning vogue for staging history marked by astonishing expenditures of creative ingenuity, which brought to life on London stages such events as *The British Glory in Egypt* at Astley's Ampitheatre (1801) and *The Battle of the Nile* at Sadler's Wells (1815). The intrinsic political resonance of these productions, whether addressed toward recent events or episodes from the more distant past, made historical drama particularly compelling as a powerful vehicle for engaging in the turbulent politics of the revolutionary era and the post-Napoleonic years.[29] For many women dramatists, however, the strong pull of historical drama's role in public affairs gained a special urgency because of its convergence with new forms of historical revisionism through which many of the period's women writers were finding significant political outlets.

I have argued elsewhere how major shifts in later-eighteenth-century historiographical theory and method created unprecedented opportunities for women authors not only to engage in various types of historical writing but also to develop revisionary modes of historical understanding that trenchantly address the politics of the present.[30] The new enlightenment historiography of such towering figures as Hume, Gibbon, Ferguson, and Robertson transformed historical inquiry into the predominant system of knowledge production during the romantic era, which consequently became the primary discursive field in which competing ideologies of nation, race, gender, class, and empire clashed.[31] This public arena of writing frequently assumed an exclusive masculine orientation productive of 'men's history', as Christina Crosby has argued,[32] particularly in the domains of political and philosophical history. Yet shifting centers of meaning in the new

---

[28]   Richard D. Altick, *The Shows of London* (Cambridge, 1978), p. 176; Michael S. Wilson, '*Ut Pictura Tragoedia*: An Extrinsic Approach to British NeoClassic and Romantic Theatre', *Theatre Research International*, 12 (1987): 206.

[29]   For an extensive discussion of the political functions of liberal drama by male and female British playwrights of the 1820s, see Diego Saglia's '"The Talking Demon": Liberty and Liberal Ideologies on the 1820s British Stage', *Nineteenth-Century Contexts*, 28/4 (December 2006): 347–77.

[30]   Greg Kucich, 'Mary Shelley: Biographer', in Esther Schor (ed.), *The Cambridge Companion to Mary Shelley* (Cambridge, 2003), pp. 226–41.

[31]   For substantial accounts of the rise of British historiography in the later eighteenth and early nineteenth centuries, see Phillips, *Society and Sentiment;* Karen O'Brien, *Narratives of Enlightenment: Cosmopolitan History from Voltaire to Gibbon* (Cambridge, 1997); and Stephen Bann, *Romanticism and the Rise of History* (New York and Oxford, 1995).

[32]   Christina Crosby, *The Ends of History: Victorians and the 'Woman Question'* (London, 1991).

history could also foster a unique kind of accessibility to women readers and writers.

Mark Salber Phillips has demonstrated how the growth of middle-class commercialism in eighteenth-century British society inspired Hume's generation of historians, dissatisfied with the dominant plots of military strife and monarchial power struggles in conventional historiography, to place a new emphasis on commerce, industry, the arts, social relations, and domestic life and its affective components. This realignment, intensified by the general rise of sentimental culture, triggered a previously unheard-of historical interest in social life and the realm of affect. Hume, for instance, features many domestic, often sorrowful, settings in his famous *History of England* (1754–62). The makers of this new history targeted women readers and addressed women's experience as part of their concentration on the social fabric of the past. Such a new emphasis converged with the rapid increase of women writers in other sentimental genres to inspire, Phillips concludes, numerous experiments by women with the 'affective possibilities' of historical narration.[33] That entryway, which opened out into an inviting range of generic avenues such as historical fiction, historical drama, biography, memoirs, and educational history for children, as well as histories of women, also encouraged women writers to capitalize on the charged new possibilities of historical writing for participating discursively in national politics. Thus Hays confidently prefaces her *Female Biography* with the goal of 'advanc[ing] ... my sex ... in the grand scale of ... social existence', and Lady Morgan aligns her history of women with 'the great impulse to social improvement and national well-being'.[34]

Despite this enthusiasm about the political agency of historical writing, Catherine Moreland's complaint in *Northanger Abbey* about the 'tiresome' and gender-biased nature of 'solemn' history also represents an underlying discontent with historical options shared by many of the women who actively exercised them.[35] In her imaginative history of women's experience, *Characteristics of Women*, Anna Jameson complains that history 'disdains to speak' of the complexity of women's character. Morgan asserts that women have been falsely marginalized and, worse, insidiously demonized throughout the records of history. 'Alluded to, rather as an incident than a principal in the chronicle of nations, her influence, which cannot be denied, has been turned into a reproach; her genius ... has been treated as a phenomenon, when not considered as a monstrosity!'[36] Why such critical perceptions of a standard masculinized history obtained in spite of the discipline's growing appeal to and inclusion of women stems from a variety of persisting, gender-based limitations in the newer modes of historical representation.

---

[33]   Phillips, *Society and Sentiment*, p. 93.

[34]   Hays, *Female Biography*, vol. 1, p. iv; Morgan, *Woman and Her Master*, vol. 1, p. 16.

[35]   Jane Austen, *Northanger Abbey* (Harmondsworth, 1985), p. 123.

[36]   Anna Jameson, *Characteristics of Women: Moral, Political, and Historical*, 2 vols (London, 1832), vol. 1, p. 11; Morgan, *Woman and Her Master*, vol. 1, p. 21.

A significant number of women writers found mainstream history much too curtailed in its explorations of affect and social life, which provoked calls like Catharine Macaulay's when openly rivaling Hume in her own *History of England* for more 'sympathising tenderness' in the shaping of 'historical knowledge'.[37] This pattern of extending or intensifying the new priorities of historical writing, following a 'different track' rather than forging an entirely new mould, serves as a useful model for comprehending the multivalent forms of historical revisionism practiced by women writers of the romantic era. As Hays puts it, her intention is not to 'astonish [with] profound research' and new material but rather to 'collect and concentrate' historical details in an 'interesting' and original 'point of view'.[38] The opportunities for political intervention through such a realignment loom largely, Morgan contends, in the process of rewriting women's history through a new kind of sympathetic outlook that traces female sufferings and wrongs 'in every region … from Indus to the Pole' and 'fearlessly … plead[s] her cause'.[39]

Pleas for many 'causes' – including the abolition of slavery; resistance to war; improved class, race, ethnic, and religious relations; scaled-back imperial ambitions, as well as female empowerment – issued from this alternative way of seeing the past.[40] A prototype for feminist historiography today,[41] its sheer volume and creative variety during the romantic period explain why the burgeoning vogue of historical drama fired the imaginations of so many women dramatists. Indeed, their theoretical pronouncements on the significance of historical drama overwhelmingly link the value of the genre to the challenge of refitting its conventions in alignment with the 'affective possibilities' of the alternative, female histories proliferating all around them. Ann Yearsley introduces her historical play, *Earl Goodwin*, with a theoretical preface emphasizing the importance of tracing sympathetic relations in history – 'the bosom warm'd by social love' – while recovering domestic pathos and, especially, women's sufferings from the more generalized annals of political history. Elizabeth Macauley outlines a related agenda in the preface to her experimental *Histrionic Delineation of Historical Character*, arguing that the 'national study' of history should turn from general events to 'personal portraiture' of sorrow, once again women's grief in particular,

---

[37]   Catharine Macaulay, *The History of England, from the Accession of James I to that of the Brunswick Line*, 8 vols (London, 1763–83), vol. 6, pp. 21, 23, 28, 130.

[38]   Hays, *Female Biography*, vol. 1, p. vii.

[39]   Morgan, *Woman and Her Master*, vol. 1, p. 21.

[40]   Examples of these forms include, among many others, Charlotte Smith's *The Emigrants*; Morgan's *The Wild Irish Girl*; Anna Barbauld's *Eighteen Hundred and Eleven*; Helen Maria Williams's *Peru*; Ann Yearsley's *On the Inhumanity of the Slave Trade*; Felicia Hemans's *The Siege of Valencia*; and Mary Shelley's *The Last Man*.

[41]   For representative developments in recent feminist historiography, see Joan Wallach Scott (ed.)'s *Feminism and History* (Oxford, 1996), Ann-Louise Shapiro's *Feminists Revision History* (New Brunswick, 1994), and Bonnie Smith, *The Gender of History: Men, Women, and Historical Practice* (Cambridge, MA, 1998).

depicted with a special eye to the 'sympathies' and 'feelings' of the 'heart'. Jane West goes even further, claiming that such an inward turn of the drama to 'the amiable virtues of domestic life' would instigate a comprehensive reform of 'the present state of our stage' and 'invigorate' its social function.[42] Making similar claims in many of her prefaces to *The British Theatre*, Inchbald complains about the generic patriotism of much historical drama and charges modern dramatists to 'bid defiance to all that [traditional] history has recorded'. 'The truth of history' on stage, she elaborates, consists of 'melting pathos', 'scenes of woe', and 'pathetic claims [on] behalf of suffering' that 'melt the soul to sympathy' in a display of what Mitford calls 'woman's truth'.[43] This feminized way of staging the past specifically replaces, Mitford elaborates, the overblown 'glorious past' (*Foscari*, p. 17) of military triumph and imperial power in traditional historical drama. In virtually every one of these cases for domesticating historical drama, such a new affective 'truth of history' assumes the even more particularized authenticity of women's lived experience and suffering brought back to life with a variety of political aims, though quite frequently directed toward the task of toppling, in Yearsley's strident phrase, man's 'despotic rule over woman'.[44]

This emphasis on social agency in theorizing a new theatre of women's historical suffering draws strategically on the political imperatives at the core of romanticism's emergent forms of feminist historiography. For the inward, domestic priorities of 'sympathetic' history did not mean circumscribing the new truths of the past to a conventionally privatized realm of feminine affect. Quite the opposite, Catharine Macaulay became a major player, Hume's chief opponent, in national debates over the political legacies of Britain's seventeenth-century revolutions. She thus infused the force of affect, which she characterized as 'shed[ding] many tears' over the sorrowful records of the past,[45] into the center of the most urgent public controversies of her time. Such a direct political application of history's affective possibilities, particularly regarding women's experience, actually stands out as one of the most widely shared maneuvers in the many different inflections of the new, feminized 'truth of history'. Arguably the most demonstrable examples of this social agenda surfaced in those innovative histories – like Morgan's *Woman and Her Master* and Hays's *Female Biography* – devoted specifically to women's experience throughout time and across the globe. These more specialized histories of women concentrate on the deep subjectivities and affective lives of illustrious women in order to counter distortive caricatures of female 'phenoms' or 'monsters' and to demonstrate women's mental capacity, as Morgan argues, for managing affairs of state and participating in 'the progress of great social and national events

---

[42]   Yearsley, *Earl Goodwin, an Historical Play* (London, 1791), p. Ia; Macauley, *Mary Stuart*, pp. v, viii; West, 'Preface to the Plays', in *Poems and Plays*, vol. 4, pp. x, vii.

[43]   Inchbald's comments appear in her prefaces to *Cato* (vol. 8, p. 7), *The Grecian Daughter* (vol. 15, p. 4), and *The Battle of Hexham* (vol. 20, p. 4); Mitford, *Foscari*, p. 67.

[44]   Yearsley, *Earl Goodwin*, p. 20.

[45]   Macaulay, *History*, vol. 6, p. xii.

... In all outbursts of mind, in every forward rush of the great march of [social] improvement, she has borne a part ...'.[46] This way of linking interior capacities with social amelioration leads, moreover, to sustained analyses of women's historical experience within oppressive social and legal systems (what we would now call sex-gender systems of power). In spite of the great historical progress of science and civilization, Morgan elaborates, the retrograde social 'institutions' regulating gender, particularly marital laws and educational restrictions, persist in forming 'a ... nucleus of evil ... [that] renders woman still a thing of sufferance and ... wrongs ... [in] every phase of society, and in every region ...'. Recovering the history of 'melting pathos' in these 'scenes of woe' works specifically toward righting women's wrongs and, even more broadly, forwarding the general march of social progress and, as Morgan puts it, the 'best of ... reforms'.[47]

Those women writers who shared Inchbald's wish to bring the revisionary history of pathos into the theatre pointedly explored the dramaturgical possibilities for enacting this precise linkage between spectacles of female suffering and models of social reform, past and present. Yearsley, for example, avidly supports the politics of Goodwin's populist rebellion against Edward the Confessor in 1042, but she ultimately subordinates political considerations to the personal trauma endured by Goodwin's family, particularly the sorrows of his wife, Emma, when she is falsely accused of infidelity by the king's faction. The 'private woe' of 'a mother's suffering' and the struggle among Goodwin's family members to regain 'dear domestic bliss' control the action on Yearsley's historical stage, eventually inspiring the rule of sympathy over 'the iron rod of Law' in national politics when Goodwin's son, Harold, advises against war on the grounds of domestic priorities.[48] Such a socialized alertness to these sympathetic priorities also informs the historical drama of Francis Burney, whose *Edwy and Elgiva* advocates a special kind of 'Retrospection' that, governed by its 'domestic charge', pierces into the story of the suffering female heart at the core of history's grand events.[49] Burney thus foregrounds the marital pathos of Elgiva, a 'Sweet Sufferer' who is abducted and murdered by the clerical enemies of her new husband, King Edwy,[50] in order to advance through her play's profound sympathy for history's sorrowful victims an affective plea for reconciliation between those conflicts of church and state – for Burney in particular, between Catholic France and Protestant England – that continue to wreak havoc in her own time. In thus featuring stage center the socially transformative effects of displaying female woes, women playwrights of the 1790s demonstrated the unique possibilities of realizing those lofty national ideals of theatrical and cultural renewal through a new kind of affective historical drama

---

[46]   Morgan, *Woman and Her Master*, vol. 1, pp. 20, 29.

[47]   Ibid., vol. 1, pp. 16, 17, 21.

[48]   Yearsley, *Earl Goodwin*, pp. 4, 31, 37.

[49]   Fanny Burney, *Edwy and Elgiva*, ed. Miriam J. Benkovitz (Hamden, 1957), pp. 19, 15.

[50]   Ibid., p. 67.

linked integrally to the still broader social project of their female contemporaries to deepen the 'sentimental register' of eighteenth-century historiography.

Baillie and Mitford offer particularly revealing examples of the strategic connection in this innovative historical drama between re-imagining the past and forging social reforms in the present. Both writers engaged in substantial amounts of historical reading, focusing particularly on the newer types of sentimental investments in eighteenth-century historiography. Baillie, for instance, drew on Robert Henry, one of the leading proponents of the new history of commerce and domestic relations, as an important model for her Saxon plays, *Ethwald, Part First and Second*.[51] In the preface to her 1821 poetic volume of historical narratives, *Metrical Legends of Exalted Characters*, Baillie invokes numerous instances of heightened affect in the new history: such as Hume's attentiveness to the 'languishing ... condition' of her own ancestor, Robert Baillie of Jerviswoode, during the Jacobite uprisings of the late seventeenth century (p. 761); and Robert Wodrow's climactic episode on the 'sufferings' of Jerviswoode in his *History of the Scottish Church* (p. 759). Mitford, who acknowledges Baillie as her inspiration in drama, similarly turns to John Moore's *View of Society and Manners in Italy* (1783) as her primary source for the 'melting pathos' of the Foscari tragedy. Mitford and Baillie both characterize their adaptations of these affective records of the past in terms that highlight the prominence of sentiment and pathos in their own historical writing. Baillie even defines her *Metrical Legends* as 'sentimental' history (p. 706), and Mitford presents *Foscari* as a 'domestic tragedy' suffused with 'pure and gentle pathos' (p. 1).

Both writers also stress, in a maneuver that grows out of the revisionary emphasis of the women's historicism of their time, the modified focus of their domestic history, particularly its deepening of the sentimental registers in their sources. Dissatisfied with the limitations of emotional interiority in what she calls 'real history' (p. 5), Baillie conceives of a 'new' kind of history that will recover the poignant inner lives of individuals hitherto 'unknown in history', especially female sufferers like her own ancestor Lady Griseld Baillie (p. 706). Following such a 'different track' strikes both writers as the most promising means for realizing that urgent ideal of a revitalized theatre that will also reform the nation. Baillie thus looks specifically to an original type of affective historical drama to fulfill her ultimate goal of a theatre of 'instruction' whose cultural work inspires 'sympathetic curiosity' among theatre audiences of societal makers and shakers – judges, lawyers, rulers – and thus renders them 'more just, more merciful, more compassionate in their public functions' (p. 4).

I have recently argued how Baillie, in constructing this new theatrical school of sympathetic history, relies on contemporary pictorial technologies and particular vogues for staging 'attitudes' and tableaux vivants to develop a new mode of

---

[51]   Phillips opens his study of the new history with a sustained analysis of Henry's representative example of the form, *History of Great Britain from the Invasion by the Romans under Julius Caesar* (1771–93).

freezing the action of her plays in tableaux scenes of intense affective exchanges.[52] This performance technique assumed a wider range of inflections, with more acute political imperatives than I have previously noted, in women's historical drama of the romantic era. Tracing the details of its broader deployment in representative scenes from Mitford as well as Baillie will deepen our understanding of the extent to which the outpouring of historical plays by women on the romantic stage drew strategic direction from both the revisionary orientation and the social activism of the period's emergent forms of feminist historiography. For both Mitford and Baillie not only conceptualize their historical drama generally in terms of a new outlook on the past. They also fashion their stage pictures as reconstructions of prominent masculine precedents in historical drama through revisionary maneuvers similar to the patterns of rewriting source material in the alternative women's historiography of their time. Their stage tableaux thus deepen the sentimental registers of their models – Shakespeare for Baillie; Byron for Mitford – and, in so doing, feature powerful examples of the socially reformative effects of sympathy, gendered in female terms, on the dynamics of justice and mercy in public sphere politics regarding empire, militarism, and national patriotism.

These transformative functions in Baillie's tableaux of sympathy emerge most notably when her arrested scenes halt the grand march of general history at critical stage moments, replacing the pageantry of wars and the intrigues of national and imperial politics with a re-engendered historical outlook and a modified political situation, both grounded on the inner life of sympathetic human relations. *Constantine Paleologus*, Baillie's large-scale drama on the fall of Constantinople to the Ottoman power in 1453 and the shift of imperial power from West to East, abounds with spectacular stage effects – smoke and fire, booming cannons, collapsing columns, troops surging across stage in the crush of combat; but this sensational flow of grand historical action dramatically stops at the play's conclusion with one of Baillie's most stunning examples of picturing the alternative impact of affective history. Immediately following the death of Constantine and the establishment of a new public court ruled by the Turkish sultan, Mahomet, Baillie brings Valeria, Constantine's grieving wife, stage center as the pivotal figure in this public arena of power. With the action of history now focused on this anguished female presence in the midst of imperial authority, Valeria flings her robe open to reveal a self-inflicted knife wound 'in her breast' (p. 477). This gripping spectacle of female suffering then develops into an elaborate tableau picturing group sympathies spread across various subject positions that unite private and public spheres while dissolving entrenched differences of gender, class, social identity, and, momentarily, even race and religion. Valeria falls back in mortal agony, and the small community of Constantine's surviving followers, male and female, gathers round her in poignant support. The soldiers Rodrigo and Othus, now rejecting their passionate dedication to military codes of honor,

---

52   Kucich, 'Joanna Baillie and the Re-Staging of History and Gender', in Thomas C. Crochunis (ed.), *Joanna Baillie, Romantic Dramatist* (London, 2004), pp. 108–29.

join Valeria's female attendant, Ella, and her servant, Lucia, to form a body of supporters physically entwined in their loving ministrations to Valeria. She draws the group into even closer union, first joining the hands of Ella and Rodrigo as she blesses their marital prospects and then catching hold of Ella and Lucia 'with a convulsive grasp' (p. 477) as she expires. Baillie highlights the statuary effect of this palpable embodiment of interlocking affections in the center of imperial power with a stage direction calling for the scene to be held motionless: a 'solemn pause' ensues (p. 478). With the frenetic and destructive action of grand history along with its conventional social behaviors thus halted by that solemn pause, an alternative historical vision of sympathy governed by female energies thus rises into striking relief as a stage tableau of the new 'truth' of the past.

The revisionary emphasis of this way of re-staging history, and its linkage to the patterns of rewriting and social intervention in the new forms of feminist historiography, becomes most apparent in Baillie's precise reformulation of similar plot lines, tableaux, and climactic interactions in Shakespeare's Roman precedents. Although Baillie's critics faulted her at times for excessive borrowing from Shakespeare throughout her dramatic writing, her abundant echoes and allusions usually work toward significant revision. Valeria's climactic choice of suicide over submission to the victorious enemy ruler obviously recalls Cleopatra's example in *Antony and Cleopatra*. Yet the parallel also highlights strategic contrasts. For Valeria displays none of Cleopatra's self-centered, albeit magnificent, vanity. Valeria's tendency at times to draw Constantine away from his martial compulsions does not serve her own desire for power and attention, as in Cleopatra's manipulation of Antony, but works instead to highlight the value of domestic affections over military glory. Indeed, Valeria functions throughout her saga, most unlike Cleopatra, in the kind of positive, unifying role that culminates in the final tableau of interlacing sympathies she inspires throughout her community. Baillie foregrounds the transformative social power of that impact through even more specific revisions of *Coriolanus*.

Undoubtedly Baillie's most important theatrical model for her own historical drama on the final days of the Caesars, *Coriolanus* features not only popular insurrections and imperial conflicts similar to those of *Constantine Paleologus* but also striking clashes, like those in Baillie's play, between the demands of military honor and the pull of domestic ties. It was famously re-mounted, after years of banishment from the London stage because of its conspiratorial overtones, with a sensational lead performance by John Philip Kemble in the year Baillie published *Constantine Paleologus*. Kemble actually produced his own edition of the play in 1806, which heightened the prominence of Coriolanus's emotional exchanges with his mother, Volumnia, as Kemble's new title declares: *Shakespeare's Coriolanus; or, The Roman Matron*. Of perhaps greatest interest to Baillie, Kemble elevated the intensity of these and related scenes by staging them as dramatic tableaux that earned universal acclaim and ensured the production's astonishingly sustained popularity until Kemble's 1817 retirement in the title role.[53] Much as Baillie may have drawn inspiration and guidance from these precedents, she also pointedly altered what both Shakespeare and Kemble offered.[54]

While Baillie incorporates many of Shakespeare's plot scenarios – the danger of popular uprisings; the self-searching treachery of political authorities; the impending doom of a besieged imperial city –, she significantly modifies the dynamics of public action and domestic affections in *Coriolanus*. Where Coriolanus alternately imposes his destructive martial will on Roman citizens as well as family members or subjects himself to the questionable, often equally militaristic influence of his mother, Baillie moves Constantine increasingly toward domestic sympathies with Valeria and affective relations with his loyal followers.[55] He even laments Othus's fatal turn from scholarly pursuits to a soldier's iron duty, and he admits his own deep preference for the quiet lot of a woodman spending 'peaceful days' and 'shar[ing] my crust' with 'her who would have cheer'd me' in domestic bliss (p. 458). His supporters remain faithful, unlike those of Coriolanus, precisely because of his expressions of such sympathy for them, figured in many stage displays of flowing affection and discarded armor that contrast markedly with Kemble's famous statuesque performances of a haughty, rigid Coriolanus. Although Baillie's Constantine finally submits with reluctance to the martial responsibilities of his public identity, this stronger inclination to 'dear domestic ties' becomes embodied in Valeria's closing tableau as the play's center of value.

Baillie's highly detailed reconstruction of a related scene in *Coriolanus* drives home the transformative social potential of this new priority. Near the end of

---

[53]   For contemporary discussions of the statuary effect of Kemble's tableaux, see William Hazlitt's commentary in *A View of the English Stage* (1818), in *The Complete Works of William Hazlitt*, ed. P.P. Howe, 21 vols (London, 1930–34), vol. 5, pp. 376–8. For more recent scholarly discussions of Kemble's various productions of *Coriolanus*, see David Rostron, 'Contemporary Political Comment in Four of J.P. Kemble's Shakespearean Productions', *Theatre Research/Researches Theatrales*, 12 (1972): 113–19; Barbara Puschmann-Nalenz, 'Using Shakespeare? The Appropriation of *Coriolanus* and *Henry V* in John Philip Kemble's 1789 Productions', *Shakespeare Yearbook*, 5 (1995): 219–32; John Ripley, *Coriolanus on Stage in England and America, 1609–1994* (Madison, NJ, 1998). For an astute reading of the politics of the Kemble productions and Hazlitt's reactions, see Charles Mahoney, 'Upstaging the Fall: *Coriolanus* and the Spectacle of Romantic Apostasy', *Studies in Romanticism*, 38 (Spring 1999): 29–50.

[54]   Kemble had played the lead male role in Baillie's *De Monfort* (1798) and then encouraged her to present *Constantine Paleologus* to the Drury Lane management. When he curtly rejected the play, however, Baillie felt 'hurt' and determined to bring her 'connexion with Drury Lane Theatre', and presumably with Kemble as well, to 'an end'. Cf. *The Collected Letters of Joanna Baillie*, ed. Judith Bailey Slagle, 2 vols (Madison, NJ, 1999), vol. 2, pp. 1106–7.

[55]   In her Preface to *Miscellaneous Plays*, Baillie states that her top priorities in modifying Gibbon's account of the fall of Constantinople were to introduce 'the character of Valeria ... and [bring] forward the domestic qualities of Constantine ...' (p. 390).

Shakespeare's play, a vengeful, ever prideful Coriolanus has split with Rome and stands now in league with his former enemies on the verge of destroying Rome. Coming into his tent, the seat of public power, his mother, wife, and son beg as pathetic ambassadors from Rome for him to relent. They are attended by the silent and unobtrusive attendant of his wife named, not coincidentally for Baillie, 'dear Valeria' (Act V, scene 3, 67).[56] As this domestic group of beseeching sufferers kneels humbly before the general, they resemble the body of supporters grouped around Valeria in the Turkish general's court at the end of Baillie's play. Their pleas, moreover, inspire a change similar to the elevation of sympathy in *Constantine Paleologus*, for Coriolanus, moved to 'sweet compassion' (Act V, scene 3, l. 196), sheds his vengeance and agrees to spare Rome. A significant model for Baillie's climactic tableau, in which Mohamet also relents in his stern designs against defeated foes, this display of feminized sorrow in the general's tent, nevertheless, falls short of her own goals.

The members of Coriolanus's domestic circle, for instance, remain disconnected from each other and from him, kneeling in gestures of self-abasing supplication rather than fully interconnected sympathy, which even strikes Coriolanus as an 'unnatural scene' (Act V, scene 3, l. 184). Kemble's famously statuesque representation of Coriolanus only heightened this unnatural distance. Even when Kemble sensationally prostrated himself before Volumnia in grandiloquent repentance, the tableau effects of alternating prostration do more to figure continuing power struggles between mother and son (with Coriolanus's own son and wife still on the margins) rather than the deep affective and physical intimacies of Baillie's stage pictures. These distortive effects worsen as Volumnia rises to separate herself from the kneeling group and harangue Coriolanus on the misery he has caused. Further compromising the presence of sympathy, Ausidius, Coriolanus's rival, takes secret glee in the awareness that Coriolanus's expression of mercy will ensure his downfall. Indeed it does, for despite his momentary softening, Coriolanus remains locked into masculine systems of power that swiftly destroy him for relenting in his destructive purpose. A brief outpouring of compromised sympathy then serves but to reinforce the violent regulations of power politics in this imperial setting.

To punctuate her corrective extension of the potential of this incomplete gesture toward social change, Baillie transforms the peripheral Valeria of *Coriolanus* into the new heroine of her own play, who is neither overbearing matron nor submissive wife but rather the unifying center of *Constantine Paleologus* in her full embodiment of domestic sympathies. In this transition between plays, the character of Valeria also undergoes a fundamental change in emotional constitution that further emphasizes Baillie's revisionary point. Not only subdued but also renowned for austerity in Shakespeare's play – as 'chaste as the icicle' (Act V, scene 3, l. 65) –, Valeria re-emerges on Baillie's stage as a radiant presence suffusing the

---

[56] All citations from *Coriolanus* refer to William Shakespeare, *The Tragedy of Coriolanus*, ed. Reuben Brower (New York, 1966).

affective influence of a 'woman's heart' throughout her community (p. 471). Such a change receives striking illustration in Baillie's strategic contrasts between the isolating statuary of Kemble's *Coriolanus* and the fluid interweaving of bodily figures around Valeria in the closing tableau of *Constantine Paleologus*.

Baillie's central embodiment of affective power in this updated tableau of group sympathies thus demonstrates a refashioning of theatrical history that, similar to the broader revisionary patterns of women's historiography, plays a crucial role in enacting ideals of social reform. Those ideals are not only modeled in tableau embraces but also featured in the altered views and actions of the main characters on stage. Rodrigo feels 'softened' and, releasing to the winds his 'stern' sense of military honor along with his 'chafed passions' (p. 478), forgives the cowardice of Justiniani. Mahomet, astounded by 'such ties' of sympathy in Valeria's group (p. 477), seeks friendship from his former enemies and generously sanctions the betrothal of Rodrigo and Ella. Othus renounces violence and commends the educational impact of the play's final tableau of sympathy, which he characterizes as a 'lesson of such high ennobling power' (p. 478). Given Baillie's vision of the theatre as a school for educating social leaders and political rulers, such a 'lesson' aims directly to inspire her audience members toward shaping a more sympathetic, just society. Her innovative ways of replacing official history and its specific manifestations in historical drama with stage pictures of communal sympathy thus foster new 'lessons' for the school of the theatre, illustrating reformed models of gender and social relations for the state of the nation.

Mitford performs similar kinds of stage pictures and revisionary moves, which also push toward ideals of female empowerment and a more merciful society, in the climactic scenes of her historical tragedy on fifteenth-century Venetian politics, *Foscari: A Tragedy* (published and staged at Covent Garden in 1826). Like Baillie, Mitford draws on the women's historiography of her time to display models of social reform by stopping the progress of conventional history on stage to re-imagine and picture forth in climactic tableaux the new truths of a more affective past.[57] Also like Baillie, Mitford illustrates the transformative social impact of communal sympathies, gendered in female terms, suffused throughout the centers of state power. She is even more direct than Baillie, moreover, in focusing these reconstructions of past and present on specific revisions of male precedents in historical drama. Her prologue, for instance, openly announces her choice to 'follow ... a different track' from Byron's 1821 play on the same topic, *The Two Foscari*. Mitford claims in her Preface to have completed her work and even submitted it to Covent Garden before Byron's publication five years earlier and without any knowledge of its existence. Nevertheless, the Prologue emphasizes her marked divergence from his 'bold Tragedy' in her production of a 'woman's play'

---

[57] For Mitford's revisionary tactics in her poetry and their critiques of the gender politics of her time, see Diego Saglia, 'Public and Private in Women's Romantic Poetry: Spaces, Gender, Genre in Mary Russell Mitford's *Blanch*', *Women's Writing*, 5 (1998): 405–22.

featuring a different kind of sympathetic historical outlook literally embodied in the author's 'trembling hand' (p. 2). What might seem like a stereotypical apology for female weakness in this self-representation will appear more like a declaration of a new kind of social power when juxtaposed with the transformative effects set in motion by the energies of Valeria's 'woman's heart' in *Constantine Paleologus*. Such a power, reinforced by pictorial 'lessons' reminiscent of Baillie's theatrical school, grows out of Mitford's strategic diversions from Byron's historical stage.

Byron had kept relatively closely to his mainstream historical sources of Pierre Daru and J.C.L. Simonde de Sismondi, featuring an appendix with extracts from their accounts, in retelling the sorrowful history of the elderly Doge Foscari, who is compelled by stern duty to exile his beloved son Jacopo, falsely accused of crimes against the city-state. As Daniel Watkins and Jerome McGann have argued, Byron's interest in his sources focuses on their attention to the tragic conflicts between justice and affection, dutiful patriotism and familial bonds, which infect the Venetian republic and inwardly shatter both the Doge and his son.[58] Byron's ideological critique of state power dramatizes its relentless annihilation of the heart's desires, which are subordinated to merciless duty and political enmity by all the protagonists. 'The *father* softens', announces Byron's epigraph, 'but the *governor's* resolved' (p. 129).[59] Much as the Doge feels inwardly lacerated by the sufferings of his 'dearest offspring' (p. 184), tortured and doomed to exile by the Senate, he clamps down his emotions in deference to his fierce civic duty. When confronted by those who 'feel deeply for your son', he justifies the necessity of carrying out the sentence by explaining, 'I am the state's servant' (p. 148). 'This means', declares Jacopo's wife, Marina, in pinpointing the tragic core of Byron's indictment of state power, 'that you are more a Doge than father' (p. 162). The contagion of such crushing power infects even the psyches of its victims, for Jacopo, despite the officially sanctioned outrages perpetrated against him, remains fanatically dedicated to the Venetian state. His wildly patriotic response to what seems an unlivable prospect of exile is to wish, disregarding all marital and familial ties, for a tempestuous storm to dash his 'broken corse upon the barren Lido, / Where I may mingle with the sands which skirt / The land I love …' (p. 185). Even Marina, the play's passionate spokesperson for the claims of human sympathy over civic justice, succumbs to the pernicious Venetian rule of vengeance. Barred from the halls of justice and despairing of her influence on state proceedings – 'what are a woman's word', she laments (p. 152) –, Marina assumes implacable hatred for her foes after Jacopo dies from his torture-inflicted wounds and the Doge expires with a broken heart. 'A thousand fold / May the worm which ne'er dieth feed upon

---

58　　Daniel P. Watkins, *A Materialist Critique of English Romantic Drama* (Gainesville, 1993), pp. 167–72; *Lord Byron: The Complete Poetical Works*, ed. Jerome McGann, 7 vols (Oxford, 1980–91), vol. 6, pp. 625–45. All subsequent references to the McGann edition of *The Two Foscari* are cited parenthetically by page number.

59　　The epigraph slightly modifies Richard Brinsley Sheridan's lines from Act II, scene 2 of *The Critic* (1779): 'The father softens – but the governor / Is fix'd!'

them!' (p. 186), she rages in furious execration, and vows stern 'retribution'. 'I have sons, who shall be men', she solemnly concludes, extending the brutal cycles of retributive justice and state violence to the next generation (p. 199).

Woman's word does make a difference in Mitford's very different version of the story. She relies on the somewhat more sentimental account of the Foscari history in John Moore's *View of Society and Manners in Italy* and departs substantially from that and other sources by inventing a fiancée for the young Foscari, Camilla, who functions somewhat like Baillie's Valeria as the affective center of the play. Also like Valeria, Camilla *does* break into the halls of justice and power. When young Foscari is falsely accused of murdering her father, the senator Donato, she rises to his defense in court and, defying 'the iron law / Of Venice' and its unyielding demand for 'justice', she cries out, 'For mercy, mercy' (p. 46). Mitford then features Camilla's power to inspire sympathy throughout this poisoned arena of masculine justice by constructing a stage tableau, reminiscent of Baillie's, in which Camilla 'supports' both Foscari – the son dying of a sword wound and the father afflicted with grief – in a group display of sympathies that even includes a former enemy, Cosmo. Glossed as an arrested moment of changed outlooks – 'What spectacle is this?', gasps an onlooker (p. 64) –, this stage picture stops the vicious, inexorable march of historical justice in Venice and foregrounds a new presence of sympathetic mercy in the public and private life of the state. The execution sentence of young Foscari is commuted; the former friends turned enemies, Foscari and Cosmo, find a brief reconciliation; the Doge pardons Cosmo; and, as the Doge throws off his ducal bonnet in a symbolic renunciation of iron justice, the cycle of dutiful retribution that drives the history of Venice gives way at the play's conclusion to heartfelt expressions of love among Camilla, Cosmo, and the two Foscari.

Mitford's abiding commitment to the social implications of this type of revisionary historicism in stage pictures registers in her deployment of similar theatrical tactics for *Rienzi: A Tragedy*. Published and staged at Drury Lane in 1828 for a highly successful run of thirty-four performances, *Rienzi* rather stunningly appears to revisit Baillie's adjustment of the famous reconciliation scene in *Coriolanus*. In her own play on Roman history, chronicling the rise and fall of the fourteenth-century populist forerunner of Italian nationalism, Cola di Rienzi, Mitford also re-writes Gibbon, acknowledged in her Preface, by inventing and giving a prominent social role to a female character, Rienzi's daughter Claudia. Demure and passively obedient throughout most of the play, Claudia, like Camilla and Baillie's Valeria, breaks down the walls of state justice and infuses the power of merciful sympathy into government policy when she pleads for her father to commute his execution sentence against her beloved Angelo Colonna, convicted of treason against the state. Mitford's stage management of this scene works even more precisely than Baillie's toward a transformative reconfiguration of the climactic exchange between Volumnia and Coriolanus.

Just like Volumnia, Claudia enters into the center of state authority and pleads for mercy to a stern, unyielding intimate relation. 'Oh, pardon,' she implores

Rienzi, 'Call him [Angelo] as thou wilt, but pardon! / Oh, pardon!'[60] Also like Volumnia, Claudia responds to the ruler's persisting implacability by collapsing to her knees: 'See, I kneel ... wilt pardon?' (p. 60). This stage moment, which inspires Rienzi to relent and '[r]aise ... up' the supplicating Claudia, virtually mirrors the scene Baillie adapted from *Coriolanus*. Reshaping that encounter even more directly, however, Mitford stages a significant reversal of Shakespeare's plot that signals a still more fruitful exchange of mutual sympathies. She replaces the warped dynamics of Volumnia's manipulative control of her son with a loving interchange between father and daughter, in which Rienzi reassumes his natural place as nurturing parent while also affirming the 'mutual' affections they share for each other. 'Rest on my bosom', he gently murmurs, 'let thy beating heart / Lie upon mine; so shall the mutual pang / Be stilled ... my sweet one! Oh, forgive – ' (p. 60). The tableau that ensues (with stage directions calling for Claudia to rush 'into Rienzi's arms') features this pair physically entwined in mutual love and forgiveness. Like Baillie's stage picture, Mitford's tableau not only softens the gestural rigidity of Shakespeare's and Kemble's models but in so doing also replaces the official history of justice and violence with a new chronicle of sympathetic relations embodied in female agency. The consequences for social transformation in the past and present, as in Baillie's play, receive immediate manifestation. Rienzi discards the law of vengeful justice for the rule of sympathetic mercy and, dramatically altering the history of Roman power, grants pardon to his enemy, Angelo.

If Baillie and Mitford could thus shape from the revisionary historicism of their time an alternative, imagined past that also pictured forth on the stage of 'a woman's play' the potential for social transformation in the present, they also flagged their strong reservations about the limits of such possibility. Valeria's final intervention comes at the cost of her life, or metaphorically her female identity, her heroic assumption of what Mohamet calls a 'manly state' ironically reinscribing a separation of gendered spheres of private and public life (p. 477). Camilla's infusion of mercy into the Venetian state does not save either Foscari, for the son dies of his wounds and the Doge, though finally preferring the dictates of the heart to those of the state, staggers on with but a 'broken heart' (p. 66). Rienzi's embrace of forgiveness comes too late for Angelo, who is executed just before the pardon arrives, and retribution cycles back to dominate Rome. Rienzi's enemies slay him for the sake of 'vengeance' and 'justice' while mortally wounding Claudia when she fruitlessly tries to protect him at the play's conclusion (p. 65). Baillie also seemed doubtful of successfully managing the static quality of her intimate tableaux in London's large patent houses, where the 'present circumstances', as she noted in a theoretical preface (p. 231), demanded large spectacle and frenetic action. Nevertheless, experiments with stage performance and historical representation like hers and Mitford's ultimately reveal the considerable degree to which they

---

[60]   Mary Russell Mitford, *Rienzi: A Tragedy* (London, 1828), p. 60. All subsequent references to this edition are cited hereafter parenthetically by page number.

both extended the possibilities and tested the limits of those efforts pervading women's historical writing and, particularly, historical drama of the romantic era to alter the structures of history and power.

Chapter 2

Historical Agency in Romantic Women's Drama

Lilla Maria Crisafulli

A discussion of historical agency in women Romantic playwrights may seem in some ways a contradictory enterprise. Between the end of the eighteenth and the beginning of the nineteenth century, women – to whatever social class they belonged and whatever trade they professed – did not seem to have the political force to argue for a radical change in national policy, and when they did so, they paid for it very dearly, as, for example, in the case of Anna Laetitia Barbauld (1743–1825), who retired from the publishing market once her 'Eighteen Hundred and Eleven, a Poem' (1812) came to the attention of a malevolent critic.[1] Apparently, to the eyes of their contemporaries, women were not in a position to represent or embody historical agency, especially if we read agency performatively, i.e. if we interpret it as an act or as the origin of action, as a living experience that produces a change. Agency would thus involve an interplay between the category of subjectivity, either individual or collective, and the process of causality, namely the effect that the act or action of the subject produces on a given reality, and as a consequence modifying it.[2] How, then, could women articulate an act of self-empowerment, as agency demands, and, at the same time, disempower the authority to which they were subordinated, when centuries of history had deprived them precisely of the political power and authoritative subjectivity they would have required in order to act in the public sphere?

It is a fact that in the Romantic period – which is traditionally made to coincide with the post-revolutionary age – women on the whole experienced a history of exclusion, historical or political agency being recognized as fundamentally male-gendered. During Romanticism, as Angela Keane points out in *Women Writers and the English Nation*,

> The masculine subject is … free to … come and go, long and belong at the same time. This *mobile* condition perhaps accounts for the 'representative' national status of male writers as peripatetic as Shelley and Byron, and for the paradoxical

---

[1]   The critic in question was the notorious John Wilson Croker, who violently attacked Barbauld in the *Quarterly Review* in 1812.

[2]   For an extensive discussion of historical agency, see William Jewett, *Fatal Autonomy: Romantic Drama and The Rhetoric Of Agency* (New York, 1997).

elevation of the male traveller/adventurer in the Romantic national tradition. In the Romantic national imagery, the woman who wanders, who defines herself beyond the home and as a subject ... divests herself of femininity and erases herself from the familial, heterosexual structure of the nation.[3]

Another reason for the exclusion of women from history was their marginalization as individual subjects, which corresponded to a progressively wider nationalization of 'Woman' as an abstract and ideal unit. Unitary Woman embodied and reproduced the national family, her virtues mirrored national virtues, just as her vices could dangerously disarm the whole community. The entire nation seemed to depend on Woman's moral integrity and familial affections. The nation became a feminized home and nurturing place where the origin and the stability of all citizens dwelled, even more so during the revolutionary and post-revolutionary years.[4]

The consequence of this national construction of Unitary Woman was that actual and plural women were entrapped in an icon of femininity that did not seem to take into account their belonging to a given social class or civil status, thereby frustrating their individual attempts at mobility and emancipation. According to the historian Diane Owen,

> ... the consistent impulse to see women in iconic rather than in narrative terms ... inevitably reduced their historical presence almost as much as those legal barriers that had kept them from a public life. Women were denied an active public persona and hence excluded from history's narrative ... In the historic age of men, these static women, frozen out of the flow of history, were best described and understood not by narrative devices but rather by iconic means.[5]

This iconic representation of women was in turn to feed into several streams of literary genres and to cause countless problems, as, for example, in the sphere of British female playwriting, especially when it dealt with history and femininity.

While women's aspirations were being forced into an iconic portrayal, the nation as a whole had undergone a process of feminization, to the point that England, at the end of the eighteenth century, came to be seen as a female in danger, and consequently in need of male protection. After the two revolutions, the American and the French, and during the long years of the war against France, the trope of female sexual vulnerability was frequently used to embody the nation's exposure

---

[3]	Angela Keane, *Women Writers and the English Nation* (Cambridge, 2000), p. 2.

[4]	Ibid, p. 3.

[5]	Quoted in Ann M. Frank Wake, 'Women in the Active Voice: Recovering Female History in Mary Shelley's *Valperga* and *Perkin Warbeck*', in Syndy M. Conger, Frederick S. Frank, Gregory O'Dea and Jennifer Yocum (eds). *Iconoclastic Departures. Mary Shelley after Frankenstein: Essays in Honor of the Bicentenary of Mary Shelley's Birth* (Cranbury, NJ, London and Mississauga, ON, 1997), 235–59, at p. 237.

to the attacks of its brutal and vulgar enemies. Virility belonged to England's male citizens, but not to their nation.

As is well known, the French Revolution had fired the mythologizing imagination of Edmund Burke, who had drawn the metonymic equation between the image of the Queen, Marie Antoinette – confined and abused in the tower by a ferocious National Assembly – and the condition of ungoverned and ruthless anarchy to which France was being led. Burke described France as a gentlewoman raped by a wild revolutionary mob:

> It is now sixteen or seventeen years since I saw the queen of France, then the dauphiness, at Versailles ... Little did I dream ... that I should have lived to see such disasters fallen upon her in a nation of gallant men, in a nation of men of honour and of cavaliers. I thought ten thousand swards must have leaped from their scabbards to avenge even a look that threatened her with insult. – But the age of chivalry is gone. – That of sophisters, oeconomists, and calculators, has succeeded; and the glory of Europe is extinguished for ever. Never, never more, shall we behold that generous loyalty to rank and sex, that proud submission, that dignified obedience, that subordination of the heart, which kept alive, even in servitude itself, the spirit of an exalted freedom. The unbought grace of life, the cheap defence of nations, the nurse of manly sentiment and heroic interprize is gone. It is gone, that sensibility of principle, that chastity of honour, which felt a stain like a wound ....[6]

But if, within the Burkean scenario, women were used to summon up the chivalric values of the nation, the same women, if left free, could become corrupt creatures, as the French women of the working class and of the petite bourgeoisie had been judged to be while demonstrating in the streets of Paris. Women had therefore to be tied up with a double knot for the security and the stability of the whole community. The 'compensatory equation', to quote Alison Sulloway, whereby 'women's segregated domesticity was supposed to compensate for man's expanding universes and to forestall revolution both at home and overseas',[7] left them struggling under the disabilities of gender or, in the case of women dramatists, under the complexities of genre, especially in the post-revolutionary years when culture and literature went through a powerful re-masculinization.[8]

In many ways, although Britannia remained female-gendered, the designation 'Britons' seems to be reserved for men; on the other hand, a large number of

---

[6] Edmund Burke, *Reflections on the Revolution in France* (1790), ed. Conor Cruise O'Brien (Harmondsworth, [1969], 1983), pp. 169–70.

[7] Alison Sulloway, *Jane Austen and the Province of Womanhood* (Philadelphia, 1989), p. 4.

[8] Gary Kelly, 'Feminine Romanticism, Masculine History, and the Founding of the Modern Liberal State', in Anne Janowitz (ed.), *Romanticism and Gender* (Woodbridge, 1998), pp. 1–18.

British women were not ready to identify themselves with every connotation that this label implied. Many women of the time not only rejected Burke's iconic image of a subdued and frozen entity, but stepped out into the political arena in order to deconstruct the gendered language of nationhood.[9]

Not by chance, some of them turned to the writing and production of drama, historical drama in particular, in order to project onto the past their current state of affairs, and, in so doing, to retrace a mechanism of causality able to explain and comment upon the events that were taking place in their own time.[10] Drama, as has been well known at least since Aristotle, is not easily reconcilable with stasis, and neither is historiography, since both discursive modes imply change, plot and development. Likewise, the community of women cannot be dealt with as a fixed and uniform extra-historical category.[11] Drama – like history or 'women' – is ruled by the flux of life and the flow of social change. In her article 'Women and History on the Romantic Stage: More, Yearsley, Burney, and Mitford', Katherine Newey discusses the use of history and genres by women playwrights, remarking how 'in using history and the high cultural form of tragedy, Romantic women playwrights were appropriating the "traditional authority of those national objects of knowledge". In this way, the authority of genre could be used to overcome the disabilities of gender'.[12] Newey goes on to draw a distinction between the use of drama (tragedy in particular) and the use of fiction, whereby

> Fiction ... can also be an instrument in the division of experience into that series of binary oppositions with which we still struggle: masculine and feminine, public and private, history and domesticity. In writing tragedies from the source material of English history, Romantic women playwrights carefully and cautiously attempted to dissolve the limits of those binaries by forcing a confrontation between the spheres of public, masculine, political action and

---

[9]   The connection between women and nation has been successfully explored by Anne K. Mellor in *Mothers of the Nation: Women Political Writing in England, 1780–1830* (Bloomington, IN, and Indianapolis, 2000).

[10]   Greg Kucich has written extensively on women and Romantic historical drama. See, among other publications, 'A Haunted Ruin: Romantic Drama, Renaissance Tradition, and the Critical Establishment', in Terence A. Hoagwood and Daniel P. Watkins (eds), *British Romantic Drama* (London, 1998), pp. 56–83; 'Joanna Baillie and the Re-Staging of History and Gender', in Thomas C. Crochunis (ed.), *Joanna Baillie, Romantic Dramatist* (London and New York, 2004), pp. 108–29. See also his essay in this volume.

[11]   For a more extended discussion on categorizing 'women' as a single community, see Joan Wallach Scott's introduction to the volume *Feminism and History* (Oxford, 1996), pp. 1–13, in particular p. 4: 'history contains examples of fundamental differences, in experience and self-understanding, among women, potentially undermining the political task of creating an enduring common identity.'

[12]   Katherine Newey, 'Women and History on the Romantic Stage: More, Yearsley, Burney, and Mitford', in Catherine Burroughs (ed.), *Women in British Romantic Theatre. Drama, Performance and Society, 1790–1840* (Cambridge, 2000), pp. 79–101, at p. 79.

feminine domesticity and feeling. Through the plotline of tragedy and its generic convention of the fall of the great man, these writers dramatized a feminist challenge to the exercise of extreme power and the actions of tyranny.[13]

In order to enquire further into women's use of history, we may direct our attention to the work of two of the pioneers among women historians, Catharine Macaulay Graham and Mary Hays: the former, Macaulay, an historian in a stricter sense; the latter, Hays, a conveyor of history through biography. In the introduction to her *Female Biography; or Memoirs of Illustrious and Celebrated Women of All Ages and Countries* (1803), Mary Hays states in straightforward fashion her gendered intentions. History and the stories of women of the past, with their fortunes and misfortunes – she affirms –, may be used to set up examples for other women to admire, if not to follow. Moreover, biographies, reaching women's sensibility more than the dry facts of history, may add 'knowledge and fortitude' to their 'grace and gentleness':

> My pen has been taken up in the cause, and for the benefit, of my own sex. For their improvement, and to their entertainment, my labour has been devoted. Women, unsophisticated by the pedantry of the schools, read not for dry information, to load their memories with uninteresting facts, or to make a display of a vain erudition. A skeleton biography would afford to them but little gratification: they require pleasure to be mingled with instruction, lively images, the grace of sentiment, and the polish of language. Their understandings are principally accessible through their affections: they delight in minute delineation of character; nor must the truths which impress them be either cold or unadorned. I have at heart the happiness of my sex, and their advancement in the grand scale of rational and social existence. I perceive, with mingled concern and indignation, the follies and vices by which they suffer themselves to be degraded. If, through prudence or policy, the generous contention between the sexes for intellectual equality must be waved, be not, my amiable country-women, poorly content with the destination of the slaves of an Eastern harem, with whom the season of youth forms the whole of life! A woman who, to the graces and gentleness of her own sex, adds the knowledge and fortitude of the other, exhibits the most perfect combination of human excellence.[14]

As is clear from the quoted passage, Mary Hays is an historian who attempts to establish women's presence and active voice in the events of history through individual lives, while also trying, like the first theorist of feminism, Mary Wollstonecraft, to reconcile the two sexes under the aegis of a unified humanity.

---

[13]   Ibid., p. 80.

[14]   Mary Hays, *Female Biography; or Memoirs of Illustrious and Celebrated Women of All Ages and Countries. Alphabetically Arranged, in Six Volumes*, printed for Richard Phillips (London, 1803), pp. III–V.

Women are portrayed by Mary Hays as historical subjects and indeed as makers of history. This is equally true of Mary Wollstonecraft, who, like Hays, was also a talented novelist and able to bring together individual stories and general history, thus creating, in a Godwinian radical vein,[15] a persuasive interplay between micro- and macro-history. Wollstonecraft creates fictional women – Mary, Maria or Jemima – that, in their vicissitudes and in the account of their personal circumstances, become 'living actions', that is to say, relentless instruments of a firm accusation of the oppression of women exercised by the social and political powers of Wollstonecraft's contemporary England. As a consequence, however, Mary, Maria or Jemima also acquire the paradigmatic value of a more general and historical representation of individuals. Wollstonecraft's aim to generalize the particular is asserted quite clearly at the beginning of her posthumously published novel, *Maria, or the Wrongs of Woman* (1798), where she states, 'my main object was the desire of exhibiting the misery and oppression, peculiar to women, that arise out of the partial laws and customs of society. In the invention of the story, this view restrained my fancy; and the history ought rather to be considered, as of woman than of an individual'.[16] In *Feminism and History*, however, Joan Wallach Scott warns us against the danger of an approach that 'simultaneously establishes women as historical subjects operating in time and makes the idea of "women" singular and timeless':

> ... those women in the past (or in other cultures) whose actions set precedents for our own are taken in some fundamental way to be just like us. They have to be like us if the comparisons and precedents are to be meaningful. ... Could a shared identity of 'women' exist at all if the conditions of life and the meanings of actions were fundamentally different from our own?[17]

Catharine Macaulay Graham seems quite aware of this risk, as displayed in her eight-volume *History of England* (1763–83), which defines in many different ways women's sense of history between the eighteenth and nineteenth centuries. But if Macaulay is willing to make precise distinctions while dealing with the particulars

---

[15]   I am thinking here of William Godwin's novel *Caleb Williams* and in particular of the unpublished essay 'Of History and Romance' in which the author theorizes the superiority of romance over history, since 'True history consists in a delineation of consistent, human character, in a display of the manner in which such a character acts under successive circumstances, in showing how character increases and assimilates new substances to its own, and how it decays.' Godwin could then rightly end his advocacy exclaiming, 'Dismiss me from the falsehood and impossibility of history, and deliver me over to the reality of romance'. See 'Of History and Romance', Appendix IV, in *Caleb Williams*, ed. Maurice Hindle (Harmondsworth, 1988), pp. 359–74, at pp. 371, 372.

[16]   Mary Wollstonecraft, *Maria, or the Wrongs of Woman*, ed. Gary Kelly (Oxford, 1980), p. 73.

[17]   Joan Wallach Scott's introduction to the volume *Feminism and History*, pp. 3–4.

and the individuals, she resists any levelling of moral values or the effacement of ethics when the judgement involves general history:

> The invidious centuries which may ensue from striking into a path of literature rarely trodden by my sex, will not permit a selfish consideration to keep me mute in the cause of liberty and virtue, whilst the doctrine of slavery finds so many interested writers to defend it by fraud and sophistry, in opposition to the common reason of mankind and the experience of every age. Absurd as are the principles and notions, on which the doctrine of arbitrary power is established, there have been ever in this country found many to adopt it ....[18]

One of Macaulay's main concerns in writing a *History of England* was in fact to 'challenge the exercise of extreme power and the actions of tyranny' by whatever sex they were perpetrated. And if she admits that her aim is to instruct her readers (didactic aims being one of the main reasons for women's resort to history), on the other hand she seems determined to use history as an instrument of virtual punishment of sinful rulers and politicians, be they men or women, bestowing on them eternal infamy and, vice versa, expressing eternal gratitude to the true patriots who have made a free country of England:

> Fame is the only reward which, in the present times, true virtue hath to hope; and the only punishment which the guilty great have to apprehend, is eternal infamy. ... Patriots who have sacrificed their tender affections, their properties, their lives, to the interests of society deserve a tribute of praise unmixed with any alloy. With regret do I accuse my country of inattention to the most exalted of their benefactors ....[19]

Macaulay then sums up her intentions:

> To do justice to the memory of our illustrious ancestors to the most extent of my small abilities, still having an eye to public liberty, the standard by which I have endeavoured to measure the virtue of those characters that are treated of in this history, is the principal motive that induced me to undertake this intricate part of the English history.[20]

Despite these good intentions, the gender of the history Macaulay narrates did not fail to arouse the malevolence of the contemporary critics who did not share her desire to transcend sexual boundaries, as stated at the end of Mary Hays's biography of Macaulay:

---

[18]   Catharine Macaulay, *The History of England from the Accession of James I to that of the Brunswick Line*, 8 vols (London, 1763), vol. 8, p. x.

[19]   Ibid.

[20]   Ibid., vol. 8, p. ix.

A female historian, by its singularity, could not fail to excite attention: she seemed to have stepped out of the province of her sex; curiosity was sharpened, and malevolence provoked. The author was attacked by petty and personal scurrilities, to which it was believed her sex would render her vulnerable. Her talents and powers could not be denied; her beauty was therefore called in question, as if it was at all concerned with the subject; or that, to instruct our understanding, it was necessary at the same time to charm our senses. She is deformed (said her adversaries, wholly unacquainted with her person ...).[21]

If these were the difficulties of a well-established historian such as Macaulay, we can begin to imagine what it was like to be a 'histor' in the world of theatre and drama in the Romantic age. Certainly the complications and anxieties of a woman playwright were no less significant than those acknowledged by Macaulay, Hays or Wollstonecraft in conducting their own professions. Women's plays were too often accused of not representing *real* life, or, with some fortunate exceptions, of not showing sufficient knowledge of the vicious but lively reality of the backstage,[22] but, paradoxically, when it was obvious that female playwrights had some familiarity with life (or with the backstage), they had to disguise it for shame or fear, just as they likewise had to conceal the uncommon circumstance of being endowed with a lively imagination from which they were able to create reality anew. Female imagination and knowledge, like female bodies, had to be bridled, and little freedom was allowed even to their dramatic offspring, whose staged lives, actions and ideologies – as Hannah Cowley (1743–1809) or Elizabeth Inchbald (1753–1821) complained on several occasions[23] – were double-checked by royal censors and dramatic critics. Hannah Cowley, for example, protests against the gender-biased notion of propriety in drawing characters and making them speak:

> [Critics] will allow me, indeed, to draw strong character, but it must be without speaking its language. I may give vulgar or low breed persons, but they must converse in a stile of elegance. I may design the coarsest manners, or the most

---

[21]   Mary Hays, *Female Biography, or Memoirs of Illustrious and Celebrated Women of All Ages and Countries. Alphabetically Arranged, in Six Volumes*, 6 vols (Philadelphia, 1807), vol. 3, p. 158.

[22]   For a representative example of such critiques, see William Hazlitt, 'On the Living Poets', in *Lectures on the English Poets*. Hazlitt claims that Joanna Baillie uses men and women in her plays in the same way as little girls use their dolls: 'She treats her grown men and women as little girls treat their dolls – makes moral puppets of them, pulls the wires, and they talk virtue and act vice'; in *The Selected Writings of William Hazlitt*, ed. Duncan Wu, 9 vols (London, 1998), vol. 2, p. 301.

[23]   Elizabeth Inchbald, who was both a well-known novelist and a respected playwright, soon discovered that being a dramatist was a very serious matter, even more so for a woman, as she points out in *Remarks for the British Theatre (1806–9)* (Delmar, NY, 1990).

disgusting folly, but its expressions must not deviate from the line of politeness
…

It cannot be the *Poet's* mind, which the public desire to trace in dramatic representations; but the mind of their characters, and the truth of their colouring. Yet in my case it seems resolved that the point to be considered, is not whether that *dotard*, or that *pretender*, or that *coquet*, would so have given their feelings, but whether Mrs. *Cowley* ought so to have expressed herself.[24]

On the other hand, regardless of all her inner conflicts or private concerns about her profession due to her sex, whenever Cowley had to deal publicly with her writing for the theatre and with her desire to see her plays staged, she was well aware of the sort of conduct and 'language' she had to use. A convincing example comes from a letter she wrote to David Garrick, in which she endeavours to persuade him to accept her play *The Runaway*. In the letter she adopts a typical female rhetoric of the time, ranging from the language of maternity to the idiom of modesty:

I have formed a design on your heart – and to make an impression on it I would show you three little Cherubs who, if they could talk, would tell you their future welfare depends in great measure on your acceptance of their mother's labour; they should promise you their infant love, and their maturer gratitude. My little Betsy would in five minutes smile you into all the sentiment I could wish. The title of an author, I assure you, Sir, I am at all ambitious of, nor could vanity have induced me to attempt making my name public. This attempt is a sacrifice to those for whose benefit every effort in my power is a duty. I think thus much necessary by way of apology for having stept out of that province which is prudently assigned to my sex.[25]

Here Cowley seems almost to echo Reverend T. Gisborne's sermons against the women playwrights who, he believed, violated the most elementary rules of female behaviour, that prescribed decorum and modesty, since the effect of theatre was 'to encourage vanity; to excite a thirst of applause and admiration'.[26]

Fortunately, Hannah Cowley, like many other women writers, infringed these limits, giving life to a considerable number of convincing plays and a gallery of credible dramatic characters. It must be admitted, however, that some questions

---

[24]   Cowley, Preface to *The Town Before You* (London, 1795), p. x, quoted in Melinda C. Finberg (ed.), *Eighteenth-Century Women Dramatists* (Oxford, 2001), p. xli (italics in original).

[25]   *The Papers of David Garrick. Pt. 1. Correspondence from the John Forster Collection of the National Art Library* (London, 1998), 48.E.20, vol. 26, let. 27/1.

[26]   See Thomas Gisborne, *An Enquiry into the Duties of the Female Sex* (1797), in Ellen Donkin, *Getting into the Act: Women Playwrights in London 1776–1829* (London, 1995), p. 15.

remain open. How, for instance, were women playwrights creating heroines who embodied their authors' principles in actions, making of them what P.B. Shelley foretold for his Beatrice Cenci, namely the heralds of a new social and political awareness? And, still more, how did they shape the category of agency in their historical plays, when they were themselves at risk of being deprived of the faculty of inscribing their own selves in the flow of contemporary events?

In *Fatal Autonomy: Romantic Drama and the Rhetoric of Agency*, William Jewett discusses how Romanticism, having extended the concept of subjectivity to new realms of knowledge and consciousness, inevitably reshaped the category of action that, losing its single association with an obvious political or military event, came to embrace a quieter and more social mode. According to Jewett, 'the romantic poets ... wish ... to probe literature's resources for bringing people to an awareness of their active powers, of their origin and limitations ... [and] awareness of literature's power to shape beliefs about the power to act.'[27] Drama in particular seemed to promote the belief in the power to act and, at the same time, to produce an ethos of active reflection on the anxieties that derive from this belief.[28]

Jewett's attempt to define agency in the Romantic period moves from Wittgenstein's famous aphorism, 'To imagine a language means to imagine a form of life', implying that 'all grammatical sentences, active or passive, convey an idea of agency'; at the same time, it goes back to David Hume's essay 'Of the Idea of Necessary Connexion', where Hume stated, 'the terms of EFFICACY, AGENCY, POWER, FORCE, ENERGY, NECESSITY, CONNEXION, and PRODUCTIVE QUALITY, are all nearly synonymous', and concluded that 'the idea of agency originates not in reason but in particular experiences'.[29] Agency, therefore, will occur whenever language is uttered, represented or staged: 'political agency is produced whenever social energies can be "embodied" by a man – and we should add, a woman – speaking on stage',[30] words being the means by which actions are both performed and represented, in life as well as within a dramatic text.[31] According to Jewett, we are allowed to think of ourselves as political beings as long as we are able 'to reflect on the genealogy of the beliefs by which we come to accept our places in history'.[32] It is in this sense, it seems to me, that agency has to be seen and interpreted in women's historical dramas; every time they disputed and renegotiated their place and their role within society through the world of drama, women were exercising an extraordinary power of agency.

There is no question that women's Romantic plays enact the origin of their subjection to authoritarian rule. They map out the tracks of women's subjected role and place in society in order to articulate the anxiety that this subjection has

---

[27]   Jewett, *Fatal Autonomy*, p. 12.

[28]   Ibid., p. 16.

[29]   Ibid., pp. xi–xiii.

[30]   Ibid., p. 56.

[31]   Ibid., p. 30.

[32]   Ibid., p. xiii

produced in their sex over time, and to understand in what way it has affected women's fate in history. Following Joan Wallach Scott's politics of history, I believe that the dramatists 'develop a way of thinking historically about gender', for they draw 'attention to the ways in which changes happen in laws, policies, and symbolic representations'.[33]

Plays such as Hannah More's *Percy*, Ann Yearsley's *Earl Goodwin* or Joanna Baillie's *Constantine Paleologus* as well as *The Family Legend*, but also Letitia Elizabeth Landon's *Castruccio Castrucani* or Felicia Hemans's *The Siege of Valencia*, to name only a few, display their authors' dissent towards the patriarchal order in which they, as much as their protagonists, were to live, but they also demonstrate that subjection to the patriarchal order did not bring about the incapacitating of female subjectivity and did not obliterate women's free will. Through their plays women bring back an audible female voice and restore a consistent female presence in history. As Katherine Newey observes,

> When women playwrights exert agency through writing history and tragedy, they inhabit the field of cultural production which resists the exclusion and abatement of female subjectivity, and they begin to make claims to the world of public policy, of history, and of power.[34]

By creating heroines who retain a strong ethical sense and a powerful social energy, and by denouncing the institutions by which they feel deceived and entrapped, women playwrights used theatre to amplify their voice and frame their needs because they believed that theatre was able, as Betsy Bolton puts it, 'to shape a mass of spectators into an audience and, by extension, its power to shape that audience into a nation', since women's theatrical engagement was 'an explicitly political act'.[35] While writing for the theatre women were busy to 'rewrite' their nation and to perform a new need for history.

Romantic women's plays often betray a deep sense of alienation, of not belonging. In many of their plays the female characters live in an estranged world, in a sort of no-woman's-land. This condition is well represented by the trope of the rock in the middle of the North Sea where Helen, in *The Family Legend*, is taken to be drowned when the tide submerges it. The rock is both no land at all, appearing and disappearing among the violent waves and rough winds, yet, at the same time, a small piece of land at risk of being swallowed at any moment. Similarly claustrophobic and *unheimlich* is Elwina's parental house in More's *Percy*, where the heroine is left unprotected and exposed to arbitrary power. On the other hand, in Landon's *Castruccio Castrucani*, Claricha's solitude and isolation are revealed

---

[33]   Denise Riley, 'Does a Sex have a History?', in Scott (ed.), *Feminism and History*, pp. 7–33, at p. 24.

[34]   Newey, 'Women and History on the Romantic Stage', p. 97.

[35]   Betsy Bolton, *Women, Nationalism and the Romantic Stage: Theatre and Politics in Britain, 1780–1800* (Cambridge, 2001), p. 3.

by her powerlessness to impose her will and her needs even on those who love her.

Such estranged and alienated worlds become a rhetorical figure for the actual social context in which much of the end of the eighteenth century and beginning of the nineteenth century were plunged, and so serve to articulate women's disappointment, exposure and pride, while appealing for political and social change. Despite everything, their appeals are effective. This is the case with Helen's refusal to deny her son's legitimate birth in Joanna Baillie's *The Family Legend*, or with Claricha's successful effort to stop the plot against Castruccio in Landon's play. Even when they lament the suppression of their identity or the repression of their desires, like Hannah More's Elwina in *Percy*, women act and make their voice heard. Interestingly, in women's Romantic historical drama the female characters are expected to be agents and to behave as if they were able to defy society and resist its rules. This is why they are significantly shown to be under continuous scrutiny by the patriarchal authority to which they are bound: inside and outside seem to coincide, leaving little room for freedom or for the expansion of the self. We might recall the obsessive inquisition of Douglas into his wife's secret desire in Hannah More's *Percy*, ironically at the precise moment when Elwina has renounced forever her love for Percy in order to honour her marital vows to Douglas. Douglas says to Elwina:

> Turn, Madam, and address those vows to me,
> To spare the precious life of him you love.
> Ev'n now you triumph in the death of Douglas,
> Now your loose fancy kindles at the thought,
> And wildly rioting in lawless hope,
> Indulges the adultery of the mind.
> But I'll defeat that with. – Guards bear her in.
>   Nay, do not struggle. *(She is borne in)*
>   [end of Act IV] [36]

On the stage, as well as in their real lives, women are seen to live under constraint, to be perpetually besieged, unable to tell the whole truth so that they have to resort to reticence and opacity, whereby their story becomes, like their history, fragmented, concealed, suppressed. 'The adultery of the mind', as Douglas defines Elwina's secrecy and desperate withdrawing from his compulsive control, involves even the proper and feminine Helen in Baillie's play. Helen prefers to die rather than tell a lie, but, nevertheless, she is unable to deliver her whole story even to her reliable chamber maid Rosa when she enquires about Sir Hubert De Grey. Helen secretly loves De Grey but has to forsake him for Maclean in a marriage of political convenience that sealed a peace treaty between the Macleans, the

---

[36]   Hannah More, *Percy, a Tragedy as it is acted at the Theatre Royal in Covent Garden* (London, 1778), p. 68.

Scottish clan of the Highlands, and the Campbells, the Lowlanders, to whom she belonged

> *Rosa.* And heaven will aid you, madam, doubt it not.
> Though on this subject still you have repress'd
> All communing, yet, ne'ertheless, I well
> Have mark'd your noble striving, and revered
> Your silent inward warfare, bravely held;
> In this more pressing combat firm and valiant,
> As is your noble brother in the field.
>
> *Helen.* I thank thee, gentle Rosa; thou art kind –
> I should be franker with thee; but I know not –
> Something restrains me here. (*Laying her hand on her heart*)
> I love and trust thee;
> And on thy breast I'll weep when I am sad;
> But ask not why I weep.
>   [Act I, end of scene ii][37]

All this suggests that the women playwrights held – to borrow one of Terence Allan Hoagwood's insights – the 'historicity of understandings no less than the historicity of that which is understood'.[38] In other words, if we believe that knowledge is preliminary to any action, the Romantic playwrights were establishing the presence of women in history while staging their heroine's achievements and catastrophes, or when recording women's voices and protests or representing their silences and subjections. They were, in a word, working out a powerful exercise in agency. Staging women in history meant to display the quality of their experience and to give evidence of their ideas and actions.[39] Therefore, if a play is a palimpsest-like social text, as Greenblatt has argued, where what is left is a trace of the 'circulation of social energy',[40] women draw on the past in their plays in order to use that energy and to seek redress as well as a restoration of lost agency in the present. Thus the past helps throw light on a present that needs to be understood and commented on but also to be 'acted upon'.

---

[37]   Joanna Baillie, *The Family Legend* (from *Miscellaneous Plays*), in *The Dramatic and Poetical Works of Joanna Baillie*, 2nd edn (London, 1851), p. 486. The play, originally written in 1805, was staged in Edinburgh in 1810.

[38]   See Terence Allan Hoagwood, 'Romantic Drama and Historical Hermeneutics', in Hoagwood and Daniel P. Watkins (eds), *British Romantic Drama: Historical and Critical Essays* (London, 1998), p. 45.

[39]   Scott, *Feminism and History*, p. 20.

[40]   See Stephen Greenblatt, *Shakespearean Negotiations: The Circulation of Social Energy in Renaissance England* (Berkeley, CA, 1988), pp. 4–7.

Agency here is memory as much as anger: it is to exercise memory, to record the 'disguised' presence of women in history and unveil the abuses and the contradictions that they went through in order to regain the present and transform the future. No wonder, then, that the view of history that women offer in their dramas is often dark, even when they miraculously rescue their heroines, as in Baillie's *The Family Legend*. The heroines of women's history plays are frequently plunged into an ocean of sighs, tears and pessimism, but, at the same time, their voices articulate a story of resistance and opposition. This happens in whatever time or setting women are placed: either when the dramatists deal with the Scottish legendary past, foreshadowing, as in Baillie's *The Family Legend*, the Act of Union, and consequently the formation of Great Britain; or when history travels through space as well as time – to Roman, Italian or Spanish history, as in Mitford's *Rienzi* or *Foscari*, in Landon's *Castruccio Castrucani*, or in Hemans's *The Siege of Valencia*. Or, again, when the plays deal with national history, as in More's *Percy*, going back to the chivalric times of medieval England, much loved by Scott and Coleridge, but viewed with a certain distrust by women, as Landon admits in her essay on the female heroines in Scott's novels.[41] In the second act of *Percy*, for instance, Elwina not only discloses her bitter feelings towards her father, who had forced her to renounce her love for Percy in order to marry Douglas, but also unveils her oppositional ideology towards the arbitrary power policy that sustained the so-called 'Holy Wars' such as the Crusades. To her father Raby, who has summoned her to dispel Douglas's suspicions and doubts about her loyalty towards him, Elwina protests:

> If he has told thee that thy only child
> Was forc'd, a helpless victim to the altar,
> Torn from his arms, who had her virgin heart,
> And forc'd to make false vows to one she hated,
> Then, I confess, that he has told thee truth.
> [Act I][42]

Soon after, when the knight Sir Hubert, on his return from the Crusades in Palestine, enters the hall of the castle, Raby, who warmly and enthusiastically welcomes him, complains of Elwina's coldness towards the knight; provoking her dissent and anger:

---

[41]   Letitia Elizabeth Landon, 'The Female Picture Gallery', in *Life and Literary Remains of L.E.L.*, by Laman Blanchard, 2 vols (London, 1841), vol. 2, p. 155.

[42]   More, *Percy*, p. 27.

When policy assumes religion's name,
And wears the sanctimonious garb of faith,
Only to colour fraud, and licence murder,
War then is tenfold guilt.
                    [Act I][43]

And again:

… O blind to think
That cruel war can please the prince of peace!
He who erects his altar in the heart,
Abhors the sacrifice of human blood,
And all the false devotion of that zeal,
Which massacres the world he died to save.
                    [Act I][44]

Elwina invalidates her father's ideology in many ways: for example, first, in calling for private justice, she challenges his power to impose on her fidelity to her domestic duties; then, on a larger scale, she calls for the redressing of global justice, rejecting the pseudo-justice of the Crusades. Similarly subversive appears Rosa's speech in *The Family Legend*, when in the admiring words she addresses to Helen, she states that female combat within the private confines of the domestic walls can be as distressing and heroic as men's fighting in the open field.

In general, women performed history in order to disclose a mechanism of causality that might explain and comment upon the events of the present, but also as a way – more hidden and perhaps more unconscious – of resisting their belonging to a nation that had hampered their lives and frozen their prospects. As Katherine Newey observes, 'in writing tragedies from the source material of [English] history, Romantic women playwrights carefully and cautiously attempted to dissolve the limits of binary oppositions. Through the plotline of tragedy and its generic convention of the fall of the great man, these writers dramatized a feminist challenge to the exercise of extreme power and the actions of tyranny.'[45] I believe that this was true every time women staged history, whether or not according to the classical canons of tragedy. They drew a scenario in which the experience of past female lives was placed, but which also mirrored in many ways their anxieties regarding the future of their own lives.

Through historical drama, women entered into a traditionally male field and challenged it, in order to gain authority or, to quote Newey again, 'to claim both aesthetic and political seriousness, using the authority of genre to overcome the disabilities of gender and establishing a presence that was proscribed from other

---

[43]   Ibid., p. 29.
[44]   Ibid., p. 30.
[45]   Newey, 'Women and History on the Romantic Stage', p. 80.

arenas of public debate.'[46] It is precisely through their conquest of the public and highly gendered arena of historical drama that women playwrights affirmed a new subjectivity, a new mode of self-empowerment: in a word, agency.

---

[46]   Ibid., p. 79.

Chapter 3

Hannah More's and Ann Yearsley's Anglo-Saxon History Plays

Cecilia Pietropoli

The presence of a considerable amount of historical drama on the English stage in the last decades of the eighteenth- and first decades of the nineteenth century was a consequence of the need to come to terms with a present characterized by many unprecedented historical events. At the same time, it was the result of a new way of approaching the past. First the French and American revolutions and then Napoleon's expansionist policy aroused a new interest in history all over Europe, which went together with the desire to revert to the past as a means of interpreting and explaining the present. Extraordinary events, such as the French Revolution, provoked two opposing reactions: they seemed to people who believed in the importance of evolution and change a perfect means to shed the last remains of feudal society. From the opposite point of view, the past was perceived as a sort of golden age forever lost. From both perspectives, literary representations of the past, when compared to documentary historical reconstructions, were able to blunt edges and overcome difficulties by suggesting possible, even if ahistorical, solutions. This is particularly true for England, where Romantic medievalism was basically conservative: the Middle Ages were perceived as the source and origin of the current cultural and social system, and as such the most promising hunting ground for answers to the conflicts that affected the modern age.

The new interest in the past drew upon an innovative, more dynamic and more popular conception of history, and found its most visible expression and diffusion, at a popular level, in the so-called legitimate theatre and in Walter Scott's historical novels. In order to outline the poetics of Romantic historical drama, therefore, we might draw inspiration from the critical revision that has recently involved historical narrative: the boundaries of this genre have been stretched to admit works whose historical background had previously been considered merely ornamental. This innovative approach has allowed scholars to reconsider the position of *Ivanhoe*, which Scott himself had significantly subtitled 'a romance' rather than 'a novel'. *Ivanhoe* had often been excluded from the list of Scott's historical novels because history appeared less accurate and more novelistic in it than in the Waverley Novels. Behind this critical reappraisal is the idea that the aim of historical fiction was to provide a glimpse of the spirit of an age, rather than reproduce it with scientific accuracy. The same applies to historical drama, especially Romantic historical drama, which was designed to dramatize a private and popular perception of history rather than a public and official version of it. Its approach to the past was therefore personal and anachronistic, and less interested in the events themselves than in the ways they were individually perceived. If this applies to Romantic historical drama in general, it is particularly true of the plays I intend to deal with, plays written by women and set in the Middle Ages. My essay will question how two playwrights in particular, Hannah More and Ann Yearsley, reconstructed certain episodes in the history of Anglo-Saxon England; my aim is to retrace their ideas on the political function of historical drama and, consequently, their contribution to the construction of modern tragedy.

Women playwrights' approach to the Anglo-Saxon world is the subject of a recent essay by Jacqueline Pearson that aims to retrace the modernity under the surface of Anglo-Saxon history, thus considering 'the historical setting merely an indirect means for examining urgent contemporary issues'.[1] It is undeniable that in their plots women playwrights openly alluded to contemporary England, where people were less affected by the American and French revolutions than by the outcomes of the industrial revolution and new economy. But they also transformed and reinvented historical drama from a gendered perspective, thus giving voice both to their own specific reception of the past and to their approach to the present. The past thus became an ideal setting in which to locate situations and conflicts that could not be otherwise taken on by women, on the assumption that the history of the nation, especially when oppressed and battered, could effectively mirror the history of women. Romantic women writers did not simply take an interest in history; they went so deep into this acknowlegedly male field as to contribute to the foundation of Romantic historiography by adding to it specific issues of gender. In Greg Kucich's words, their 'consuming engagement with history actually entailed a shared effort to re-envision mainstream history as a critical means of altering contemporary gender practice and ideology.'[2]

Women's historical literature encompassed and mingled mainstream and gendered ideas of history, with the consequence that their idea of tragedy was likewise peculiar and gendered. Jeffrey Cox has stated that 'Romanticism brought, after all, the rebirth of romance and thus of the quest that breaks out of the enclosed world of tragedy',[3] thus suggesting that the Romantic hero, confined within a bourgeois anti-heroic world, went in search of a different, more imaginative and liberated idea of adventure among the ruins of a more glorious past. What I

---

[1]   Jacqueline Pearson, 'Crushing the Convent and the Dread Bastille: The Anglo-Saxons, Revolution and Gender in Women's Plays of the 1790s', in Donald Scragg and Carole Weinberg (eds), *Literary Appropriations of the Anglo-Saxons from the Thirteenth to the Twentieth Century* (Cambridge, 2000), pp. 122–37, at p. 125.

[2]   Greg Kucich, 'Women's Historiography and the (dis)Embodiment of Law: Ann Yearsley, Mary Hays, Elizabeth Benger', *Wordsworth Circle*, 33/1 (2002): 3–7, at p. 3.

[3]   Jeffrey N. Cox, 'Romantic Redefinitions of the Tragic', in Gerald Gillespie (ed.), *Romantic Drama, a Volume in A Contemporary History of Literature in European Languages* (Amsterdam and Philadelphia, 1994), pp. 153–65, at p. 153.

wish to argue here is that at the beginning of the nineteenth century mainstream historical literature and tragedy adopted conventions and perspectives that were already aspects of women's approach to history and literature. If we go back to Scott's approach to historical narrative we notice that his 'medieval' novels differ entirely from the previous ones, which were set in recent Scottish history. While history was rapidly turning into a science based upon original and indisputable documents, literature took upon itself to provide a popular version of official history and to explore aspects that mainstream history was not allowed to touch upon. Literary works therefore offered a private version of history, which was paradoxically anachronistic because the past was reconstructed by juxtaposing episodes belonging to different ages; even historical characters could be turned into hybrid, fictional figures, and submitted to revision and reinterpretation.[4] Another important aspect of Romantic historicism is that it took into consideration not only public figures but also common people, and the way they were affected by and reacted to history. Romantic historicism was therefore largely pragmatic, and focused on the true maker of history, the social body, and on its everlasting conflict with great historical figures.[5] Obviously, to re-write history appeared easier when literature drew upon a far-away past rather than the recent one. These new concepts of history and historical narrative rapidly spread among the members of the middle class, to which most readers of historical fiction and most theatre-goers belonged. This explains how women managed to take part in the creation of innovative concepts of historical fiction and drama, and of new narrative and theatrical techniques. A politically oriented interpretation of historical literature, which considered its realistic elements more important than its fictional ones, was sure to ignore women's contribution to historical literature. Their contribution has been reconsidered by the recent critical revision, which has been based upon aesthetic rather than political principles.

A wider definition of historical drama admits a larger number of plays, in which romance and fiction are more relevant than history itself. In trying to devise a list of Romantic history plays, however, a first difficulty arises from the fact that most texts resort to the generic subtitle 'a tragedy', thus making it difficult to retrace the playwright's original aim. According to the way they deal with history, Romantic history plays can be roughly divided into three groups. The first gathers plays whose historical background is merely ornamental: in this case, the Middle Ages are seen as the most appropriate setting for a gothic plot in which a fair and worthy heroin is oppressed by a stereotypical villain. A significant example can be found in Baillie's 'serious musical drama in two acts' *The Beacon*, whose action draws upon the traditional topos of the relationship between a virtuous

---

4   See Michel Maillard, 'L'antinomie du référent: Walter Scott et la poétique du roman historique', *Fabula*, 2 (1983): 65–76.

5   See my 'Il Medioevo nel romanzo storico europeo', in Piero Boitani, Mario Mancini and Alberto Varvaro (eds), *Lo spazio letterario del Medioevo, L'attualizzazione del testo*, 5 vols (Roma, 2004), vol. 4, pp. 39–65.

and patient lady and a knight who is far away in the Holy Land. Baillie's play differs from the majority of historical dramatic works in that it reaches a happy ending when Ermingard, back from Palestine, marries the heroine, who has been able meanwhile to resist the persecution of the villain, Lord Ulrick. This kind of drama rests upon some general ideas about past societies and does not show any sense of the unique features of each epoch; the characters are black or white and foreshadow the stereotypical characters of popular melodrama.

In the plays belonging to the second group, an historical character is seen in its private domestic dimension, usually in conflict with a wife or daughter. The possibility is soon suggested that familial abuse can be symbolic of political tyranny. The characters are more complex and morally ambiguous than in the first group, satisfying 'Hegel's prescription for the dialectical basis of tragedy'.[6] The plots, however, lack historical consciousness, in the sense that they do not consider history as a process in which every event has its own place in a pattern of evolution. An example of this approach to history and drama will be provided in this essay by Hannah More's *Percy* (1777).

The third group comprises plays in which both the private dimension and the public function of historical characters are taken into consideration. They look self-consciously historical, in the sense that they show awareness of the fact that any event has a double effect: on the historical process and also on the daily life of all individuals. The present is perceived as a consequence of the past, but also as something utterly different from it. A significant example will be found in *Earl Goodwin*, written in 1791 by Ann Yearsley, who significantly subtitled it 'an historical play'.

The contrast between political concern and private desire takes the form, in Romantic historical drama written by women, of a clash between a traditional tyrant and a woman determined to undermine the old patriarchal system. A general social question is reduced to a single individual problem. Allusions to macrocosmic crises can be perceived, however, in what takes place in the domestic microcosm, because, as Betsy Bolton has stated, 'sentimental politics relied on natural feeling and familial relations to provide a model for political action'.[7]

The two early plays I wish to discuss, *Percy* and *Earl Goodwin*, are both set in Anglo-Saxon England, at the origin of the British nation and its political system, and both go back to past times in order to retrace the sources of collective and individual history. It is documented that David Hume's *History of England* was well known among women who took an interest in history, so much so that even Ann Yearsley, who had little time for books, was likely to have heard of it.[8] In it, Hume asserted that English civilization had in fact begun with the Norman

---

6   W.D. Howarth, 'Assimilation and Adaptation of Existing Forms in Drama of the Romantic Period', in Gillespie (ed.), *Romantic Drama*, pp. 81–97, at p. 85.

7   Betsy Bolton, Women, Nationalism, and the Romantic Stage: Theatre and Politics in Britain, 1780–1800 (Cambridge, 2001), p. 21.

8   Pearson, 'Crushing the Convent and the Dread Bastille', p. 126.

Conquest; selecting an episode in Anglo-Saxon history therefore implied a precise political project, which required that all characters were provided with historical significance, if not historical accuracy. In terms of the theory of history behind them, the two plays represent different stages in the transition from Enlightenment to Romanticism; from the point of view of their structure, they are both instances of the transition from a neoclassical- to a Romantic concept of historical drama. Even if they differ one from the other in many ways, they can in my opinion be dealt with together because both playwrights seemed to share a principle that Walter Scott would shortly after make explicit in a footnote to the second edition of *Ivanhoe*: 'I will not allow that the author of a modern antique romance is obliged to confine himself to the introduction of those manners only which can be proved to have absolutely existed in the time that he is depicting, so that he restrain himself to such as are plausible and natural, and contain no obvious anachronism'.[9]

The same applies to the authors of historical drama, especially to women dramatists who touched upon an aspect of history that was less clearly documented and more subject to speculation and reconstruction. If we want to go beyond the old assumption that all Romantic writers intended 'to transcend historical condition through an act of consciousness' to assume that 'Romanticism is ... a movement of withdrawal from society in which a new form of individuality is constructed, followed by a social return in which the reinstitutionalization of this new individual subjectivity is begun, and thus the construction of a new social formation',[10] Romantic women's plays can be of great help, because no one could dramatize the double role of dramatic characters, public and private, social and domestic, better than a woman. No one better than a woman could offer a private and therefore marginalized and liminal vision of history. Romantic women playwrights alone could, in the words of Katherine Newey, 'structure and contextualize what might otherwise be a domestic family tragedy'.[11] Not all journeys into history were successful and not all playwrights could accomplish the entire process, but they were more and more successful as they became conscious of their function in history on the one hand, and of their right to deal with history and the theatre on the other.

The earlier of the two plays, Hannah More's *Percy*, was first staged in 1777 and published in 1778.[12] *Percy* is set in a nondescript 'gothic hall', and the action is set in motion by two secondary characters, Birtha and Edric, who inform us that the lord of the castle, Douglas, is tormented by some secret pain that he is

---

9   Walter Scott, *Ivanhoe*, ed. A.N. Wilson (Harmondsworth, 1984), p. 552.

10   Hans Löfgren, 'Romanticism, History, and the Individual Subject', in David Robertson (ed.), *English Studies and History* (Tampere, 1994), pp. 89–101, at p. 90.

11   Katherine Newey, 'Women and History on the Romantic Stage: More, Yearsley, Burney, and Mitford', in Catherine Burroughs (ed.), *Women in British Romantic Theatre: Drama, Performance and Society, 1790–1840* (Cambridge, 2000), pp. 79–101, at p. 85.

12   Hannah More, *Percy, A Tragedy, as it is acted at the Theatre-Royal in Covent-Garden* (London, 1778).

anxiously trying to conceal. Immediately after that, we learn that the problem arises from two diverging ideas of married love of Lord Douglas and his fair and virtuous wife Elwina:

> … Ill are their spirits pair'd.
> His is the seat of frenzy, her's of softens,
> His love is transport, her's, is trembling duty,
> Rage in his soul is as the whirlwind fierce,
> While her's ne'er felt the pow'r of that rude passion.[13]

Douglas's frenzy is the effect of jealousy, which has even prevented him from joining the Christian army at the Crusade. Edric suggests that,

> Perhaps the mighty soul of Douglas mourns,
> Because inglorious love detains him here,
> While our bold knights, beneath the Christian standard,
> Press to the bulwarks of Jerusalem.[14]

In reality Douglas is concerned with a single knight, Percy of Northumberland, who had once been Elwina's lover whom she had been obliged to give up because of a trivial feud between him and her 'barbarous' father Lord Raby:

> My barbarous father forced me to dissolve
> The tender vows himself had bid me form –
> He dragged me trembling, dying, to the altar,
> I sigh'd, I struggled, fainted, and– complied.[15]

The gothic hall becomes the home of resentment and suspicion to the point that Douglas is turned into 'a savage tyrant'. To her husband's passions, Elwina opposes her steady sense of honour and duty, which can more easily be preserved in a solitary and retired life:

> Then leave me here to tread the safer path
> Of private life, here, where my peaceful course
> Shall be as silent as the shades around me,
> Nor shall one vagrant wish be e'er allowed
> To stray beyond the bounds of Raby Castle.[16]

---

[13]   Ibid., Act I, p. 2.
[14]   Ibid., Act I, p. 2.
[15]   Ibid., Act I, p. 10.
[16]   Ibid., Act I, p. 11.

And again:

> My lord, retirement is a wife's best duty,
> And virtue's safest station is retreat.[17]

Before she can find peace, however, the plot is complicated by some unexpected events: first the news of Percy's death reaches the castle, then he suddenly appears, totally unaware of the fact that his ex-fiancée is now married to a very jealous man. In the final duel between the two, Douglas kills Percy and then stabs himself after he has discovered that Elwina has poisoned herself.

More than once Lord Raby tries to make this domestic tragedy take on wider significance by comparing the present turmoil to a more tranquil and honourable past:

> Where is the antient, hospitable hall,
> Whose vaulted roof once rung with harmless mirth?
> Where every passing stranger was a guest,
> And every guest a friend. I fear me much,
> If once our nobles scorn their rural seats,
> Their rural greatness, and their vassal's love,
> Freedom, and English grandeur, are no more.[18]

And again:

> All private interests sink at his approach:
> All selfish cares be for a moment banish'd!
> I've now no child, no kindred but my country.[19]

When facing a crisis (More wrote her play before the French Revolution, but after the American one), all nations nostalgically revert to a better and more glorious past. In England, in particular, eighteenth-century medievalism was built on the concept that the history of the British nation was less fragmented and more consistent than that of other European countries. Politically conservative Hannah More was certainly affected by this idea, but was also aware that historical drama in the late eighteenth century was meant to have a political and pedagogical function. Her play therefore underlines the dependence of individuals upon history. More's idea of history is far from innovative: what she searches for is an array of exemplary models that are in fact trans-historical. The characters, designed to be either utterly bad or sublimely good, act as exempla of vice and virtue, and reveal a neoclassical background, since they operate within the parameters of fixed cultural conventions.

---

[17] Ibid., Act I, p. 12.
[18] Ibid., Act II, p. 15.
[19] Ibid., Act II, p. 21.

The opposition between good and bad, right and wrong, can be easily transferred to contemporary England. Past and present are juxtaposed and the line between them blurred in order to suggest that the same ethical purposes and standards can be applied to both. History is perceived as an unchangeable sequence of recurring events, which always ends tragically, as it is impossible for individuals to intervene in and change the historical process. Nonetheless, More's heroine refuses to submit to patriarchal power. The political message of the play is to be found in this soft but unabated opposition to domestic tyranny. *Percy* is therefore the story of a familial fight and at the same time a revenge tragedy, but can also be considered an history play. We could call this kind of play historical tragedy in order to mark its difference from domestic tragedy *tout court* on the one hand, and history play based on a less conservative theory of history on the other.

The second play, *Earl Goodwin* by Ann Yearsley, was staged at the Theatre Royal in Bristol in 1789 and printed in 1791. She consciously subtitled it 'an historical play', even if in the Prologue to her drama she appeals to the muse of poetry rather than to the muse of history. Her source of inspiration is Shakespeare, who '... holds, from his unmeasur'd height / The talisman of fancy to my sight'.[20] Her declared intent is to 'Prove active virtue only can be right'[21] and to do so she resorts to the Middle Ages, which in her opinion are characterized by heroism and brutality at the same time. At this stage we are led to expect that the play will follow the same ethical and dramatic criteria we have already found in *Percy*. In her Exordium, Yearsley states: 'For the few incidents (except imaginary ones) which compose the whole of this piece, the Reader must advert to the year 1042 of English history, at which period Edward the Confessor was crowned. The king was blindly zealous, and, if we judge from externals, the dupe of designing men'.[22] And she concludes: 'Goodwin is seriously what I wish every man to be: but the whole is meant to influence the judgement, shield it from credulity, and teach the mind to act more from reason than superstitious romance'.[23] The image of the Middle Ages as a time of superstition and credulity derives from the eighteenth-century approach to the past; the suggestion that individuals should try to act in accordance to reason is equally based upon past conventions. Utterly Romantic, on the contrary, are the characters of Emma, the king's mother, and Editha, his wife: it is historically documented that Edward, after accusing his mother of being an adulteress, compelled her to undergo an ordeal, or *judicium dei*, to prove her innocence. The historical background is therefore accurate, and Emma is constructed both as a woman who in a precise historical moment opposed tyranny and oppression, and as a generic exemplum of female virtue. She is a liminal

---

[20]   Ann Yearsley, *Earl Goodwin, An Historical Play* (London, 1791), Prologue, page not numbered.

[21]   Ibid., Prologue, page not numbered.

[22]   Ibid., Exordium, p. 1.

[23]   Ibid.

character, as she has been marginalized by her gender and by her sin; this allows her to observe and judge from a privileged perspective.

In *Earl Goodwin*, the first character to come on stage is the title character himself. Goodwin informs the audience that,

> The day is spent, and England's records hold
> Its circumstance unparallel'd, when Kings,
> Trust e'en a Mother's virtue to report,
> Throwing its essence on the casual act
> Of blind purgation: where shall dow'rless maids,
> Unjoyful widows, or the faithful wife,
> Find shelter from detraction? – Furious zeal![24]

Ann Yearsley was perfectly aware that the interest in the past is often provoked by crises or by unexpected events. But the crisis at the basis of this play is not a battle, or a war, or regicide or usurpation. The day Goodwin alludes to is the day of Emma's trial, while the unprecedented event is the King's lack of respect for his own mother, the consequences of which will fall upon all women, be they maids, widows or wives. This event sets off the long sequence of upheavals that forms the action of the play: the rebellion of Goodwin and his sons against the King is caused less by his religious zeal than by the excessive number of Norman counsellors at court, above all the terrible Archbishop of Canterbury, who was in fact a Norman, Robert de Jumièges:

> And must our England, still be made their prey?
> No, leave king Edward in their bait; but save!
> Oh, Father, save thy country![25]

Goodwin:

> I will not sleep till Edward turn his ear
> To the complaint of England. Private woe
> Spreads not a gen'ral malady; and we
> Must see Editha pine, through lengthen'd hours,
> In grief we may not notice; but the wrongs
> Of this much-injur'd land shall have redress,
> Batt'ring the foul of Edward till her pow'rs
> Dissolve 'mid hideous ruin …[26]

---

24 Ibid., Act I, p. 1.
25 Ibid., Act I, p. 3.
26 Ibid., Act I, p. 19.

The opposition between Saxons and Normans was soon to become the subject of Scott's novel *Ivanhoe*; but while in *Ivanhoe* the Saxons appear as solid, matter-of-fact men when compared to the corrupted and effeminate Normans, here corruption, irrationality and superstition are men's faults, while honesty and rationality are female qualities. Emma and Editha together embody the literary idea of past Englishness and represent the fictional image of the nation. The same words and images are employed to describe the suffering of the two women and the oppression suffered by Anglo-Saxon England.

Edward's words can be used to justify oppression over a whole people:

> O feeble woman! lost when unrestrain'd,
> And virtuous but from terror, how may man
> Believe you innocent? ...
> ....
> Thus shall you live suspected, ev'ry joy,
> Tho' guiltless, be arraign'd by the hot fiend,
> Inhuman Jealousy! your sex's freedom
> Be lost, and tyranny alone secure you.[27]

To masculine brutality Emma opposes her resolute temper:

> How weak the woman who dissolves in tears
> At undeserv'd disgrace! *Insult*, well borne,
> Affords a stubborn energy of soul.[28]

And again:

> *When woman* dares *perfection*, on her breast
> She wears an aegis, which no poison'd dart
> Of calumny can pierce.[29]

Even Edward seems to wonder at Emma's strength:

> With what pow'rs
> Is Emma form'd! what stubbornness upholds
> Her dauntless spirit! am I not too weak?[30]

---

[27]   Ibid., Act II, p. 20.
[28]   Ibid., Act II, p. 26 (italics in original).
[29]   Ibid. (italics in original).
[30]   Ibid., Act II, pp. 27–8.

Editha's comment summarizes the qualities of noble women's souls:

> ... I only grieve
> For Emma – Ah, my Lord, she deeply feels!
> The mind of woman is most finely wrought,
> Pure, modest, self-denying; e'en when love
> Demands a chaste return, unthinking man
> Ne'er comprehend us. Rudely urg'd are Queens
> When vulgar voices may aloud pronounce,
> They're virtuous or dishonour'd.[31]

The power of the unworthy Saxon king is therefore questioned, and appears more and more oppressive and illegitimate. On the contrary, Goodwin's main concern is England: 'My son, we must not yield to private woe',[32] says Goodwin to his son Harold, the future and last Saxon king. And later on:

> Nor *mine*, or *thine*, shall ever raise my arm
> To plunge a guiltless nation deep in blood.
> Already do the groans of lab'ring hinds
> Make the winds heavy, while their troubles roll
> Like billows to the foot of Edward's throne,
> And dashing *there*, are lost in wide dispersion.[33]

Historical documents tell us that Goodwin was in fact one of the richest landowners of the time and that he was mainly interested in securing access to the throne for one of his sons. Nonetheless, the Saxon England described in the play is historically acceptable and the spirit of the age is well reproduced. Saxon England ruled by a Saxon king but in fact prey of the Normans can be easily compared to contemporary England under King George III. The French Revolution, however, cannot be ignored (and is in fact mentioned in the Epilogue of the play written by Mr. Meyler and spoken by Mrs. Smith). In such a critical moment conservative England glances nostalgically at its own past and tends to idealize it. Even an openly progressive woman, as Ann Yearsley was, seems to be affected by this general nostalgia for the golden age, but the consequent sense of loss soon becomes a fresh stimulus for new fights, new rebellions and new political ideas. She cannot ignore the fact that the past bears on the present, or that the present is a direct consequence of the past. The present is, however, utterly different from the past and requires different action and different characters. The tragic end of the play, far from giving way to inconsolable grief, bears the message that evolution and change are possible – perhaps not immediately, but certainly in the distant future.

---

[31] Ibid., Act I, p. 11.

[32] Ibid., Act I, p. 4.

[33] Ibid., Act I, p. 5 (italics in original).

Wars and revolutions are therefore necessary to allow a nation and its people to rebel against an unbearable situation and start again on a new basis.

Women's Romantic drama is open at the same time to collective dreams and nostalgia, and to more radical analyses and projects, as a consequence of the combination of two different ideas: on the one hand the desire to retrace a more heroic and less fragmented past, on the other the awareness that history also means unrenounceable changes and acquisitions.

We can therefore conclude that the historical tragedy and the history play belong to the same genre because they are both ambivalent, or even ambiguous, and equally divided between nationalism and internationalism, progressivism and conservatism, nostalgia for the past and expectations for the future. This mixed genre, partly tragedy and partly history play, was peculiar of the Romantic age as a result of its approach to history and the tragic. While popular history was turning into a private and familial matter, tragedy was likewise no longer the prerogative of a superior hero, but was being domesticated. Furthermore, Romantic tragedy was becoming a spiritual and social quest, which often resorted to fiction and fantasy. This quest could be quite readily undertaken by women playwrights, who at the end of the eighteenth century had already provided excellent examples of plays based on romance and tragedy, historical truth and fantasy; plays that were also to influence and give shape to mainstream male drama.

Chapter 4

Historical Sieges in Women's Romantic Drama: Felicia Hemans, Joanna Baillie and Frances Brooke

Serena Baiesi

Alive your passion tho' our play may keep,
Behind the curtain you must have a peep.
Tho' bright the tragic character appear,
Our private foibles you delight to hear.
In life's great drama the same rule we find:
When on the stage the patron of mankind
Performs his part – the public virtue strike,
But 'tis the secret anecdote we like. ...
A Female Poet draws the tender tear.
True to her sex, she copies from the life
The Mother, Daughter, and the faithful Wife.
Let her this night your kind protection gain,
The Critic then will parody in vain.
And let fair Virtue, ere she quit the age,
Here pause awhile – and linger on the stage.[1]

In investigating Romantic theatre and drama, one is struck by the large number of plays – written by both men and women – dealing with the specific subject of the 'siege' of a city. Many writers of the period set their plays in a location where an assault takes place from outside, in a variety of historical locations and epochs – from ancient times to the recent past – usually in the form of the attempted conquest of a capital by foreign invaders. The siege dramatizes the violent clash not only between opposing political factions but also between different cultures, religions and sexes, each struggling for power and supremacy. The final goal of the siege is invariably the military control of a city, or even a state, and, on a metaphorical plane, it implies the assertion of power over the vanquished 'other'. In some cases, it can be read as a symbol of masculine defloration of the 'weaker'

---

[1]   Epilogue written by unknown called 'a friend' and spoken by Mrs Yates as presented on 31 January 1781 at Covent Garden after the performance of the tragedy written by Frances Brooke, *The Siege of Sinope*.

sex. In any case, gender roles and the interaction between the sexes are important aspects of siege plays, especially when composed by woman writers, as is the case with the examples discussed here.

In this essay I would like to suggest some lines of interpretation of three theatrical sieges, written respectively by Frances Brooke, by Joanna Baillie and by Felicia Hemans. These writers stage a historical siege in order to express their viewpoints on political aspects of the past and especially of their own time. More specifically, they show how the private concern of family affection is strictly connected with political reality and with the protection of the state. Finally, they create male and female characters whose behaviour and speech does not follow the traditionally separated sphere of action of gender rules.

Before analyzing these three plays, however, it might be useful to trace the sources of the literary and theatrical topic of the siege in its widespread dissemination during the Romantic period. Between 1760 and 1830, more than twenty plays had the term 'siege' in their titles.[2] Some of these dramas, such as Joanna Baillie's *Constantine Paleologus*, were conceived for the stage; others for the closet, for example *The Siege of Jerusalem* by Mary Bowes, the one-act *Siege of Valencia* by Felicia Hemans, and the single-scene *The Siege* by Mary Russell Mitford. The majority of these plays are historical dramas and tragedies, but there were siege comedies as well: for example, the comic opera *The Siege of Belgrade* written by James Cobb; or Joanna Baillie's comedy entitled simply *The Siege*. We can also find more complex theatrical representations that mixed together drama and comedy, as in the case of Astley's Amphitheatre production of *Tippoo Sultan; or, The Siege of Bangalore* (1792), an amalgamation of action, animal husbandry and complex scenic effects, referred to in its advertisement as a 'Compiled, Whimsical, Original, Tragic, Comic, Pantomimical Sketch, in Three Parts'; Astley's composition involves a double siege displaying military

---

[2]   See, for example, William Hawkins, *The Siege of Aleppo* (1758); John Home, *The Siege of Aquileia* (1760); Mary Eleanor Bowes, *The Siege of Jerusalem* (1774); Frederick Pilon, *The Siege of Gibralter* (1780); Frances Brooke, *The Siege of Sinope* (1781); Fanny Burney, *The Siege of Pevensey* (1789); Elizabeth Forsyth, *The Siege of Quebec* (1792); Julius William Mickle, *The Siege of Marseilles* (1794); William Preston, *The Siege of Ismail: or, a Prospect of War. An Historical Tragedy* (1794); Henry James Pye, *The Siege of Meaux* (1794); William Sotheby, *The Siege of Cuzco* (1800); Joanna Baillie, *Miscellaneous Plays* [*Constantine Paleologous; or, the Last of Caesars*] (1804); Joanna Baillie, *A Series of Plays*; [*The Siege* (Comedy)] (1812); Anonymous, *The Siege of Malta. A Tragedy* (1823); Felicia Hemans, *The Siege of Valencia* (1823); Jonathan Smith, *The Siege of Algiers* (1823); Mary Russell Mitford, *Dramatic Scenes* [*The Siege*] (1827); John Augustus Stone, *The Siege of Antioch* (1827); James Cobb, *The Siege of Belgrade* (a Comic Opera) (1828); John Nicholson, *The Siege of Bradford* (1831); Alexander Macomb, *The Siege of Ditroit* (1835).

techniques and technical innovations on stage in order to promote English colonial dominance.[3]

Many of these sieges took place in Europe, and concerned the struggle for political power between Eastern and Western cultures. There are likewise many American sieges – set, for example, in Quebec or in Detroit – that deal with English colonization and attempts at de-colonization. The theme of the siege was also employed in prose and poetry, and it was usually associated with masculine quest and conquest. This is true of Byron's *The Siege of Corinth*, published in 1816, and Nicholas Michell's historical poem *The Siege of Constantinople* of 1831, to mention two texts from a much longer list. Many other plays, poems and novels published in this period also present the topos of the siege as a marginal event. In the 1820s Lord Byron narrated the 'Siege of Ismail' in *Don Juan*, and Mary Shelley, in her apocalyptic novel *The Last Man* in 1826, described the adventures of the last surviving member of the human race after a devastating visitation of the plague during the siege of Constantinople in the year 2092, in which the Greeks, led by an English hero, finally recapture the city from the Turkish enemy.

Several genres and sources contaminated the theatrical output of the Romantic period, and we frequently discover situations and characters within the siege-plays that are taken directly from novels and poems, as well as other dramatic forms. As Jeffrey Cox observes in his study of Romantic tragic drama, 'The romantics did not write one type of play, but rather engaged a disparate set of dramatic forms', taking inspiration for their plots from a wide range of sources and from their precursors. This is why 'there is a sense in which the romantic drama attempts to incorporate all past and present dramatic forms, to experiment with every embodiment of the tragic vision',[4] and this is true for siege-plays in particular.

In the three siege-plays by women playwrights that I wish to discuss, the historical and political significance of the conquest of a city is linked to the creation of a new female protagonist who struggles to survive through the political and social consequences of a war that also affects her private life. The plays in question are Frances Brooke's *The Siege of Sinope*, performed at the Theatre Royal in Covent Garden in 1781; Joanna Baillie's *Constantine Paleologus*, published in 1804 as a part of her *Miscellaneous Plays*, and staged in Liverpool in 1808; and *The Siege of Valencia*, written for the closet by Felicia Hemans in 1823. Although these plays were composed over a relatively long period of time, they have nevertheless several issues in common, which I wish to explore here.[5] First, Brooke, Baillie and

---

[3]   For a general introduction to this representation, see Daniel O'Quinn's 'War and Precinema; Tipu Sultan and the Allure of Mechanical Display', chapter 7 in O'Quinn, *Staging Governance; Theatrical Imperialism in London, 1770–1800* (Baltimore, 2005), pp. 312–48.

[4]   Jeffrey N. Cox, *In the Shadows of Romance: Romantic Tragic Drama in Germany, England, and France* (Athens, OH, 1987), p. 13.

[5]   Felicia Hemans also wrote a poem entitled 'The Last Constantine', inspired by Joanna Baillie's siege-play.

Hemans use specific historical events set in the past and in distant countries in order to criticize indirectly the contemporary political situation in England. Second, the virtues and faults of their male and female heroes are linked to a gendered system of values. Third, these plays all prove to be attempted deconstructions of the traditional idea that men and women occupy separated domains of action. These plays demonstrate, on the contrary, that women had a fundamental role in history and in politics, which they carried out without neglecting their responsibilities in the domestic sphere.

Brooke, Baillie and Hemans made skilful use of historical events that were probably familiar to the audience of their time: Brooke's *The Siege of Sinope* recalls ancient Roman history, namely the conquest of Pontus by the king of Cappadocia, aided by the Romans, in the tenth century BC; Baillie's *Constantine Paleologus* deals with the final siege of Constantinople by the Turks in 1453, at the expense of the Greek emperor Constantine; Hemans's *The Siege of Valencia* invokes the attack on the Christian kingdom of Spain, at the castle of Valencia, by the Moorish prince during the thirteenth century. These different historical contexts all frame the cultural clashes at the heart of these plays, where Eastern and Western Europe fight to conquer land and to gain military power. At the same time, the relocation of political conflicts in a distant past and in remote geographical venues allowed these women writers to assert their opinions about contemporary historical issues such as colonialism and tyranny. As Adriana Craciun and Kari E. Lokke note, women writers were involved in the political life of their time, and women playwrights too often staged past historical events in order to take part in the contemporary ideological debate:

> That British women's voices did claim a powerful presence in the ideological debates surrounding the French Revolution and the Napoleonic wars does not, however, mean that British patriarchy sanctioned the breakdown of barriers between masculine and feminine roles, between public and domestic realms. Rather, the writings of the eighteenth-century authors confirm that in the decades following the American revolution, separate spheres were being increasingly prescribed in theory, yet increasingly broken through in practice.[6]

Since theatrical, as well as literary, censorship was particularly strict at that time,[7] 'this procedure of symbolic substitution (putting current events in ancient costume)

---

[6]   Adriana Craciun and Kari E. Lokke, 'British Women Writers and the French Revolution', in Craciun and Lokke (eds), *Rebellious Hearts: British Women Writers and the French Revolution* (New York, 2001), pp. 3–32, at p. 16.

[7]   'By 1737, the Licensing Act legalized blanket restrictions on the kind of political or religious content in the plays. This overt censorship had drastic consequences for the kinds of plays allowed into production for the next two centuries. It was particularly true of the last quarter of the eighteenth century ... that the French Revolution created widespread paranoia in England and that the Licensing Act made it possible to eliminate at the source

enabled writers to represent revolutionary content when more direct enactments were not permitted on the London stage'.[8]

In particular, Baillie and Hemans describe the invaders from a 'colonialist' point of view, referring to the Muslims as an uncivilized and barbarous culture. The audiences of the time were very anxious and often alarmed at contact with people from distant countries, and especially with devotees of non-Christian religions. Imperialism and colonialism had created not only a sense of English supremacy over the 'other', but at the same time they gave rise to a sense of the threat of the unknown. As Beth H. Friedman-Rommel observes in her discussion of *Constantine Paleologus*,

> Baillie's text refines dominant British stereotypes about Muslim government, and reminds audiences of the contemporary international political struggle for control of the Mediterranean, a vital strategic and commercial region. Britain partially justified its own imperialism by asserting its moral superiority and capability to rule.[9]

Women playwrights often adopted in their plays the characterization of the 'other' to emphasize the difference of what was accepted by society and what was excluded, placing women in a dialectical position between these two situations. The colonial space is used here as background to criticize homeland politics and society by creating stereotypes of culturally different agencies. Felicia Hemans, like Joanna Baillie, was ready to attribute to the invaders some qualities and merits, by way of a critique of English weakness, especially in the battlefield. The siege of Constantinople ends with the city being won by the Turkish sultan, while the city of Valencia will be saved thanks only to the providential arrival of the king of Spain, and not through the resistance of the city itself.

On the other hand, the three playwrights also make the invaders acute observers of the cultural differences they encounter, since they can recognize from the very outset of the siege the true qualities of the adversaries they are facing. The enemy, acting according to his senses, embodies the repressed instincts of the English, showing a less conservative attitude towards morality and behaviour. We can detect in these plays a cultural dislocation of feelings and instincts that have been lost the natives of England – where manners and ideals imposed by religion and codes of conduct have irrevocably shaped the human subject – yet are still vigorous in their

---

plays making any reference to social struggles' – Ellen Donkin, *Getting into the Act: Women Playwrights in London, 1776–1829* (London, 1995), p. 5.

[8]   Terence Allan Hoagwood, 'Elizabeth Inchbald, Joanna Baillie, and Revolutionary Representation in the "Romantic" Period', in Craciun and Lokke (eds), *Rebellious Hearts*, pp. 293–316, at p. 303.

[9]   Beth H. Friedman-Romell, 'Staging the State: Joanna Baillie's *Constantine Paleologus*', in Tracy C. Davis and Ellen Donkin (eds), *Women and Playwriting in Nineteenth-Century Britain* (Cambridge, 1999), pp. 151–73, at p. 167.

non-Christian adversaries. Women play a role in between these two poles, acting as behavioural intermediaries both in the home and on the battlefield.

Indeed, the Moors are particularly surprised by the strong will displayed by European women, who are truly willing to change the course of history thanks to their strength of character, their obstinacy and determination; in a word, through their masculine qualities along with the feminine. As Gary Kelly stresses in his study on Mary Shelley and Felicia Hemans, these writers depict historical events from a male standpoint:

> Like many other post-Revolutionary and post-Napoleonic writers, they [women writers] represent history as 'masculine', that is, characterized by ambition, conflict, war, and imperialism, and thus as a relentless cycle of destruction and oblivion for historic individuals, peoples, states, and empire.[10]

They also depict the female counterpart of history, however, staging brave heroines not only fighting for their countries but also struggling for the safety of their families. The dramatists endeavour to adopt a double perspective, the military and the domestic one, usually privileging the weaker of the two opponents in the battlefield. This is why the faction attacked from outside – the Greeks or the Spanish in these cases – is always the one foregrounded by the authors. In Baillie's and Hemans's plays Turkish and Moorish aggressors are sources of death and suffering, bearers of pestilence. Here again we cannot fail to recall Mary Shelley's fatal plague, which likewise comes from the Middle East. But Baillie, instead of choosing a man, elects a woman, Valeria, as 'the last tender remnant of our race'.[11]

Gender relations are an important dimension in these plays, marked by love and affection in women, and by hardness and sterile heroism in men. In Baillie's play male Moors are dangerous not only as soldiers but also as brutal rapists, while, on the contrary, Turkish women in Hemans's siege have the same maternal love for their children as Christian women. Women, traditionally associated with children and identified as the weakest members of society, are depicted in these plays as brave and strong figures, who enter into battle in order to defend their countries as well as their homes and families, thereby combining 'masculine' public action with 'feminine' private affectivity:

> Even though both Baillie and Hemans want to explore the 'epic' masculine world of combat and conquest, they always domesticate that interest by showing

---

[10]   Gary Kelly, 'Last Men: Hemans and Mary Shelley in the 1820s', *Romanticism*, 3/2 (1997): 198–208, at p. 199.

[11]   Joanna Baillie, *The Dramatic and Poetical Works of Joanna Baillie: Complete in One Volume* (London, 1851), p. 458.

its limitations, how it is limited by its relation to the supposedly smaller and more trivial world of the domestic affection.[12]

Distant place and time are not depicted here in a 'romanticized' way, but are employed in order to show forth a new form of female patriotism. In this way, erstwhile forgotten heroines, who possibly never existed, have a chance to play an active role in history.

Besides the clash of different cultures, religions and genders in these plays, we find open references to contemporary political events that directly involved the troubled relations between the British government and its people, especially the poorest strata of society. In his study of the colonial issue and its theatrical representations during the nineteenth century, Daniel O'Quinn explores the role of playwrights, especially women, in English politics and how they dramatized their anxieties in their plays, since 'in a time of political corruption, when monarchy has devolved into despotism, the playwright, not the politician, finds herself in an auspicious situation, for she is the arbiter of manners and morals, and thus of the spirit of the nation'.[13]

We find this conflict especially in Baillie's play, where she deals quite openly with the political implications of the siege, dedicating great importance to the role of the citizens during the battle, and to the relationship between the soldiers and the king. Baillie continually stresses the necessity of dialogue and trust, which should link a leader to his military forces and to his people. For example, she sets up an opposition throughout the play between Constantine's attitude towards his soldiers, with whom he acts in social brotherhood – calling them 'loving', 'brave', 'good' and 'zealous friends' –, and the Turkish sultan who calls his closest soldier 'slave' or 'worm', and considers him mere 'dust beneath his feet'. Moreover, Constantine does not dare command his soldiers, but simply asks them to act, whereas the sultan is always addressed as the 'mighty sultan', 'your highness' and 'mighty prince'. At the end, Constantine's soldiers, who are also his companions, display their loyalty to him at the cost of their own lives. The sultan, by contrast, even if victorious, is forced to recognize his solitude and to reveal his lust towards everything that he cannot conquer in the battlefield, shouting to his humble slave: 'Away! Away! Thy humble zeal I know; / Yea, and the humble zeal of such as thou art. / The willing service of a brave man's heart, / That precious pearl, upon the earth exists, / But I have found it not.'[14] Significantly the final speech by the dying Othus, one of the more faithful of Constantine's soldiers, recalls this principle: 'Great Sultan, thou hast conquered with such arms / As power has given to thee,

---

12   Marlon B. Ross, *The Contours of Masculine Desire: Romanticism and the Rise of Women's Poetry* (New York and Oxford, 1989), p. 287.
13   O'Quinn, *Staging Governance*, p. 146.
14   Baillie, *Dramatic and Poetical Works*, p. 478.

the imperial city / Of royal Constantine; but other arms, / that might the friends of Constantine subdue, / Heaven has denied thee'.[15]

The relationship between the Greek king and his non-military subjects in Baillie's play is more complex. Not all of them wish to follow Constantine in the final battle against the Turks, since they are aware of the imminent defeat. Peasants and common people do not aspire to glory and honour as the soldiers do; they seek a peaceful life, preferring to surrender to the enemy because this means putting an end to their sufferings and the danger of losing their loved ones. Indeed, in this play, the citizens are prepared to come out armed in the streets in order to protest openly against the king.

Here Joanna Baillie evokes European pivotal historical events of her time involving crowds threatening the absolute power of the authorities: the first historical event to which she refers is certainly the French Revolution and the successive period of terror; Pitt's Terror in England and the treason trials against the radicals are also alluded to, likewise the popular insurrection that took place in 1798 in Ireland and was suppressed by military forces. Such uncontrolled, dangerous and violent popular reactions, and the subsequent measures taken by governments to put them down, are staged in Baillie's drama in order to show the necessity of dialogue and mutual care between the ruling class and its subjects: of the prevention of tyranny, on the one hand, and of the violent reaction of the population on the other. As Beth H. Friedman-Rommel points out,

> Constantine's exemplary behaviour toward the mob functioned as a collective fantasy of what a patriarchal ruler should do: love and defend the 'children' in his care. But the patriarchal contract is mutually binding: whereas rulers must remain vigilantly aware of their subjects' needs, subjects should eschew desire for luxury and rise up to serve their country at home and abroad, lest liberty, in the absence of discipline become license.[16]

Moreover, Baillie, like Hemans and Brooke and many other writers of their time, following the consequences of contemporary revolutionary events, staged not only the conflict between governmental power and the citizenry but also a clash between the different social classes. This can be seen as an expression of discomfort towards a general situation whereby 'in England the tension between repressive government, popular discontent and intellectual detachment was not as violent as in Revolutionary France, but the shock waves of revolution and war stimulated the most palpable class conflict in Britain since the Stuart period'.[17]

In Baillie's play the brave foreign patriots (Constantine's soldiers, except Othus, are in fact Italians from Genoa) represent the Greeks as an unfaithful,

---

[15]   Ibid.

[16]   Friedman-Romell, 'Staging the State', p. 169.

[17]   George Taylor, *The French Revolution and the London Stage, 1789–1805* (Cambridge, 2000), p. 2.

irrational and ugly mob, but this is not entirely fair since their poor life conditions push them to invoke 'Bread and wine, and peaceful days!'[18] They are, however, ready to surrender to the Turks, and even threaten their king: 'Surrender', they cry; 'Surrender, devils, or you shall pay the cost!'[19] It is the task of the king to placate this turmoil: Constantine first appeals to patriarchal relationship between a father and his 'children', asking them to trust him and believe his words, because 'children do / Support, and honour, and obey their sire'.[20] He then invokes civic responsibility and patriotism towards the state, since it is absolutely necessary 'To save your city, your domestic roofs, / Your wives, your children, all that good men love'.[21] Brave men are indeed ready to sacrifice their lives to the good of the city; the king needs their support in terms of love and devotion, but also in terms of practical action. It is Constantine who first shows a deep trust in his people, when he goes out among them unarmed. But while some of the citizens are genuinely persuaded to follow the king, many others are still opposed to military conflict. This explains why a struggle breaks out among the people, who cannot reach a compromise between the necessity of revolt and loyalty towards the king. The scene ends with a soldier confirming his mistrust towards the Greeks: 'No, faith! I know you well: you are at large a set of soft, luxurious, timid slaves.'[22]

Joanna Baillie therefore presents a humble and humane king facing an angry mob only partially seduced by his words and actions. She recognizes that an idyllic relationship between the king and his subjects is rare and probably unachievable. Moreover, we should not forget that in England, at the beginning of the nineteenth century, political stability was a utopian dream, and that the people, especially the poor, were tired of wars, famine and the fear of death, all of which seemed constantly to afflict the whole of Europe. At the very end of the play, Baillie stresses the failure of absolute power, both that imposed by the government and that imposed by the ruling class upon the lower components of the social ladder. Despotism without control is too dangerous, and neither tyranny nor anarchy is a solution in the preservation of the wealth and welfare of a nation. On the contrary, Baillie seems to suggest a balanced relationship between the two factions based on reciprocal loyalty, morality and sacrifice: 'Words will, perhaps, our better weapons prove, / When used as brave men's arms should ever be, / With skill and boldness. Swords smite single foes, / But thousands by a word are struck at once'.[23]

The Spanish citizens of Valencia are also tired of fighting a battle that seems to lead only to defeat. In her siege, Felicia Hemans underlines the unfairness of the sacrifices and struggles of the poor on behalf of a small and privileged group. In her time, reforms were needed to prevent a potential English insurrection similar

---

18   Baillie, *Dramatic and Poetical Works*, p. 453.
19   Ibid.
20   Ibid.
21   Ibid., p. 454.
22   Ibid.
23   Ibid., p. 452.

to the French Revolution, since the disparity between classes was becoming all too evident. In the play, citizens openly comment on the waste of money and the loss of lives caused by the battle: 'Why, this is just!', one of them declares; 'These are the days when pomp is made to feel / Its human mould!'[24] And again: 'Sickness, and toil, and grief, have breathed upon us, / Our hearts beat faint and low.'[25] Only the encouragement of a woman, in this case Ximena, will persuade the citizens to be loyal to their king, and to keep on battling for the general good of the city. The sense of the community is strongly perceived in this play as well as it is in others, especially those written by women writers, who stage not a solitary hero struggling for his own survival, but rather men and women battling for the general interest.

A radically different historical setting is presented by Frances Brooke: the Middle East during the Roman invasions of Cappadocia and Pontus. The conflict takes place between two factions: that of Pharnaces, King of Pontus, and that of Athridates, King of Cappadocia. Supported by the Romans, who are defined as 'the remains / Of an unhappy race',[26] Athridates breaks the peace with Pharnaces in a surprise attack on the city of Sinope. Here Frances Brooke is clearly endeavouring to restore the ancient pride of Mediterranean civilizations, corrupted and usurped by the Romans who had invaded them and brought negative sentiments of revenge among a peaceful people. Even though Brooke died in 1789, she had had the chance to witness another important insurrection, the American Revolution, whose dynamics and consequences inevitably influenced her writings.

In *The Siege of Sinope*, one of the more prominent generals of the battle says to the king:

> When I view
> The dreadful carnage of this day of blood;
> See this fair city, which the dawn beheld
> The pride of Asia, humbled in the dust;
> Her slaughter's citizens; her blazing dome;
> Her infants, clinging round their dying mothers;
> Forgive me, sir; if, loyal as I am,
> I drop the tear humane.[27]

Men who weep and women who go to battle are certainly not rare in these siege plays. Constantine, in Baillie's play likewise, not only displays feminine qualities and attitudes – especially towards his companions –, but cries in front of and for

---

24   Felicia Hemans, *The Siege of Valencia. A Parallel Text Edition. The Manuscript and the Publication of 1823*, eds Susan J. Wolfson and Elizabeth Fay (Peterborough, ON, 2002), p. 173.

25   Ibid., p. 177.

26   Frances Brooke, *The Siege of Sinope* (Cambridge, 1994), p. 39.

27   Ibid., p. 24.

them, and the last night before the final battle he says to them: 'I put off / all form and seeming; I am what I am, / A weak and heart-rent man. Will thou forgive me? / For I in truth must weep'.[28]

It must be stressed that women playwrights do not separate traditional female and male attitudes and skills in fashioning their characters. As Ann Mellor observes with reference to *The Siege of Valencia* in her study on the relationship between romanticism and gender, 'it is here that Hemans stages her most powerful dialogue between the public and the private sphere, testing her domestic ideology against the social real of history'.[29] This is why in these plays women's role is not strictly limited to a private sphere of action, but also begins to influence the public sphere. And vice versa, as we have seen, men are not always stereotypes of strength and rationality, but, like women, sometimes act under the influence of feelings.

Brooke's and Hemans's female characters clearly betray this mixture of political and domestic concerns, which are difficult, if not impossible, to reconcile. As Marlon Ross asserts,

> What women must learn is that heart-knowledge cannot protect them from the demands of public life, from the political strife of the state. What men must learn is that heart-knowledge is the basis for all the public actions, for all of the motivations and aims that make them the more visible agents of the state guardianship.[30]

Women are above all concerned with the safety of their children who are captured by the invaders, and in both these dramas – Brooke's and Hemans's – they react instinctively with an unshakeable firmness of intention. Both Thamyris in the Sinope siege and Elmina in Valencia betray their cities and break promises made to their husbands in order to save their children. Blinded by fury, the outraged mothers behave like soldiers in the open battlefield, facing the enemy without fear:

> Bereft of all her familial bonds, deprived of her domestic security, Elmira at last realizes the larger significance of affectional sacrifice. She realizes that her heroic attempt to save her children, though empowered by the right affection, has been misplaced. Her affection is then transferred to the state, as she comes to realize the continuity between political freedom and domestic happiness.[31]

Here again private concerns clash with public actions, and women who desire to reconcile these opposing aspects of their lives are inevitably unsuccessful. Even though Thamyris's son survives, her father commits suicide, and she thereby loses

---

28   Baillie, *Dramatic and Poetical Works*, p. 458.

29   Anne K. Mellor, *Romanticism & Gender* (New York and London, 1993), p. 135.

30   Ross, *The Contours of Masculine Desire*, p. 275.

31   Ibid.

a close family member. On the contrary, Elmina's sons are murdered, and her husband Gonzales also dies during the battle. Thamyris is the emblem of a woman endorsed with female virtues and masculine strength of will. She is described as having 'All the strength / Of manly wisdom, mix'd with woman's sweetness',[32] but she also has to admit that 'our unhappy sex is born to suffer'.[33] When she is reproached by her husband because she has not killed their child before he was captured, however, she replies: 'Learn to know / This heart, which beats as proudly as thy own'.[34]

Similarly Elmina, in Hemans's play, goes cross-dressed as a soldier to Abdullah's tent in the Moorish camp in order to beg for her sons' liberation. When she discloses her identity, Abdullah is incredulous at her courage, but she reassures him:

> Think'st thou there dwells no courage but in breasts
> That set their mail against the ringing spears,
> [...] Thou little know'st
> Of nature's marvels! – Chief! My heart is nerved
> To make its way through things which warrior-men ...
> Would look on, ere they braved! – I have no thought,
> No sense of fear!'[35]

In the same way, Valeria, in Baillie's drama, is 'a wondrous mixture of woman's loveliness with many manly states', and she is also 'strange, perplexing, and unsuitable'.[36] Even if initially she seems to accept her confinement to the traditional role of wife and mother within the world of domesticity, she eventually goes on to assert her will and influence in the public sphere.

Most probably Brooke, Hemans and Baillie were all acquainted with the famous Greek heroine who is evoked by all the three women characters they put on stage: Thamyris, Valeria and Elmina are all reminiscent of Antigone in her determination to take care of her loved ones, even if it meant breaking the law and losing her own life. All three of them, like Antigone, are ready to give up their lives in order to assert their will and preserve the freedom of their loved ones: Valeria commits suicide in order to escape the invaders; Thamyris states at the outset of the battle, 'My soul's unshaken purpose, Thamyris / Will die as a queen, and free'; Elmira shows her readiness to die with her children as soon as she meets the Moorish king. These romantic protagonists, however, are not, unlike the figures from ancient tragedy, supported by gods in their actions, nor do they live in a perfectly ordered and hierarchically organized society. On the contrary, they

---

32   Brooke, *The Siege of Sinope*, p. 14.
33   Ibid., p. 47.
34   Ibid., p. 54.
35   Hemans, *The Siege of Valencia*, p. 129.
36   Baillie, *Dramatic and Poetical Works*, p. 477.

must struggle to survive in an 'unheroic' world free of divine control, in a chaotic society where the hero cannot simply go about accomplishing his pre-ordained duty but must face political reality and revolutionary impulses.[37]

Wives like Thamyris, in Brooke's siege, and Valeria, in Joanna Baillie's tragedy, do not passively accept the war, but impel their husbands to stop risking their own lives. Both evoke again and again the 'power of the affections', a feminine source of authority rarely understood and shared by men. It is in recalling this power that Thamyris asks Pharnaces to 'stay, and guard with pious care / The place of thy fathers – guard thy son! / Thy wife! Thy people! Who with ardent eyes / Look up to thee for safety'.[38] With similar words Valeria confronts Constantine, who replies: 'Thy woman's hand is stronger, sweet Valeria, / Than warrior's iron grasp'.[39]

Frances Brooke, Joanna Baillie and Felicia Hemans, in conclusion, use the historical pretext of the siege in order to investigate both gender and political issues. Private and public spheres in these plays have equal weight, and the moment one prevails over the other balance and stability are definitively compromised. To privilege exclusively only the public or the private sphere can be fatal, as these three tragedies effectively demonstrate. The power of affection is not merely a domestic and female affair, but crosses the border separating the genders and becomes a public issue, involving women and men equally and linking love for the family with love for the state.[40]

The heroes and heroines of these plays in the end have to die because of the impossibility of solving the contradictions existing between private and public, between political interest and personal affection, between intimate emotions and social duties. Hemans, Baillie and Brooke all present female characters actively involved in important historical events, throwing new light not only on the interpretation of history *tout court* – including the possibility of the existence of women taking part in it – but also on the specific history of Romantic drama. As Gary Kelly observes, Hemans – and I would add, like Baillie and Brooke – has turned in her play,

> … to the victimization of women by 'masculine' history and to feminine kinds of heroism, more decisively to the representation of (afflicted) subjectivity as the 'other' side of history constituted by the 'records' of the public political sphere, more fully to imagined, fictionalised 'records' to fill the gap in 'masculine' history, to supplement and thus destabilize and challenge it, more clearly to the

---

37 See Cox, *In the Shadows of Romance*.

38 Brooke, *The Siege of Sinope*, p. 20.

39 Baillie, *Dramatic and Poetical Works*, p. 452.

40 '[Hemans] presents the continuity of affection as the only means through which resolution (both incidental denouement and moral resoluteness) can be achieved. Because affection has the power to transfer love of family to love of state' – Ross, *The Contours of Masculine Desire*, p. 276.

creation of 'national' literature of such records as a foundation of the feminized modern liberal state.[41]

Women playwrights, challenging the traditional ideology of the separate spheres of action between the sexes, opened up the possibility of contributing to the canon of Romantic drama by establishing a tradition of historical plays, which stage history and gender relations from the point of view of the vanquished and the socially emarginated members of society. They give voice to heroines who are not supported by a well-balanced social and political system or by divine power but are obliged to fight for their state and for their family at the same time in a chaotic world surrounded by war and revolution. Finally, they invoke the ideal of peaceful life in a community all of whose members can attend to their family affections without facing the threat of government interference or invasion from without.

---

[41]   Kelly, 'Last Men', p. 206.

Chapter 5

Felicia Hemans, Schillerian Drama, and the Feminization of History

Gary Kelly

Felicia Hemans was the leading female voice of European Romantic liberalism within the English-speaking world of her time. She acquired this voice partly by relentlessly adapting European liberal Romantic literature into forms appropriate for the British cultural and political situation, though she did little actual translating. Hemans opened this process with her first collection, *Poems*, published in 1808, and sustained and developed it through the rest of her career. Continental European drama was an important element in this literary, cultural, and political relationship. By the time Hemans began publishing, Continental dramatic literature, in translation, was well known to British readers and theatre audiences, and it continued to be a force in British Romantic literature throughout Hemans's career. Familiar with western European literature and languages from her childhood, Hemans turned for her own dramatic practice, not surprisingly, to perhaps the most famous and influential contemporary European dramatist – Schiller. Schiller was not Hemans's only model – her countrywoman Joanna Baillie was also important; but Hemans's plays would have been recognizably Schillerian to her readers, and thus have signaled to them her participation in a broadly liberal program of the kind being pursued by a wide range of writers and artists on the Continent, most of whom admired Schiller. More important, however, is Hemans's alteration of the Schillerian form to represent her own Romantic feminism and thereby influence Romantic liberalism as well as the cultural politics of her English-speaking readers. Yet Hemans's adaptation of Schillerian drama had less to do with Romantic drama or theatre than with Hemans's own carefully constructed literary career, and it is in terms of this career that I examine her dramas here.

Hemans's career as exemplary European liberal voice had five related phases – and one blind alley –, each built on the preceding one, and each responding to the changing public political scene in Britain, Europe, and beyond. In her first phase, in the collections *Poems* (1808), *England and Spain* (1808), and *The Domestic Affections* (1812), Hemans constructs herself as a female poet of the European culture of Sensibility, addressing Britain and Europe at the time of the Napoleonic crisis. Here, she followed late eighteenth-century British women poets in speaking to the public political sphere, its internal as well as international conflicts, from and for the domestic sphere and the feminine perspective from that sphere. Like such predecessors as Anna Laetitia Barbauld, Elizabeth Ryves, Helen Maria Williams, Elizabeth Bentley, Mariana Starke, and Charlotte Smith, writing during earlier British imperial crises of the American and French Revolutionary wars, Hemans posits a specifically feminine public poetry by adopting themes that are irenic, philanthropic, mediatory, and patriotic in an earlier sense of public-spirited.[1]

In her next phase, Hemans adapted and extended this work for the immediately post-Napoleonic period by constructing herself as feminine poet of Romantic cultural nationalism, addressing the United Kingdom's situation as *the* global superpower, but one with potentially disastrous social tensions within. In major poems of this period, *The Restoration of the Works of Art to Italy* (1816) and *Modern Greece* (1817), Hemans represents Britain's national and imperial situation in terms of the history of empires, and relies on the conventionally accepted feminine entitlement to the aesthetic sphere in order to address the public political sphere.

At about the same time, however, Hemans made an excursion into another poetic mode – one that was risky for a female poet. In 1816/17 she wrote two heroic couplet verse satires, 'The Army' and 'Reform'.[2] 'The Army' addresses the public controversy over the 'problem' of demobilized servicemen flooding back into Britain after the final defeat of Napoleon. Many in the middle-class, tax-paying public wanted drastic cuts in the military budget, and some claimed that returning and disgruntled servicemen constituted a threat to public order and the state. Hemans, with two brothers and a husband returning as war veterans, satirized the anti-military voices in 'The Army'. 'Reform' deals with a related issue. The post-Napoleonic period, with its fiscal and economic crises and relaxation of war-time restraints, also saw renewed agitation for political and social reform in Britain. Though Hemans sympathized with liberal causes in Continental Europe and its colonies and former colonies, like many liberals she was a gradualist reformer and was leery of what was then called 'radical' reform, or reforms that would further the interests and power of the lower middle class and politicized working class. In 'Reform', a heroic couplet verse satire filled with allusions to *Paradise Lost*, she attacks the voices of radical reform. 'The Army' and 'Reform' are accomplished poems, would have done their author no discredit, and resembled many topical satires published in newspapers and magazines of the time. Hemans may have published them there; if so, she did not republish them, for, as she well knew, satire, especially on public political events, was conventionally considered unsuitable for female readers or writers.

At the same time, she turned to a theme considered more acceptable for the woman writer, as long as she avoided 'controversy' or display of 'learning' – the theme of religion. To varying degrees and at various moments from the mid-1810s

---

[1]   It was during Hemans's lifetime that 'patriot' began to be associated with devotion to one's nation, in particular, against other nations, in the construction of Romantic nationalism.

[2]   Manuscripts are in the Liverpool (England) Public Library.

to the mid-1820s Hemans represented herself as a female Christian poet, though of liberal attitude. Here, too, Hemans follows earlier British women poets, as well as writers in Elizabeth Montagu's 'Bluestocking' circle of the second third of the eighteenth century, whose letters were published during Hemans's early career. These writers criticized the irreligion, 'freethinking', and anti-clericalism of men of the European Enlightenment; Hemans criticizes similar aspects of male culture in her own day associated with British reformers, French Revolutionaries, and Napoleon's enforced modernization of Europe. The Bluestocking writers specifically promoted Anglicanism and supported the established state church, however, whereas Hemans follows other female predecessors in promoting a generalized Protestantism, representing religion as a force of social conciliation and philanthropy, in tune with a conservative strain in emergent European liberalism. Hemans experimented with this theme in several ways. In the extensively revised second edition of *The Restoration of the Works of Art to Italy* (1816) she argues that Christian art, more than the art of pagan antiquity, represents the true glory of Italy and the aspirations of Italians and all peoples for the liberty that is the best condition for producing great art. In *Tales and Historic Scenes* (1819) the theme of religion is not nearly so prominent, but in *The Sceptic* (1820) Hemans attacks religious scepticism for undermining personal integrity, the domestic affections, and society itself. In *Dartmoor: A Poem* (1821) Hemans deplores false religion such as those of Britain's prehistoric past, perhaps opposing the vogue for Britannic primitivism in Romantic culture at that moment. In her historical drama *The Siege of Valencia* (1823) she again stresses religion as a prime motivation in national unity and emancipation, but in her other historical drama, *The Vespers of Palermo* (1823), religion is not a major theme. Only in the last phase of her career, in the 1830s, would religion become a consistently central theme in her writing.

Meanwhile, from the late 1810s to the late 1820s Hemans produced a series of works more fully in tune with Romantic liberal nationalism as it was expressed in Continental European literature. In this period Hemans presents herself as a female poet of liberalism resisting monarchist and Catholic post-Napoleonic Restoration and Reaction. Now Hemans clearly represents history as a masculinist project that is destructive of the subjectivity and domesticity central to post-Revolutionary, post-Napoleonic bourgeois ideology and culture. This phase of Hemans's work was the most sustained and produced her most substantial, diverse, and accomplished work. In these works she critiques both masculinist history and male-authored historiography, and does so both thematically and formally. Thematically, she represents masculine history's destructive impact on women and the feminine in a wide range of times, places, societies, and cultures. Formally, she resists masculine history and historiography by using pathetic romance – or verse narrative in which a prominent narrator explicitly sympathizes with the victims of masculine history. Hemans devoted great energy to this literary and ideological task in a diverse range of highly accomplished works.

Tales and Historic Scenes (1819) collects a variety of narrative and reflective poems set in various times and places from antiquity to the early modern era.

These poems are dominated by the sympathizing narrator already found in the bestselling verse narratives of Byron, Scott, Campbell, and others. Hemans emphasizes more than they do, however, the destruction and waste caused by masculine action in history and the suffering inflicted on women and the domestic sphere by such action, and she focuses on female or feminized male protagonists. After experimenting with Christian discursive poetry, Hemans returned in the mid-1820s with renewed vigor to the problem of masculine history, now reflecting on the European liberal revolts and their suppression in the early 1820s. She addresses the European and global situation of liberalism directly in two volumes – *The Siege of Valencia: A Dramatic Poem*; *The Last Constantine: with Other Poems* (1823) and *The Vespers of Palermo: A Tragedy, in Five Acts* (1823). The dramas will be discussed later, but having only mixed success with them, Hemans turned to a form that she, with Letitia Landon, pioneered in the 1820s – the dramatic monologue. *The Forest Sanctuary* (1825), which Hemans considered her major work, is the verse monologue of an unnamed Spanish conquistador who recounts events leading to his exile in the 'forest sanctuary' of North America. As a former soldier and thus instrument of masculine history, he is feminized through the suffering inflicted by that history, and comes to represent the feminized subject of a liberal state that has not yet been realized – the Spanish liberal revolt was suppressed by a French army just as Hemans was composing the poem. *Records of Woman* (1828) is another set of 'tales and historic scenes', all centred on female protagonists, drawn from history and literature, including Romantic historical drama. In another virtuosic display of formal and stylistic range, thus validating her literary–historical authority, Hemans again shows women, the feminine, and the feminized in culture and society crushed by forces of masculine history.

In the final phase of her career Hemans makes *herself* the protagonist of that theme, constructing herself as a religious, Wordsworthian female poet of afflicted femininity and domesticity. In 1826 the *Literary Magnet* published a series of essays on 'The Living Poets of England'; the first was on Wordsworth, but the second was on Hemans.[3] She responded to this living canonization with a flow of personal lyrics in Wordsworthian style, on Wordsworthian subjects, and tagged with Wordsworthian quotations and allusions. Hemans's strategy is to present herself, rather than some historical or fictitious figure, as the exemplary subject of liberal ideology and the proleptic sovereign subject of some future modern liberal state. Hemans had earlier asserted this subjectivity intensely but indirectly in dramatic monologues such as *The Forest Sanctuary* and 'Arabella Stuart' (first poem in *Records of Woman*), and in pathetic narrative romances. By the late 1820s, however, she turned decisively to the lyric, publishing a large number of such poems in the literary magazines and annuals. In part Hemans was exploiting the market for these kinds of poems, rather than longer narratives, in such publications; but she also had to publish such poems in large number in order to assert, validate, and authorize her claim to exemplary feminized liberal subjectivity. These numerous

---

[3]   *Literary Magnet*, n.s., 1 (January 1826): 17–22, and n.s., 3 (March 1826): 113–21.

poems were then collected into volumes in the 1830s: *Songs of the Affections; with Other Poems* (1830), *Hymns on the Works of Nature, for the Use of Children* (1833), *Scenes and Hymns of Life; with other Religious Poems* (1834), and *Poetical Remains of the Late Mrs Hemans* (1836), put together by her family after her death in 1835. Hemans was not only following Wordsworth's canonization as national poet and essentially lyric poet; she was also rewriting this model in her own terms, and her own, liberal version of the lyric Romantic voice, in such poems as the 'Sonnets Devotional and Memorial' and 'Thoughts during Sickness'.[4]

In summary, Hemans's generic–ideological career progressed from the early personal lyric voice characteristic of the feminized literature of Sensibility, through indirect voices of various kinds (including Byronic and Campbellian verse narrative, Schillerian drama, and dramatic monologue), to feminized Wordsworthian personal lyric voice. Each of the moves in this trajectory negotiated between Hemans's previous work, new political events and situations, and developments in the literary field.[5] These developments were of two kinds – British and Continental –, which Hemans aimed to merge in her own work through quotation, allusion, epigraph, and appropriation. First there was the work of her leading male British predecessors and contemporaries: Thomson, Mason, and the Sentimental poets in her early career; Southey and especially Campbell, with other early Romantic poets, in her early middle career; Byron and (though less obviously) Shelley in her middle career; and Wordsworth in the last stage of her career. Hemans recontextualizes this British dimension of intertextuality in her work, however, by juxtaposing it with European Romantic literature, mostly of liberal tendency, including such writers as Foscolo, the early Chateaubriand, Germaine de Staël, Schiller, Pellico, Alfieri, Jean Paul, Goethe, Novalis, Pindemonte, Oehlenschläger, von Arnim and Brentano, Sismondi, Fouqué, Körner, Manzoni, Grillparzer, Lamartine, and many others.

Hemans's career comprises, then, a continuing spectacle of a liberal Romantic feminist rewriting contemporary literature and past history in relation to unfolding current events. After Hemans's death this situation changed, but by then Britain itself was beginning to modernize into a liberal state, and such states were being founded or fought for in many parts of the world. Hemans's career of liberal writing, which had unfolded temporally, was consolidated after her death and made historically transcendent by successive collected and selected editions of her works, down to the Oxford University Press edition (1914), which, ironically, was the death knell of her status as a popular classic. These editions formed, for middle-class readers in English-speaking communities around the world, a home verse encyclopedia of European Romantic liberal themes of subjectivity, domesticity,

---

4   'Sonnets Devotional and Memorial' are from *Scenes and Hymns of Life, with Other Religious Poems* (1834), and 'Thoughts during Sickness' were first published in the *New Monthly Magazine*, 43 (March 1835): 328–30.

5   Pierre Bourdieu, *The Rules of Art: Genesis and Structure of the Literary Field*, trans. Susan Emanuel (Stanford, 1995).

and progressive feminization of history, society, and the state. Hemans's dramas, though not very successful with readers, theatre audiences, or critics, nevertheless constituted a significant moment in her career as feminist Romantic liberal writer and a significant element in her reception. I would argue that these significances are disclosed less by reading her plays in the context of Romantic drama, women's drama, or closet drama than by reading them in the context of Hemans's career and her sustained project of constructing an authoritative feminine and feminist Romantic liberal public voice.

Hemans pursued this project mainly by feminizing history – or history and historiography viewed as masculine and masculinist projects – in four main ways. First, she romanticized, or put into romance narrative form, moments from all periods and places of history, and she did this in the cultural context of her day, where romance and history were gendered feminine and masculine respectively and widely viewed as incompatible if not inimical. Second, she constructed herself as a transhistorical yet feminine consciousness at a time when many considered women to be immersed in the immediacy of quotidian life and thus unable to achieve a critical and transhistorical perspective on it. Third, she appropriated, adapted, and altered the work of both British and Continental European contemporaries, at a time when many of her countrymen and countrywomen regarded Continental European literature as something to be avoided, as corrupt and corrupting, as un-British if not anti-British. Finally, she gave a specifically feminist turn to her appropriation of Romantic liberalism.

For Hemans aimed, like many contemporaries, especially women such as Germaine de Staël, to promote the broad European liberal revolution against its reactionary monarchic and Catholic opponents.[6] In Romantic liberal literature this revolution is often figured as the struggle of a feminine or feminized culture and politics against masculinist and yet paradoxically effeminate ones, or the struggle of constitutional, progressive, secular, middle-class, and irenic values against the monarchic, reactionary, Catholic, unmodernized, ignorantly plebeian, and militarist ones. Like European liberals, Hemans also aimed to detach liberalism from residual attachments to *ancien régime* culture and thereby to 'rescue' it from possible lapse into historic masculinism, and thus from repetition of the masculinist history characteristic of past centuries. In other words, Hemans proposes to change the course of history by feminizing it; furthermore, her chosen instruments for doing so are ones associated with feminine cultural spheres, or in which women are at least licensed to participate, namely literature. This project may be compared to Mary Wollstonecraft's work in the context of British reformists' and French Jacobins' revolutionary masculinism of the early and mid-1790s, or Helen Maria Williams's somewhat different project in the context of French Jacobin and Napoleonic masculinism of the mid- and late 1790s, or Mary Shelley's in the

---

[6]   Hemans's anti-Catholicism may now seem illiberal, but like many liberals she saw Catholicism and especially the Papacy as a prop of despotism, largely by fostering plebeian ignorance, 'superstition', and resistance to modernization.

context of post-Napoleonic masculinism of Restoration and Reaction, from 1815 through the 1820s.

Unlike Wollstonecraft, Williams, and Shelley, however, Hemans was a career poet, and in her project three poetic modes are central – narrative, lyrical, and dramatic. Like other Romantic writers, she merges genres and modes, particularly these three, and more than any contemporary besides Byron she fuses the dramatic with lyric narrative. Many of her poems centre on a dramatic incident or tableau, as in 'The Wife of Asdrubal', 'The Widow of Crescentius', and 'The Death of Conradin' (*Tales and Historic Scenes*, 1819), 'Casabianca' (from *The Forest Sanctuary*, second edition, 1829), 'The Landing of the Pilgrim Fathers in New England' (from 'Other Poems' in *Records of Woman*, 1828), and 'Scene in a Dalecarlian Mine' (in *National Lyrics, and Songs for Music*, 1834). She fuses lyric, narrative, and drama in her dramatic monologues, notably *The Forest Sanctuary* and 'Arabella Stuart'. She fuses lyric with dramatic as another innovative form in the series 'Scenes and Hymns of Life' (1834), where a dialogue, or 'scene', establishes a conflict that is transcended in the concluding 'hymn'. A rare piece of published prose by Hemans is a critique of Goethe's drama *Tasso* (1790) in which Hemans contrasts Goethe's representation of Tasso's vicissitudes at the court of Ferrara with Byron's representation (in 'The Lament of Tasso') of the poet determined to transform his inward sufferings into transcendent narrative poetry.[7] Hemans also links narrative poems to plays by herself or others: 'The Last Constantine' (published with her verse tragedy *The Siege of Valencia*, 1823) is inspired by Joanna Baillie's drama *Constantine Paleologus*, and 'The Death of Conradin' (from *Tales and Historic Scenes*) is linked to Hemans's play *The Vespers of Palermo*. Hemans not only inserts lyrics into her dramas, as many contemporaries did, but makes the lyric instrumental in the action, as when Ximena sings a ballad of El Cid in *The Siege of Valencia*, stirring the populace into renewed resistance to the besieging Moors.

As in her work generally, Hemans's dramatic models were both British and Continental. She admired the dramas of Joanna Baillie, and corresponded with her. She based her narrative–reflective poem 'The Last Constantine' on Baillie's *Constantine Paleologus* (published in *Miscellaneous Plays*, 1804; staged at Liverpool, Hemans's home town, in 1808). She admired Mary Mitford's *Our Village*, corresponded with Mitford, and evidently knew her historical dramas, though all but one of these (*Julian*, staged as *The Melfi* at Covent Garden in March 1823) postdated Hemans's own dramas. It is possible that Hemans, a voracious and wide-ranging reader, also knew female predecessors' dramatic work, such as Hannah Brand's historical play *The Huniades* (staged at Norwich in 1791 and at London in 1792), Mary Deverell's *Mary, Queen of Scots: An Historical Tragedy, or, Dramatic Poem* (published 1792; not staged), Sophia Lee's *Almeyda, Queen of Granada* (staged and published 1796), or Anne Plumptre's adaptation from Kotzebue, *The Count of Burgundy* (published 1798; adapted and staged 1799).

---

[7]   Felicia Hemans, 'German Studies, By Mrs. Hemans', *New Monthly Magazine*, 40 (January 1834): 1–8.

Even these native sources seem to have been viewed by Hemans through the template of Schillerian dramatic form, however. Hemans clearly drew on Schiller, in various ways. Schiller's poems were among her favourites, and she even tried to convert Wordsworth to a liking for them. Though Hemans makes no direct reference to Schiller's literary and theoretical essays, her interest in art as a form of national aesthetic education for sovereign subjectivity is in tune with his arguments. A number of Hemans's important poems refer directly to Schiller, as a signal to the informed reader. One of two epigraphs to *The Forest Sanctuary* is from Schiller's *Die Jungfrau von Orleans*; the other is from Coleridge's *Remorse*. Two poems in Hemans's *Records of Woman* are based on scenes in Schiller's dramas – 'The Switzer's Wife' (*Wilhelm Tell*) and 'Joan of Arc in Rheims' (*Die Jungfrau von Orleans*). In her correspondence and notes Hemans also refers to Schiller's plays *Wallenstein, Die Jungfrau von Orleans*, and *Wilhelm Tell*, and to dramas inspired by Schiller, including those of Adam Oehlenschläger (who also promoted Schiller's dramas in his essays) and Manzoni's *Il Conte di Carmagnola*. Hemans engages directly with Schiller as a major voice of European liberal Romanticism, however, in her dramas *The Vespers of Palermo* and *The Siege of Valencia*, rewriting Schillerian drama in terms of her feminist Romantic liberalism.

This relationship may seem to have been unavoidable. Schiller was the major dramatist and one of the major writers of any genre in Hemans's day to represent the conflict of history and the feminine in terms of emergent liberal ideology. The theme may be discerned in both of the distinct but related phases of Schiller's career as dramatist. Schiller's early plays participated in the pre-Revolutionary German Sturm und Drang, related to the European culture of Sensibility in a broad movement against upper- and lower-class cultures, interests, and hegemony.[8] After a period as historian and essayist, Schiller returned to drama, addressing the European and global post-Revolutionary Napoleonic crisis. Schiller, like many writers across Europe and beyond, promoted state-formation as cultural revolution in the interest of the middle classes, first as a reformist, anti-aristocratic participant in Sturm und Drang, then as an anti-Jacobin, anti-Bonapartist, (German) liberal Romantic nationalist. Like the similar work of Kotzebue, Schiller's Sturm und Drang dramas from *Die Räuber* to *Kabal und Liebe* represent a critical intersection of class and gender conflict, and had great impact across Europe; in England, significantly, they were taken up by women dramatists, among others, with adaptations by Elizabeth Inchbald and Ann Plumptre. After Schiller's death in 1805, however, his later, historical dramas became more influential, and in her own plays Hemans rewrote these dramas, and the Schillerian dramatic form evolved by a number of European playwrights from the Dane Adam Oehlenschläger to the Italian Alessandro Manzoni, both of whose work she knew.

Schillerian dramaturgy, as a form including Schiller's plays and also developed from them, involves a particular relationship between certain kinds of settings,

---

8   For an account of Schiller's career, see Lesley Sharpe, *Friedrich Schiller: Drama, Thought and Politics* (Cambridge, 1991).

plot, characters, and themes. The settings fictionalize periods of supposed nation-forming in the past – periods that, according to Schillerian historicism, saw the emergence of unified nations from resistance to external threat through the overcoming of internal divisions. In Schiller's historical dramas, for example, there is the vaguely historicized period of Sicilian history in *Die Braut von Messina*, the reign of Elizabeth I of England in *Maria Stuart*, the time of Joan of Arc in *Die Jungfrau von Orleans*, and the (largely fictitious) era of Swiss independence in *Wilhelm Tell*. In the Romantic period, such eras were represented in a variety of historiographical and literary works, creating for the plays' audiences an effect of retrospective irony: the audience (or at least the reasonably well read members of the audience) would already know roughly what transpired, during and after the dramatic action, from their general knowledge of history. The geo-historical setting is represented as a site of conflict through plots of social and family division, which are in turn microcosms of larger, national divisions; the plot is resolved through establishment of familial, social, and national unity, or the anticipation of such unity – perhaps even in the period inhabited by the play's audience. The logic of this plot is driven by two factors: history and the structure of action–reaction.

Three kinds of history come into play here: local, general, and implied. First there is local historical 'fact', that is, roughly what did happen or plausibly could have happened in the particular event dramatized in the play, as told by historiography available at the time of the play's staging or publication, though this historiography was often fictitious, as in the case of *Wilhelm Tell*, or fictionalized, as in *Die Jungfrau von Orleans*. Second was general history, or the history of the West as context for the particular set of events dramatized; in Schillerian drama this general history has two patterns – masculine history as cycles of empires achieved by male action in wars, conquests, and colonizations, and repetition of and parallels between these cycles. Finally, there is implied history: the 'history' represented in the drama is understood by the audience as a parallel to the history unfolding in their own present. Most important is that all three kinds of history involved in the drama place the audience in history, as observer but also as implied participant, implied agent. This is precisely the kind of agent, as sovereign subject, on which liberal ideology was founded, and this dramatic–historical effect on the audience may help explain the popularity of Schiller's plays through the period of formation of modern liberal states that his dramas implicitly call for and anticipate.

The Schillerian plot's logic of action–reaction dramatizes the creation of the modern liberal nation state. In this plot, the external threat discloses or accentuates internal divisions of two kinds – between characters or groups of characters and within individual characters, as subjective conflict. In the end, or plot closure, conflicts are resolved, or at least eliminated, through suffering and sacrifice and meaningful death, thereby enabling or enforcing unity as the necessary condition for defeat of the external threat. The emphasis is not on action but on the internal, subjective suffering or transformation in exemplary individuals, who are thereby represented as proleptic sovereign subjects of a future liberal state. For in Schillerian historical drama, action as such is less important than suffering and sacrifice – the forge or proof (in the sense of both test and evidence) of sovereign subjectivity in the cultures of Sensibility and Romanticism. In Schillerian drama, even those who act do so reluctantly, or are forced to do so, and when forced to do so try to avoid implication in what they have done; action as such is often minimal, and crucial action often occurs entirely offstage, being reported or implied rather than represented (in the theatrical sense). This shift of emphasis from action to subjective undergoing not only keeps sovereign subjectivity at the centre but also represents Schiller's and his audiences' ambivalence about revolutionary and Napoleonic violence and preference for representation of their central ideal of sovereign subjectivity as a mode of being rather than doing. A consequence of this approach to plot is to throw particular emphasis onto character and characterization, dialogue, and scene structure.

In Schillerian drama, characters have two major functions. First, characters fit the drama's social–historical themes: minor characters represent social groups and major characters represent historical forces, passing or emergent (as seen from the Romantic period). Second, the themes of Schillerian drama require particular prominence for female characters, elaborated according to conventions of gender difference circulating widely in middle- and upper-class European culture of that time. Women are important and sometimes central figures in Schiller's dramatic works across his career, from *Die Räuber* to *Wilhelm Tell*. As in much literature of Sensibility and Romanticism, female characters enable the writer to elaborate major issues of the conflict between public and private spheres, between the political and the personal, affective, and domestic. Female characters, built on the convention of woman's 'natural' aptitude for patience, endurance, forbearance, and fortitude, also enable elaboration of the central Schillerian themes of sacrifice for the national good, defeminization of women by masculine history, and the incompatibility of the feminine, including sovereign subjectivity and domesticity, with the public, political sphere. These themes are central in Schiller's plays, from the early *Kabal und Liebe* to the later *Die Braut von Messina, Maria Stuart*, and *Die Jungfrau von Orleans*.

Schillerian drama uses parallel and contrasting figures to elaborate this structure of female characters. Different female characters play out varieties of femininity, positive and negative, within the broad themes of the play. For example, in *Die Braut von Messina*, Isabella's maternal feelings lead her to evade patriarchal rule in the form of her husband's command, based on a monitory prophecy, to have their infant daughter killed. The evasion ironically brings about the destruction of her sons foretold by the prophecy – sons who are the needed military leaders for a Sicily facing external aggressors. Beatrice, the daughter, is the unwitting agent of political forces that result in national political disaster. The males – her brothers – are aggressive and violent; women are victims who attempt in vain to resist patriarchy. In *Wilhelm Tell* the female characters are secondary but significant in their differences. Hedwig Tell, the hero's wife, is fearfully maternal and uxorial; by contrast, Gertrud Stauffacher (the character on whom Hemans based her poem 'The Switzer's Wife') is domestic but inspiringly patriotic. Berta, the aristocratic patriot, converts the noble youth Ulrich from courtier to warrior, from Austrophile to Swiss patriot. Female difference is represented on a grander scale in *Maria Stuart*, which contrasts the vulnerably feminine Maria to the defeminized Elizabeth, while both are shown to be pawns of ambitious men. The contrasts are on a lesser scale in *Die Jungfrau von Orleans*, which offers Agnes Sorel, royal mistress but ardent patriot, and Johanna, female warrior and patriot, set against Johanna's sisters, who are entirely domestic. In Schillerian drama, with its emphasis on nation formation, love is a personal absolute, as in all Romantic literature, but its function is to support or disrupt national and social unity and the national cause; if love is an obstacle to the national cause, it is sacrificed. Hemans will make this issue central in her dramas.

In summary, Schillerian drama gives crucial roles to female characters in relation to the public, political sphere, for good or ill. For good, the female character is less a representation of a woman than a symbolic embodiment of the idealized revolutionary nationalist middle class of Schiller's day. Examples are Johanna in *Die Jungfrau von Orleans* and Gertrud Stauffacher in *Wilhelm Tell*. For ill, the female character takes several forms, all negatively feminine and either excessive or transgressive in relation to idealized domestic yet patriotic femininity. Examples are Isabeau in *Die Jungfrau von Orleans*, who troubles the political sphere out of 'unfeminine' political ambition, or Berta Tell in *Wilhelm Tell*, whose fears for her family's safety impel her to oppose her husband's patriotic mission. To bring out these different female roles in the history of nation formation, Schillerian drama uses the familiar device of character contrast. Hemans will, again, make more of such figures.

Hemans's adaptation of Schillerian dramaturgy is informed by her liberal Romantic feminism. Her literary career began after Schiller's death, in the Napoleonic crisis of global warfare and the post-Napoleonic crisis of Reaction and Reform; she writes her dramas, in particular, during the repression of liberal revolt in southern Europe. Hemans carries Schillerian dramaturgy forward to the period of emergent Romantic nationalism and liberalism, therefore placing greater emphasis on masculine history's affliction of the feminine and the domestic and on the value of the positively feminine, in men or women, to the liberal Romantic project. More decisively than Schiller, however, Hemans emphasizes the cost, especially to women and the feminine, of this project. This emphasis guides her adaptation of Schillerian dramaturgy.

As in Schillerian drama, the settings in Hemans's plays are periods of supposed nation-forming in the past – emergence of a unified nation from resistance to external threat and overcoming internal divisions. In Hemans's case, these periods are the so-called vespers of Palermo, or uprising of Sicilians against French rule in AD 1282, and the period of the Christian reconquest of Spain from the Moors in the eleventh and twelfth centuries. In Hemans's dramas, too, the historical setting creates an effect of retrospective historical irony: the audience already knows roughly what transpired, during and after the dramatic action. In Hemans's dramas, as in Schiller's, plots of social and family division parallel national divisions, with resolution in unity or anticipation of unity on all levels. In Hemans's dramas, too, the plot logic is driven by history and the structure of action–reaction, and local, general, and implied history are invoked. In Hemans's dramas, however, the collision of masculine history with the feminine is even more destructive; implied history, as the audience's present, is more sharply topical by reference to the liberal revolts in southern Europe and their suppression by leagued absolute monarchies, while Britain stood by – a situation deplored by many Britons of liberal sympathies. Finally, in Hemans's dramas the sense of reconciliation and national unity at the close is less certain and secure than in Schillerian drama; for Hemans's readers and audience, Britain's apparent social tranquility in the early 1820s could not mask a sense of deeper social antagonisms ready to burst into the open, as happened by the late 1820s.

In Hemans's dramas, as in Schiller's, the interplay of these three kinds of history places the audience in history, as observers yet also, and more important, as implied participants and agents. Hemans, however, represents the historical process as alien and even hostile to the plays' pathetic or affective centre – certain female characters and feminized males. These include Constance and Raimond in *Vespers of Palermo*, and Elmina and her young sons as well as Gonzalez and Theresa in *Siege of Valencia*. In Hemans's dramas, this alien, hostile element is represented by two kinds of character: super-masculine characters who conceive of themselves as forces of history, such as the antagonists Procida and Eribert in *Vespers of Palermo*, or the antagonists Abdullah and Hernandez in *Siege of Valencia*; and terminally masculinized female characters, such as Vittoria in *Vespers of Palermo* and Ximena in *Siege of Valencia*, who consciously sacrifice for the national cause not just their feminine character, desires, and social sphere, but their very lives. In the last phase of Hemans's career, when she represented herself as exemplary liberal subject, she would construct *herself* as such a sacrifice, assuming the character of de Staël's Corinne, who becomes a national voice at the cost of feminine kinds of domestic happiness.[9]

To reinforce her dramas' more critical and negative representation of masculine history, Hemans makes the plot logic of action and reaction starker than in Schillerian drama. In Hemans's dramas, the external threat doesn't just disclose or accentuate internal divisions; it creates them. It is true that, as in Schillerian drama, such divisions are resolved through suffering and sacrifice. There is much more emphasis in Hemans's dramas on the suffering and sacrifice, however, especially on the part of female characters. Furthermore, the reconciliation, resolution, and national unity seem more fragile and precarious – and hardly a consolation for the sacrifice. As in Schillerian drama, onstage action is infrequent, minimalist, and less important than representation of suffering and sacrifice – in fact, much of the action in Hemans's dramas is debate between masculine and feminine viewpoints

---

[9]   See, for example, 'Corinne at the Capitol', from *Songs of the Affections, with Other Poems* (1830), and also 'Woman and Fame', first published in *The Amulet* (1829).

and depiction of female suffering and sacrifice.[10] As in Schillerian drama, there is little action onstage; crucial physical or martial action occurs offstage, being reported or implied rather than represented – and those who act do so reluctantly, are forced to do so, and try to avoid implication in what they have done. In Hemans's dramas, however, this restraint in representing physical or violent action and shift of emphasis to representation of subjective action go beyond Schiller's and his audiences' ambivalence about revolutionary violence and their preference for representing sovereign subjectivity as a mode of being rather than doing. More clearly than in Schillerian drama, Hemans's dramas reject violence, even in an apparently good (i.e. national) cause, as a lapse into masculine history, into what has caused the sacrifice and suffering that are the real drama.

As in Schillerian drama, Hemans's approach to plot throws emphasis on character and characterization and dialogue, but with different implications. Hemans's dramas have fewer characters than most Schillerian dramas, with the notable exception of *Die Braut von Messina* – Schiller's experiment in ancient Greek tragic form, and the play that comes closest to Hemans's emphasis on female suffering caused by masculine forces, values, and politics. That there are fewer characters in Hemans's dramas concentrates attention on personal relationships, giving greater emphasis to the dramatic representation of the conflict of masculine and feminine viewpoints and of female suffering, and shifting emphasis in terms of characters' social representativeness. As in Schillerian drama, characters still fit the dramas' social–historical themes: minor characters represent social groups; some characters represent historical forces, passing or emergent (in terms of Hemans's era); and the dramas' themes require particular prominence for female characters. In Hemans's dramas, however, the reduced array of characters gives greater emphasis to issues of gender in the processes of nation formation. The drama discloses not so much the value of the feminine to nation formation as the need to feminize history in order to change it, and more particularly and by implication, to change it from a (masculinist) monarchic–ecclesiastical order to a (feminized) liberal constitutional one.

In short, women are thematically, symbolically, and dramatically more important in Hemans's dramas than in Schiller's. In both dramatists' work, female characters are used to represent central conflicts of public versus private spheres, the political versus the personal, affective, and domestic, but the conflict is sharpened in Hemans. Not only does Hemans dramatize the theme of sacrifice for nation formation; she shows that involvement of women in the public political sphere results in defeminization of various kinds. Not only is the feminine incompatible with life in the public political sphere; it is destroyed by it. Similarly, love in

---

[10]   For example, in *The Siege of Valencia* the debate between Elmina and Gonzalez in scene 1 and between Elmina and Hernandez in scene 2, and the agony of Elmina and Ximena in scene 8, culminating in the latter's death; in *The Vespers of Palermo*, the protest of the feminized warrior Raimond against the bloodthirsty vengefulness of his father Procida and the Sicilian conspirators in Act 2, scene 4 and his debate with Procida in Act 3, scene 2.

Schillerian drama can support or disrupt national unity and nation formation, but in Hemans's dramas it must be repressed in the national cause and is crushed by masculine history: Constance loses Raimond in *Vespers of Palermo*, Vittoria never even discloses her love in *Siege of Valencia*, and the reconciliation of Gonzalez and his wife Elmina, at the end of that play, is barely a consolation.

Schiller's dramas were much more successful theatrically than Hemans's; they entered the European and global stage repertory, were staged again and again through the nineteenth century, and some remain current today, besides the *Wilhelm Tell* staged annually at Interlaken, Switzerland, and New Glarus, Wisconsin.[11] One reason may be that Schiller made full use of stage resources, especially once he had access to Goethe's theatre at Weimar; Schiller's dramas offered spectacle of the kind nineteenth-century theatre-goers expected. Hemans's dramas do not do so, and in dramatic scope and theatrical requirements are suited, though not only suited, for reading more than for theatrical representation. This does not mean that Hemans's dramas were failures as dramas or did not function as dramas for her readers. Hemans was certainly keen to have her dramas staged, if she could – she was a professional writer and knew the financial and other rewards possible from successful stage presentation. Nevertheless, the form of Hemans's dramas and their function within her oeuvre indicate that she designed them primarily, if not solely, as closet drama – in the positive sense asserted by Joanna Baillie and developed by other female Romantic playwrights.[12] Hemans's dramas function within the private and domestic sphere appropriate to closet drama.

This was not their only function within her oeuvre, however. Hemans's dramas take their place in a body of work mostly made up of narratives and lyrics, but much of which also includes dramatic narrative and dramatized lyric. Most of Hemans's work, be it narrative, lyric, dramatic, or a mixture of these, dramatizes critical moments in history when public and private, masculine and feminine spheres collide. In masculine history, these various works imply, the outcome of such collision is inevitably tragic, and tragedy was at that time still the most prestigious historic genre besides epic. Yet tragedy and epic were long regarded as beyond women's experience, education, and creative powers, and few women writers ventured on them, even in Hemans's day. By their mere presence in her oeuvre, Hemans's dramas made a feminist assertion and conferred cultural prestige and generic validation on her work. At the same time, by their presence in her oeuvre the dramas validate Hemans's dramatization and heroization of bourgeois subjectivity, domesticity, and everyday life, thereby serving a bourgeois cultural revolution exemplified, as many of her female contemporary writers exemplified it, in the feminine spheres of society and culture, and in the female, feminine poet herself.

---

[11]   For Interlaken, see http://www.tellspiele.ch/index.html; for New Glarus, see http://www.wilhelmtell.org/contact/ (both accessed 3 February 2004).

[12]   See Catherine Burroughs, *Closet Stages: Joanna Baillie and the Theater Theory of British Romantic Women Writers* (Philadelphia, 1997).

Most important, however, was the function of Hemans's dramas as closet dramas within her oeuvre. As just asserted, throughout her career, in various genres and forms, Hemans dramatizes and heroizes the emergent liberal subject, as the feminine or feminized subject suppressed by masculine history, and therefore, she implies, requiring something like the modern liberal constitutional state in order to remake history. In addition, however, Hemans's oeuvre is designed to call into being the liberal subject as the new agent of and in history. Dramatic form is central to this call. In her oeuvre, gathered or selected into successive one-volume editions published everywhere English was read, and ranging across full-scale dramas, dramatic narratives, lyrics, and other forms, Hemans helped teach successive generations of readers not only how to be liberal subjects but also that to be such a subject was necessarily heroic and dramatic. It may not be coincidental that Hemans's popularity, always challenged by masculinist critics and canons, fell steeply when those kinds of heroism and drama lost their prestige, in the early twentieth century and bloody global warfare of nations and empires. Nevertheless, it can be argued that Hemans's dramas, circulating widely throughout the English-speaking world in the many different editions of her work, together with all her proliferated dramatic forms of narrative and lyric, perhaps contributed more to the cultural revolution that effected the modern liberal state than even Schiller, or perhaps more than any Romantic poet, or dramatist, or poet–dramatist.

PART II
Dramaturgical and Cultural Processes

Chapter 6

The Erotics of Home: Staging Sexual Fantasy in British Women's Drama

Catherine Burroughs

What connections do we find between eighteenth-century British erotica[1] and the dramas written by women during the Romantic period, and what do these

---

[1]   Those who study erotic writing before the twentieth century realize that the words 'pornography' and 'erotica', as well as the phrase 'libertine writing', require contextualization and historical perspective. It is important to recall that, etymologically, 'porne' is the Greek word for 'prostitute'. But, as Lynn Hunt states in *The Invention of Pornography*, '[p]ornography did not constitute a wholly separate and distinct category of written or visual representation before the early nineteenth century'. Hunt writes: 'If we take pornography to be the explicit depiction of sexual organs and sexual practices with the aim of arousing sexual feelings, then pornography was almost always an adjunct to something else until the middle or end of the eighteenth century. ... But the main lines of the modern pornographic tradition and its censorship can be traced back to sixteenth-century and seventeenth-century Italy and seventeenth- and eighteenth-century France and England (albeit with important antecedents in ancient Greece and Rome)' – Lynn Hunt, 'Introduction: Obscenity and the Origins of Modernity, 1500–1800', in Hunt (ed.), *The Invention of Pornography: Obscenity and the Origins of Modernity, 1500–1800* (New York, 1993), pp. 9–45, at pp. 9–10. Bradford K. Mudge, following Walter Kendrick's argument in *The Secret Museum* (1987), reminds us that, in distinction from the word 'obscenity' (with its Greek meaning 'off or behind the stage'), pornography is a 'nineteenth-century neologism, and it refers specifically to graphic images or narratives that have been mass-produced for the sexual use of their consumers'; see Bradford K. Mudge, 'Romanticism, Materialism, and the Origins of Pornography', *Romanticism on the Net*, 23 (August 2001), at: http://users.ox.ac.uk-scat0385/23mudge.html, accessed August 2004, p. 2. Mudge writes that '... recent scholarship suggests the following: although we have numerous examples in Britain of sexually explicit literature and art before 1800, the function of that material was not exclusively to arouse the audience, nor was it mass-marketed for commercial gain by authors, printers, publishers who understood and presupposed its "illegitimate" pleasures. More accurately termed "proto-pornographic", this material may have included sexually explicit scenes, but those scenes were at the time experimental. ... Before 1800, in other words – and *Fanny Hill* (1749) notwithstanding – "pornography" simply did not exist as a recognizable generic category. ... In short, pornography as we know it emerged over the course of the eighteenth century ... [and by] 1820, the year of Queen Caroline's trial for adultery, pornography had become a popular sub-genre of political invective' (p. 2). As a result of his research, Mudge dates modern pornography as emerging around

connections reveal about the ways in which erotic literature has influenced female playwriting? Where in the plays composed by British women do we locate descriptions of female sexual desire and sexual fantasy, and what conclusions can we draw from the form and content of these (mostly implicit) textual moments?

Eros in the Home: Aphra Behn versus Mary Pix

Scholars have rightly argued that plays composed between the Restoration and Romantic eras reveal an increasing priggishness about staging sexual conduct. Indeed, in only a short period of time, we can identify a tension that shapes female dramaturgy during the eighteenth century. Between 1678 and 1696 – in less than two decades – we find Aphra Behn's vision of female sexuality giving way to Mary Pix's more cramped discussion of the same subject. A brief look back at Behn's comedy, *Sir Patient Fancy*, for instance – which was first staged in 1678 and performed throughout the eighteenth century – reveals so strong a commitment to the fulfilment of female desire that the title character, Sir Patient, is actually grateful at the play's end that he has been cuckolded by his wife. To the company gathered on stage, he makes clear that a wife who cheats – rather than rendering a man miserable – can be the source of sexual liberation:

1820 – and coming into full bloom in the 1830s and 1840s. Additionally, Ian Frederick C. Moulton cautions us not to assimilate 'the history of erotic representation to the history of pornography ... because not all explicit representation of sexual activity can be meaningfully defined as pornographic' – Moulton, *Before Pornography: Erotic Writing in Early Modern England* (Oxford, 2000), p. 3. In his study of pre-eighteenth-century erotic writing, Moulton distinguishes between 'erotica' and 'erotic writing'. According to his classification, 'the term "erotic writing" refers to any text, regardless of genre or literary quality, that deals in a fundamental way with human physical sexual activity' (p. 5). The term 'has the advantage of being a descriptive, not a generic, term, and it is relatively free of moral judgment' (p. 6). In perhaps his most helpful assertion, Moulton writes: 'In thinking about debates over what pornography is and is not, I have often thought that it might make more sense to see pornography as a way of reading rather than a mode of representation. As a way of reading, pornography would be characterized by an obsessive interest in the material read, an abstraction of the self and an abdication of critical faculties, and a sense of voyeurism – of observing without being observed in return' (p. 11).

I … will turn spark; they live the merriest lives – keep some City
mistress, go to Court, and hate all conventicles.
You see what a fine City-wife can do
Of the true breed; instruct her husband too:
I wish all civil cuckolds in the nation
Would take example by my reformation.

(Act V, p. 123)[2]

By contrast, Mary Pix's *The Spanish Wives* – performed in 1696 and revived
several times in the early 1700s – is less concerned with women's sexual freedom
than with the appearance of scandal. Those who have read the play will recall
that Elenora is married to an insanely jealous husband, who has stolen her from
her betrothed, the count Camillus. Camillus is intent upon claiming the legality
of his betrothal, and the play ends happily, in the sense that the young lovers are
reunited. As Katharine Rogers has observed, 'Pix's devaluation of the importance
of physical virginity' is notable,[3] since the rightful husband does *not* regard the de-
virginated Elenora as used goods. In the play's dichotomous terminology, Elenora
has only 'staggered' but not 'fallen'. Yet Elenora's main concern at play's end
is to 'hope my future conduct will satisfy the world of my innocency'.[4] Her aim
is to be treated as if her hymen has been metaphorically restored. This theme of
redemptive virginity will resurface throughout the eighteenth century, appearing
as late as 1780 in Sophia Lee's popular comedy *The Chapter of Accidents*, based
on a play by Diderot.[5]

A tension that we might describe as 'Behn versus Pix' structures eighteenth-
century dramaturgy to the point where women who even 'stagger' in their sexual
behaviour are often regarded as already 'fallen', forecasting much of Victorian
melodrama. In plays by eighteenth-century women, as in the novel, celebrations
of female sexual fulfilment are countered by restrictions on female desire;
monogamy is increasingly a value, along with the idea that the modern couple
will spend all of its erotic satisfaction on each other. And, after 1785 and into the

---

[2]   Aphra Behn, *Sir Patient Fancy. The Meridian Anthology of Restoration and
Eighteenth-Century Plays by Women*, ed. Katharine M. Rogers (New York, 1994), pp.
23–130, at p. 123.

[3]   Katharine M. Rogers, 'Introduction', in Rogers (ed.), *The Meridian Anthology of
Restoration and Eighteenth-Century Plays by Women* (New York, 1994), pp. vii–xviii, at
p. xv.

[4]   Mary Pix, *The Spanish Wives. The Meridian Anthology of Restoration and
Eighteenth-Century Plays by Women*, ed. Katharine M. Rogers (New York, 1994), pp. 131–
84, at p. 182, Act V, scene 6.

[5]   For an analysis of the sexual fantasies encoded in this play, see my 'British Women
Playwrights and the Staging of Female Sexual Initiation: Sophia Lee's *The Chapter of
Accidents* (1780)', *Romanticism on the Net*, special issue: Romanticism and Sexuality, 23
(August 2001), at http://www-sul.stanford.edu/mirrors/romnet, accessed August 2001.

early nineteenth century, the dramaturgy of many plays by women presents the following equation: the reward for a man's increasing effeminization (in the sense that he is expected to be more monogamous) is a domestic arrangement that *may* allow for erotic exploration but which, more importantly (in terms of political and social consolidation) promises that deception and cuckoldry – plot devices that drive so many seventeenth- and eighteenth-century comic plays – will be eradicated. Admiration for the libertine, the deceptive young wife, and the sexually active older woman – elements that constitute an eroticized domesticism in the late seventeenth century – gives way to what we might be called a 'domesticated eroticism'. Even in the very text that scholars pinpoint as inaugurating modern-day pornography (1748/49), John Cleland's *Memoirs of a Woman of Pleasure* – there is, as Randolph Trumbach has noted, an attempt to make companionate marriage the site of the sexy.[6]

This vision of uniting the domestic with the erotic takes an interesting turn in certain plays by women writers of the Romantic period. There are, for instance, several dramas from the 1820s and 1830s that raise the question of what it would be like to have one's sexuality nurtured – during sexual initiation and thereafter – by the very communities in which one has been raised.

This question comes to the fore in two scripts that I want to discuss in this article – Joanna Baillie's *The Bride* (1828) and Frances Anne Kemble's *An English Tragedy* (comp. 1833–1843). These plays interest me because they deal with the topic of heterosexual intercourse through an approach that is both feminist *and* conservative.

I have observed that certain British women playwrights feature incest in order to express a desire for a different kind of sexual initiation rite, one that allows the initiate to take more control of the sexual experience. Moreover, dramatic representations of incest can serve to express a longing to have one's sexual

---

6   Randolph Trumbach, 'Modern Prostitution and Gender in *Fanny Hill*: Libertine and Domesticated Fantasy', in G.S. Rousseau and Roy Porter (eds), *Sexual Underworlds of the Enlightenment* (Chapel Hill, 1988), pp. 69–85, at p. 69. J. Douglas Canfield has written that eighteenth-century comedy 'becomes less about the socializing of the centrifugal sexual energy of the male rake than the socializing of the centrifugal sexual energy of the female coquette'; cf. J. Douglas Canfield, 'Introduction', in Canfield (ed.), *The Broadview Anthology of Restoration and Early Eighteenth-Century Drama* (Peterborough, ON, 2001), p. xi. Yet the focus on the coquette does not unleash her erotic energies; rather, the trend is to de-eroticize her and make the management of the home her source of fulfilment. Ruth Perry has described this impulse – in relation to the eighteenth-century British novel – in terms of the century's growing de-sexualization of the female breast and an intensifying focus on women breastfeeding their own children: 'maternity came to be imagined as a counter to sexual feeling, opposing alike individual expression, desire, and agency in favor of a mother-self at the service of the family and the state' – Ruth Perry, 'Colonizing the Breast: Sexuality and Maternity in Eighteenth-Century England', in John C. Fout (ed.), *Forbidden History: The State, Society, and the Regulation of Sexuality in Modern Europe* (Chicago and London, 1992), pp. 107–37, at p. 112.

initiation – one's defloration – managed by the family compound. The fantasy of endogamy may be motivated *not* by a desire to have real intercourse with the father or the brother or the sister or the mother, or, as in the aristocratic tradition of the Renaissance, by a desire for economic consolidation.[7] Rather, explorations of incest can be read as ways of fantasizing about how to fortify one's self against losing access to the privileges of the child–parent relationship: the being cared for; the eschewing of adult worries and responsibilities; the luxuriating in the parental home and body. Paradoxically, then, the incest fantasy may convey *not* a wish to sleep with the parent but a desire to avoid initiation into adult sexuality – a condition identified in profiles of the 'sexual anorexic'.[8] Incest fantasies thus become a vehicle for re-imagining female sexual initiation as the antithesis of casual, violent, or traumatic encounters performed by a non-relative.

Women and Pornography: Female Sexual Initiation

Because the line between British dramaturgy – especially in comedy – and the scenarios explored by eighteenth-century writers of erotica is not as rigid as it might seem, studying the ways in which these genres resemble each other (at certain moments) can provide us with useful information about what a culture does and does not value. As scholars of 'Porn Studies' have observed, fantasies articulated in erotic writing can open a door to the priorities of the cultural 'center' even though that literature may be regarded as residing on 'the margin'.[9] But while sexual fantasies certainly can provide outlets for an imagined rebellion against cultural restraints or, at the least, express a desire for adventurousness, they can also be used to ward off fears of anticipated or actual sexual experiences. Therefore, erotic fantasies articulated in literature can be read as providing access not so much to the fantasier's actual desires as to the source of her conflict about sex and sexuality.

In contrast to some of the erotica produced in eastern cultures, erotic literature by western writers – especially in Great Britain, France, and America – typically teaches us that female sexual initiation has historically been a rite reserved for the exogamous – or for strangers, or for those who believe ceremonies of defloration should violate, rather than consecrate, the body.[10] I am reminded of

---

[7]   See Bruce Boehrer, *Monarchy and Incest in Renaissance England* (Philadelphia, 1992), for a fascinating discussion of endogamy and exogamy in the Renaissance – in the context of his analysis of Shakespeare's history plays.

[8]   For more on this phenomenon, see Patrick Carness, *Sexual Anorexia: Overcoming Sexual Self-Hatred* (Center City, MN, 1997).

[9]   For a representation of the approaches and methodology of 'Porn Studies', see Linda Williams's edited volume, *Porn Studies* (Durham, NC, and London, 2004).

[10]   Dorelies Kraakman delineates 'two models of sexual initiation' in western pornographic writing, and it is the issue of 'curiosity that makes the difference' in a

the contemporary research of Naomi Wolf, who has studied how young girls in American culture become sexually active. For her 1997 study titled *Promiscuities*, she interviewed pre- and early-adolescent girls to see how they describe, or represent, the moment when they first had heterosexual intercourse. Even in the 1990s Wolf found a disturbing inability on their part to speak about this event in anything but negative or vague terms. She cites as examples selected comments from over 400 girls interviewed by sociologist Sharon Thompson:

> I tell you, I don't know why or how I did it. Maybe I just did it unconsciously
> …
> I don't know what came over me that night. I really don't. I mean, I can't really answer it. But it happened.
> I had no idea. I had no idea at all. I knew I would be taking off my clothes, and I knew he'd be taking off his clothes. But as far as what would happen, I didn't know …
> I didn't really know what I was doing. I knew what I was doing but I didn't actually *know* what I was doing.[11]

If as recently as this past decade these women seem not to have a vocabulary for talking about defloration, or an audience to address, it is unsurprising that even the most personal writings by women from previous eras (such as journals and diaries) will reveal so little information at the explicit level about their sexual lives and fantasies. As Amanda Vickery has written in her excellent history of 'genteel' British women in Georgian England, 'two topics that were virtually

---

girl's enjoyment and control of [sexual] experience. Cf. Dorelies Kraakman, 'Reading Pornography Anew: A Critical History of Sexual Knowledge for Girls in French Erotic Fiction, 1750–1840', *Journal of the History of Sexuality*, 4.4 (1994): 517–48, at p. 531. There is 'la petite curieuse', a figure that appears in eighteenth- and early nineteenth-century erotic fiction in France. Curiosity 'may not leave the virgin intact, but it provides her with understanding and practical knowledge' (Ibid., p. 526). 'The girl who lacks curiosity is left in blind ignorance, the plot being constructed as to exclude any possibility of her becoming enlightened at any time' (Ibid., pp. 534–5). Over the nineteenth century, Kraakman discovers that the 'disappearance from dominant discourse … of the curious girl desiring to experience and to know is not just a matter of locking her stories behind the closed doors of secret museums or private cabinets; it may also be read as the disappearance of a theory of knowledge' (Ibid., pp. 521–2). As Julie Peakman has noted, young women often lost their virginity to older women in eighteenth-century erotic writing, but male sexual initiators were 'classed' as superior. Julie Peakman, 'Initiation, Defloration, and Flagellation: Sexual Propensities in *Memoirs of a Woman of Pleasure*', in Patsy S. Fowler and Alan Jackson (eds), *Launching Fanny Hill: Essays on the Novel and Its Influences* (New York, 2003), pp. 153–72, at p. 159.

[11] Sharon Thompson, *Going All the Way: Teenage Girls' Tales of Sex, Romance and Pregnancy* (New York: Hill and Wang, 1995), pp. 135–6.

never' committed to paper 'were spirituality and sex'.[12] Women wrote of childbirth, breastfeeding, marriage, and courtship in their non-fictional writing (such as letters) but not of defloration, sexual initiation, masturbation, or erotic scenarios.[13]

And yet we know from the recent research on seventeenth- and eighteenth-century British erotica that women were consumers, sellers, and sometimes producers of 'the lewd and licentious'. This, despite the fact that, as Jacqueline Pearson's analysis of women reading in Britain between 1750 and 1835 has shown, the woman reader in general was cause for great anxiety. In 1775, Dr Edward Sloane Wilmot even contended that '"the perusal of the novel" can constitute the first fatal stage of a woman's decline that may culminate in a frightful case of *furor uterinus*'.[14]

While it is well documented that men were the primary consumers of erotica, the extent to which women were also reading erotic books may have been greater than we have realized. So-called dangerous texts of the period – Rousseau's *Julie, ou la Nouvelle Eloise* (1761), his *Confessions* (1781–88), Goethe's *The Sorrows of Young Werther* (1774), and LaClos's *Les liaisons dangereuses* (1782) –, though they would not typically have appeared in circulating libraries, would likely have been available to any woman who worked or lived in a household with a private library, as might medical books and sex manuals.

But women were not only *readers* of such material. As Julie Peakman describes in her recent study, *Mighty Lewd Books* (2003), they might *see* erotica as a young girl in boarding school where 'obscene prints' were known to have been

---

[12]   Amanda Vickery, *The Gentleman's Daughter: Women's Lives in Georgian England* (New Haven and London, 1998), p. 11.

[13]   Masturbation hysteria was fanned by the publication of *Onania: or, The Heinous Sin of Self-Pollution, And All its Frightful Consequences, in Both Sexes, consider'd, etc.* (1707). G.S. Rousseau and Roy Porter have observed that, while the age had 'an unusually prominent and public sexual culture', it was also 'less an age of erotic pleasure than as a new era of sexual anxiety ... moral scare over the evil consequences of masturbation grew to panic proportions, associated with new fears of personal and national decay arising from the debilitating effects of waste of semen in what Barker-Benfield has called the "spermatic economy" ... official attitudes toward homoeroticism hardened, turning the occasional sin of buggery into the more terrifying stereotype of the sodomite ... the dread figure of the nymphomaniac began to loom large in the protopsychiatric imagination ... an anticipation of the Freudian dilemma that sexual happiness and the order of civilised society was utterly incompatible' – 'Introduction', in Rousseau and Porter (eds), *Sexual Underworlds of the Enlightenment* (Chapel Hill, 1988), pp. 1–24, at pp. 2–3. In short, 'this brave new world of sexual liberation may have represented almost an all-time *crisis* in women's own sense of the construction and control of their sexuality' – a problem replicated for homosexual men (ibid., p. 5; italics in original).

[14]   Michael Shinagel, '*Memoirs of a Woman of Pleasure*: Pornography and the Mid-Eighteenth-Century English Novel', in Paul J. Korshin (ed.), *Studies in Change and Revolution: Aspects of English Intellectual History, 1640–1800* (Menston, 1972), pp. 210–36, at p. 230.

sold.[15] Sexual information could also reach women and girls on the streets. Roy Porter writes about a James Graham, who established for a period the 'Temple of Hymen' at the Adelphi Theatre in the Strand where he 'lectured to fashionable crowds about the invigorating properties of happy sexuality', 'advocated the use of pornography', recommended 'various sexual positions for women who had failed to get pregnant', and 'hired out his "celestial bed" to barren couples for L50 a night'.[16]

Yet the extent to which women *wrote* erotica has only begun to be explored. And, when it comes to determining which erotic *playscripts* were female-authored, much work lies ahead. Karl Toepfer has suggested a rich direction for research in his fascinating study of 'the clandestine theatre' in pre-Revolutionary France. In these settings, aristocratic women – including Marie-Antoinette – played a central part in the staging of private performances for elite audiences, some including 'pornographic entertainments'.[17] According to Toepfer, the 'most lavish sponsor of clandestine theatre' was Marie-Madeleine Guimard – an opera star who built at the mansion of Prince Soubise a 'demi-elliptical' auditorium, which could accommodate 240 people with '[g]rilled loges and curtained vestibules' for aroused spectators to satisfy themselves in private.[18]

Dramas written for public theatre – especially for the commercial London stage between 1780 and 1830 – would seem the least likely texts to in-script erotic fantasies. For even though the Romantic period coincides with, in Bradford K. Mudge's phrase, the 'emergence of the pornographic imagination',[19] its dramatists were battling numerous pressures on free expression, including the Stage Licensing Act of 1737, which enacted repressive restrictions on political, religious, and sexual discourse, and which, by the time of the French Revolution, served – along with fears of social unrest and war – to make playwrights more cautious about addressing contemporary topics, especially if they had commercial ambitions. But, as I will argue, Romantic women playwrights *did* find ways to explore the sexual fantasies of their cultural period, and one of these ways was to feature the topics of defloration and incest.

---

[15]   Julie Peakman, *Mighty Lewd Books: The Development of Pornography in Eighteenth-Century England* (Basingstoke and New York, 2003), p. 37.

[16]   Roy Porter, 'A Touch of Danger: The Man-Midwife as Sexual Predator', in Rousseau and Porter (eds), *Sexual Underworlds of the Enlightenment*, pp. 206–32, at p. 208.

[17]   Karl Toepfer, *Theatre, Aristocracy, and Pornocracy: The Orgy Calculus* (New York, 1991), p. 66.

[18]   Ibid., pp. 64–5.

[19]   Mudge, 'Romanticism, Materialism, and the Origins of Pornography', p. 3.

Defloration Fantasies and Joanna Baillie's *The Bride* (1828)

Joanna Baillie's *The Bride* (1828) suggests how the dramaturgy of even this 'model of an English gentlewoman' – to use William Wordsworth's phrase[20] – attends to the era's preoccupation with defloration. Indeed, Baillie's play has an erotic power that one might not expect to find in a work constructed as a vehicle for Christian pedagogy.

Baillie's composition of *The Bride* was triggered by a belief (typical of her era) that the duty of a good Christian was to help 'reform' the cultural practices of a colonized people – in this case the natives of Ceylon, which had been made a British colony in 1802.[21] We are rightly critical of this mindset today, but, as Baillie wrote to her friend Margaret Holford Hodson, although it 'was somewhat presumptuous at my age to venture on such a subject ... I could not withstand the *temptation* laid in my way of perhaps doing *real good* in my vocation, before I should lay it aside for ever which my grey hairs and encreasing listlessness admonish me to do'.[22] Even as Baillie uses the word 'temptation' – an interesting choice given the erotic content of her play –, she tries to compensate for her sense of trespass (of writing about something she knows little about) with the hope that such an endeavour might do 'real good'.

Explaining the circumstances of the play's composition, Baillie tells Holford that the advocate-general of Ceylon, Sir Alexander Johnston, asked her 'to write a Drama for the moral improvement of the Cyngalese, he furnishing me with a story characteristic of their own manners &c to work upon'. This was not an unfounded request on Johnston's part; Baillie's drama, *The Martyr*, had already been translated into Sinhalese in 1826.[23] 'It seems all the instruction which they [the natives of Ceylon] receive is in dramatic form', Baillie wrote; 'their dramas are performed in the open air, and assembly of ten thousand people will attend to them [plays] without wearying for nine or ten hours at a streach [*sic*]'.[24]

Baillie thought deeply about the audiences who might see her plays, even though fewer than ten of the twenty-seven were staged during her lifetime. Baillie's extensive body of theatre theory makes clear that she sought – through writing drama – to trace the ways in which different passions (love, jealousy, hate) can teach audiences 'sympathetic curiosity'. If audiences could be compelled to study the ways in which a particular 'passion' affects a particular character, then they

---

[20]   Margaret Carhart, *The Life and Work of Joanna Baillie*, Yale Studies in English 64 (New Haven, 1923), p. 3.

[21]   For a helpful analysis of the colonial contexts and textual form of *The Bride*, see Christine Colon's 'Christianity and Colonial Discourse in Joanna Baillie's *The Bride*', *Renascence*, 54/3 (Spring 2002): 163–76.

[22]   Judith Bailey Slagle, *Joanna Baillie: A Literary Life*, 2 vols (Cranbury, NJ, 2002), vol. 2, p. 609 (my emphasis).

[23]   Ibid., vol. 1, p. 268.

[24]   Ibid., vol. 2, pp. 597–8.

might be prompted to watch with an intensity that might result in the development of a more acute sensibility.

This idea is actually dramatized in the third and final act of *The Bride* when two spectators speak lines designed to describe to an audience how to read the body of the main character in his emotional crisis. The stage directions state that '*Rasinga throws himself into his seat and buries his face in his mantle*', and the second spectator says '*in a low voice to the 1st [spectator]*: Look, look, I pray thee, how Rasinga's breast / Rises and falls beneath its silken vesture'. The first spectator responds by describing what we, the audience, are primarily to notice – the protagonist's bodily response to his emotional confusion: 'There is within a dreadful conflict passing, / Known by these tokens, as swoln waves aloft / Betray the secret earthquake's deep-pent struggles'. The second spectator then rejoins – voice still low: 'But he is calmer now, and puts away / The cover from his face: he seems relieved'.[25]

As this brief passage suggests, a paradox in Baillie's theory is that moral development is triggered by a dramaturgy that features the body's physicality, and thus Baillie's enterprise is, in concept, decidedly sensuous. Like her brother, Matthew – a noted anatomist whose *The Morbid Anatomy* (1793) featured detailed engravings of the vagina and uterus –, and like her uncle, John Hunter – a renowned surgeon who sought to calm the hysteria over masturbation by becoming an 'informed and enlightened spokesman' on the practice –, Joanna Baillie chose to tell her stories through that genre most ineluctably tied to the body, the drama.[26] In short, throughout her career she made the mind's effects on the body her main object of study. In this sense, then, as Dorothy McMillan has demonstrated, Baillie resembled her physician relatives, or a proto-psychiatrist, anatomizing the mind/ body complex for the collective examination of a theatre audience.[27]

Baillie's preface to *The Bride* makes clear that this is a work of her imagination, rather than a historical drama. This point is worth emphasizing since Baillie's statement throws into relief the fantasy-driven aspect of *The Bride*'s dramaturgy. While she provides several references to Ceylon that indicate she has done some research about the culture, she tells readers that she 'wished to have found some

---

[25]   Joanna Baillie, *The Bride*, in *The Dramatic and Poetical Works of Joanna Baillie: Complete in One Volume* (London, 1851); repr. 2nd edn, *The Dramatic and Poetical Works* (Hildesheim and New York, 1976), p. 683.

[26]   Shinagel, '*Memoirs of a Woman of Pleasure*', p. 230.

[27]   For more information about Baillie's brother, Matthew, and the connections between sister Joanna's plays and Matthew's study of anatomy, see Dorothy McMillan, '"Dr." Baillie', in Richard Cronin (ed.), *1798: The Year of the Lyrical Ballads* (Houndmills and London, 1998), pp. 68–92; Deidre Gilbert, 'Joanna Baillie, Passionate Anatomist: Basil and Its Masquerade', *Restoration and Eighteenth-Century Theatre Research*, 16/1 (2001): pp. 42–54 (at pp. 42–3); and Frederick Burwick, 'Joanna Baillie: Matthew Baillie, and the Pathology of the Passions', in Thomas C. Crochunis (ed.), *Joanna Baillie, Romantic Dramatist: Critical Essays* (London and New York, 2004), pp. 48–68.

event *in the real history* of Ceylon, that might have served as a foundation for my drama; but not proving successful in my search … I have of necessity had recourse to imagination'.[28] *The Bride*, then, is patently a product of an Englishwoman's imagination of Ceylonese culture, and it is a strikingly eroticized view.

Chock-full of gothic elements (secret passages, castles, a besieged heroine), *The Bride* grapples with a problem that pornographic writing often foregrounds for titillating effect: how a married man can sleep with more than one woman, and, if he has a predilection for virgins, how he can satisfy that desire.[29] *The Bride* features a Cingalese chieftain, Rasinga, who decides to introduce into his household (as a second wife) a virgin whom he has glimpsed during a mountain excursion. While struggling to overcome his guilt at planning to sexually displace his first wife, Artina, he calls his situation an 'ecstasy […] / Though cross'd with darkness black as midnight'; this fraught passion makes him determined to 'enjoy this momentary radiance'.[30] But Rasinga's brother-in-law, Samarkoon, has other plans. He is outraged that the heterosexual life of his sister would be ended to make way for another woman, and, because Samarkoon also lusts after the bride, he steals her, is put in jail, and Artina is sentenced to die for trying to help him escape.

Aiming to write a play that would 'reform' the Ceylonese, whom Baillie had been told elevated vengeance over forgiveness, she introduces to the plot a Spanish physician named Juan de Creda. (A stand-in, perhaps, for the doctor-uncle and doctor-brother that Baillie so admired?) Juan de Creda has visited Rasinga long ago and healed him when he was gravely ill. Now, two years later, de Creda appears on the scene, like a deus ex machina, to restore the household's 'peace and order and domestic bliss'.[31] Like Baillie, who, in 1831, several years after *The Bride*, published an essay on her religious beliefs – called 'A View of the General Tenour of the New Testament Regarding the Nature and Dignity of Jesus Christ' –,[32] de Creda uses the rhetoric of Jesus Christ to persuade Rasinga to forgive both

---

28   Baillie, *The Bride*, p. 666 (my emphasis).

29   Tassie Gwilliam has studied the cultural obsession with virginity, maidenheads, and defloration, observing that 'eighteenth-century narratives of falsified virginity testify to an increasingly complex negotiation of the cultural contradictions involved in celebrating female virginity as a central value while at the same time treating women – and their virginity – as objects of commerce, both literary and actual' – 'Female Fraud: Counterfeit Maidenheads in the Eighteenth Century', *Journal of the History of Sexuality*, 6/4 (1996): 518–48, at p. 519.

30   Baillie, *The Bride*, Act I, scene 3, p. 671.

31   Ibid., p. 663.

32   In two papers given recently at conferences in Italy, Isabella Imperiali argues that the roots of Baillie's project, the *Plays on the Passions*, 'lie in ancient sacred theatre', a medieval tradition that (during an informal conversation) Imperiali traced into the present – in the practice and theory of contemporary director Peter Brook (see his chapter on 'holy theatre' in *The Empty Space* [1968]). Imperiali's research reminds us that religious aspects

Samarkoon and Artina (the former for trying to steal his bride; the latter for trying to help her brother escape prison).

To teach others to choose forgiveness over revenge is unflinchingly the thrust of Baillie's play. But, by making polygamy the vehicle through which to foreground the subject of forgiveness, she introduces a problem for her dramaturgy: how to purge it of what Juan de Creda calls 'sensual excess'?[33] For it is precisely the play's 'sensuality' that animates Baillie's drama. Although the unnamed 'bride' appears in only one scene where she speaks seven short lines, her body provides a powerfully erotic spectacle; and the bride's anticipated defloration – alluded to symbolically when she keeps dropping her costume veil – dominates the thoughts of the play's characters.

Erica Rand has written about a moment in Diderot's life (in 1767) when he saw a painting that outraged him because it violated his sense of how a virgin on the eve of her wedding night would, or should, respond to 'the sacrament of bridal defloration'.[34] In 1767 Diderot 'launch[ed] a diatribe against pornography' in response to Antoine Baudouin's *Le Coucher de la mariée*. But it is interesting to note that Diderot's own imaginings of how true virgin brides are to behave conform to the period's pornographic scenarios in which 'fear' and 'trembling' exemplify the virgin's physical intactness and, more importantly, add to the arousal of the male initiator.

Here is Diderot's fantasy of hymen loss, as it appears in his critique of Baudouin's painting, which showed 'a young woman, well-born and well-bred, with one knee on the bed, solicited by her spouse in the presence of her female attendants who prepare her'. In France, Diderot expostulates, one would expect to find a different sort of bridal scene, and it goes like this:

---

of Baillie's work have been under-analyzed, and, in a provocative discussion of one of Baillie's late works, *A View of the General Tenour of the New Testament Regarding the Nature and Dignity of Jesus Christ* (1831), she explores Baillie's Unitarianism in the context of the late eighteenth-century Dissenters movement. Laying the groundwork for a better understanding of the contradictory impulses that run through Baillie's writing, Imperiali's insights into Baillie's religious works (including her plays, *The Martyr* [1826] and *The Bride* [1828]) suggest that Baillie's progressivism is more apparent if one investigates the nonconformist Unitarian beliefs of the larger Dissenting community. (I appreciate the author's permission to cite from her work.) In a similar impulse, Sean Carney compares Baillie's theory of spectatorship and the passions with Adam Smith's philosophy in *The Theory of Moral Sentiments* in order to complicate earlier evaluations of Baillie's writing; perhaps it was 'failed', according to Baillie's own standard, because 'it was not *safe* enough … there was not enough *connaisance* of the autonomous self in her work, and instead her plays were soaked through with dangerous, anti-social *jouissance*' – Sean Carney, 'The Passion of Joanna Baillie: Playwright as Martyr', *Theatre Journal*, 52 (2000): 227–52, at p. 252.

[33]   Baillie, *The Bride*, Act III, scene 1, p. 680.

[34]   Erica Rand, 'Diderot and Girl-Group Erotics', *18th-Century Studies*, 25/4 (1992): 495–516, at p. 500.

An innocent girl endlessly prolongs her evening toilet; she trembles; she tears herself away only sorrowfully from the arms of her father and mother; she has her eyes lowered, she doesn't dare to raise them toward her attendants; she sheds a tear. When she finishes her toilet to move toward the nuptial bed, her knees buckle under her; her women have retired, she is alone when she is abandoned to the desires, to the impatience, of her young husband.[35]

This Diderotian image of the dawdling, trembling, tearful, downcast bride who, with knees 'buckling', moves slowly to the site of her sexual initiation, was everywhere in eighteenth-century English erotic literature, and it is an image that resembles Baillie's dramatic portrait of 'the bride' from Ceylon.

In the single scene in which the bride appears onstage – Act II, scene 2 – she has just been kidnapped by Samarkoon, unmarried and younger than Rasinga. Recalling Diderot's image of the ideal bride on her wedding night, she appears in 'tears and alter'd state', 'shrinking' and 'drooping in cheerless silence'.[36] Nevertheless, in keeping with the pornographic scenarios of defloration that pervaded the eighteenth and nineteenth centuries, the bride's ardour inevitably emerges as she undergoes a metaphorical initiation into sex. The stage directions tell us that Samarkoon attempts to '*draw aside her veil, while she gathers it closer*' and then '*the upper fastening of the veil gives way and falls over her hand*'.[37] At this event, Samarkoon remarks – like the sexual initiator that he will eventually become –, 'And look, the silly fence drops of itself; / An omen of good fortune to my love. ... / I am young, unmarried, and my heart / Shall be thine own, whilst thou reignst mistress here, / As shares the lion's mate his forest cave, / In proud equality'. Perpetuating the erotic fantasy that a true virgin always sheds tears during her initiation as a sign of her physical intactness, Samarkoon tells the audience that the bride 'smiles' at his description of his prediction – 'yea, a *tear* / Falls on that smiling cheek; yes, thou art mine'.[38]

Yet, in spite of Samarkoon's desire to have the virgin bride for himself, the play is preoccupied with the married Rasinga's desire to have the erotic endlessly available to him in his home. That he urges his first wife Artina to imagine herself in the role of the bride's 'elder sister' underscores the fact that Rasinga's fantasy of deflowering a virgin is tied up with other fantasies from pornographic literature in which, in the hunt for sexual pleasure, taboos can be transgressed with impunity. One of these taboos is incest.

Reassuring Artina that she will still occupy a 'loved and honour'd' position', Rasinga chides her: 'Why didst thou think it could be otherwise, [that you would not be "loved and honour'd"] / Although another mate within my house / May take her place, to be with thee associated, / As younger sister with an elder born?

35 Ibid., p. 497.
36 Baillie, *The Bride*, Act II, scene 2, p. 673.
37 Ibid., p. 674.
38 Ibid. (my emphasis).

/ Such union is in many houses found'.[39] As if to underscore the naturalness of what western audiences would have regarded as 'unnatural' (a polygamous arrangement) – a move which is one of the seductions of pornography –, once Rasinga announces his desire for the bride, Artina's brother, as well as her young son, is thrown into the position of playing Artina's husband. In fact, one of the most striking images in the play occurs near the end of Act III when Artina is facing death and her son, Samar, hurls these husband-like words at Rasinga, his father: 'The death that is appointed for my mother / Is good enough for me. We'll be together: / Clinging to her, I shall not be afraid, / No, nor will she'.[40]

The play argues that Rasinga's passion for a young and beautiful virgin is the product of an unreformed mindset likely to be encountered in non-Western, non-Christianized settings. And yet the dramaturgy complicates Baillie's intended message. For the intensity of Rasinga's fantasy – to have all of his erotic objects in the home – is one of the play's more interesting features. In spite of having to relinquish the bride to Samarkoon at play's end – overpowered by the Christian teaching of Juan de Creda and by the traumatized pleas of his son to save his mother's life –, Rasinga is still dwelling upon what 'the bride' might have been 'worth' to him in sexual pleasure had he had her, and – for this reason – an audience will also be dwelling on this fact as the play ends. Even as Rasinga chastises himself to 'cease! / Speak not of this – … if it be possible, / We'll think of this no more',[41] we do not believe him, because 'this' – the virgin defloration, the proposed incestuous-like living arrangements – have taken centre stage. When the two spectators to whom I referred above ask us to contemplate Rasinga in his emotional turmoil – pulled between Juan de Creda's Christian theology, the tears of his son, and his anticipation of taking the bride's virginity –, it is hard not to feel sympathy for Rasinga's plight.

For even as Baillie's dramaturgy presents Rasinga's sexual desires as 'un-Christian' and anti-domestic, it also arouses 'sympathetic curiosity' about Rasinga's drive to eroticize his home. And, as the play traces the bodily responses of numerous characters to Rasinga's desire, it invites us to imagine what it would be like to be the initiator of a scheme to unite the erotic with the domestic. Additionally, in a move that I do not have space to discuss here, the play allows us to experience the perspective of a woman fighting to keep her sexual place in her husband's life. In short, if *The Bride* had been staged with English actresses wearing an imagined version of eastern dress, it would have presented a stirringly complex representation of a household turned upside down by *eros*. That Juan de Creda is trying to teach forgiveness in the midst of this erotic scenario may have been approved by conservative playgoers, but I wager that, long after the play had ended, they would remember not the play's moral but its erotic charge.

---

39   Ibid., Act I, scene 3, p. 671.
40   Ibid., Act III, scene 2, p. 683.
41   Ibid., Act III, scene 2, pp. 683–84.

Fantasies of Incest and Fanny Kemble's *An English Tragedy* (comp. 1833–1843)

The connections between Baillie and Frances Anne Kemble, whose play I will next discuss, are numerous and worth noting in light of the fact that both playwrights dramatize a domestic 'erotics' as an indirect way of confronting the sexual fantasies of their culture.[42] Kemble's famous aunt, Sarah Siddons, had originated the role of Jane de Monfort in the 1800 production of Baillie's tragedy *De Monfort*; Kemble's uncle, John Philip Kemble, played the lead male role. Kemble's long life was very dramatic, and Baillie was a witness to the start of a career that would take an even more dramatic turn when Kemble married a wealthy American and found herself the mistress of a slave plantation near Sea Island, Georgia, in the late 1830s. Like Baillie, who wanted to use her writing to do some 'real good' in the world by reforming those she considered in moral need, Kemble drew upon her penchant for keeping journals to produce one of the most vivid portraits of slavery in the antebellum South. (In distinction from Baillie, however, Kemble actually exerted direct influence on world events; the publication of her journal in 1863 is credited with keeping England from supporting the Southern cause.)

Between 1831 and 1843 Kemble composed two plays in which the topic of defloration is indirectly addressed through a focus on quasi-incestuous relationships. Furthermore, in the copious journals and letters written throughout her long life, Kemble portrays her early acting career as itself a kind of sexual ceremonial, one that alternately thrilled and threatened her. In an entry in one of Kemble's journals, she wrote that the stage 'was the very reverse of my inclination. I adopted the career of an actress with as strong a dislike to it as was compatible with my exercising it at all'.[43] But she also found the process of performing extremely compelling and sensuous.

Especially in the early stages of her acting career (in the 1830s), Kemble quite often frightened herself with the wealth of emotion that issued forth from her person, as if she were a conduit for someone else's expressive history. For example, not having rehearsed the moment in Thomas Otway's *Venice Preserved*

---

[42]   Baillie and Kemble admired each other. In 1825 or 1826 – it is not clear from her letter in which year Baillie wrote – Baillie was first introduced to Kemble at Siddons's house when Siddons gave a reading of *King John*. At the same time she got to hear a play that Frances had written. (This play was *Francis the First*, which was later performed.) Baillie writes to Sir Walter Scott: 'at 16 she has written a Tragedy which, read in company by her Father, has struck every body as wonderfully forcible and Shakespearian' – Slagle, *Collected Letters*, vol. 1, p. 431). Later, watching Kemble perform on stage, Baillie observed that, while 'one of the few faults she has' is 'a little over-acting' (ibid., vol. 1, p. 493), '[s]he has saved Covent Garden from ruin & above a hundred Actors from being turned adrift to starvation and must feel a proud satisfaction in the success of her powers, and long may she enjoy it!' (ibid., vol. 1, p. 468).

[43]   Frances Anne Kemble, *Records of a Girlhood* (New York, 1879), p. 70.

when Belvidera is to 'utter a piercing scream', Kemble discovered in the first performances of that role that she 'uttered shriek after shriek without stopping, and rushing off the stage ran all round the back of the scenes, and was pursuing my way perfectly unconscious of what I was doing, down the stairs that led out into the street, when I was captured and brought back to my dressing-room and my senses'.[44] Kemble writes that she experienced a similar moment when first performing as Juliet. The 'passion I was uttering [was] sending hot waves of blushes all over my neck and shoulders', she recalled in *Records of a Girlhood*, 'while the poetry sounded like music to me as I spoke it, with no consciousness of anything before me, utterly transported into the imaginary existence of the play. After this, I did not return into myself till all was over ...'.[45] These kinds of experiences – and her reflections on them – prompted Kemble to confess that it is 'not the acting itself that is so disagreeable to me, but the public personal exhibition, the violence done (as it seems to me) to womanly dignity and decorum in thus becoming the gaze of every eye and theme of every tongue'.[46]

What makes this early acting career more complicated, in my view, is that Fanny's rite of passage occurred not because she was attracted to the theatre as a profession (even though she was the niece of Sarah Siddons), but because her parents urged her to take the stage in order to help them out of financial trouble. (They were managers of Covent Garden.) Therefore, Fanny's initiation into acting – which served also as an initiation into sexual expression, as the quotations above suggest – was strongly associated with her nuclear family, especially with her father.

In fact, Fanny Kemble's acting debut as Juliet in 1829 was the ultimate family affair. Her mother, playwright and actress Marie Therese De Camp, came out of retirement to perform Lady Capulet, and her father, Charles Kemble, took the part of Mercutio. On occasion, Charles Kemble would act Romeo to Fanny's Juliet when they toured the United States. And, in 1832, when Fanny's play, *Francis the First*, was produced in London, Charles performed his daughter's potential lover, rejecting her character for another female character in the script.

Kemble's journals and letters reveal a young woman eager to quit her acting career and transfer her allegiance from a parent who was also an acting partner to a husband to whom she could legitimately direct her sexual longings, even though sex seems not to have been her focus. Rather than desiring romantic mutuality in which the physical life throbs – as it did in those onstage performances that troubled her so greatly –, Kemble suggests in her writing that she regarded marriage as legitimately directing her 'affections' toward a legally sanctioned love object.

Yet in the several plays she wrote (in which incest is a component), Kemble also implies that such a transfer was complicated by the fact that she had once been a performing daughter encouraged to take the stage by her own family. By

---

44	Ibid., p. 236.
45	Ibid., p. 220.
46	Ibid., p. 432.

marrying shortly after her acting career had begun and while on tour with her father, Kemble seems to have participated in a kind of rebellion, in the sense that marriage – as an institution – always potentially threatens the nuclear family. But although she ran away from her father into the arms of a legitimate lover, she seems not to have been able to let go of a fantasy in which she might stay in the bosom of her family forever.[47]

What evidence do I have for this assertion?

I want to turn to one of Kemble's two plays – *An English Tragedy*, composed between 1833 and 1843 (the decade of her marriage) – because I believe it underscores how certain British women writers have used playwrighting to register the difficulty they have encountered in having to shift their loyalty from the father to the husband, the person designated to initiate daughters into a heterosexual stage.

Kemble tells us in her preface to *An English Tragedy* that it was inspired by 'an anecdote of real life, which I heard my father relate', and it is fascinating to contemplate the conversation that evidently took place between father and daughter as they discussed the story that became the impetus for Act III, scene 3 – the climactic scene. According to Kemble's play, the story her father told her focused on the extra-marital affair of a beautiful woman named Anne (Kemble's middle name), whose lover, growing tired of her, tries to pay his gambling debts by pimping her to another man. (One could read this as the allegorical story of Kemble's own life: her father, in debt as theatre manager, prostitutes Fanny to the stage.)

Fanny took this story and added a further plot twist. She created a quasi-incestuous relationship between a brother and a sister, Judge Winthrop (who is Anne's husband) and his sister Mary. Given that Kemble's culture frequently represented sexual initiations as brutal and bloody for the initiate, might Kemble have written her play in order to fantasize – through her discussion of incest – that the heartache of Anne's infidelity can be avoided by keeping one's sexuality all in the family?

We cannot, of course, know, although the evidence that accrues in a study of Kemble's work is provocative. When *An English Tragedy* opens, Winthrop appears to be happily living with both his wife, Anne, and his sister Mary in a country setting that is described as an Eden, but he soon finds his world endangered by the prospect that his sister might wed. When asked by James Forrester to give his consent for the marriage, Winthrop responds in the tormented language of the lover: 'Sir, I cannot give that child away! / You might as well ask me for half my

---

47   For an analysis of this conflict in reference to Kemble's poetry, see Catherine Burroughs, '"Be Good!": Acting, Reader's Theatre, and Oration in the Writing of Frances Anne Kemble', in Harriet Kramer Linkin and Stephen Behrendt (eds), *Romanticism and Women Poets: Opening the Doors of Reception* (Lexington, KY, 1999), pp. 125–43.

heart! / I cannot *want* her – I can't live without her'.[48] (The word 'want' expresses the ambivalence of incestuous longing, since it means both 'I can't lack' [in the sense that I don't want to 'need' or to be 'destitute'] and 'I can't desire' [as in 'require'].) A few lines later, Winthrop tries to explain his refusal by saying that Mary 'oft has sworn to me, she never / Should love a man, to have him for her husband', and, in response to James's suggestion that 'Mistress Mary heeds my suit', Winthrop bursts forth:

> O Heaven! this is the way! a whole dear life
> They [sisters] live upon our knees, and in our arms,
> The darlings of our very souls – and lo!
> A stranger, passing by, but beckons them,
> And straight they turn their back upon their *homes*,
> And make their *lodging* in a new-found *heart*.
> Oh! I had dreamt of this – but it is bitter,
> Now that 'tis come to pass![49]

Moaning that a 'husband is a wall that builds itself / Between a woman and all other things', Winthrop portrays Mary's future marriage as not only depopulating his household but also doing so through a seeming act of ingratitude and even betrayal. He compares Mary to 'the young bird, in our hedge elm trees here, / Warmed in the nest', who nevertheless 'drives thence / The ancient brood, who made their proper home there'.[50] Here, Mary is figured as the cuckoo bird, who would 'cuckold' her brother by marrying another, thus evacuating 'the ancient brood' from its 'proper home'. Moreover, Winthrop calls her potential marriage 'her burial', in the sense that he 'scarce could feel [it] more sadly'.[51]

But rather than upbraiding Winthrop for an inappropriate desire to keep his sister at home, *An English Tragedy* rewards him for his wishes by requiring the death of his adulterous wife, Anne, and installing Mary into the *position* of spouse. In fact, by including references to the fact that a number of men throughout the Judge's district are being cuckolded by their seemingly virtuous spouses, the play's dramaturgy argues that endogamy is the best defence against these threats.

This fascinating play deserves more attention than I can give it here, as does Kemble's discussion of the emotional incest between another brother–sister pair in her first drama, *Francis the First*. But, in concluding, the point I want to emphasize is that certain British plays linking defloration with incest are sometimes the product of conservative longings translated into erotic scenarios, conveying a poignant desire to stay within familiar regimens of behaviour and expression (to manage

---

[48]   Frances Anne Kemble, *An English Tragedy*, in *Plays* (London, 1863), Act II, scene 3, p. 61 (my emphasis).

[49]   Ibid, p. 62 (my emphases).

[50]   Ibid., p. 63.

[51]   Ibid., p. 65.

one's sexual initiation, for instance). For what could communicate resistance to change – and a search for comfort – more dramatically than desiring to keep the erotic within the home? Indeed, the juxtapositions of conservatism and feminism that one encounters in Kemble's and Baillie's writing – too numerous to delineate here – can help us to consider how profoundly conflicted some eighteenth- and nineteenth-century women may have been about the appropriateness of wanting a permanent role in the sexual drama of their families of origin.

Chapter 7

When Mitford Met Baillie: Theatre, Sociability and the Networks of Women's Romantic Drama

Diego Saglia

In *Recollections of a Literary Life*, published in 1852 when she was 65, Mary Russell Mitford devotes a chapter to 'Female Poets' in which she focuses on her acquaintance, both as a reader and as a personal friend, with two older women writers, themselves friends and neighbours in the village of Hampstead: Catherine Fanshawe and Joanna Baillie.[1] In her remarks on the latter, Mitford expresses admiration for her art and praises her outstanding output, while also pleading guilty to an '*esprit de corps*' which in this context, she confesses, specifically means 'pride of sex'.[2] Baillie, who had passed away the previous year, is celebrated as 'the first woman who won high and undisputed honours in the highest class of English poetry', and Mitford is especially proud of 'the honour of claiming acquaintance with this most gifted person'.[3] Thus, it might seem incongruous that, in addressing the merits of Baillie's production, Mitford also discusses it in terms of a quasi-masculine achievement:

> Her tragedies have a boldness and grasp of mind, a firmness of hand, and a
> resonance of cadence, that scarcely seem within the reach of a female writer;
> whilst the tenderness and sweetness of her heroines … would seem exclusively

---

[1]   See Mary Russell Mitford, *Recollections of a Literary Life; or, Books, Places, and People*, 3 vols (London, 1852), vol. 1, chapter 13. Catherine Maria Fanshawe (1765–1834), artist and poet, was one of the contributors to Baillie's *A Collection of Poems, Chiefly Manuscript, and from Living Authors* (1823). Her best-known poem was a riddle on the letter H, often mistakenly attributed to Byron. Most of her poetical compositions, unpublished at her death, are contained in *Memorials of Miss C. M. Fanshawe* (1865) edited by her nephew William Harness (1790–1869), an early friend of Lord Byron from their Harrow days, a life-long personal friend of Mary Russell Mitford, as well as intimately acquainted with Barbarina Brand, Lady Dacre. Ordained in 1812, Harness was a *Quarterly* reviewer, published an edition of *The Dramatic Works of Shakespeare* to which he prefixed a life of the author (1825), and edited Fanshawe's *Literary Remains* (1876).

[2]   Mitford, *Recollections of a Literary Life*, vol. 1, p. 241.

[3]   Ibid., pp. 241, 242.

feminine, if we did not know that a true dramatist – as Shakespeare or Fletcher – has the wonderful power of throwing himself, mind and body, into the character that he portrays.[4]

If Mitford acknowledges her own bias in favour of Baillie's 'female' achievements, she also recurs to a conventional comparison with masculine skills in order to assess the effective value of her dramatic powers. Yet, after all, since Mitford's own abilities as a playwright were frequently compared to masculine ones, her assessment of Baillie may be read as a mere rehearsal of contemporary critical commonplaces.[5] In fact, it may be no more than a nod to convention in a text that firmly places dramatic practice within the female sphere, a position that Baillie would have found entirely consonant with her own awareness of belonging to a group of women writers at the forefront of a different, specifically female, development in British literature. This is especially visible in Baillie's letter of 18 April 1829 to the American divinity professor and literary editor and reviewer Andrews Norton, where she says:

> I am much pleased ... that you should give your testimony in favour of the healthful influence of our female writers on the sentiments & manners of the present day. Indeed I think, while you do us honour you do us justice, and it is from men like yourself that we receive it and prize it: the half-learned & weaker part of your sex have always set their faces against us. Mrs Hemans & Miss Edgeworth you cannot well prize more highly than I do; with Miss Mitford's Village I am only acquainted from a few extracts ... I am not, however, ignorant of another excellent work of hers which has appeared since you left England, her Tragedy of Rienzi, acted this last winter many times to full Houses in Drury Lane, and deserving its success.[6]

---

[4]   Ibid., p. 242.

[5]   Famous, or indeed notorious, are Byron's words in a letter to John Murray of 2 April 1817: 'When Voltaire was asked why no woman has ever written even a tolerable tragedy? "Ah (said the Patriarch) the composition of a tragedy requires *testicles*!" – If this be true Lord knows what Joanna Baillie does – I suppose she borrows them' – *Lord Byron's Letters and Journals*, ed. Leslie Alexis Marchand, 12 vols (London, 1973–80), vol. 5, p. 203. On the common belief that the anonymously printed, first issue of Baillie's *Plays on the Passions* were the work of a male author, see Margaret Carhart, *The Life and Work of Joanna Baillie* (New Haven, 1923 [1970]), pp. 14–16. In addition, Macready defined Mitford's talents as 'semi-masculine'. See Marjorie Astin, *Mary Russell Mitford: Her Circle and her Books* (London, 1930), p. 135. In a pamphlet on *Rienzi* published in 1828, the editor of 'Cumberland's British Theatre' remarked that, 'in the character of Rienzi, Miss Mitford has shown that she can write with masculine energy'; quoted in Vera Watson, *Mary Russell Mitford* (London, 1949), p. 184.

[6]   *The Collected Letters of Joanna Baillie*, ed. Judith Bailey Slagle, 2 vols (Madison, NJ, and London, 1999), vol. 2, p. 912. The literary and Biblical scholar Andrews Norton (1768–1850), appointed divinity professor at Harvard in 1819, undertook a long

Here, Baillie delineates a community of female authors centred on the outstanding achievements of Hemans, Edgeworth, Mitford and herself, a community that she boldly pitches against the 'half-learned & weaker part' of the male sex. Tellingly, she singles out for praise Mitford's *Rienzi*, first staged at Drury Lane on 11 October 1828 and the most popular and successful dramatic work by a woman playwright on the later Romantic-period stage. And, just as Baillie acknowledges Mitford's achievement as a high point in a developing tradition of women's writings, in her *Recollections* Mitford pays homage to the epiphanic effects of Baillie's drama on her own youthful imagination. There, she evokes her attendance, as 'a girl of thirteen' and in the company of her younger friend William Harness, at a performance of *De Monfort* 'by John Kemble and Mrs. Siddons', that is during the initial run of the production that had opened at Drury Lane on 29 April 1800 and lasted eight nights.[7] Yet, in *Recollections* Mitford also records how, forty years later, she had discussed that performance with Baillie herself at Lady Dacre's:

> Forty years after, we [Baillie and Harness] had the pleasure of talking over that representation with the authoress, in Lady Dacre's drawing-room, a place where poets 'most do congregate', and we both agreed that the impression which the performance had made upon us remained indelible. Now, the qualities in an acted play that fixed themselves upon the minds of children so young, must have been purely dramatic.[8]

For Mitford, these long-lasting impressions prove beyond doubt that Baillie's plays are made for the stage and constitute a model of *acted* theatre: 'That Mrs. Joanna *is* a true dramatist, as well as a great poet, I, for one, cannot doubt, although it has been the fashion to say that her plays do not act'.[9] In point of fact, the first run of *De Monfort* had been an impressive one. The play was perfectly suited to the performing skills of Kemble and Siddons, both personal friends of Baillie, whose acting style she probably had in mind when composing the play, especially since it allows ample scope for their universally celebrated (and extremely

---

correspondence with Baillie and promoted her works in the United States. He also edited *Poems of Mrs Hemans* (1826–28) and wrote several articles on Hemans's works for the American reviews.

[7]   See Mitford, *Recollections of a Literary Life*, vol. 1, pp. 242–3. After the first run, Baillie's play was revived by Edmund Kean, for whom she rewrote the conclusion, at Drury Lane on 27 November 1821; and again in Bath on 19 June 1822, and Birmingham on 4 July 1822. See *The Collected Letters of Joanna Baillie*, ed. Slagle, vol. 2, pp. 1075–6, and Carhart, *The Life and Work of Joanna Baillie*, pp. 110–30.

[8]   Catherine Burroughs briefly refers to this episode in *Closet Stages: Joanna Baillie and the Theater Theory of British Romantic Women Writers* (Philadelphia, 1997), p. 104.

[9]   Mitford, *Recollections of a Literary Life*, vol. 1, p. 242.

effective) alternation of statuesque fixity and sudden bursts of action.[10] In his *Lectures on the English Poets* (1818), William Hazlitt remarked on the perfect fit between actor and character in *De Monfort*, asserting that 'There is in the chief character of that play a nerve, a continued unity of interest, a setness of purpose and precision of outline which John Kemble alone was capable of giving'.[11] In addition, the performance was heightened by impressive staging effects, from the circumscribed suspense produced by the use of the veil with which Jane de Monfort conceals her identity in Act II, scene 1, to the more spectacular devices in the catastrophe set in a Gothic chapel designed by William Capon, the senior designer at Drury Lane since 1794. Placed at the centre of a darkened, 52-feet deep stage, Capon's chapel was only half-visible, its gloomy structure surrounded by a variety of Gothic effects from a freshly dug grave to a religious procession.[12] Commentators praised the elaborate décor, and the play itself was indicated as a model of contemporary tragic excellence. Thus, for instance, after the premiere of Maturin's *Bertram* in 1817, *The British Lady's Magazine* declared that it was 'by far the nearest approximation to a good tragedy that we have seen on the stage since the De Monfort of Miss BAILLIE'.[13] If Mitford joined this chorus of appreciative voices, however, other women writers expressed less favourable views, among them Elizabeth Inchbald and Anna Seward, who criticized the play for its unlikely development of the passion of hatred.[14]

---

[10]   If Margaret Carhart observes that it is difficult to ascertain whether the play was written especially for Siddons and Kemble (*The Life and Work of Joanna Baillie*, pp. 115–16), Paul Ranger is in favour of this interpretation: *'Terror and Pity Reign in Every Breast': Gothic Drama in the London Patent Theatres, 1750–1820* (London, 1991), p. 100. Siddons's acting style and her alternation of the 'frozen moments' and 'outbursts of grief or frenzy' are examined by Frederick Burwick in 'The Ideal Shatters: Sarah Siddons, Madness, and the Dynamics of Gesture', in Robyn Asleson (ed.), *Notorious Muse: The Actress in British Art and Culture 1776–1812* (New Haven and London, 2003), pp. 129–49. On Baillie's use of 'techniques for arresting stage motion', see Greg Kucich, 'Joanna Baillie and the Re-Staging of History and Gender', in Thomas C. Crochunis (ed.), *Joanna Baillie, Romantic Dramatist: Critical Essays* (London and New York, 2004), pp. 108–29, at p. 116.

[11]   *The Complete Works of William Hazlitt*, ed. P.P. Howe, 21 vols (London and Toronto, 1930–34), vol. 5, p. 147.

[12]   On the original production of *De Monfort*, see Carhart, *The Life and Work of Joanna Baillie*, pp. 110–22.

[13]   'Review of Charles Robert Maturin's *Bertram*', *The British Lady's Magazine*, 3 (June 1816): 429.

[14]   See *Letters of Anna Seward: Written between the Years 1784 and 1807*, 6 vols (Edinburgh and London, 1811), vol. 5, p. 243. Among other things, in her prefatory 'Remarks' to her edition of *De Monfort* for *The British Theatre*, Inchbald observes that the play 'denotes that the authoress has studied theatrical productions as a reader more than as a spectator' – *The British Theatre*, 25 vols (London, 1808), vol. 24, p. 5. The customary critique of Baillie's 'monopathetism' is summarized in Thomas Campbell's *Life of Mrs Siddons*, 2 vols (London, 1834), vol. 2, p. 254.

Baillie and Mitford are well-known figures in the vignette depicted by *Recollections of a Literary Life* of women dramatists talking about one of the central plays in Romantic-period legitimate dramaturgy and theatre. Yet, albeit less familiar, the other two figures present at the meeting are equally important members of what was a close-knit and particularly well-connected social and artistic network. As we shall see, William Harness plays an important role in Mitford's social and literary circles,[15] while Barbarina Brand, Lady Dacre (1768–1854) is the pivotal figure in this significant picture, as well as the least familiar.[16] Born Barbarina Ogle, she was the daughter of Admiral Sir Chaloner Ogle, and in 1789 married the officer in the Guards Valentine Henry Wilmot. After his death, in 1819 she married Thomas Brand, twentieth Baron Dacre. She was a playwright and a poet, and her works appeared in a volume of *Dramas, Translations, and Occasional Poems* (1821). Ugo Foscolo, whose close friend she was, dedicated his *Essays on Petrarch* to her, and her substantial 'Translations from Petrarch' are included in its Appendix. Frequently praised for her artistic skills, Dacre was a friend of the sculptor John Flaxman and the painter Edwin Landseer, among others. A friend of both Fanshawe and Baillie, the authors evoked in Mitford's *Recollections*, Dacre was one of the leading figures in London's cultural circles.

---

[15]   See Caroline M. Duncan Jones, *Miss Mitford and Mr Harness: Records of a Friendship* (London, 1955).

[16]   Evidence of this is provided by the fact that biographers often confuse her with other contemporary women. Thus, Mitford's Victorian biographer, the Reverend L'Estrange, observes (incorrectly) that 'Sheridan's second wife, a Miss [Esther] Ogle, was a sister of Lady Dacre and cousin of Miss Mitford' – *The Friendships of Mary Russell Mitford as recorded in letters from her literary correspondents*, ed. A.G. L'Estrange, 2 vols (London, 1882), vol. 1, p. 11. In fact, Lady Dacre was a cousin of Sheridan's second wife. Dacre was the daughter of Admiral Sir Chaloner Ogle, first baronet, whereas Esther Ogle (Sheridan's wife) was the daughter of Newton Ogle, Dean of Winchester. Esther had three sisters (Anne, Kate and Susan), and Lady Dacre two (Sophia and Arabella). See Walter Sichel, *Sheridan*, 2 vols (London, 1909), vol. 2, p. 264. Moreover, in her *memoirs*, Dacre's granddaughter, Barbarina Lady Grey, specifically wrote, 'Hester Ogle, a cousin of my grandmother's'; see *A Family Chronicle Derived from Notes and Letters Selected by Barbarina, the Hon. Lady Grey*, ed. Gertrude Lyster (London, 1908), p. 25. L.A. Marchand misspells the title of Dacre's 1815 play *Ina* as 'Ian', and wrongly remarks that Mrs Wilmot's, that is Lady Dacre's, spangled dress had inspired Byron's lyric 'She walks in beauty like the night', composed in June 1814 and published in *Hebrew Melodies* (1816). See *Lord Byron's Letters and Journals*, ed. Marchand, vol. 4, p. 290, n. 1. In fact, as Jerome McGann observes, the poem was inspired by Anne Wilmot (1784–1871), the wife of Byron's first cousin Robert John Wilmot. See Lord Byron, *The Complete Poetical Works*, ed. Jerome J. McGann, 7 vols (Oxford, 1980–93), vol. 3, p. 467. Furthermore, in her recent biography of Baillie, Judith Bailey Slagle defines Lady Dacre as a 'gothic Romanticist', thus obviously confusing her with Charlotte Dacre, the poet known as 'Rosa Matilda' and author of *Zofloya*. See *Joanna Baillie: A Literary Life* (Madison, NJ, and London, 2002), p. 215.

As a playwright, Lady Dacre knew how to use social and cultural connections to promote her work both in the private and the professional circuits.[17] While her granddaughter recorded that Dacre 'wrote several plays and comedies for amateur theatricals, which were given at Hatfield and the Hoo, and which were very successful', she also wrote with a view to professional staging and performance.[18] In the entry for 2 May 1813 of his extensive diary, the artist Joseph Farington noted that the author William Sotheby had recommended to Lady Dacre that she submit one of her plays to the painter William Lawrence for an opinion on its merits. As Sotheby had already done so himself, receiving incisive and encouraging observations, Farington reports that 'She had a similar work in hand, which she also submitted to his judgment, & Miss Joanna Baillie has also solicited his observations'; he then transcribes Sotheby's praise of Lady Dacre: 'He spoke very highly of Mrs. Wilmot as being a woman possessed of extraordinary talents'.[19] But Dacre's operations to get people interested in her play did not stop here, as, on 5 May, Farington records how Lawrence informed him that, the previous day, together with Sotheby, the antiquarian Richard Payne Knight and the connoisseur Sir George Beaumont,[20] he had paid a visit to

> ... Mrs. Wilmots & there heard a Play (a Tragedy) written by Her read by *Young*, the Actor, who Lawrence thought read it very ill. His principal fault seemed to be his having fixed upon one particular character as if He had been the actor of it, and laying stress on this He made the other characters subservient to it. – Lord & Lady Grey, Sir H Englefield & several others were present & much approbation was expressed, Lawrence thought the play would be well received if brought upon the stage. The Company did not separate till two oClock.[21]

That Dacre could get a celebrated professional actor, Charles Maine Young, to give a private reading of one of her plays to a distinguished company is clear evidence of her far-reaching connections, as well as of her determination to see her works staged. The play read by Young was most probably *Ina*, a historical tragedy set in Anglo-Saxon times, staged at Drury Lane, then under Richard Brinsley Sheridan's management, on 22 April 1815 with Edmund Kean in the leading role of

---

[17]   On Dacre's extensive social circles, see *A Family Chronicle*, ed. Lyster, pp. 18–19.

[18]   Ibid., p. 19.

[19]   *The Diary of Joseph Farington*, ed. Evelyn Newby, 17 vols (New Haven and London, 1998), vol. 12, pp. 4339–40. Baillie, for instance, had asked Lawrence's opinion about her tragedy *Henriquez*. See Slagle (ed.), *Joanna Baillie: A Literary Life*, pp. 223, 258.

[20]   Farington additionally records that Sir George Beaumont read Baillie's *De Monfort* to his assembled family and guests on two consecutive evenings, 30 September and 1 October 1800: *The Diary of Joseph Farington*, ed. Newby, vol. 4, pp. 1438, 1439.

[21]   Ibid., vol. 12, p. 4342.

Egbert.[22] The performance was a failure, although the published version ran to three editions in the same year. Its resounding unsuccess on the stage prompted Byron's acerbic commentary, in a letter to Thomas Moore of 23 April 1815, that 'Women (saving Joanna Baillie) cannot write tragedy; they have not seen enough nor felt enough of life for it. I think Semiramis or Catherine II might have written (could they have been unqueened) a rare play'.[23] Baillie, however, was a close friend of Dacre and, supportive of her theatrical ambitions, in 1815 wrote to Sotheby about *Ina* and the possibility of securing a box for her family and friends at Drury Lane to see the performance.[24] Years later, their literary contacts and exchanges were strengthened further when Dacre contributed 'Stanzas suggested by a Canzone of Petrarch' to Baillie's 1823 *A Collection of Poems, Chiefly Manuscript, and from Living Authors*, a work that testifies to the networks of contact, exchange and collaboration among female (and male) writers in the later Romantic period, as well as to Baillie's central position in this context.[25]

As the animating presence of a literary and artistic *salon* where poets, as Mitford says, 'most do congregate', Lady Dacre is fully representative of that climate of Romantic-period sociability that Gillian Russell and Clara Tuite have described as an evolution of eighteenth-century models of 'coffee-house sociability' and as fundamentally related to the fact that 'in Romantic-period Britain ... imaginative literature assumes a fully-fledged cultural and political authority'.[26] In the case of Baillie, Mitford and Dacre, however, this more generalized notion of sociability is

---

[22]   L.A. Marchand adds that, for its first performance, the play featured a prologue by William Lamb and an epilogue by Thomas Moore: *Lord Byron's Letters and Journals*, vol. 4, p. 290.

[23]   Ibid.

[24]   On 26 August 1818, Baillie had written to Lady Dacre to express her appreciation of her plays, and especially *Xarifa*, which she read twice. Then, on 15 August 1821, Baillie wrote to inform Dacre that she had read her plays in the printed version, adding that they read better than in manuscript and that *Pedrarias* was her favourite. See the letters in *A Family Chronicle*, ed. Lyster, pp. 30–31, 39.

[25]   See Baillie's letter of 27 January 1822, in which she invites Dacre to contribute a poem (ibid., pp. 42–4). Other contributors to the collection, published for the benefit of Baillie's needy friend Mrs James Stirling, were Felicia Hemans, Anne Home Hunter, Anna Letitia Barbauld, William Wordsworth, Walter Scott, Thomas Campbell, Charles Brinsley Sheridan, George Crabbe, Anna Maria Porter, Samuel Rogers, Anne Grant of Laggan, Margaret Holford, Elizabeth Benger, Sir George Beaumont and Baillie herself. The volume was very successful and 'earned well over £ 2,000 with its subscription' (Slagle [ed.], *Joanna Baillie: A Literary Life*, p. 165).

[26]   'Introducing Romantic Sociability', in Gillian Russell and Clara Tuite (eds), *Romantic Sociability: Social Networks and Literary Culture in Britain, 1770–1840* (Cambridge, 2002), pp. 1–23, at p. 19.

compounded by the sisterly feelings and deep ties of friendship that connected so many women writers of the Romantic period.[27]

The drawing-room vignette in Mitford's *Recollections* features not just two, but three women playwrights (with the inclusion of the Reverend William Harness as an early enthusiast of Baillie and Mitford's chaperon[28]) discussing theatrical and dramatic subjects, as well as strengthening their links of mutual affection, respect and collaboration. Moreover, this scene yields even more fascinating insights, if we seek to establish the exact date of this meeting and its context. In *Mary Russell Mitford: Her Circle and Her Books* (1930), Marjorie Astin reports the encounter as follows: 'It was at Lady Dacre's that Miss Mitford became acquainted with Joanna Baillie. She was much attracted by the learned and pleasant old poetess, whose name she afterwards took for one of her finest geraniums'.[29] If Astin domesticates the scene, envisaging a kind of balmy and 'floral' sequel to it, by contrast, I intend to highlight that, in actual fact, the three women were talking business, and that this highly dramatic and 'drama-centred' meeting took place in the context of intense theatrical activities.

The idea of organizing a meeting between the two playwrights had been on Lady Dacre's mind for some time. On 11 March 1836 she wrote to Mitford:

> I believe I am doing an odd thing, dear Miss Mitford, in enclosing to you a letter from the glorious Joanna, in which she agrees with me in all I said of your 'Rienzi.' The *knocking your heads together* is an allusion to my saying I should wish to bring you together if you came to town, and to 'knock your clever heads together.' She agrees with me also that 'Ion' is of too highly poetical a cast for the uneducated people who form the mass of an audience.[30]

Furthermore, in the same letter, Dacre discusses the staging of Baillie's tragedy *The Separation*, which had opened at Covent Garden on 25 February 1836 yet ran for only one night, as did *Henriquez*, a tragedy on remorse, premiered at Drury Lane on 19 March 1836.[31] Both plays were destined to be surpassed in fame and success by Thomas Noon Talfourd's tragedy *Ion*, first staged at Covent Garden on

---

[27]   A model study of a circle of women writers intimately linked by ties of friendship and literary collaboration is Norma Clarke's *Ambitious Heights: Writing, Friendship, Love, The Jewsbury Sisters, Felicia Hemans and Jane Carlyle* (London and New York, 1990).

[28]   Harness was an admirer of Baillie well into his later years, when he fondly remembered an evening spent at Mrs Siddons's, on which occasion the actress had read Shakespeare's 'Lear to Milman, Joanna Baillie and myself'. See also his statement that 'Joanna is perhaps one of the greatest geniuses that ever lived' – Duncan Jones, *Miss Mitford and Mr Harness*, pp. 54, 64.

[29]   Astin, *Mary Russell Mitford*, p. 68.

[30]   *The Friendships of Mary Russell Mitford*, ed. L'Estrange, vol. 1, p. 314 (italics in original).

[31]   See Carhart, *The Life and Work of Joanna Baillie*, p. 164.

26 May 1836 for Macready's benefit, and one of the greatest theatrical triumphs of the season. In view of the poor reception of Baillie's own tragedies, Dacre concludes in half-despondent, half-hopeful, tones: 'The theatre is now at so low an ebb, it must mend, I think'.[32]

The theatrical circumstances of the meeting become even more significant when we consider that it took place in 1836, during Mitford's stay at the Talfourds' London home. The latter were family friends, and Mitford had promised she would attend the first performance of *Ion*. Baillie herself had gone to see the theatrical triumph that was to eclipse her own dramas of the same year. She was present at the premiere of 26 May and, just before the performance, shook hands with Wordsworth, who was in the adjoining box.[33] As Baillie says in a letter of 15 June 1836 to her friend the writer Margaret Holford about her own failed plays, 'Whether either piece will be revived seems to be very doubtful', and promptly adds: 'M[r] Serg[t] Talfourd's beautiful Drama of Ion, which you no doubt have read, followed soon after on the Covent Garden boards with most brilliant success, so he immediately became the Dramatic Lion of the day, and I took my modest station as appointed for me'.[34]

It was the premiere of *Ion* that ultimately brought Baillie and Mitford together within a context that was eminently literary and theatrical, and conspicuously male-dominated. The writer, politician and judge Thomas Noon Talfourd was an old friend of Mitford's father, Dr Mitford, a trusted friend of Mitford herself, one of her regular correspondents and her 'literary advisor'. A writer and friend to many established and emergent authors of the period (Dickens dedicated the *Pickwick Papers* to him), he was the first *memoirist* of Ann Radcliffe (1826), the editor of Charles Lamb's letters (1837, 1848), the drama critic for the *New Monthly*

---

[32]   *The Friendships of Mary Russell Mitford*, ed. L'Estrange, vol. 1, p. 314.

[33]   On Baillie's presence at the first performance of Ion, see David Watson Rannie, *Wordsworth and his Circle* (London, 1907), p. 305. Margaret Carhart confirms that, in 1836, Baillie was in London for 'the première of Talfourd's Ion at Covent Garden' – *The Life and Work of Joanna Baillie*, p. 63.

[34]   *The Collected Letters of Joanna Baillie*, ed. Slagle, vol. 2, p. 658. Margaret Holford (1778–1852) was a poet, translator and prose writer, and the daughter of Margaret Holford, poet, novelist for the Minerva Press, and playwright. She began to publish poetry at an early age, and her poem on Scottish history *Wallace, or the Fight at Falkirk* (1809) was noticed in the *Quarterly Review* and caused Walter Scott's jealousy. On 3 July 1810, Mitford wrote to Sir William Elford, 'Have you read a poem which is said to have excited the jealousy of our great modern minstrel, "The Fight of Falkirk?" I was delighted with the fire and genius which it displays, and was more readily charmed, perhaps, as the author is a lady; which is, I hear, what most displeases Mr. Scott' – [William Harness], *The Life of Mary Russell Mitford*, ed. Rev. A.G. L'Estrange, 3 vols (London, 1870), vol. 1, p. 107. Her *Warbeck of Wolfstein* (1820) was dedicated to Baillie and she contributed two poems ('On Memory' and 'Lines Suggested by a Portrait of the Queen of France') to Baillie's 1822 collection of collected original verse. In 1826 Holford married the Rev. Septimus Hodson. On Baillie and Holford, see Slagle (ed.), *Joanna Baillie: A Literary Life*, pp. 205–10.

Magazine (1820–31), and in 1836 he proposed a bill (that was ultimately defeated) to extend copyright to 60 years. His greatest and most resounding success was his classical tragedy *Ion*. After the play's first night, its enthusiastic reception and Talfourd's birthday were celebrated by a company of over sixty guests gathered at the author's house at 56 Russell Square. As Henry Crabb Robinson records in his diary entry for 26 May 1836,

> At night I attended the first performance of Talfourd's *Ion* with a party of friends at Covent Garden. Wordsworth, Landor, my brother, the Jaffrays, etc. The success complete. Ellen Tree and Macready were loudly applauded, and the author had every reason to be satisfied, in anticipation of which he gave a supper largely attended by actors, lawyers, and dramatists. Miss Mitford there. No sign of ill-will then nor of want of cordiality among the literary candidates for praise. Yet Landor thought proper to reproach Wordsworth with a want of cordial approbation […] mixed up with other matter; but I never knew on what grounds. Other jealousies soon sprang up among the dramatic poets, whose position most exposes them to jealousy and envy.[35]

An event fraught with tensions, this evening rivals in importance with that other 'immortal dinner' of Romantic-period London held at the studio of the painter Benjamin Robert Haydon at 22 Lisson Grove on 28 December 1817, and which brought together Wordsworth, Keats, Charles Lamb and Thomas Monkhouse, as well as the surgeon Joseph Ritchie and the 'comptroller of the Stamp Office' (and thus Wordsworth's superior) John Kingston.[36] Organized on a grander scale, Talfourd's event surpasses this earlier dinner also in terms of intergenerational exchanges and the sheer concurrence of literary figures. Among these was Macready, who had just acted in the play's title-role for his benefit night, after giving the author a substantial hand in adapting the original 'tragic poem' for the stage. Wordsworth and Landor were there and, sitting close to each other, ended up quarrelling as Landor resented Wordsworth's opinions about his friend Southey and his dislike for Goethe, as well as for a variety of other reasons. Apparently Landor even went as far as parodying 'We Are Seven'.[37] These tensions probably paved the way for Landor's attack on Wordsworth in *A Satire on Satirists*, published later in 1836, where he also accuses the Lake poet of sitting unmoved through the performance of *Ion* (what Robinson calls a 'want of cordial approbation').

---

[35]   *Henry Crabb Robinson on Books and their Writers*, ed. Edith J. Morley, 2 vols (London, 1938), vol. 2, p. 494. He also records, 'I sat by Miss Tree and near Miss Mitford but left early to accompany Wordsworth who wanted someone to shew him the way' – *The London Theatre 1811–1866: Selections from the Diary of Henry Crabb Robinson*, ed. Eluned Brown (London, 1966), p. 151.

[36]   See Penelope Hughes-Hallett, *The Immortal Dinner: A Famous Evening of Genius and Laughter in Literary London, 1817* (London, 2000).

[37]   See Rannie, *Wordsworth and His Circle*, p. 305.

Others in attendance were a young Robert Browning, all fired up with theatrical ambition; the painters Clarkson Stanfield and John Lucas; the young writer Henry Fothergill Chorley;[38] John Forster, the literary critic of the *Examiner* and the future biographer of Landor and Dickens; the playwrights Henry Hart Milman, James Sheridan Knowles and Barry Cornwall; the actress Ellen Tree (who had also acted in the play); and Mary Russell Mitford herself.[39] Apart from the argument between Wordsworth and Landor, another critical moment in the evening took place when Macready told Wordsworth that a few lines he had included in the play had been inspired by some lines from the older poet's yet unpublished *The Borderers* – a minor, but possibly annoying, instance of plagiarism.[40]

When we shift the focus to consider this event from Mitford's point of view, her description is contained in a letter to her father dated from Talfourd's home on 26 May:

> Mr. Wordsworth, Mr. Landor, and Mr. White dined here. I like Mr. Wordsworth of all things; he is a most venerable-looking old man, delightfully mild and placid, and most kind to me. Mr. Landor is a very striking-looking person, and exceedingly clever. Also we had a Mr. Browning, a young poet (author of 'Paracelsus'), and Mr. Proctor, and Mr. Chorley, and quantities more of poets, &c. Stanfield and Lucas were also there, and young Brown, Lord Jeffrey's nephew ... You cannot think how much I like Ellen Tree and Stanfield; so would you.[41]

Mitford's evocation of Talfourd's momentous literary dinner depicts a preponderantly male world in which a single woman dramatist (or, indeed, writer) awards herself a relatively marginal position and self-effacing attitude. The marginality, however, must not be exaggerated, for, in fact, Mitford was the most repeatedly successful dramatist present at the gathering. And if, here, she

---

[38] Born in Lancashire, Chorley (1808–72) moved to Liverpool where he met, and became a close friend of, Felicia Hemans. He began to contribute to the *Athenaeum* in 1830, and achieved fame as a musical journalist and the author of books on music. He wrote plays and novels, all unsuccessful, as well as *Memoirs of Mrs Hemans* (1836) and published an edition of Mary Russell Mitford's letters (1872).

[39] See also Macready's account of this event, in *The Diaries of William Charles Macready 1833–1851*, ed. William Toynbee, 2 vols (London, 1912), vol. 1, pp. 318–20.

[40] As Macready notes, Wordsworth had read these lines (beginning 'Action is transitory – a step – a blow') to him during their first meeting in June 1823. See *The Diaries of William Charles Macready*, ed. Toynbee, vol. 1, p. 319. The same lines from *The Borderers* were used as one of the epigraphs to Wordsworth's *White Doe of Rylstone* (first published in 1815) in the six-volume edition of *The Poetical Works of William Wordsworth* (1836–37). See William Wordsworth, *The White Doe of Rylstone; or The Fate of the Nortons*, ed. Kristine Dugas (Ithaca and London, 1988), p. 77.

[41] *The Life of Mary Russell Mitford*, ed. L'Estrange, vol. 2, pp. 44–5.

describes herself as a secondary *dramatis persona*, and elsewhere repeats how generous Wordsworth was towards her own 'poor' works, in another letter to her father of 30 May she places herself firmly at the centre of the picture: 'I am living in the midst now of all that is best of London conversation'.[42]

The male-dominated and intensely 'dramatic' occasion of Talfourd's dinner constitutes the wider context of Mitford's meeting with Baillie, and events began to develop quickly thereafter. In a letter dated 28–29 May 1836, Mitford wrote to her father: 'I find that half the literary world is invited to meet me at Lady Dacre's'.[43] In the letter of 30 May, she confirmed: 'William Harness came to settle about our going to Lady Dacre's tomorrow'.[44] And, eventually, on 31 May:

> At seven William [Harness] came to take me to Lord Dacre's. It is a small house, with a round table that only holds eight. The company was William, Mrs. Joanna [Baillie], Mrs. Sullivan (Lady Dacre's daughter, the authoress),[45] Lord and Lady Dacre, a famous talker called Bobus Smith (otherwise the great Bobus)[46] and my old friend, Mr. Young the actor, who was delighted to see me, and very attentive and kind indeed. But how kind they were all![47]

Dated 'Tuesday night', this letter was written immediately after her return from the evening at the Dacres' where she met Baillie for the first time, so that it seems plausible to suggest that the meeting fondly evoked in *Recollections* took place on 31 May. On 6 June 1836, Mitford wrote to Lady Dacre to thank her for 'one of the most delightful evenings of the short visit to London which the kindness of many friends, and in some cases, perhaps, accident, have crowned with gratifications'.[48] Her gratitude was no conventional expression, since she saw this meeting as the high point of her stay in the capital, when she met an impressive number of contemporary women writers. As she wrote to her friend Emily Jephson (the great-niece of the Irish playwright Robert Jephson) on 19 June 1836, 'I spent

---

[42]   Ibid., vol. 3, p. 50.

[43]   Ibid., vol. 3, p. 48.

[44]   Ibid., vol. 3, p. 49.

[45]   Lady Dacre's daughter, by her first marriage, was Arabella Jane Wilmot (1796–1839), the wife of Rev. Frederick Sullivan and author of *Recollections of a Chaperon* (1831) and *Tales of the Peerage and Peasantry* (1835). Elizabeth Barrett Browning commented on Sullivan's death in a letter to Mitford of 7–12 March 1839; see *The Letters of Elizabeth Barrett Browning to Mary Russell Mitford 1836–1854*, ed. Meredith B. Raymond and Mary Rose Sullivan, 3 vols (Waco, 1983), vol. 1, p. 112.

[46]   Robert Percy Smith (1770–1845), brother of Sydney Smith, literary author, judge in India, and MP.

[47]   *The Life of Mary Russell Mitford*, ed. L'Estrange, vol. 3, p. 51.

[48]   See *A Family Chronicle*, ed. Lyster, p. 113. Here, among the guests, she also mentions the painter Edwin Landseer, and Mr and Mrs Milman. In the same letter Mitford records talking to Lady Dacre about the young Elizabeth Barrett.

ten days in London – ten days crowded with gratification ... I saw, on terms of the most agreeable intimacy, Lady Dacre, Lady Morgan, Lady Mary Shepherd, Mrs. Trollope, Mrs. Marcet, Mrs. Callcott, Jane Porter, Joanna Baillie, and I know not how many other females of eminence, to say nothing of all the artists, poets, prosers, talkers, and actors of the day'.[49]

Moreover, Baillie's letters also contribute to confirming the date of the meeting. On 15 June 1836, she wrote to Margaret Holford: 'I had the pleasure of meeting the other evening at Lady Dacre's a writer I had often wished to see – Miss Mitford'.[50] That their dramatic activities were a strong reason for their mutual interest is made clear in the same letter, as Baillie praises Mitford's tragedy *Rienzi*: 'Have you read her "Rienzi?" it has been one of the most successful of our modern Tragedies and worthy to be so'.[51] She goes on to deplore the fact that 'this clever, accomplished woman at her age should live as the slave of a selfish Father, who has spent two fortunes belonging to her on his own indulgences and leaves her to drudge on with her pen for his maintenance'.[52] As indicated by Mitford's discussion of *De Monfort* and Baillie's mention of the younger woman's work, the meeting effectively functioned as a catalyst for their interest in each other's output.

The relevance of the acquaintance between Mitford and Baillie at Lady Dacre's against the background of the first performance of *Ion* and Talfourd's dinner lies in that this episode brings into focus a whole series of connections that are normally relegated to the margins in biographical and critical accounts more inclined to consider authors and playwrights (especially female ones) in isolation. Located at the far end of a Romantic period that, by this date, has already conventionally given way to pre-Victorian cultural manifestations, the 1836 meeting reveals the interconnections between female protagonists of the contemporary dramatic and theatrical worlds, as well as their links with male colleagues. In addition, it offers a fascinating glimpse of the sociability and conviviality of intellectual and literary circles in late Romantic-period London. Centred on Lady Dacre's *salon*, the meeting confirms and enriches our knowledge of the contacts between women writers and playwrights, throwing light on their shared 'esprit de corps' and their exploitation of the period's channels of social interaction in order to debate, criticize and exchange ideas, and to offer mutual support. This use of sociability indicates that Mitford, Baillie and Dacre were deeply conscious of the cultural impact of

---

[49]   *The Life of Mary Russell Mitford*, ed. L'Estrange, vol. 3, pp. 53–4.

[50]   *The Collected Letters of Joanna Baillie*, ed. Slagle, vol. 2, p. 659.

[51]   Ibid.

[52]   Ibid. Baillie is here alluding to the fact that, on her tenth birthday, Mary Russell Mitford had won £20,000 on the lottery, a fortune that was quickly spent by her father to build Bertram House, near Reading. However, owing to Dr Mitford's prodigality and his increasing financial problems, the house had to be sold in 1820, and the family moved to a small cottage in Three Mile Cross, south of Reading. When Dr Mitford died in 1842, he left his daughter to face debts of up to £1,000.

their work and its place within recent developments in women's drama. At the same time, it illuminates their desire to emphasize the existence of this female tradition by debating it in the semi-public circles of *salons* and correspondences.

Moreover, the meeting had consequences. In a letter probably written in 1837, Mitford informed Dacre that she had been invited to take up the editorship of the second issue of *Finden's Tableaux*. The publishers of this annual expected her to contribute all the prose passages (although Henry Chorley had volunteered a tale), while Elizabeth Barrett and Mrs Procter (possibly Barry Cornwall's wife) had offered to write poems for it. In her letter Mitford extends the invitation to Dacre, and adds:

> I applied to dear Mrs. Joanna for her aid, and received an answer so kind and so gracious that, although she could not comply with my request after refusing so many applications, her letter was in the highest degree gratifying and characteristic. What a glorious creature she is! So true and simple-hearted and unspoilt as a woman! such an honour to her sex as a poetess! Once again, dearest Lady Dacre, I look back to all I owe you in her acquaintance. She speaks with great pleasure of a visit from your ladyship and Lady Becher – another glorious person in another way – how one always longs to turn her into Miss O'Neill again![53]

As on other occasions, Mitford praises Baillie's qualities, talent and work, yet also awards her a central role in the world of women, drama and theatre by mentioning the visit paid to her by Lady Dacre and Eliza O'Neill, the latter of whom, in 1819, had left the stage to marry the Irish MP William Wrixon Becher, baroneted in 1831. If this letter provides further confirmation of the importance of women's dramatic, theatrical and literary networks for Mitford's identity and activity as a writer, the consequences of the 1836 meeting also included more material forms of support. On 20 May 1837, Mitford wrote to Harness to inform him that Lady Dacre had been working her cultural and political circles in order to convince Lord Holland to support Mitford's application for a state pension and, ultimately, the prime minister, Lord Melbourne, to grant it. Just eleven days later, on 31 May, an elated Mitford wrote to Emily Jephson: 'I have had today an announcement from Lord Melbourne of a pension of 100*l*. a year. The sum is small, but that cannot be considered as derogatory, which was the amount given by Sir Robert Peel to Mrs. Hemans and Mrs. Somerville'.[54]

---

[53]   *A Family Chronicle*, ed. Lyster, p. 143.

[54]   *The Life of Mary Russell Mitford*, ed. L'Estrange, vol. 3, pp. 73–5. In the same letter to Jephson she writes that the idea of the application for a state pension 'originated with dear William Harness, and that most kind and zealous friend, Lady Dacre; and the manner in which it was taken up by the Duke of Devonshire, Lord and Lady Holland, Lord and Lady Radnor, Lord Palmerston, and many others [...] has been such as to make this one of the most pleasurable events of my life' (vol. 3, p. 75).

Baillie valued the younger woman's contributions to contemporary literature and drama, and, in turn, Mitford repeatedly celebrated the figure and production of Baillie as a major model and influence. Nonetheless, the respect and reverence characterizing the meeting at Lady Dacre's must not blind us to the fact that, at the same time, Mitford and her circle assessed Baillie's work from a variety of perspectives, some of which were indeed less decidedly sanguine about 'great Joanna''s achievements.

Baillie's literary production and *persona* had been at the centre of Mitford's reflections on literature and fame since her earliest literary attempts. In a letter to Sir William Elford of 20 September 1810, when she was already attracting attention as a promising poet before making a name for herself as a prose writer and dramatist, Mitford expresses very clear ideas about her career as a writer in an unquestionably female context: '[Maria Edgeworth] and Miss Baillie and Mrs. Opie are three such women as have seldom adorned one age and one country. Of the three, I think I had rather (if such a metamorphosis were possible) resemble Miss Baillie'.[55] At this initial stage in her career, Mitford repeatedly invokes Baillie as the culmination of success and fame for a woman writer, and an example of literary excellence in general. In a letter to her father of 7 June 1811, she writes: 'To be, some time or other, the best English poetess (Miss Baillie is a dramatist, you know,) is the height of my ambition'.[56] A year later, writing to Sir William Elford on 1 July 1812, Mitford reviews (and expresses her reservations about) the acting style of John Philip Kemble, and concludes by observing that, after Sarah Siddons's retirement from the stage in the same year, the tragic muse will be deprived of one of its most devoted votaries. Fortunately, however, its other great female support is still well and active: 'Tragedy, poor Tragedy! must now fly from her superb arena and take shelter in the pages of Shakespeare and the bosom of Miss Baillie'.[57]

As Mitford's literary interests shifted from the poetry of the 1810s to the prose sketches of *Our Village* (1824–32), she simultaneously developed a clear sense of her dramatic vocation.[58] On 12 April 1822 she wrote to Elford:

> To confess the truth, my dear friend, I am so thoroughly out of heart about 'Foscari' that I cannot bear even to think or speak on the subject. Nevertheless

55 *The Life of Mary Russell Mitford*, ed. L'Estrange, vol. 1, p. 108.

56 Ibid., vol. 1, p. 133. On Mitford's early poetic production and use of literary networks, see my essay 'Private and Public in Women's Romantic Poetry: Spaces, Gender, Genre in Mary Mitford's *Blanch*', *Women's Writing*, 5 (1998): 405–19.

57 *The Life of Mary Russell Mitford*, ed. L'Estrange, vol. 1, p. 201.

58 Mitford began to compose the tales of *Our Village* in 1821. As Vera Watson remarks, at this stage 'Mitford does not appear to have considered her magazine articles as anything more than a side-line, a means to obtain much needed money. She certainly never dreamed it would be through them that her fame would descend to posterity. Her principal preoccupation at this time was with the theatre' – *Mary Russell Mitford*, p. 144.

the drama is my talent – my only talent – and I mean to go on and improve. I *will* improve – that is my fixed determination. Can you recommend me a good subject for an historical tragedy? I wish you would think of this, and if you have none in your own mind, ask any likely person. It should have *two* prominent male parts – and I should prefer an Italian story in the fourteenth, fifteenth, sixteenth, or seventeenth century, as affording most scope, and being less liable to blame for any deviation from truth in the plot than any well-known incident in the greater States.[59]

By this time, Macready and the Covent Garden manager – probably Charles Kemble, who had become chairman of the management committee in March 1822 – had held *Foscari* 'hostage' for at least a year. Already on 19 April 1821 Mitford had written to her friend the writer Barbara Hofland, saying, 'I have no news to tell you of "Foscari", which is still in the hands either of the manager or of Mr. Macready; but I already feel sure that it will be rejected'.[60] Delays in production and authorial anxieties were mostly caused by rivalries among male actors and theatre managers, as in the emblematic instance of Mitford's *Rienzi*, which suffered an even lengthier deferral than *Foscari*.[61] To reassert her intention to become a dramatist in the midst of these difficulties and squabbles reveals Mitford's readiness to grapple with the problems of staging, the most daunting and 'public' aspect of dramatic activity, and work towards their solution. Even during these fraught negotiations, Baillie remained a crucial point of reference and a model that supported Mitford's development of a sense of her own dramatic career and her 'fixed determination' in achieving success and fame as a playwright.

Thus, in her letter to Hofland of 19 April 1821 Mitford reiterates her resolve to become a successful dramatist, and, although despairing of *Foscari*, announces her intention to begin a new project, inviting her friend to suggest an idea for a play 'with a high, ample, magnificent plot', preferably 'something middle-aged and Italian'.[62] Later, in another letter to Hofland dated 8 June 1821, Mitford thanks her

---

[59]   Letter of 12 April 1822 to Sir William Elford, in *The Life of Mary Russell Mitford*, ed. L'Estrange, vol. 2, p. 149.

[60]   *Letters of Mary Russell Mitford: Second Series*, ed. Henry Chorley, 2 vols (London, 1872), vol. 1, pp. 104–5. Hofland (1770–1844) was mainly a prose writer, having published books for children and young adults in the earlier part of her career, and Victorian three-deckers, later. She also published some verse, and in 1810 had tried her hand at playwriting with a collection of *Little Dramas for Young People on Subjects Taken from History*. Here relation with Mitford was one of close friendship and mutual professional respect, as is demonstrated by her poem 'To Miss Mitford', which praises her friend's literary genius in enthusiastic terms. See Thomas Ramsay, *The Life and Literary Remains of Barbara Hofland* (London, 1849), and Dennis Butts, *Mistress of Our Tears: A Literary and Bibliographical Study of Barbara Hofland* (Aldershot and Brookfield, 1992).

[61]   See Watson, *Mary Russell Mitford*, pp. 161–84.

[62]   *Letters of Mary Russell Mitford: Second Series*, ed. Chorley, vol. 1, p. 105.

for her suggestion of a theme that 'appears quite fit for a tragedy' and is better than the idea she has received from 'Miss J—' (probably Emily Jephson).[63] However, before beginning to work on it, she will need to discuss Hofland's proposal with her 'Adviser-General, Mr. Talfourd, without whom I cannot stir a finger, to know if it meets his approbation'.[64] Then, she turns to the subject of actors' skills and their suitability for different roles: 'The only thing is, whether the hero will be quite the thing for Macready, my main stay, the vigorous prop that is to support my flowers and leaves', 'Charles Kemble's assistance is valuable in a play', 'Young, too, will be at Covent Garden next year, and may do one of the fathers', and 'Miss Foote, the beautiful Miss Foote, will be a Seraphina ready made'.[65] Finally, she exclaims: 'Oh, how glad I shall be to thank you in a preface, some fine day, after the first representation, if ever it should come to that! How happy and how proud!'[66] This epistolary exchange, indicative of yet another link in the chain of women's dramatic collaborations, seems to combine, if the dating and chronology of the letters are correct, Mitford's concerns about *Foscari* and the most appropriate cast for a successful performance with her initial ideas for *Julian*, the 'middle-aged' and 'Italian' play begun on 30 December 1821 and eventually staged, well before *Foscari*, on 15 March 1823 at Covent Garden.

Furthermore, in the same letter, Mitford responds to the objection, possibly voiced by Hofland's husband, and in contrast to the opinions of the writer and editor John Thelwall, that 'A woman who could paint history must first have renounced her sex'. In answer to this, she observes that, not only may women write about history, but also 'why should not a woman conceive and embody the tender passions? Why should she not write such a play as "Romeo and Juliet", for instance? Did he never [*sic*] read "Count Basil?" the finest, in my mind, of modern plays, always excepting the exquisite "Virginius" of Mr. Knowles'.[67] Mitford advocates freedom of literary action for women over and against male-regulated prescriptions and injunctions, claiming both history and the tender passions as areas available to women playwrights. And it is no coincidence that one of Joanna Baillie's plays, *Count Basil* (first published in 1798 and never acted), is pointed out as a model of female excellence in both thematic fields. In addition, Mitford reinforces her defence of women's dramaturgy through a

---

[63]   Ibid., vol. 1, p. 106.

[64]   Ibid.

[65]   Ibid.

[66]   Ibid.

[67]   Ibid., vol. 1, p. 107. The reference is to John Thelwall (1764–1834), political and literary writer, and editor, among other literary ventures, of the *Panoramic Miscellany* to which Mitford contributed. In a letter to Barbara Hofland of 20 September 1826, Mitford complains that 'Mr. Thelwall's magazine has stopped, and he has not paid me a farthing' (*Letters of Mary Russell Mitford: Second Series*, ed. Chorley, vol. 1, p. 132). See also William A. Coles, 'Magazine and Other Contributions by Mary Russell Mitford and Thomas Noon Talfourd', *Studies in Bibliography*, 12 (1959): 224.

remark on Byron, who, in her opinion, 'can imagine the passions, but not the affections; and his way of forming a pure woman is to mould her out of snow, like the companion of Laila, in "Thalaba"'.[68] Even the most popular writer of the day does not succeed in depicting the 'tender passions', something at which women dramatists (with the notable exception of James Sheridan Knowles) excel.

Nevertheless, a picture in which women dramatists share in a sense of unflagging camaraderie and mutual support would be an incomplete account, not to say a misleading one. Nearer the date of Mitford's meeting with Baillie, on 4 February 1836, Mary Howitt (poet, editor and translator, working in team with her husband William) writes to Mitford to celebrate her dramatic achievements. Quite surprisingly, she does so by giving qualified praise to Joanna Baillie's dramatic art:

> Joanna Baillie is, as you say, 'a glorious old lady'. She has a glorious mind. It is impossible for you to admire her more than I do; but one thing I must remark, you will see now the whole world of criticism exalt her to the skies, and not on the strength of her own noble intellect, but at the expense of every other woman who has written tragedy. It is the fashion of modern criticism; the idol of the day must be the head of a pyramid, erected on other men's fame ... I never deny the wonderful excellence of Joanna Baillie, but no one shall persuade me that 'Rienzi' is not as good as any drama by her. Do not be discouraged, dear Miss Mitford. I know how mortifying these invidious comparisons are, but everything will find its level, and thinking people will contradict by their own firesides these unjust and invidious comparisons.[69]

Howitt's reflections evidently fly in the face of Mitford's much repeated, and already amply quoted, praise of Baillie, which she would rehearse a few months later, before and after her London meeting with the 'grand old lady' of contemporary British drama. But Howitt's words are an interesting introduction to the fact that, in spite of Mitford's long-standing worship of Baillie, her own views on her great predecessor's art often express more (or, possibly, less) than mere enthusiasm. More qualified statements, for instance, emerge from Mitford's letters to Emily Jephson, and particularly from a series of extracts from their long correspondence copied into one of Jephson's letters dated 19 January 1853.[70] Among other things, these fragments record how Jephson, a descendant

---

    68   *Letters of Mary Russell Mitford: Second Series*, ed. Chorley, vol. 1, p. 107. In a previous letter to Elford of 9 January 1822, Mitford discusses Byron's plays and concludes: 'Altogether, it seems to me that Lord Byron must be by this time pretty well convinced that the drama is not his forte' – *The Life of Mary Russell Mitford*, ed. L'Estrange, vol. 2, p. 144.

    69   *The Friendships of Mary Russell Mitford*, ed. L'Estrange, vol. 1, pp. 307–8.

    70   Jephson's letter is a 'cento' of letters from Mitford aimed at illustrating her friend's life. Mitford's first letter to Jephson in *The Life of Mary Russell Mitford*, ed. L'Estrange, is

of the late eighteenth-century playwright Robert Jephson, sought to attract the publishers' interest in reprinting her great-uncle's plays.[71] Always ready to help, Mitford contacted Henry Colburn through Talfourd, 'with an understanding that [an edition of the plays] might come out in the winter or spring of 1832'.[72] At the same time, she also informed Miss Jephson: 'I have desired W. Harness to ask Mr. Kemble and Mrs. Siddons if they can give us any help, which I think not unlikely, especially in the affair of the "Conspiracy"'.[73] However, 'the *necessity* of finishing her play' and other pressing engagements eventually discouraged Mitford from pursuing the project of Jephson's works any further.[74] It is in the same *collage* of excerpts that Mitford expresses her reservations about Baillie:

> W. Harness certainly underrates the plays [of Jephson]. His taste is a little warped by his love of the poetry of Joanna Baillie's style ... The fact is that Joanna Baillie had imbued her mind with the fine rich style of the old writers, and had herself a fancy full of poetical imagery; but she entirely wanted construction, had less of character than Mr. Jephson, and had not had an idea of that real and great thing, stage effect (of course I do not mean pageants and processions), but the turns of fortune and development of story in which Shakespeare is quite unrivalled ... If Mr. Jephson's plays be less poetical than Joanna Baillie's, they are more eloquent, and eloquence seems to me far more akin to passion than mere beauty of imagery, however delightful ... One proof is that Mr. Jephson's plays did act successfully ... and that Joanna Baillie's do not.[75]

These general remarks on the differences between Jephson's dramatic art and Baillie's may be connected with the reservations Mitford had already expressed in the early 1810s about the Kemble style of acting, usually perceived to be closely related to Baillie's dramatic writing as in the case of *De Monfort*. Indeed, in her letter to Sir William Elford of 1 July 1812, she observed: 'Messrs. Kemble and Co. never do converse – they always declaim, and that not in the very best manner; so that between long pauses and unnatural cadences, the audience have nothing for it but to fall asleep and dream of Shakespeare. That he and all the writers of Elizabeth's days (the real Augustan age of English poetry) were of my

---

dated 10 July 1824 (vol. 2, pp. 181–3).

[71]   The Irish dramatist Robert Jephson (1736/7–1803) was the author of *Braganza* (performed in 1775); *The Law of Lombardy* (1779); *The Count of Narbonne* (1781), an adaptation of Horace Walpole's *The Castle of Otranto*; *Julia* (1787); and *The Conspiracy* (1796), based on Metastasio.

[72]   *The Friendships of Mary Russell Mitford*, ed. L'Estrange, vol. 2, p. 247.

[73]   Ibid., vol. 2, p. 248.

[74]   Ibid., vol. 2, p. 247 (italics in original).

[75]   Ibid., vol. 2, pp. 248–9.

opinion, I am quite sure'.[76] These are strong words for a young woman who has just begun to make a name for herself thanks to a handful of books of poetry. For here she criticizes an idol of the theatre and the manager of Covent Garden and his style of acting, as well as the whole family theatrical business – 'Messrs. Kemble and Co.' – and its performing tradition. In voicing her opinionated and strongly held views, Mitford even calls on Shakespeare and his contemporaries as authorities that would support her opinion, as she is confident that 'Ford, Massinger, and Fletcher', then relatively known and soon to be brought back to attention by William Hazlitt's lectures *On the Dramatic Literature of the Age of Elizabeth* (1818), would agree with her critique of the Kemble school of acting.[77]

These strategies of critical self-positioning make clear that Mitford begins very early to stake out her own field of literary activity and accumulate 'cultural capital', to invoke Pierre Bourdieu's term, by demarcating lines of difference, as well as continuity, with the male and female dramatic tradition and the dominant style of acting.[78] The doubts, provisos and critiques she voiced from the 1810s to the 1830s reveal that Mitford was constantly trying to situate herself and her art within a shifting field of aesthetic codes and staging conventions. Thus, if in her *Recollections* she emphatically maintains that Baillie's dramas are a model of *acted* theatre, 'although it has been the fashion to say that her plays do not act', this statement conceals a much more conflicted and mutable attitude.[79] Mitford is inspired by Baillie's magisterial example to emulate achievements that constitute an important precedent for a woman writer, while, at the same time, she feels in a position to criticize certain aspects in Baillie's craft – anticipated by her youthful strictures on the Kembles' style of acting – and thus delineate the peculiar features of her own writings for the stage.

Mitford therefore emerges as a crucial figure for the reconstruction and reassessment of the interconnections among women playwrights in the Romantic period, their circles of creative discussion, and their interaction with male advisers, writers, managers and actors. The latter could be either helpful and supportive, as with Harness, Elford and Talfourd, or more ambivalent, as in the case of Macready. As for the women, Mitford was at the centre of an intricate series of networks of collaboration, support and exchange, from which

---

[76]   *The Life of Mary Russell Mitford*, ed. L'Estrange, vol. 1, p. 200.

[77]   Ibid. On Romantic-period acting styles, see Alan S. Downer, 'Nature to Advantage Dressed: Eighteenth-Century Acting', *PMLA*, 58 (1943): 1002–37, and 'Players and the Painted Stage: Nineteenth-Century Acting', *PMLA*, 61 (1946): 522–76, and Alan Hughes, 'Art and Eighteenth-Century Acting Style, III: Passions', *Theatre Notebook*, 41 (1987): 128–39.

[78]   See Pierre Bourdieu, *Distinction: A Social Critique of the Judgment of Taste*, trans. Richard Nice (Cambridge, MA, 1984).

[79]   *Recollections of a Literary Life*, vol. 1, p. 242.

her playwriting, the productions of her plays, and her own income as a writer undoubtedly benefited.

A good instance of this is offered by *Rienzi*, the tragedy that Baillie repeatedly praised in her letters, singling it out as 'worthy' of the title of 'the most successful of our modern Tragedies' in her letter to Margaret Holford of 15 June 1836 quoted above. Indeed, the play's inception owed much to Mitford's friendship with yet another woman writer, Eleanor Ann Porden, as recorded in the Preface to the 1854 two-volume edition of Mitford's *Dramatic Works*: 'It was during the run of "Julian", that seeing much of my dear friend of Miss Porden (afterwards married to Sir John Franklin), and talking with her of subjects for a fresh effort, one or the other, I hardly know which hit upon "Rienzi"'.[80] When the play met with the usual obstacles in the production process, it was another woman writer and friend, the energetic Frances Trollope (Mitford called her 'a lively, brilliant woman of the world' and one of 'many accomplishments'),[81] that undertook to help Mitford's play to find its way to the stage. She had read it in the spring of 1826 and started to promote it in all her 'sociable' circles and through her contacts and connections with influential people. Thus she suggested to Mitford that she submit *Rienzi* to the author and playwright Henry Hart Milman for an opinion ('would you indulge Mr. Milman with a sight of the tragedy?').[82] Milman, the author of the popular Italianate tragedy *Fazio* (Covent Garden, 5 February 1818) and the theatre critic for John Murray's *Quarterly Review*, had also helped Felicia Hemans to rework her *Vespers of Palermo* and prepare it for the stage.[83] After Mitford had assented and Milman read the play, Trollope wrote encouragingly to the author: 'I hear in many directions of Mr. Milman's high admiration of "Rienzi"'.[84] Another of Trollope's strategies was to try to revive her friend Macready's interest by playing him off against Edmund Kean, whom she also knew, taking advantage of the rivalry between the two male stars in order to promote a woman's work of genius. Her letters to Mitford give lively accounts of her attempts at working on Macready's ego: 'No, we will not intreat ... Trust me, dear William would rather eat his heart than see Kean appear in "Rienzi"'.[85] In spite of all these efforts, her plans failed and *Rienzi* opened at

---

[80]   *The Dramatic Works of Mary Russell Mitford*, 2 vols (London, 1854), vol. 1, p. xxvii.

[81]   *The Friendships of Mary Russell Mitford*, ed. L'Estrange, vol. 1, p. 160.

[82]   Ibid., vol. 1, p. 159.

[83]   *The Vespers of Palermo* (unsuccessfully staged at Covent Garden on 12 December 1823) was revived for another night in April 1824 at the Edinburgh Theatre in the Scottish capital, after Joanna Baillie had persuaded Walter Scott to influence the theatre manager, Mrs Harriet Siddons, to produce it. In May 1824 Baillie thanked Scott for his 'friendly exertions in favour of Mʳˢ Heman's Tragedy' (*The Collected Letters of Joanna Baillie*, ed. Slagle, vol. 1, p. 426).

[84]   *The Friendships of Mary Russell Mitford*, ed. L'Estrange, vol. 1, p. 163.

[85]   Ibid., vol. 1, p. 159.

Drury Lane much later, on 11 October 1828, with Charles Maine Young in the title-role and an initial run of thirty-four nights.[86] Eventually, the play went to the United States also through Trollope's contacts and influence, and she saw it acted at the Chatham Theatre in New York, as she wrote in a letter to Mitford of 31 May 1831.[87]

Although always inevitably looming large, the presence of male figures in this reconstruction appears less oppressive if we recover the existence of a close-knit community of female writers involved in developing a drama and theatre of their own. For Mitford's reliance on male circles and circuits coexists with her awareness of belonging in a female tradition and its social and artistic practices. Implicit in her 'fixed determination' to become an acknowledged protagonist of the contemporary theatre is also her unflagging interest in evaluating the figures and legacies of her predecessors, and soliciting the help and advice of friends for her own projects. At the same time, her acts of self-positioning can be especially polemical with respect to male playwrights, as clearly emerges from her judgements over those who, in her opinion, had spectacularly failed in the drama: Byron and Scott.[88]

While not entirely setting female playwrights apart from male circuits of cultural influence, the networks examined here testify to the existence of an intellectual, literary and dramatic community of women writers who provided each other with vigorous support, encouragement and sponsoring. If, on 15 June 1836, Baillie wrote to Margaret Holford, 'I had the pleasure of meeting the other evening at Lady Dacre's a writer I had often wished to see – Miss Mitford',[89] the pleasure was reciprocal, as well as more genuine than a mere expression of

---

[86]   Mitford recounts the play's varying fortunes in Macready's hands and refers to Trollope's help in a letter to Barbara Hofland of 20 September 1826. See *Letters of Mary Russell Mitford: Second Series*, ed. Chorley, vol. 1, p. 133.

[87]   On Trollope and *Rienzi*, see Astin, *Mary Russell Mitford*, p. 62, and Watson, *Mary Russell Mitford*, p. 184. See also Trollope's letter to Mitford from New York of 29 May 1831 (*The Friendships of Mary Russell Mitford*, ed. L'Estrange, vol. 1, pp. 226–8). In addition, on Trollope's exertions in favour of Mitford's play, and their friendship more generally, see Pamela Neville-Sington, *Fanny Trollope: The Life and Adventures of a Clever Woman* (London, 1997), pp. 94–6.

[88]   In a letter to Sir William Elford of 9 November 1824, Mitford tells him of a discussion she had with the painter Robert Benjamin Haydon – one of her closest friends and also present at the 1836 dinner at Talfourd's – about Byron and Wordsworth. If Mitford is entirely in favour of Wordsworth for moral reasons, about Byron she says: 'I have never had any respect for Lord Byron's talents since he failed so egregiously in the drama, and did not find it out. Scott failed in the drama too, but then he made the discovery and drew back, and, accordingly, nobody remembers "Halidon Hill", and everybody adores the novels' – *The Life of Mary Russell Mitford*, ed. L'Estrange, vol. 2, p. 194. For a similar critique, see also Baillie's words on Byron's *Manfred* in a letter of 30 June 1817 to an unidentified correspondent: *The Collected Letters of Joanna Baillie*, ed. Slagle, vol. 1, pp. 1126–7.

[89]   Ibid., vol. 2, p. 659.

conventional feelings. It was the pleasure arising from the confirmation of the existence of a network of female playwrights, its ramifications, and its central position in the dramatic and theatrical debates of Romantic-period Britain.

Chapter 8

Dramatic Theory and Critical Discourse in Elizabeth Inchbald's *Remarks on The British Theatre*

Franca Dellarosa

This paper focuses on some key aspects of Elizabeth Inchbald's *Remarks* on the plays included in *The British Theatre* series (1806–1809), which are considered here as a self-sufficient and consistent critical and theoretical corpus. The pioneering activity of this dramatist and actress as 'Britain's first woman drama critic' has been the object of much meta-critical investigation,[1] in the context of the current rediscovery of the fundamental contribution of Romantic-era women writers, which has fostered a renewed perception and consequent reshaping of a much more complex and variegated cultural configuration of the age.[2] My

---

[1]   See Katharine M. Rogers's essay 'Britain's First Woman Drama Critic: Elizabeth Inchbald', in A.M. Schofield and C. Macheski (eds), *Curtain Calls: British and American Women and the Theater* (Athens, OH, 1991), pp. 277–90. More recently, Catherine Burroughs has discussed the dialogic relationship between closet and stage in Inchbald's criticism, in the context of her study of Baillie's dramatic theory, in *Closet Stages: Joanna Baillie and the Theater Theory of British Romantic Women Writers* (Philadelphia, 1997). Marvin Carlson has emphasized the relevance of Inchbald's groundbreaking experience in the panorama of nineteenth-century drama criticism as such, even transcending issues of gender: see 'Elizabeth Inchbald: A Woman Critic in Her Theatrical Culture', in Catherine Burroughs (ed.), *Women in British Romantic Theatre: Drama, Performance and Society, 1790–1840* (Cambridge, 2000), pp. 207–22. In the same volume, Thomas C. Crochunis focuses on specific aspects of both Inchbald's and Baillie's complex negotiation as playwrights and theorists in the (male-oriented) theatrical culture of their time: see 'Authorial Performances in the Criticism and Theory of Romantic Women Playwrights', pp. 223–54. Mary A. Waters, explicitly singles out Inchbald as a central case study, and focuses on a variety of issues emerging in the prefaces, such as her problematic attitude towards the supposed formative function of British drama in the shaping of English national character, and her singularly modern awareness of the collaborative quality of 'the genesis, production and reception of drama': see her *British Women Writers and the Profession of Literary Criticism, 1789–1832* (Houndmills and Basingstoke, 2004), pp. 57–81.

[2]   In the last few years a number of important studies have been published, drawing a growingly and fruitfully complicated map of women's contribution to Romantic-era drama and theatre. These include individual studies (Burroughs, *Closet Stages*, 1997), collections

attention will be devoted in particular to enquiring into the dynamic relationship that is posited throughout the prefaces between reading and performance, an issue to which Inchbald was acutely sensitive. The writer's critique of Joanna Baillie's *De Monfort* proves to be a significant case in point, providing an instance of Inchbald's perspective on such issues as the handling of theme in relation to theatrical efficacy, and the need for the dramatist to be fully aware of all factors relating to stagecraft. On the other hand, a parallel reading of Baillie's own theories offers further possibilities of identifying both divergences and cross-connections between the individual profiles of the two writers.

Roaming through the *Remarks* on the 125 plays forming *The British Theatre*, one gets the feeling of a consistent project, despite the unavoidable fragmentariness due to its very range. The project had been started – as Inchbald herself half-humorously stated in an often-quoted letter to George Colman the Younger – '[i]n one of those unfortunate moments which leaves us years of repentance'.[3] Its consistency lies in the bifocal perspective that pervasively features in the critic's presentation of many individual plays, and which takes positively into account, in Catherine Burroughs's words, 'the movement *between* closet and stage',[4] i.e. the inclusiveness of the dramatic text as object of different possible forms of fruition, where reading and performance fulfil different potentialities of the text itself.

A useful counterpoint to Inchbald's monumental achievement is provided by the authoritative voice of Joanna Baillie, both in her dramatic practice and in the extensive theoretical essays in the form of prefaces, directed 'To the Reader',

---

of essays on miscellaneous subjects, such as those edited by Tracy C. Davis and Ellen Donkin (*Women and Playwriting in Nineteenth-Century Britain* [Cambridge, 1999]) and Burroughs (*Women in British Romantic Theatre*, 2000), as well as monographic volumes collecting essays on individual authors, such as the collection edited by Thomas C. Crochunis on Joanna Baillie (*Romantic Dramatist* [London, 2004]), together with substantial biographies on the most important writers and new scholarly editions of individual or collected works and letters. This intensive scholarly activity as a whole testifies to the kindling of critical interest towards an area of study that is both compelling and demanding, requiring, as it does, the tracing of the outline of an entirely new pattern, where literary historiography, cultural history and gender studies meet.

[3]   Richard Brinsley Peake, *Memoirs of the Colman Family*, 2 vols (London, 1841), vol. 2, p. 319. The complex relationship Inchbald established as an actress and playwright with the Colman family is reconstructed in Ellen Donkin, *Getting into the Act: Women Playwrights in London, 1776–1829* (London, 1995), pp. 110–31. Commentary on the exchange of letters with Colman the Younger is given in Frank Felsenstein (ed.), *English Trader, Indian Maid: Representing Gender, Race and Slavery in the New World, An Inkle and Yarico Reader* (Baltimore and London, 1999), pp. 18–19, 170–71. See also Waters, *British Women Writers and the Profession of Literary Criticism*, pp. 60–65, and Annibel Jenkins's biography *I'll Tell you What: The Life of Elizabeth Inchbald* (Lexington, KY, 2003), pp. 478–87. Jenkins's volume also provides a detailed account of the circumstances of writing, as well as extended summaries of the *Remarks* (pp. 452 ff.).

[4]   *Closet Stages*, p. 84.

which accompany her various collections of dramas, together with her early and celebrated 'Introductory Discourse'. These essays offer illuminating pieces of self-criticism, but also knowing evaluations of the material conditions of staging in early nineteenth-century theatre, together with recurring observations on the nature of theatrical communication and on the supposed stage/page dichotomy.

The point where the two dramatist–theorists' experiences meet is in Inchbald's opening note to *De Monfort*, which was included in volume XXIV of *The British Theatre* collection.[5] Baillie's 1798 'play on the passion' of hatred had been staged between April and May 1800 at Drury Lane, running for eight nights, with John Philip Kemble as the tormented protagonist and Sarah Siddons as a memorable Jane De Monfort;[6] this is the production the Longman edition of *The British Theatre* refers to:

> Amongst the many female writers of this and other nations, how few have arrived at the elevated character of a woman of genius! The authoress of 'De Monfort' received that rare distinction, upon this her first publication. There was genius in the novelty of her conception, in the strength of her execution; and though her play falls short of dramatic excellence, it will ever be rated as a work of genius. (XXIV: 4, 3)

The warm and somewhat emphatic appreciation of 'a woman of genius' who has elevated herself 'amongst the many female writers of this and other nations', which opens Inchbald's note, is soon qualified by the immediate identification of a major fault: the play, according to the critic, 'falls short of dramatic excellence', even though it 'will ever be rated as a work of genius' (the word 'genius' occurs three times in the space of a few lines). Inchbald seems in fact to be willing to balance her genuine admiration for Baillie's ability to depict the progressive catastrophe awaiting the protagonist – immediately perceptible to the *reader* of the play – with a negative evaluation of its dramatic efficacy:

> The spirit, the soul, the every thought and sensation of the first character in this piece, De Monfort, is clearly discerned by the reader, and he can account for all the events to which they progressively lead: but the most attentive auditor, whilst he plainly beholds effects, asks after causes; and not perceiving those diminutive seeds of hatred, here described, till, swollen, they extend to murder, he conceives the hero of the tragedy to be more a pitiable maniac, than a man acting under the dominion of natural propensity.

---

[5] All quotations from the *Remarks* are from the 25-volume edition of *The British Theatre* (London, 1806–1809). References will be given in parentheses; as plays are paginated separately in each volume, this order will be followed: volume number, order of the play in the volume, page number.

[6] Judith Bailey Slagle, *Joanna Baillie: A Literary Life* (Madison, NJ, 2002), pp. 88 ff.

Even to the admiring reader of this work, who sees the delineation of nature in every page, it may perchance occur, that disease must have certain influence with hate so rancorous; for rooted antipathy, without some more considerable provocation than is here adduced, is very like the first unhappy token of insanity. (XXIV: 4, 4)

What seems to be at stake here is the very definition of the passions that are the object of Baillie's dramatic enterprise: if the causes of the overwhelming passion are not *shown* before the eyes of the beholders, the hero of the tragedy *appears* to be 'more a pitiable maniac than a man acting under the dominion of natural propensity'. Inchbald's qualification, then, pertains to the handling of theme: a 'lunatic' (XXIV: 4, 4) does not make an especially suitable hero for a tragedy, while *probability*, which is a constant priority in Inchbald's dramatic criticism, is not at stake in this case, since 'the delineation of nature' is offered to the eyes of the reader 'in every page', despite the fact that it is devoted to showing mental deviation. On the other hand, this level of Inchbald's critique is intertwined with, and reinforced by, her emphasis on the dubious *theatrical* efficacy of a psychological investigation that might prove to be too subtle to pass the test of the playhouse reception:

Authors may think too profoundly, as well as too superficially – and if a dramatic author, with the most accurate knowledge of the heart of man, probe it too far, the smaller, more curious, and new created passions, which he may find there, will be too delicate for the observation of those who hear and see in a mixed, and, sometimes riotous, company. (XXIV: 4, 3)

These words entail a qualified evaluation of Baillie's approach to dramaturgy, and its supposed limitations, which takes pragmatically into account the actual conditions of theatrical life in London, while exposing the difficulty of the search for an effective balance between the seemingly irreconcilable exigencies of psychological investigation, on the one hand, and the interests of spectacle on the other.[7] Accordingly, the somewhat patronising notes that close the article point to the quality of *De Monfort* as a not-entirely-satisfactory attempt on the part of a talented writer, whose main defect seems to be that of having 'studied theatrical productions as a reader more than as a spectator': as often happens with Inchbald,

---

[7]   This was, in fact, a constant preoccupation, which can be traced throughout Baillie's dramatic career, and finds oblique confirmation in the very texture of her dramatic practice, which, as Thomas C. Crochunis suggests, 'places textuality and theatricality in dialogue' – 'Joanna Baillie's Ambivalent Dramaturgy,' in Crochunis (ed.), *Joanna Baillie, Romantic Dramatist*, pp. 168–86, at p. 169. On Baillie's attention to stagecraft and her sensitiveness to spectacular potential in her plays, see also, in the same volume, the contributions by Greg Kucich, 'Joanna Baillie and the Re-staging of History and Gender', pp. 108–29, and Jeffrey N. Cox, 'Staging Baillie', pp. 146–67.

it is of course Shakespeare who is elected as the example to follow, since he 'gained his knowledge of the effect produced from plays upon an audience ... by his constant attendance on dramatic representations, even with the assiduity of a performer' (XXIV: 4, 5–6).

Among the Shakespearian plays that form a substantial part – a fifth – of the *British Theatre* collection as a whole, an interesting and in a sense ironical case in point for our discussion is provided by *The Winter's Tale*, which, in Inchbald's assessment, 'seems to class among those dramas that charm more in perusal than in representation' (III: 5, 2). The variety in time, place and action, which is part of the fascination of this play, but also its dramatic limit, Inchbald argues, makes for its full enjoyment as a unified whole in the act of reading, in the same way as 'some of the poetry is less calculated for that energetic delivery which the stage requires, than for the quiet contemplation of one who reads' (III: 5, 4). And yet it is the very handling of the hero's motivations – i.e. the credibility of the psychological representation, in this 'play on passion', of King Leontes's folly – that Inchbald finds less acceptable in terms of imaginative truth:

> Shakespeare has said in his tragedy of Othello, that a man is 'Jealous, because he is jealous.' This conceit of the poet seems to be the only reason that can be possibly be alleged, for the jealousy of the hero of the present work; for the unfounded suspicion of Leontes in respect to the fidelity of Hermione, is a much greater fault, and one with which imagination can less accord, than with the hasty strides of time, so much censured by critics, between the third and fourth acts of the play. It is easier for fancy to over leap whole ages, than to overlook one powerful demonstration of insanity in that mind which is reputed sane. (III: 5, 4)

One cannot help being reminded of the critic's censure of Baillie's characterization of De Monfort in terms of dramaturgically unjustified insanity. It is the Baillie text itself, on the other hand, that explicitly echoes its Shakespearian antecedents in dramatizing the progressively uncontrollable passion of jealousy, which, in the case of De Monfort, renders his overwhelming hatred towards his rival all the more excruciating. While *Othello* has been identified as the source of De Monfort's strategy to discover the two supposed lovers (III.iii),[8] his misinterpretation of the attitudes and movements of Jane and Rezenvelt is voiced in terms that echo almost verbatim Leontes's own sudden burst of anger against Hermione and Polixenes:[9]

---

[8]   See Joanna Baillie, *Plays on the Passions*, ed. Peter Duthie (Peterborough, ON, 2001), p. 356.

[9]   All references to Baillie's works are from *The Dramatic and Poetical Works* (1851; repr. Hildesheim and New York, 1976). References to *The Winter's Tale* are from the Arden edition, ed. J.H.P. Pafford (London, 1963).

De Monfort. See! See they come! *He strutting by her side.*
JANE, REZENVELT *and* COUNTESS FREBERG *appear through the glass door* pursuing their way up a short walk leading to the other wing of the house.
 See, his audacious face he turns to hers;
 Utt'ring with confidence some nauseous jest.
 And she endures it too – Oh! This looks vilely!
 Ha! Mark that that courteous motion of his arm! –
 What does he mean? – he dares not take her hand!
 (Pauses and looks eagerly.) By heaven and hell he does!
   De Monfort, IV. ii

Compare this passage with the following:

Her. 'Tis Grace indeed.
Why lo you now; I have spoke to th' purpose twice:
The one, for ever ear'd a royal husband;
Th' other, for some while a friend. [*Giving her hand to Pol.*]
Leon.   [*Aside*] Too hot, too hot!
To mingle friendship far, is mingling bloods.
I have *tremor cordis* on me: my heart dances,
But not for joy – not joy. This entertainment
May a free face put on, derive a liberty
From heartiness, from bounty, fertile bosom,
And well become the agent: 't may, I grant:
But to be paddling palms, and pinching fingers,
As they now are, and making practis'd smiles
As in a looking–glass; and then to sigh, as 'twere
The mort o' th' deer – O, that is entertainment
My bosom likes not, nor my brows.
(*The Winter's Tale*, 1.2.105–19)

The knowing 'improbability', then, that is ascribed to Shakespeare's tragicomedy both for the 'unprovoked jealousy of the Sicilian king' and its contrived plot, becomes, in Inchbald's evaluation of her contemporary Baillie, the imperfect control of the dramatic material. That same charge of improbability is also at the basis of the reservations Inchbald expresses with respect to the theatrical effectiveness of the Shakespeare play as a whole. Ironically, though, the 'Remarks' on *The Winter's Tale* end up with a reference to one particular scene in the drama 'which is an exception to the rest, in being far more grand in exhibition than the reader will possibly behold in idea. This is the scene of the Statue, when Mrs. Siddons stands for Hermione.' (III: 5, 6). That is to say, what is generally acknowledged as the most *improbable* situation in the drama turns out to be the most effective in performance, where theatrical ostension can even prevail over the imaginative capability of the individual – his/her capacity of 'beholding in idea' – in relation to the 'exhibition' of Mrs Siddons's body on stage, 'standing for' the character she is impersonating, namely Hermione. The latter, in turn, 'stands for' the supposed statue representing 'her likeness', which, as Paulina suggests, 'lively mocks life' (*The Winter's Tale*, 5.3, *passim*). A mirror-like effect is conjured up, therefore, which is also the icon of the relationship theatre establishes with the reality beyond the fictional world of drama.

The two prefaces that have been discussed so far can be considered as viable paradigms of Inchbald's characteristic way of approaching the dramatic texts under consideration, in relation to the underlying presence of a series of parameters that are connected both with the author's personal background as an experienced practitioner of the theatre, and with the context of reference of the prefaces themselves. Marvin Carlson has dealt with these aspects extensively, focusing on the specific qualities that single out the uniqueness of Elizabeth Inchbald's enterprise in the cultural context of her time, in terms both of scope and of the nature of the commentaries provided.[10] 'Printed under the authority of the managers from the prompt book[s]', as the opening pages read, the plays that are included in the *British Theatre* collection provide in fact less a diachronic thesaurus of British drama from the time of Shakespeare than a synchronic panorama of what was on in London's legitimate theatres around the turn of the nineteenth century. The combination of these factors accounts for the extreme attention Inchbald pays to issues pertaining to the level of performance, including notes on the specific quality of acting in one particular production – as, for example, in the 'Remarks' on such Shakespearian plays as *Richard III* (I: 5), where the emphasis is laid on the modulation in acting as displayed in different performances, by actors such as Garrick, Henderson or Kemble – or generalizations regarding the need of certain plays for a high quality in the acting as a necessary element to the achievement of the full potentialities of the drama itself, as in the exemplary case of the 'Remarks' on Beaumont and Fletcher's *Rule a Wife and Have a Wife* (VI: 1).

The critic's sensitivity to the complex interaction of diverse factors, where the language of words combines with the language of the body and the other systems of signs involved in theatrical communication, can be perceived in many of her comments, together with her awareness of the different mechanisms at work, whether the play be enjoyed in the private sphere of the individual reading or experienced in the shared dimension of the theatre. Textual evidence abounds: by way of exemplification, I wish to focus my attention on Inchbald's comments regarding Edward Moore's tragedy *The Gamester*. First performed at Drury Lane in February 1753, the play, in the words of Nicoll, was 'frequently revived in later years', and performed in 1783 at Drury Lane again with 'Kemble as Beverley and Mrs. Siddons as his wife';[11]

---

[10]   'Elizabeth Inchbald: A Woman Critic in her Theatrical Culture', pp. 207–22.

[11]   Allardyce Nicoll, *A History of English Drama 1660–1900* (Cambridge, 1955), vol. 3, pp. 88–9.

This tragedy is calculated to have a very different effect upon the stage and in the closet. An auditor, deluded into pity by the inimitable acting of a Mrs Siddons and a Mr. Kemble, in Mr. and Mrs Beverley, weeps with her; sighs with him; and conceives them to be a most amiable, though unfortunate, pair. But a reader, blessed with the common reflections which reading should give, calls the husband a very silly man, and the wife a very imprudent woman: – and as a man without sense, and a woman without prudence, degrade both the masculine and the feminine character, the punishment of the author is rather expected with impatience, than lamented as severe. (XIV: 3, 3–4)

Inchbald's comments testify to her awareness of the sympathetic identification that the experience of the performance entails on the part of the audience. The combination of these factors, depending strictly on the acting, activates the emotional response of the beholders that is stimulated by the very exhibition of the actors' physicality: it is the flesh-and-blood substance of the bodies exposed on stage that justifies the more immediate identification that the auditor, 'deluded into pity', experiences, while being somehow deprived of the power of rationalization that accompanies the private act of reading.

The implications of Inchbald's observations are far from being unproblematic, and invite comment at different levels. Implicit reference is made to the potential dangerousness of drama as a potentially misleading instrument of teaching. Inchbald's moral and didactic aims are well known, and account for the sharp dismissal of 'licentious' plays such as Farquhar's. On the other hand, the *Remarks* are interspersed with references to the ambiguity entailed in the gap that is sometimes opened between theatrical effectiveness and moral instruction. A useful case in point is given by the severe observations attached to Susanna Centlivre's comedy *A Bold Stroke for a Wife* (first performed in 1717), where Inchbald laments that,

... at the time the most ingenious and witty of the English dramatists lived, there was no restraint, as at this period, upon the immorality of the stage. Plays would have come down to the present age, under such restrictions less brilliant in humour and repartee, with fewer eulogiums from the admirers of wit, but with fewer reproaches from the wise and the good, upon the evil tendency of the dramatic art.

The happy effect of the moral dramas of this æra, in impressing those persons with just sentiments who attend no other place of instruction but a theatre, has not yet erased from the mind of the prejudiced former ill consequences from former plays.

Mrs. Centlivre, as a woman, falls more particularly under censure than her contemporary writers: though her temptations to please the degraded taste of the public were certainly more vehement than those of the authors who wrote at that time, for they were men whose fortunes were not wholly dependent on their mental exertions; yet the virtue of fortitude is expected from a female, when delicacy is the object which tries it; and the authoress of this comedy should have laid down her pen, and taken, in exchange, the meanest implement of labour, rather than have imitated the licentious example given her by the renowned poets of those days. (XI: 3, 3–4)

This disturbing asymmetry silently at work in many of her comments between the ethic and the aesthetic is one possible object of enquiry, which, however, needs to be set in the context of the general parable of the 'Comic Stage' in the eighteenth century, with the progressive enervation of the model of the comedy of manners and the development of sentimental comedy: both phenomena respond to major transformations in the political and economic spheres, and operate to 'socializ[e] the newly mobile middling classes for their role in an emerging public order'.[12]

I would like, however, to shift the focus back to what seems to me a key note of the *Remarks* as a whole, i.e. the continuous dialectical flow that arises between the act of reading and the experience of the performance, which implies a response-oriented aesthetic position. In this respect, the paramount role of acting as a mode of mediation between dramatic text and audience is once again reaffirmed: 'Poetry, with all its charm, will not constitute a good play', Inchbald observes in the opening paragraph of the 'Remarks' on George Colman's *The Mountaineers* (Haymarket, 3 August 1793), included in volume XXI of the collection:

Those persons, who have never seen Mr. Kemble in Octavian, will yet receive delight in reading this well written play: but those who *have* seen him, will weep as they read, and tremble as they weep, for it is most certain they have not forgotten him. Those again, who have seen any other actor in the character, will peruse the play, possessed of all its claims to attention, with indifference. (XXI: 1, 3)

The emphasis is placed here not only on the difference between the act of reading and the direct fruition of the dramatic text, but also on the very quality of these respective acts: the possibility, we might say, of 'recollecting the emotions in tranquillity' and restoring their sympathetic value as provided by a previous experience at the theatre, seems to establish a sort of hierarchy in the forms of fruition of drama within which the actor's performance plays a key role.

The excitement of human sympathy – although Inchbald, as far as I know, never employs the term – as an integral part of the aesthetic fruition of drama immediately conjures up the figure of Joanna Baillie. The latter's elaboration of the concept of 'sympathetic curiosity', as it appeared in her 1798 'Introductory Discourse', had established a viable paradigm for the explanation and exploration of the psychological mechanisms presiding over the reception of drama. Not only did Baillie elaborate a complex and deceptively rationalistic construction, intended to illustrate the motivations of human behaviour in the context of an aesthetic

---

[12]   Lisa A. Freeman, *Character's Theater: Genre and Identity on the Eighteenth Century Stage* (Philadelphia, 2002), p. 147. See, in particular, chapters 4 and 5.

reflection, but she had also embedded that construction in a fascinating texture of literary, historical, and even anthropological references. The theoretical corpus of Joanna Baillie, then, offers a highly significant counterpoint to Inchbald's radically different experience of drama criticism, while opening new perspectives of reading and unexpected coincidences. A glance at Baillie's preface to her *Miscellaneous Plays* (1805) proves to be rewarding in this respect. While justifying 'To the Reader' her unwilling decision to have these plays published in a single volume, and discussing the difficult negotiation between publication and stage production, she sets off a cursory but quite intense reflection on the act of reading, which is strictly tied to the actual, material form of the publication itself. Plays, she argues, should be read one at a time, and not following hurriedly one after another, as is bound to happen when a series of interesting plays appears together, appealing to man's (or woman's) imagination and curiosity. She then goes on to establish certain prescriptive forms of behaviour, which are all meant to improve pleasure 'in perusal'. The reader is thus asked 'to have the goodness not to read it hastily, but to pause, some days at least, between each play, that they may have in this respect the same advantages which new plays generally have' (388). Hidden in a footnote, a few compressed lines comment on an interesting issue, i.e. to what extent the act of reading is shaped by genre. Not surprisingly, it is the reading of drama – precisely through the enactment of that same emotional identification that is at stake in Inchbald's scattered notes – that offers the most intense aesthetic as well as emotive and intellectual experience, acting out, one might say, a vicarious form of reality. Drama is therefore the genre bound to suffer most from the artificial intensification of effect that is synonymous with a hasty reading:

> It may be urged, indeed, that unconnected poems bound up together, and almost every other species of composition, must suffer for being read in hasty succession in the same way. And in some degree they do. But in reading descriptions of nature, successions of thoughts, and narratives of every kind, the ideas they represent to the mind are as troops drawn out before it in loose marshalled array, whose most animated movements it surveys still as a spectator; whilst in reading a drama, where every character speaks immediately in his own person, we by sympathy rush, as it were, ourselves into the battle, and fight under every man's coat of mail by turns. This is an exercise of the mind so close and vigorous, that we retire from it exhausted; and if curiosity should urge us on without sufficient rest to the next engagement that calls for us, we enter the field bewildered, and spiritless, and weak. (388)

Embedded in the miniaturized formulation of the footnote, we recognize the same line of reasoning as developed in the 'Introductory Discourse'. A response-oriented discussion of forms emerges, however obliquely, and one which is linked in this case to the very modality of reception, with the emphasis being placed on the way the act of reading seems to establish a difference in degree of intensity in the aesthetic experience, a factor that is directly connected with the form involved.

Thus, whereas in the reading of poetry, descriptive passages and 'narratives of every kind' excite participation on the part of 'the mind' as 'spectator', with drama, we may infer by the same token, the feeling mind becomes actor: direct involvement is thus experienced, and the participation is integral. While we cannot fail to note that Baillie makes use of self-reflexive theatrical imagery in her reasoning, it is her emphasis on *theatricality* as experienced in different forms and to different effects that is worthy of note here. In other words, not only is drama the form of writing that is most suitable to rendering the workings of the mind, in that it offers direct access to them and for this reason fosters instruction – as the key argument developed in the 'Introductory Discourse' suggests –, but drama is also the psychic mould, as it were, that shapes our aesthetic reception in the experience of reading. The radical, psychological-oriented quality that can be traced in Baillie's reflection is characteristically her own; the similarly dynamic understanding of the interplay between the dimensions of reading and performance, as modulated in Inchbald's *Remarks*, clearly takes a more pragmatic direction, and is less designed to explore the psychodynamics of aesthetic fruition than to describe its effects in production. Thus, whether the focus be on acting, on dramatic probability, or on the way the use of poetic language might turn out to be detrimental in terms of the play's performability, Inchbald is entirely consistent in providing the perspective of 'a performer' ('Remarks' on *De Monfort*, XXIV: 4, 5). However, this does not entail any disparagement of the dimension of reading, which indeed is regarded as *adding* potential meaning. Evidence of such an attitude can be traced throughout, and takes on a particularly significant value in her comments on Nathaniel Lee's *The Rival Queens*, where attention is given to the dimension of reading aloud, which is a somewhat in-between act, entailing an emphasis on the individual, private response to a performance activity that is, however, public. Thus Inchbald, referring to the author's talent in reading, remarks:

> He was so excellent a reader of his own plays at the rehearsals, Cibber says, – that the very first actors have thrown down their parts, in despair of giving equal force or pathos in performing them ... To persons well acquainted with theatrical qualifications, there is nothing wonderful in this intelligence. The relater of it himself must have known, from long experience, that many a fine reader cannot act; and that many a fine actor cannot read. This observation, of course, applies to a superlative degree of excellence in either art. (VI: 4, 3–4)

Reading aloud, a performative act that mostly pertains to the closet dimension, is singled out by Inchbald as an *art*, in the same way as the actor's is, offering potential for reception that is just as meaningful and as enriching as that of stage production. Possessed with all 'theatrical qualifications', Inchbald knowingly evaluates the entire range of possibilities for signification that are inscribed in the dramatic text, while her profound awareness of the conditions of the theatrical culture of her time emerges powerfully in the trenchant topicality of her observations on current dramatic production: 'Now, plays are written to be seen, not read,' she remarks in her notes on Reynolds's *The Dramatist* (XX: 1, 3), 'and present authors gain their views; for they, and the managers, are enriched, and the theatres crowded.'

Chapter 9

Elizabeth Inchbald: Translation as Mediation and Re-writing

Vita M. Mastrosilvestri

This paper focuses on the practice of drama translation by Elizabeth Inchbald, one of the most emblematic figures in the late eighteenth-century British theatrical panorama. Actress, dramatist and theatre critic, Mrs Inchbald was perfectly familiar with the dynamics underlying the London theatrical market: her adaptations for the English stage are the products both of a complex adjustment of the original to the constraints of practical stage conventions and an in-depth reformulation of the culture-bound qualities of the source dramas to the advantage of the social and political representation of her own culture. If, on one hand, the 'acculturation of the foreign text' – as Susan Bassnett suggests in her definition of drama translation as a task constantly undermined by 'labyrinthine difficulties' [1] – entails the loss of some basic traits of the original, Inchbald is nonetheless able to establish a dialogue between the two cultures. Such a negotiation is particularly evident when the dramatist represents femininity. The translation of stage conventions and sociocultural realities is enriched with the transposition of female characters from a stereotyped image, established by the dominant ideology, to a new ideal, in which emancipation is achieved within the private sphere. Through the act of translation, therefore, the woman dramatist is able to enter the domain of public discussion, without disrupting a realm in which patriarchal values prevailed.[2]

'Received with unbounded applause',[3] at the Covent Garden première on 11 October 1798, *The Lover's Vows*, Elizabeth Inchbald's adaptation of *Das Kinde Der Liebe*, by the controversial German dramatist August von Kotzebue, was nonetheless not exempt from some sharp criticism. While admitting her undeniable skill in touching the right chord with the London public through her dramatic art,

---

[1]   Susan Bassnett, 'Still Trapped in the Labyrinth: Further Reflections on Translation and Theatre', in Susan Bassnett and André Lefevere (eds), *Translating Cultures: Essays on Literary Translation* (Clevedon, 1998), pp. 90–108, at pp. 92–3.

[2]   See F. Moreux, *Elizabeth Inchbald et la Révendication Féminine au Dix-Huitième Siècle* (Lille, 1974).

[3]   James Boaden, *Memoirs of Mrs. Inchbald: Including her Familiar Correspondence with the Most Distinguished Persons of her Time*, 2 vols (London, 1833), vol. 2, p. 22; quoted in Annabel Jenkins, *I'll Tell You What: The Life of Elizabeth Inchbald* (Lexington, KY, 2003), p. 419.

the play's detractors attacked especially Mrs Inchbald's radical deviations from the original, raising more general questions about the extent to which theatrical adaptations may reshape the substance and form of the source text to the advantage of the target culture. Anne Plumptre, the principal English translator of Kotzebue, and Mary Berry, editor, diarist and society figure, expressed severe disapproval of the great number of 'alterations and omissions' Mrs Inchbald had made to the original text, betraying – in Miss Plumptre's words – 'the mind, the principles and the genius of Kotzebue'[4] and 'destroying the effects of many situations and sentiments', as Mary Berry affirmed, overtly declaring her preference for the never-performed but more faithful version by Miss Plumptre:

> *Lover's Vow* disappointed me. The necessary curtailments which have been made from the German *Natural Son*, to avoid *longueurs*, and to suit it in some degree to our manners upon the stage, destroy the effects of many situations and sentiments, by having a great degree taken away their efficient or at least sufficient cause, and consequently making them appear awkward or misplaced, or more or less than enough to the minds of the spectators: in short, a good play must ever be a whole form which it is quite impossible to take out a bit here and put in a bit there without disfiguring and degrading the original, even when the original would not succeed in representation, as is certainly the case with *Natural Son*, as I read it closely translated from the original.[5]

Mrs Inchbald's response was not immediate. Ten years later, in her *Remarks on Lovers' Vows*, included in volume 23 of *The British Theatre* collection, the celebrated dramatist, now in the most mature phase of her career, explained the strategies she had employed in the adaptation of Kotzebue's play, thus providing her only testimony concerning the complex enterprise of transposing a playtext from one *stage* into another. 'Wholly unacquainted with the German', she points out, she had been forced to work on an anonymous literal translation, 'tedious and vapid as most literal translations are'.[6] After a brief account of the state of the text, 'which came to [her] in broken English', the author points out that the changes were the result of a careful consideration of her audience's taste:

> … in no one instance, I would suffer my respect for Kotzebue to interfere with my profound respect for the judgment of a British audience. But I flatter myself

---

[4]   A. Plumptre, 'Translator's Preface to *The Natural Son*', at: http://www.etang. umontreal.ca/bwp/1800/essays/plumptre_natural_preface.html, accessed October 2009.

[5]   M. Berry, 'Extracts', quoted in Catherine B. Burroughs, *Closet Stages: Joanna Baillie and the Theater Theory of British Romantic Women Writers* (Philadelphia, 1997), p. 7.

[6]   Elizabeth Inchbald, 'Remarks on *Lover's Vows* by Elizabeth Inchbald', in *The British Theatre, or, a Collection of Plays which are Acted at the Theatres Royal Drury Lane, Covent Garden and Haymarket*, 25 vols (London, 1808), vol. XXIII, pp. 3–4.

such a vindication is not requisite to the enlightened reader, who, I trust, on comparing this drama with the original, will at once see all my motives ....[7]

Mrs Inchbald, as an experienced actress and dramatist, was obviously aware that the main task of a dramatic author is the success of theatrical communication. The knowledge of every aspect of the theatrical system of her epoch, along with her infallible instinct for the exigencies of London's entertainment industry, are the main features of Mrs Inchbald's adaptation and translation practice, which is regulated by what has been described by Susan Bassnett as the principle of 'performability', namely, the need for a dramatic text to be rewritten according to the general norms of theatrical performance, considering, at the same time, the particular stage conventions of the target culture.[8]

The study of the process of transposition of the substantial number of comedies taken from the French in her dramatic output corroborates these observations. In this case, the originals are the direct source for Inchbald, who had an excellent knowledge of the language. Accordingly, translation proper combines with techniques of adaptation, giving birth to totally fresh theatrical products. The successful realization of such a task entailed the recognition of the differences existing between the British and the Continental stages, an awareness that clearly emerges from Mrs Inchbald's remarks on Ambrose Phillips's *The Distress't Mother* (1712), a successful adaptation of Racine's *Andromache*. The acknowledgement of the immense popularity of the tragedy, which 'remained in the repertoire right through the eighteenth century',[9] is a pretext for a wide-ranging reflection on the receptive aspect of dramatic translation:

> Every Drama requires great alteration, before it can please a London audience, although it has previously charmed the audience of Paris. The gloomy mind of a British auditor demands a bolder and more varied species of theatrical amusements, than the lively spirits of his neighbour in France. The former has no attention, no curiosity, till roused by some powerful fable and intricate occurrences, and all the interest which variety creates – whilst the latter will quietly sit, absorbed in their own glowing fancy, to hear speeches after speeches,

---

[7]   Ibid., vol. XXIII, p. 3.

[8]   Bassnett, 'Still Trapped in the Labyrinth', pp. 90–108. As an example of the problems involved in 'determining the criteria for the translation of a theatre text', Bassnett considers two adaptations of Racine's *Andromache* for the British stage. The first version (Dorset Garden, August 1674) by John Crowne, which is very close to the original text, was not successfully received, since, as the author himself suggests in his 'Epistle to the Reader', it did not fulfil the expectations of an audience unwilling to respond to the 'thin Regalios' of the French Theatre tradition. On the contrary, Ambrose Phillips's adaptation, written less than forty years later, was received as a peerless masterpiece, as the radical alteration to the original made it more suitable for the English stage.

[9]   Susan Bassnett, *Translation Studies* (London and New York, 1980), p. 125.

of long narration, nor wish to see anything performed, so they are but told that something has been done.[10]

According to Inchbald, profound modifications not only in the overall structure of the source drama, but also in its stylistic details, are necessary in order for a drama of French origins to be appreciated by a 'British auditor' who is used to greater variety in 'theatrical amusements' and would not appreciate the long narrative monologues, typical of the French theatre. Once again, the focus is on the theatrical translator's ability to fulfil the expectations of her audience.

Mrs Inchbald's critical observations are substantiated by her consolidated experience in adapting foreign plays according to the demands of the British theatrical market. In her dramatic practice the playwright rejects dialogue in rhymed verse, adopting prose, which was undoubtedly more suitable to the heterogeneous English audience, whose attention was to be focused on the dramatic action, given the conditions of the performances that took place in huge theatres with bad acoustics.[11] For the same reason, plots are reduced to the essential, with the elimination of all the parts that are not strictly functional to the development of the story, and undergo mutations that blur the boundaries between theatrical genres. *Young Men, Old Women, Lovers not Conjurers* (Haymarket, 30 June 1792) transforms Gresset's five-act comedy *Le Méchant* into a farce; *Le Philosophe Marié* (1727), by Néricault Destouches, is transformed into a three-act pièce (*The Married Man*) where the pathos of the sentimental drama, and the mimicry, typical of farce, coexist.

In the former play, the original is irretrievably altered by the act of transference from one culture into another,[12] with the result that it is 'exhausted by translation ... negated by the act of transfiguration'[13] – as George Steiner defines those texts that have been somehow surpassed by their originals. The adaptation of Destouches's

---

[10]   Elizabeth Inchbald, 'Remarks on *The Distress't Mother* by Ambrose Phillips', in *The British Theatre*, vol. VII, p. 3.

[11]   J. Cox and M. Gamer (eds.), 'Introduction', to *The Broadview Anthology of Romantic Drama* (Peterborough, ON, 2003), p. vii.

[12]   The abridgement and the reduction of Gresset's comedy into a farce imply a radical alteration of plot and characterization: in the original the male protagonist Valère is a young bohémien with an aversion to marriage, whereas, in Mrs Inchbald's farce, Sylvan is the prototype of the wealthy young English man sent to Paris, the city of sin, and willing to get married. Similarly, Mrs Ambilogy, a woman who is trying to repair a compromising mistake made in her youth, has very little in common with the female protagonist's wicked, immoral mother who tries to imprison her daughter in a convent, for fear of losing the man she loves. Moreover, while in the French comedy the author highlights the dialectic between Paris's perverted, decaying refinement and the countryside, *custodian* of the domestic morals, Mrs Inchbald's farce is intended to establish the limits between national identities, making fun of 'the other' and celebrating, as a consequence, British natural righteousness.

[13]   G. Steiner, *After Babel: Aspects of Language and Translation* (Oxford, 1975), pp. 296–7.

play, on the other hand, is closer to its source text and discloses divergences that seem to be a more regular and systematic attempt, on the part of the translator, to 'inscribe' the foreign text 'with the domestic intelligibilities and interests', to use Venuti's definition of translation as a practice that has increasingly become instrumental to the requests of both the market and the dominant ideology.[14]

Conceived in historical and cultural circumstances that were totally different from those in which its original was written, *The Married Man* (Haymarket, 15 July 1789) clearly unveils the strategy employed by Mrs Inchbald in order to adapt an early eighteenth-century French play – on which the artistic inheritance of Molière still weighed, as in most of the comic works of that period[15] – for the 'despotic government'[16] of the London stage at the dawn of the 1790s. Together with the rejection of the rhymed verse, designed to achieve what Paula Backsheider defines as an 'ordinary workmanlike prose', more attuned to the stage and acting, and more perceptive about human nature,[17] the most evident formal change is the compression of the plot, without altering the number of the dramatis personae or their respective functions in the plot itself. As a result, the dramatic action is accelerated and concentrated, and the audience's attention is kept constantly alive.

Act I of the French version, for instance – made up of seven scenes, whose succession is signaled by the entrance or the exit of a given character – is condensed into a long single scene, in which lengthy monologues and soliloquies (1.5, 1.7) are reduced or drastically omitted, and the opening lines of the first exchange between the philosopher and his wife (1.6) are significantly shortened. Céliante's long soliloquy (1.3), Ariste's reflections at the end of each act, and the cynical, vindictive intrigues of Marquis du Lauret are left out or reduced to more concise, but no less effective, versions. Such examples plainly indicate the translator's deliberate decision to avoid any break in the sequence of the events. As a result, in *The Married Man* the character's intentions and inner thoughts are enacted directly on stage, to the advantage both of the rapid development of the plot, and of the emergence of the farcical element in each character's actions. Such a process has weighty consequences on the role of the characters in the scene, especially the minor ones: the role of the chambermaid, Lucy, is drastically diminished in importance, if compared to her French counterpart. In the original, Finette is a sarcastic, pitiless commentator on the events she is involved in, who unmasks the contradictions of a decaying society doomed to complete ruin; in Mrs

---

[14]   L. Venuti, 'Translation, Community, Utopia', in Lawrence Venuti (ed.), *The Translation Studies Reader* (New York, 2004), p. 482.

[15]   See Marvin Carlson, 'Introduction' to *The Heirs of Molière: Four French Comedies of the Seventeenth and Eighteenth Centuries*, trans. and ed. Carlson (New York, 2003).

[16]   Elizabeth Inchbald, 'To The Artist', *The Artist*, 1/14 (1807): 16.

[17]   Paula Backsheider, 'Introduction', in *The Plays of Elizabeth Inchbald*, ed. Backsheider, 2 vols (New York and London, 1980), vol. 1, p. xxviii.

Inchbald's version, Lucy is a marginal character and lacks the pessimistic sarcasm of Destouches's *femme de chambre*.

Beyond the formal aspects I have discussed so far, the source drama underwent deeper transformations that were the result of forces more difficult to decipher and control, including the diverging social and political profiles of the two cultures. As Judith Pascoe has observed, in the ebullient decades around the turn of the century theatre and politics were closely intertwined: both radical and conservative forces called theatricality into play, with the aim of strengthening their sphere of influence,[18] whereas theatre, in its very proliferation of forms, made the social conflicts, power struggles and beliefs of a whole nation visible.[19] Such a 'translation of politics'[20] acquired further complexity when the drama did not stem from native soil but was transplanted from a foreign culture. In that case, the efficient functioning of theatrical communication required that the translator provide the audience with a recognizable horizon in terms of cultural, social, as well as national, identity. To quote George Steiner's metaphors for the second and third phases of the hermeneutic circle, the source text must experience both an 'aggression', in which 'the density of the hostile or seductive "otherness" is dissipated', and, subsequently, an 'assimilation' producing a sense of 'at homeness at the core'[21] in the target text.

Hence, social identities – such as the aristocracy – that were in the foreground on the German or the French stage would not be easily recognized on the British stage of the late eighteenth century; the audience wanted *Britishness* and *British* social dialectics to be performed. Elizabeth Inchbald, who was perfectly aware of the needs of her public, and deeply involved in the climate of social and political unrest of the period, like most of her contemporaries translating for the theatre, enacted a 'reterritorialization' of the foreign plays, mediating between the social identities of the source and the target cultures.[22]

The Married Man also provides evidence of the 'annexation'[23] of the interference existing in the foreign text. The substitution of *philosophe* with 'man' in the title indicates the cultural gap between French Enlightenment culture and British

---

[18]   Judith Pascoe, *Romantic Theatricality: Gender, Poetry and Spectatorship* (Ithaca, NY, and London, 1997), pp. 42–3.

[19]   Betsy Bolton, *Women, Nationalism and the Romantic Stage: Theatre and Politics in Britain, 1780–1800* (Cambridge, 2001), p. 19.

[20]   Ibid.

[21]   Steiner, *After Babel: Aspects of Language and Translation*, p. 297–9.

[22]   See the concept of reterritorialization in translation as discussed in André Levefere, *Translation, Rewriting and the Manipulation of Literary Fame* (London and New York, 1992).

[23]   Antoine Berman, 'Translation and the Trials of the Foreign', trans. Lawrence Venuti, in Venuti (ed.), *The Translation Studies Reader*, pp. 276–89, at p. 278, where by 'annexationist' translation the scholar means a practice that tends to be 'ethnocentric' and 'hypertextual', incorporating and obscuring the culture-bound features of the original. Such

Georgian society at the outbreak of the revolution that would shake the political balance of the whole continent to its foundations. Destouches's sarcasm towards his conformist *philosophe*, incapable of bearing the contradiction between his status as a philosopher and his simultaneous condition as a married man,[24] would hardly have been grasped by an audience that did not identify such a social type as part of its own milieu. Thus, the audience's expectations are cleverly fulfilled by overshadowing the social characterization of the protagonist in favour of a greater consideration of the private domain. Similarly, the French author's harsh criticism of a new set of values exalting libertinism over marriage, intrigue over truthfulness, is dissolved into laughter. Le Marquis du Lauret, like the German count in *Das Kinde der Liebe*,[25] is deprived of his hedonistic cynicism, usually associated with aristocratic opulence, and is reduced to a puppet-like figure: a tribute, in late eighteenth-century England, to an increasingly powerful middle class, eager to see its ideological adversary ridiculed. Further clues of this process of *naturalization* of the foreign play may be detected in the remodeling of the minor character of Céliante. While the 'capricieuse'[26] is molded on an existing person, the author's sister-in-law,[27] in the English version the mutability and indiscretion of the French counterpart are defused, so as to stress Emily's envy at her sister's new status as a wife.

The emphasis, on the whole, seems to be not so much on the edifying purpose of the drama as on the rapid and effective flow of the scenes and on the ridiculous quality of a paradoxical domestic *querelle*. The basic divergence between the two texts, in the present case, lies therefore in what Hans Vermeer terms *skopos*,

---

a process, as a consequence, prevents the 'trial of the foreign', an act of highly ethical value, in which the Other is recognized and accepted.

[24]   See 'Notice sur la Vie et Les Ouvrages de Destouches', in N. Destouches, *Oeuvres Dramatiques, Précédées d'une Notion sur la Vie et les Ouvrages de Cet Auteur*, 6 vols (Paris, 1832), vol. 1, p. XVIII. In the introduction to the 1832 edition of Destouches's complete works, *Le Philosophe Marié* is presented as a successful attempt at depicting the paradox between early eighteenth-century intellectual non-conformity to established values and prejudices, and the degeneration of such an attitude into a mere fashion, a form of banalized conventionality: in Act I. ii, the protagonist is absolutely unable to give a rational explanation for his reluctance to make his marriage public. What emerges is an illogical, ridiculous fear of the others' judgement.

[25]   See Plumptre, 'Translator's Preface to *The Natural Son*', and Inchbald, 'Remarks on *Lovers' Vows*'.

[26]   Destouches, 'Deuxième Lettre a M. Le Chevalier de B****', in *Oeuvres Dramatiques*, vol. 5, pp. 158–61, at p. 158.

[27]   Ibid. In this letter, exalting the success of those characters taken from real life, the author cites the example of Céliante. Like the bizarre, capricious adversary of the couple, Destouches's sister-in-law is alleged to be the imprudent revelation of his marriage, which had to be kept under silence, in relation to his diplomatic career.

namely 'the aim or purpose of a translation'.[28] The translation, intended by the German linguist as a meaningful action, 'leads to a result, a new situation or event, and, possibly to a new object'.[29] As a consequence, especially in drama translation, where some culture-bound features of the source text are not suitable for performance in the target culture, the two versions are likely to 'diverge from each other quite considerably, not only in the formulation and the distribution of the content, but also as regards the goals that are set for each'.[30] This clearly entails a manipulation of the original, on the basis of the requirements of the client who 'commissions' the work, prescribing, either implicitly or explicitly, the aim of the translational action. Such a process is not carried out in a vacuum. The translated text is subject to the action of several forces, the most important of which may be identified, to use André Lefevere's terminology, as 'patronage',[31] an entity within the literary system, which, according to Foucault's definition of power, manifests itself as a hidden, enveloping regulatory body that creates and controls knowledge, rather than as a repressive force.[32] The ideological, economic and social elements composing this all-embracing institution have profound consequences on the *translatum*,[33] the product of an unlimited set of extra-linguistic variables.

The total assimilation of the socio-cultural defining features of the original implies, however, the risk of obliterating the fruitful cultural interaction generated by the encounter between two different cultures. The ambivalence of such an attitude is evident: if on one hand the version is the product of a steady 'play of deforming forces',[34] privileging the aesthetic and moral set of values of the translator's culture, at the same time this kind of 're-writing' may be considered an act of mediation between two different realities in which, as Susan Bassnett states in her description of the 'Horatian model', the translator is 'not faithful to the text but to [the] customers'.[35] Collusion with the dominant ideology is the price to pay in order to reach general consensus on stage. Yet, in the historically determined case of Elizabeth Inchbald, the woman dramatist is able to establish a silent dialogue between the original culture and her own.

---

[28]   Hans Vermeer, 'Skopos and Commission in Translational Action', trans. Andrew Chesterman, in Venuti (ed.), *The Translation Studies Reader*, pp. 227–32, at p. 227.

[29]   Ibid.

[30]   Ibid., p. 229.

[31]   André Lefevre, 'Mother Courage's Cucumbers: Text, System and Refraction in a Theory of Literature', in Venuti (ed.), *The Translation Studies Reader*, pp. 239–55, at p. 242.

[32]   Michel Focault, *Power/Knowledge: Selected Interviews and Other Writings*, ed. C. Gordon, trans. L. Marshall, J. Mepham and K. Soper (New York, 1980), p. 119.

[33]   Vermeer, 'Skopos and Commission in Translational Action', p. 228.

[34]   Berman, 'Translation and the Trials of the Foreign', p. 278.

[35]   Susan Bassnett and André Lefevere, 'Introduction: Where Are We In Translation Studies?', in Bassnett and Lefevere (eds), *Constructing Cultures: Essays on Literary Translation* (Clevedon, 1998), pp. 1–11, at pp. 3–7.

The case of *The Massacre* (1792), Mrs Inchbald's single tragic composition – never performed by virtue of its explicit references to the French Revolutionary Terror, stigmatized as a menace to the European political balance –, is exemplary in this regard. Taken from an unidentified and clearly fictitious French source, the drama is a rewriting of 'the unhappy fate of a neighbouring nation',[36] from a *British*-oriented perspective, as outlined in the advertisement to the drama. Lacking an original, *The Massacre* is a peculiar type of rewriting, a form of transposition that Susan Bassnett, retrieving an expression coined by Gideon Toury to describe 'those text[s] that claim[s] falsely to be a translation', defines as 'pseudotranslation'.[37]

'The idea of an original authentic source outside the text'[38] is both a useful device for the author to distance herself from the numerous theatrical representations of the French Revolution, which were deemed to be 'illegitimate',[39] owing to their disruptive ideological potential, and a means to express nonetheless her own vision of the slaughter of innocent people during the Terror. In practice, the 'hidden' source text is historical reality itself, which, through an extremely complex and subtle act of *déplacement*, is questioned and analyzed.

The chronological distancing of the setting – the catastrophe that destroys Tricastin's family takes place during the notorious St Bartholomew's Night, 1572 – gives the author the opportunity not only to reflect on the total failure of the ideals of liberty, equality and fraternity, but also to shape a broader vision of history, seen as a destructive force sweeping away domestic stability and genuine interpersonal relations. Mrs Inchbald's questioning of history, in order to conciliate her radical political orientation with inexorable reality, coexists with the repeated attempts in the text to define British national identity. In the drama, England is referred to as a land of liberty where an ideal familial order – a small-scale reproduction of the overall stability of a whole nation – might be restored.

By way of a conclusion, I wish to call attention to still another, more carefully concealed feature shared by the adaptations I have taken into consideration so far, namely Elizabeth Inchbald's exploration of femininity, through which the author offers her personal contribution to the process of female emancipation. The alterations to the original made from this specific perspective shed light on the divergence between the established representations of femininity and the translator's own ideal.

Mrs Inchbald rejects the traditional female stereotypes created by the male authors of the foreign plays, which are inevitably and deeply affected by the predominance of an age-long patriarchal ideology. The vain, selfish, deceitful

---

[36]   Inchbald, 'Advertisement to The Massacre', in *The Plays of Elizabeth Inchbald*, ed. Backscheider, vol. 2, p. 29.

[37]   Susan Bassnett, 'When is a Translation not a Translation?', in Bassnett and Lefevere (eds), *Constructing Cultures: Essays on Literary Translation*, pp. 25–40, at pp. 27–8.

[38]   Ibid., p. 30.

[39]   Jane Moody, *Illegitimate Theatre in London, 1770–1830* (Cambridge, 2000).

coquette, who uses her sexual power unscrupulously to climb the social ladder, or the characterless, futile female protagonists of the sentimental plots, are two sides of the same coin, both leading to the shared idea of the female characters as objects at men's disposal. The dramatist–translator chooses deliberately to vary important features of the female characters of the source text, even to the detriment of her audience's laughter. The disruption of the stereotypes imposed by the traditional theatrical representation of the female subject, however, does not imply a violent attack on the rigid behavioral strictures imposed on women. The idea of female submission to male authority, for instance, is reshaped in order to present women's faithfulness from a different perspective: far from being inanimate objects that accept their husband's commands patiently, the female protagonists are able to affirm their own will, through the exploitation of the resources provided within the narrow, claustrophobic spaces in which they are confined, silently eroding the limits of such spaces.[40]

Theatrical translation, therefore, turns out to be a further instrument in the hands of the woman dramatist in the construction of an ideal of femininity that she endeavoured to work out throughout her life. Constantly oscillating between unconditioned fidelity and painful betrayal, the act of translating becomes a mask behind which the woman writer, while remaining faithful to the models suggested by the dominant ideology, is able to express her own vision of social and sexual identities.

---

[40]   Betsy Bolton, 'Farce, Romance and Empire: Elizabeth Inchbald and the Colonial Discourse', *The Eighteenth Century*, 39/1 (1998): 3–24, and Daniel O'Quinn, 'Scissors and Needles: Inchbald's *Wives as They Were, Maids as They Are* and the Governance of Sexual Exchange', *Theatre Journal*, 51 (1999): 105–25.

Chapter 10

Negotiating Voices in Romantic Theatre: Scottish Women Playwrights, Gender and Performativity

Gioia Angeletti

In the last twenty years the British drama produced between 1737 and 1832 has undergone a considerable critical revival in Great Britain and throughout the English-speaking world.[1] As part of this revival, important and pioneering work has been made on the contribution of women dramatists, managers and critics to the theatrical development of the period, a contribution that had long been largely ignored in most literary and cultural histories.[2] A number of distinguished critics have expressly recognized the roles women played in this age of dramatic experimentation, their centrality in professionalizing relations among authors, actors and managers, and their position as technical innovators, bringing about revolutions in acting theory and staging techniques.

There are, however, still more than a few important female voices in the Romantic theatrical world that remain silent in recent critical recuperations, and it is one of the primary aims of this essay to allow them to be heard and rehabilitated. This reassessment aims to work on two levels. On the one hand, it will focus on the relatively understudied aspect of the complex struggles women playwrights of the Romantic era experienced in a male-dominated theatrical world; on the other hand, it will involve in particular a re-evaluation of some female dramatists from a somewhat peripheral area, Scotland, which after the 1707 Union of Parliaments was regarded even more as the 'exotic' northern region of Britain, a rural savage country opposed to industrial and civilized England. Scottish women

---

[1]   The 1737 Licensing Act and the 1832 Dramatic Literature Act and Reform Act mark crucial turning-points in the history of British theatre, although it must be said that the latter was less revolutionary than expected since it did not manage to bring about the abolition of the patent system introduced by the former.

[2]   A simple glance at the playbills in the National Library of Scotland or at special theatre collections such as the Larpent Collection of Plays at the Huntington Library in California would erase all doubt concerning women playwrights' productivity between the 1770s and 1820s (also considering that a great number of plays were published anonymously).

dramatists, therefore, had to confront this double gender-based and geopolitical marginalization, and rarely were they able to find definite solutions for it.[3]

As Adrienne Scullion has suggested, women involved in the nineteenth-century Scottish stage have been generally undervalued, while, in fact, they were very influential as actresses, managers, playwrights, critics and theatre historians, as well as spectators and readers of plays.[4] Thus the quality of the writings of such authors as, among others, Jean Mar(i)shall, Eglantine Wallace, Christian Carstair(e)s,[5] Mary Diana Dods (alias David Lyndsay) and Frances Wright invites us to reflect upon and possibly reconsider some of the most compelling issues in recent studies of Romantic-era women dramatists: first, the problematic situation of those writers suffering from a 'minority complex' due to their ex-centric status in relation to the dominant culture; secondly, the issue of particular, gendered obstacles to their participation in theatrical life, and the related question of how effectively they negotiated these barriers.[6] I will focus on these writers because

---

[3]   The theatres in Scotland were licensed by the magistrates or justices of the peace, and they had to apply for the renewal of these licences each year. Patent theatres, on the other hand, including the Theatre Royal in Edinburgh, were under the control of the Lord Chamberlain. In nineteenth-century Scotland the main venues were: the patented Theatres Royal in the major cities; minor playhouses in smaller towns, often competing with the theatres of Glasgow and Edinburgh, and producing a strong local tradition of performance and illegitimate theatres; the *geggy* theatres, or the 'Scottish version of the booth or fit-up theatres which strolling companies used to perform in. Like circus tents, they were made from wood and canvas, were easily dismantled and sorted between performances'; and finally the music-hall. Cf. Adrienne Scullion, 'Some Women of the Nineteenth-Century Scottish Theatre: Joanna Baillie, Frances Wright and Helen MacGregor', in Douglas Gifford and Dorothy McMillan (eds), *A History of Scottish Women's Writing* (Edinburgh, 1997), pp. 158–78, at p. 175n.

[4]   The manager of the first regular theatre in Edinburgh was the actress Sarah Ward, to whom we owe the opening of a new theatre in the Canongate in 1747; Jessie Jackson was the manager of the Edinburgh Theatre Royal before Henry Siddons (Sarah Siddons's son); the pantomime actress Florrie Ford, the comedian Ruth Stanley, and the singer Helen Kirk were among the most applauded performers of the time. Cf. Scullion, 'Some Women of the Nineteenth-Century Scottish Theatre'.

[5]   Biographical and bibliographical studies report different spellings for Carstairs and Marshall (the latter also variously called Jane or Jean), but in this essay I will consistently use the names spelt without the extra vowels, since that is how they appear on the front page of their printed works.

[6]   General information on these authors and their works can be found in, among others, Ralston Inglis, *The Dramatic Writers of Scotland* (Glasgow, 1868); Terence Tobin, *Plays by Scots, 1660–1800* (Iowa City, 1974); Philip H. Highfill, Jr., Kalman A. Burnim and Edward A. Langhans (eds), *A Biographical Dictionary of Actors, Actresses, Musicians, Dancers, Managers & Other Stage Personnel in London, 1660–1800* (Carbondale, [1973–93]); Virginia Blain, Patricia Clements and Isobel Grundy, *The Feminist Companion to Literature in English: Women Writers from the Middle Ages to the Present* (New Haven, CT, 1990); Gwenn Davis and Beverly A. Joyce, *Drama by Women to 1900: A Bibliography*

of their particularly revealing and complex negotiation of the above-mentioned double marginalization effect.

In other words, this essay is an attempt to determine if and how Scottish women playwrights, given their double exclusion from the British theatrical establishment, managed to 'get into the act'. The social stakes for achieving this were very high, since 'getting into the act' often involved substantial and subversive critiques of social, political and ideological structures established to limit women's rights and personal identities, including the creation of a domestic ideology that conceived anything 'public' as improper to a lady.[7] It was therefore necessary for women dramatists to develop forms of negotiations with the theatrical and the publishing worlds, and to accept compromises in order to have a play printed, even only by subscription, or, if they were lucky, performed.

Being a woman and a Scot enhanced those difficulties that were in any case inherent in the theatrical career as such. In Jean Marshall's *Sir Harry Gaylove*, the Prologue, by the contemporary blind poet Dr Blacklock, humorously alludes to this 'scandal' from the very beginning:

> May one in conscience credit what you say?
> A Scotch production! Heaven and earth! a play!
> What mortal prov'd so hardy to achieve it?
> Repeat your tale to such as will believe it.
> …
> This night, you say, the critics may abuse
> A Female Comedy, a Virgin Muse.
> Luxurious scandal, let me join the fray,
> In its damnation hiss my breath away;
> Teach native taste and genius to subside,
> And yield the palm to literary pride.[8]

Likewise, the author of the second Prologue, a certain 'Dr M'Clurg' – probably a fictional persona doubling for the author – addresses the audience ('Belles' and

---

of American and British Writers (Toronto, 1992); David D. Mann and Susan Garland Mann (eds), with Camille Garnier, *Women Playwrights in England, Ireland and Scotland, 1660–1823* (Bloomington and Indianapolis, 1996); Leslie Stephen and Sidney Lee (eds) *Dictionary of National Biography*, 22 vols, (London, 1908–1909); Margaret Drabble (ed.) *The Oxford Companion to English Literature*, (Oxford, 2006); Scullion, 'Some Women of the Nineteenth-Century Scottish Theatre'.

[7]   That women did not often conform to this prescribed paradigm and had, on the contrary, a strong impact on the formation of public opinion, is testified by the popularity of Richard Polwhele's satirical poem on the influential women authors and artists of the day 'The Unsex'd Females' (1798).

[8]   Jean Marshall, 'Prologue by Dr Blacklock', in *Sir Harry Gaylove; or, Comedy in Embryo. In five Acts* (Edinburgh, 1772), p. [xi] (in fact the page is unnumbered).

'Beaux'), the 'crusty' critics and, implicitly, the censors in apparently patronizing words testifying indirectly to the hostility women generally met when they attempted a literary career. The language used to describe the author is effusive in an intentionally stereotyped style, according to the clichéd icon of the 'sweet poetess', virtuous and gracious, that would become popular later in the century:

For your protection, Sirs, a Lady sues;
Which of you can a Lady's pray'rs refuse?
O! think—if hardy man, by nature brave,
When he turns author, trembles like a slave;
If, the first night his blood cold fear congeals;
O! think what gentle female softness feels![9]

Although she may seem to succumb to the conventional stereotype of the weak female 'poetess', Marshall actually turns her seemingly humble preface and prologues into stinging attacks on male critics and their gendered resistance to women authors.

For Marshall, Wallace, Carstairs, Dods and Wright, as for many other women writing between the passing of the Licensing Act and the Dramatic Literature Act, the stage became a space for conveying underlying political ideas and a new historical consciousness, in which the conflict between 'public' ethics and the ambiguous and contradictory 'domestic ideology' plays a fundamental part.[10] In most cases these social and cultural critiques emerge in generally – albeit often feigningly – self-submissive introductory discourses and prefaces, in which the female authors can hide their audaciousness behind remorseful tones and obsequious attitudes, while in fact they are confronting such topics as the oppression of women, monarchy and state religion, imperialism and colonialism, sexual roles, the mind and the self in relation to society, female (mis)education, and literary and moral censorship.

---

[9]   Jean Marshall, 'Prologue by Dr M'Clurg', in ibid., p. [xii] (the page is also unnumbered).

[10]   My view of 'the doctrine of the separate sphere' is indebted to Anne Mellor's study of women's political writing and involvement in the public sphere in *Mother of the Nations: Women's Political Writing in England, 1780–1830* (Bloomington and Indianapolis, 2000). As she clarifies from the introduction, 'if women participated fully in the discursive public sphere and in the formation of public opinion in Britain by the late eighteenth century, then the assumption that there existed a clear distinction in historical practice between a realm of public, exclusively male activities and a realm of private, exclusively female activities in this period is also erroneous. ... It may be time to discard this binary, overly simplistic concept of separate sexual spheres altogether in favour of a more nuanced and flexible conceptual paradigm that foregrounds the complex intersection of class, religious, racial, and gender differences in this historical period' (p. 7).

All the key issues involved, however, can best be explored by attending to the performative quality of these women's plays. As Catherine Burroughs suggests, 'women turned to theatre as a medium for recording their responses to their experiences as women on both cultural and theatrical stages'.[11] Contrary to a shared commonplace, a large number of women's plays written between the 1760s and the 1830s do prove apt for the stage, and were, in many cases, intended for the professional stage. Given their general exclusion from public sphere politics, women often use the theatre to dramatize their own conflicts between the pressure to conform to a domestic ideology and the imperative to engage in public issues. As Marjean Purinton observes,

> Frequently, political issues are debated in the domestic spaces of a play and staged as meta-theatrics or meta-dramatics … Through meta-theatrics, the risky public nature of women's presence could be safely enclosed within the structure of a drama in which women perform socially accepted domestic roles. … As a strategy with gender-specific ideological implications, meta-theatrics enable women playwrights to stage subversive public-sphere performances … For female dramatists and performers whose public presence was complicated by separate-sphere ideology, meta-dramatics offered a conceptual disguise for their engagements with public (masculinist) issues, a framework within which they could stage transgressions and subversions (or compliances with and endorsements) of dominant cultural practices.[12]

In other words, women's texts often retain a performative or, better, self-performative dimension, which becomes particularly interesting in those plays that were never actually staged. In staging, for example, the issue of forced marriages, as in, for instance, Eglantine Wallace's *Diamond Cut Diamond* (1787), not only do they cause the blurring of the boundaries between the public and private spaces, but they also perform and question their own role and place within contemporary society by hiding behind the masks of fictive characters. However, various mechanisms obscured the real meaning of these plays: first, censorship on the part of critics, theatre managers and committees; and secondly, various forms of self-censorship necessary to have the plays performed or sometimes just published. These restrictions were particularly encumbering for women, and, as we said earlier, even more so for Scottish women. Hence their resorting to specific 'survival' strategies in order to make a breach into the world of theatre.

---

[11]   Catherine Burroughs, 'Teaching the Theory and Practice of Women's Dramaturgy', *Romanticism on the Net*, 12 (November 1998), at: http://www.erudit.org/revue/ron/1998/v/n12/005823ar.html, accessed November 1998.

[12]   Marjean D. Purinton, 'Revising Romanticism by Inscripting Women Playwrights', *Romanticism on the Net*, 12 (November 1998), at: http://www.erudit.org/revue/ron/1998/v/n12/005822ar.html, accessed November 1998.

In Scotland censors were especially severe towards plays containing references or even slight allusions to contemporary politics or recent Scottish history, like the 1745–46 Jacobite Risings. In order to evade the strictures of censorship, some Scottish women playwrights resorted to the masquerading of controversial issues under the guise of dealing with domestic or sentimental themes (for example the 'disguised' topic of racial discrimination in Carstairs' *The Hubble-Shue*); adopted male pseudonyms (as is the case with Dods, who published her *Dramas of the Ancient World* under the pen name of David Lyndsay); or chose anonymous publication (like Porter's *The Fair Fugitives*). Few Scottish female authors, actresses and managers, on the other hand, made a more extreme choice: they exiled themselves voluntarily and attempted a literary career in the New World.

This was the case of Frances Wright. She was born in Dundee in 1795, and at the age of 18 she entered the household of James Mylne, her uncle, one of the most influential philosophers in Scotland at the time. Here she came into contact for the first time with radical intellectual circles, which were later to influence her work and personality. In 1818 she travelled to America with her sister Camilla, and was so impressed by the democracy of the New World that she decided to move there. She became involved in various public undertakings, including the establishment in 1826 of a utopian community in Tennessee aimed to promote racial and sexual freedom, and the editorship in 1828 of the *New Harmony Gazette* founded by Robert Owen. Her liberal ideas constitute the central political message in her tragedy *Altorf* and in the Preface preceding it. The play was premiered (at first anonymously) at the Park Theatre, New York, on 19 February 1819, published in Philadelphia the same year and in London three years later (this time without including the Preface, but with a sarcastic address 'To the Reader' also denouncing the management of the English stage for promoting low-quality works).

Despite the rather conventional plot, indebted to the romances of Scott and the drama of Baillie in its mountain and forest scenarios reminiscent of the Scottish Highlands, the play succeeds as 'an allegory of democracy recounting the frustrations of personal and national bondage and insisting upon the integrity of the individual within society.'[13] *Altorf* is an overtly political play, exhibiting Wright's socialist ideology and her concepts of democracy, human rights and freedom. It is especially in the Preface that she expounds her liberal and democratic thought, using little diplomacy in launching an invective against the contemporary theatre establishment and organization in Britain, recalling Joanna Baillie's observations in the Introductory Discourse to the *Plays on the Passions* (1798):

> It is I believe, generally felt and acknowledged, by the public of Great Britain as of America, that the dignity of English tragedy has now degenerated into pantomime; and that rapid movements, stage tricks and fine scenery have filled the place of poetry, character, and passion. The construction as well as the management of London Theatres perhaps present insurmountable obstacles to

---

13   Scullion, 'Some Women of the Nineteenth-Century Scottish Theatre', p. 170.

any who might there [have the] ambition to correct the fashion of the stage. No such difficulties exist here. America is the land of liberty. Here is a country where Truth may lift her voice without fear; – where the words of Freedom may not only be read in the closet, but heard from the stage ... there is not a stage in England from which the dramatist might breath the sentiments of enlightened patriotism and republican liberty. In America alone might such a stage be formed; a stage that should be, like that of Greece, a school of virtue; – where all that is noble in sentiment, generous and heroic in action should speak to the hearts of free people, and inspire each rising generation with all the better and noble feelings of human nature.[14]

It is interesting to note that Wright equates stage and political limitations by showing how the American, unlike the British, stage is not confined to scenic extravaganza and, being exempt from censorship, can become a site for the expression of radical politics. If this were really the case, one might wonder why Wright resorts to a *Verfremdung* strategy, or temporal and geographical dislocation, to confront contemporary political issues. This might be explained in part by the Romantic fascination for and revival of medieval history, together with the opportunity offered by this form of estrangement to bestow a universal value on local historical episodes. As Wright explains in the 'Advertisement', the play recounts '[T]he story of the insurrection of the Swiss Cantons in the fourteenth century; the violent and wanton tyranny exercised by Austria and her Deputies over that intrepid race of Mountaineers'.[15] Nonetheless, the Cantons' battles for independence are a clear historical transposition of the United States' War of Independence, as well as an image of political and ideological struggle against tyrannical power, imperialist rule and anti-democratic actions in general, including the despotism of father figures putting political duties before emotional bonds.[16]

The historical setting acts as a backdrop to the story of a love triangle, namely the dilemma of the young soldier Eberard de Altorf, torn between his passionate love for Rosina, the daughter of a Swiss Royalist, and his filial duty to marry Giovanna, the daughter of a Swiss Republican belonging to his father's party. By focusing on the opposition between the more rational, devoted Giovanna and the passionate, rebellious Rosina, Wright introduces a feminist theme in line with radical ideas on 'illegitimate' love liaisons and the abolition of marriage constraints. Though aware of Altorf's attachment to another woman, Giovanna insists on his respecting the codes of honour both in marriage and in war, while the subversive heroine Rosina reclaims his love and aspires to fulfilling her personal desires regardless of his public responsibilities. Without diminishing the stoic

---

[14] Frances Wright, 'Preface', *Altorf* (Philadelphia, 1819).

[15] Frances Wright, 'Advertisement', *Altorf* (London, 1822), pp. vii–viii, at p. vii.

[16] Jane Porter also deals with the theme of liberty in her play *Switzerland*, performed once at the Drury Lane on 15 February 1819 after Edmund Kean's wife, Mary, interceded in her favour.

heroism of the protagonists, the tragic denouement – the two clandestine lovers are discovered and finally kill themselves – shows that those social and political bonds cannot be readily undone.[17]

Frances Wright, however, is somewhat exceptional within the panorama of late eighteenth- and early nineteenth-century Scottish women playwrights. Most of them were forced to make compromises imposed by state censors, but they were, nevertheless, able to develop innovative 'survival strategies' to unleash their social critique in modified forms. For example, Jean Marshall published her play *Sir Harry Gaylove* by subscription thanks to the support of distinguished men of letters such as, among others, James Boswell, Dr. Beattie, Wes Digges, David Hume, Lord Lyttleton and Adam Smith. It is regrettable that the play was never staged, but at least she managed to promote it through print and to bring it to the attention of eminent intellectuals.

Though our knowledge of Marshall's life remains limited, some significant facts emerge from Henry Mackenzie's letters to Elizabeth Rose of Kilravock.[18] The exact dates of her birth and death are missing, but we know that she was born in Edinburgh, that she lived many years in London, and that her most productive phase falls between 1765 and 1788 (respectively the years of publication of her first novel, *The History of Miss Clarinda Cathcart, and Miss Fanny Renton*, and of *A Series of Letters for the Improvement of Youth*).[19] Whereas her novels met a favourable reception, her only play, *Sir Harry Gaylove, or Comedy in Embryo* (1772) was rejected by all the theatre managers she contacted. Like Wright, Marshall wrote a Preface that can be read as an important document of cultural

---

[17]   In fact, Wright married the French Owenite Phiquepal D'Arusmont since she was expecting his child. The marriage did not work, however, and she had to face a whole series of legal complications in order not to lose her entire property and win the custody of their daughter. Indeed, no definite agreement had been achieved at her death in 1852.

[18]   See Henry Mackenzie, *Letters to Elizabeth Rose of Kilravock, on Literature, Events and People 1768–1815*, ed. Horst W. Drescher (Edinburgh and London, 1967), pp. 18, 21, 72, 117–20, and Leslie Stephen and Sidney Lee (eds), *Dictionary of National Biography*, 22 vols (London, 1908–1909), vol. 12, p. 1124, where the play is judged 'a poor and amateurish piece, written like her novels under the influence of Richardson'. Mackenzie's opinion of Marshall's work, instead, is very high. Talking about the novel, he writes, 'it is a Sort of Composition which I observe the Scottish Genius is remarkably deficient in; except Smollett, & one female Author' (p. 18). The identity of this 'female Author' is revealed in the following letter: 'The Lady I meant is Miss Marshall who has wrote the Histories of Clarinda Cathcart, & Alicia Montague ... and has lately produc'd a Comedy also, which, if I am not mistaken, is now accepted of at Covent Garden' (p. 21). Unfortunately he was mistaken.

[19]   Marshall wrote two novels, *The History of Miss Clarinda Cathcart, and Miss Fanny Renton* (1766) and *The History of Alice Montague* (1767), both strongly beholden to Richardson's fiction but staging much stronger and more venturesome heroines. *A Series of Letters* is an important, and overlooked, contribution to eighteenth-century women's involvement in educational reforms and humanitarian activities.

and social history, a crucial testimony to the destiny awaiting most texts by women playwrights. It documents her determination to have her play performed, describing how unyielding the theatre authorities were and how eventually she lost her battle against the prejudiced theatre managers of Drury Lane, Covent Garden and the Edinburgh theatre.

Marshall complains in her Preface, among other things, that 'Mr Garrick, without reading the play, said he had more new ones in his hand then he could possibly bring on the stage for a number of years'.[20] Similar negative responses came from Mr Dagg, one of the patentees for Covent Garden Theatre; Mr Foote, then the manager of the Edinburgh Theatre (to whom she offers to make any changes he wants as long as they are not 'unbecoming one of her sex to write'[21]); and Foote's successor Mr Digges, who deemed the comedy 'deficient in both plot and character', thus ill-suited to the Edinburgh stage.[22] Despite these negative responses, Marshall asserts in the Preface that the play was written to be staged, adding that 'it may still be doubtful, whether it would have succeeded or not; it not being always the case, that the plays they do bring on either deserve or meet with the approbation of the public'.[23] Finally she reports the judgements of the two gentlemen who read her comedy, both utterly confuting the opinions of the theatre managers, even if in somewhat paternalistic terms: of these, Lord Chesterfield's evaluation is particularly revealing where he states that 'the dialogue, the sentiments and the moral of the play do honour to a virgin-muse'.[24] As her request to Foote shows, gender plays a central role in Marshall's experience: despite her overt recrimination against the contemporary theatre establishment, she did not intend to lose her feminine status but, on the contrary, aimed to prove how that status was not at all conflicting with dramatic production, even if it involved public exposure.

Another significant case of conflict with the theatre managers is that of Eglantine Wallace, who had her comedy *The Whim* printed in 1795, after it had been prohibited from the stage by the royal licenser because of its anti-aristocratic sentiments and unflattering allusions to the Regent's mistress, Lady Jersey.[25] The play is preceded by an acrimonious 'Address to the public' condemning the

---

[20] Jean Marshall, 'Preface', in *Sir Harry Gaylove; or, Comedy in Embryo. In Five Acts* (Edinburgh, 1772), pp. iii–x, at p. iv. The play does not report the author's name, but simply 'by the Author of Clarinda Cathcart, and Alicia Montague'.

[21] Ibid., p. vii.

[22] Ibid., p. viii.

[23] Ibid., p. ix.

[24] Ibid., p. x. This letter is included in *The Letters of Philip Dormer Stanhope, 4th Earl of Chesterfield*, ed. Bonamy Dobrée, 6 vols (London, 1932), vol. 6, p. 2936.

[25] Cf. Tobin, *Plays by Scots, 1660–1800*, p. 185. The Larpent manuscript in the Huntington Library (San Marino, California) reports the prohibition on the first page ('prohibited from being acted', LA. 1093) while the censored passages are underlined.-

injustice she had suffered. Her attitude is unusually direct and daring for a woman of her time:

> Whatever motives the Licenser may have, for giving a preference to particular people, he has no right to affix odium to the reputation of any individual, by such unjust and injurious remarks ... wherever power may be placed, I defy those who enjoy it, to possess a more honourable and heart-felt attachment to the British Constitution, than I do ... [A]s to the Comedy, or its authoress, being branded with the suspicion of *exceptionable principles*; I am totally indifferent to that. – Let him, who has more sound principles, him who has more independent ones, him, who has done more to prove the rectitude of his opinions and actions, censure; but, until such appear in the lists to disapprove; I shall rest satisfied with self-approbation.[26]

Wallace intended to devolve earnings from the performances to the poor, a fact that, to her eyes, made the Licenser's rejection even meaner and more indicative of the restrictiveness and conservatism of English constitutional laws, hostile towards any form of social improvement and towards liberal views (symbolized in the comedy by the switching of roles between the social classes and in particular by the nobles' surrender of their titles). Wallace's belief in the didactic as well as the political function of the stage emerges clearly when she writes,

> The Stage is the only school which overgrown boys and girls can go to, and did the Licenser permit more satire, more sentiment, and less ribaldry, *outré* pantomime, and folly, to appear under his auspices, it would be doing the State more service, than thus taking the alarm at The Whim of renewing the Saturnalia Feast'.[27]

Throughout the Address she displays an atypical 'un-woman-like' interest in satire aimed at denouncing public degeneration and corruption, 'private slanders', 'falsehood', 'the rascality of some News-paper Devil', in short all the 'follies of the age'.[28]

Given that the censors' strictures were often related to particular theatrical genres that, like satire, were deemed improper to a lady, one of the ways in which Scottish women dramatists sought to avoid the establishment's denunciation was the adoption of hybrid forms and trans-generic modes. The disruptive commixture of farcical and dramatic elements in Carstairs's *The Hubble-Shue* is a significant example of this tendency. *The Hubble-Shue* is a piece of sheer eccentricity, like most of the things its rather obscure author produced, including her *Original Poems* published in Edinburgh in 1786, marked by the same oddities characterizing her

---

26 Eglantine Wallace, 'Address to the Public', in *The Whim*, pp. 3–18, at pp. 4–9.
27 Ibid., p. 14.
28 Ibid., p. 17.

quirky 'playlet', as Tobin defines it.[29] Edwin Morgan describes the farce as 'a bizarre, anarchic comedy, more like Jarry or Ionesco than *Douglas* or *The Gentle Shepherd*'; in other words, ex-centric in relation to the canonical Scottish theatrical tradition, and more in line with future developments in drama.[30] According to Mann and Garland Mann it was performed in Edinburgh in 1786, but no details of the playhouse or the duration of the production are given.[31] Unfortunately the contemporary press, the playbills of the Edinburgh theatres, James C. Dibdin's *Annals of the Edinburgh Stage* (1888) and general studies on Scottish theatre do not provide any evidence for Mann and Garland Mann's reference.[32] What we know for sure is that Carstairs managed to publish both her poems and her play thanks to the support of members of the upper-class, which explains her dedication of *The Hubble-Shue* 'To the Honourable Antiquarian Society'.[33]

Whether it was produced or not, however, Carstairs's apparently ludicrous fragment-play[34] is worthy of discussion not only because it qualifies as an *ante-litteram* example of the theatre of the absurd, owing to its inconsequential speeches, eccentric (often illogical) dialogues, and almost incomprehensible storyline and situation, but especially because, amidst its general confusion (by no coincidence

---

[29]   Tobin, *Plays by Scots, 1660–1800*, pp. 69–70.

[30]   Edwin Morgan, *Scottish Drama: an Overview*, *ScotLit*, 20 (Spring 1999), at: www.arts.gla.ac.uk/ScotLit/ASLS/Scottishdrama.html, accessed October 2009, pp. 1–12, at p. 4.

[31]   The author entry for Carstairs mentions that the play was produced in Edinburgh in 1786, whereas the text entry for *The Hubble-Shue* seems to contradict this when it reports: 'It seems unlikely that this farce could have been produced' – *Women Playwrights in England, Ireland and Scotland, 1660–1823*, p. 177.

[32]   For example Robb Lawson, *The Story of the Scots Stage* (Paisley, 1917), and Bill Findlay (ed.), *A History of Scottish Theatre* (Edinburgh, 1998).

[33]   The Society of Antiquaries of Scotland was founded by another Scottish eccentric, David Erskine, Eleventh Earl of Buchan, in 1780; he intended, among other things, to open a museum of antiquities, having been himself an enthusiastic collector all his life. Both the Faculty of Advocates and the University of Edinburgh, however, objected to the idea because they feared that it might have competed with their own collections. This is an interesting detail, entitling us to interpret the play as an anti-establishment work challenging the cultural status quo.

[34]   It is composed of two short scenes: it starts *in medias res* and ends abruptly, as if there were one final part missing. The *dramatis personae* are not listed, and in some cases they are just indicated by an initial or a title (like 'M.' and 'Mrs—'). On the other hand, considering its brevity, the play abounds in stage directions, though insufficient to determine the setting. Nothing really happens in the play, except, as Mann and Garland Mann sum up, a 'talk at cross purposes' between eccentric characters who do not listen to one another; 'a discussion of the author's poetry that moves on to a wacky dinner party whose participants finally adjourn to the theatre where events end in a wild melee', or, in other words, a general 'hubble-shue' – see *Women Playwrights in England, Ireland and Scotland, 1660–1823*, pp. 177–8.

echoed in the title, a Scots word for uproar, commotion and riot[35]) it encompasses three very interesting features: first, the use of metatheatrical devices and self-inscription by which Carstairs can have herself performed; second, a critique of the contemporary theatrical establishment and, more generally, a satire on pseudo-intellectual circles; and finally, a racial issue cleverly encapsulated within a sentimental narrative.

The first feature becomes especially apparent in the opening and in the denouement of the play, both paradigmatically absurd. After an *in-medias-res* overture in which two anonymous characters and a mysterious Lady Gundie make use of unidentifiable anaphoric references to indicate a 'she' and a 'he' engaged in some obscure relationship, the two unnamed characters at least add some clearer information about the 'she':

> *N.*
> No—no—he was in no passion. For God's sake let us hear some of her poems.
> *M.*
> Her poems!—some of them are pretty—enough to be sure—and feeling—as one might say, (takes a great snuff). But, for the dramatic piece, certainly never was any thing so ridiculous.[36]

The dramatist Carstairs is at her best in self-ironic passages such as this, when she implicitly shows her awareness of the critical responses that her bizarre writing provoked, possibly undisturbed by the fiercest critiques coming especially from male readers who approved of women writing 'pretty' poems but regarded their unconventional plays as 'ridiculous'. Carstairs parodies these critics while at the same time suggesting that the insanity of her little play was deliberate and not due to a lack of writing skills on her part.

The second feature, metatheatre, materializes at the end of the play, when the weird characters move from the dinner party to the playhouse to see a performance. It is probably from this tumultuous finale that the play derives its

---

[35] In Alexander Warrack, *A Scots Dialect Dictionary, Comprising the Words in Use from the Latter Part of the Seventeenth Century to the Present Day* (London, 1911), the expression 'hubble-show' (also spelt 'hubble-shew' and 'hubble-shoo') occurs on p. 275 and is denoted as 'hubbub, tumult'. It also appears as one word on p. 266, variously spelt as 'hobbleshow', 'hobbleshaw', 'hobbleshew' and 'hobblishue', and similarly defined as 'tumult, hubbub, commotion, rabble, tumultuous gathering', the last being particularly appropriate for the play. The 1834 edition reports a quote from a poem, 'The Crying of ane Playe', attributed to the medieval Scottish poet William Dunbar, which contains this phrase in an older spelling: 'Harry, harry, hobillischowe! / Se quha is cummyn nowe'. Given that Carstairs was a well-educated governess, she was likely to have come across and deliberately chosen this poem.

[36] [Christian Carstairs], *The Hubble-Shue, Dedicated to the Honourable Antiquarian Society* (Edinburgh, 1780), p. 4. This edition was published anonymously.

title: a Mr Woods comes on the stage to announce that, because of an accident, the play must be postponed for half an hour; a Mrs Kennedy tries to make up for the inconvenience by singing a song, but the audience responds badly by protesting it is 'poor entertainment'[37] and by throwing oranges at the hapless performers till everything ends up in a general hubbub in a parodic gothic setting ('a dreadful storm—a dark night—a Nabob's carriage driving like Jehu—the coachman being drunk overturns one of the hackneys ...'[38]).

One wonders whether it is Carstairs's farce that is being performed, so that the play within the play not only offers her an opportunity to critique ironically the degeneration of contemporary theatre into low-quality forms of entertainment, but also functions as another ploy to inscribe herself in the play and use self-mockery as a means of sneering at her detractors. Her lampoon is addressed not only to the theatrical establishment but, more generally, to the intellectual and literary circles of the time. During the dinner party, the characters, obviously belonging to the upper class,[39] entertain themselves in a conversation on trivial matters, their speeches seeming to deny all cooperative principles; at a certain point the Fat Minister asks his daughter to sing an Italian song, which turns out to be pure gibberish – an allusion to the contemporary Scottish mania of importing Italian singers.

The third noteworthy aspect of the farce, the racial and colonial issue, emerges when Mrs Consul's grandchild is frightened after hearing the little black girl's tale:

> **Child.** The little girl says a great fish (a crocodile) came out of the water (the Ganges) and devoured her father—and a fine gentleman came running with a sword and stab'd the monster—and her father was all bloody, and she would have been killed; but the fine gentleman took her away, and they were carried by black mans with muslin on their head (turbans)—and the fine gentleman gave her to a great lady—All the fine things could not make her forget her poor father—He was very hungry, and as she lay on his arm, beneath the tree where the ugly monster came, he was giving her a little rice—it is all—the last—morsel.[40]

Who is this little black girl? In her innocent imagination the Briton snatching her from her father becomes a monstrous crocodile, while the gentleman consigning her to the 'great lady' is seen as her saviour. In spite of the context of children's talk, the underlying message is clear: the sentimental narrative encloses the subplot representing all those Indian girls carried to Britain to be trained as maids

---

[37] Ibid., p. 13.

[38] Ibid., p. 14.

[39] Among the characters, there is Lady Gundie (the Lady of the House), a Fat Minister and a Colonel.

[40] [Carstairs], *The Hubble-Shue*, p. 10.

or servants. This allegory becomes even more unsettling for a Scottish audience aware of the strong Scottish presence in Britain's Indian Empire. This was probably one of the reasons why *The Hubble Shue* had no success on the stage.

Tobin regards Carstairs as 'a likely candidate for the most *outré* dramatist of the century', and similarly Maidment recognizes her creativeness when he writes, 'If originality be a test of genius, the authoress of the *Hubble-Shue* bids fair to rank highest amongst the dramatic writers of the last century.'[41] Some of these judgements may sound hyperbolic when we read the play, but the significance of certain passages cannot be denied, so much so that one wonders what impact they could have had on the audience if they had been performed, since *The Hubble Shue* was certainly conceived as a production to be staged, aiming to rouse in the public the same kind of disturbance that its dramatic fiction enacts.

Social and cultural critique is a *fil rouge* running through many of these Scottish texts. In some cases, as with Carstairs, this critique is not always veiled but recurs more openly and forcefully through strategic treatments of certain topics that were acceptable for women to address publicly. For example, a central preoccupation in some plays is a concern with moral education, or the aim to produce a drama in accordance with the precepts established by Mme de Genlis in her *Théâtre à l'usage des jeunes personnes* (1779, translated in 1781) and exemplified in her own plays. This is why so many women playwrights recurrently use the word 'virtue' in their works; in order, that is, to prove that the very feminine value men thought endangered if women were to become professional writers could be reiterated and ironically enhanced by becoming a central *leitmotif* of their works.[42] In other words, some female writers realized that they could avail themselves of the prescriptions of the conduct books in order to facilitate their forays into the publishing world, even if it involved their upholding of the dominant masculinist discourse and their explicit acceptance of certain stereotypes it attached to them. Jean Marshall, as I will shortly endeavour to demonstrate, made a complex contribution to the contemporary debates on female virtue and education by reversing the feminist perspective of those who wished women's education to be more like men's, and showing instead that men's education should perhaps become more similar to women's.

Likewise, the heroines in Eglantine Wallace's *The Ton*, in particular Lady Raymond and Lady Clairville, as the author's Prologue explicitly underlines,

---

[41]   Tobin, *Plays by Scots, 1660–1800*, p. 70; James Maidment, 'Introductory Notice', in [Carstairs], *The Hubble-Shue*, pp. 3–10, at p. 3.

[42]   What Anne Mellor writes about Baillie's, Cowley's, More's and Inchbald's heroines can also be applied to the virtuous women staged by some of these Scottish playwrights: 'these powerful female dramatists and their characters assertively occupy the discursive public sphere in order to stage intellectually and emotionally persuasive versions of a New Woman, a rational, just, yet compassionate, benevolent, and peace-loving woman, the person best suited to govern the new British nation' – *Mother of the Nations*, p. 68.

personify virtue whereas most of the men, especially the exponents of the 'Ton',[43] are shown as corrupt and vicious, prone to excess and lack of self-control. The female characters in this comedy embody the civilizing force chastening and then amending the 'follies' of men, 'Some trifling faults, perhaps intriguing, gaming, / Pride, and the like ...',[44] which the author intends to sanction. Addressing the audience she declares:

> ... She fights for *you* and *virtue*;
> Ye great, support her! – for she cannot *hurt* you;
> Ye rich, ye poor; above, below the laws,
> Applaud her, and promote the common cause;
> And, if there live who still disgrace the age,
> Bid them *revere* the vengeance of the *stage*.[45]

Women's righteousness was clearly one of those themes that female playwrights could safely explore. What is particularly remarkable in Wallace is that her gendered promotion of female virtue delivers an even stronger form of social critique in its attacks on social norms and its flattening out of social distinctions – the stress on the 'common cause' must have conveyed a pointedly radical import in 1788, when the play was performed.

The marriage-motif, with all its implications and variants, represented another innocuous field for women, reflecting the requirements of the contemporary domestic ideology. In none of the plays under discussion marriage is condemned *per se* or in its institutional value, not even in *Altorf*, whose author, as has been mentioned, publicly denied its sanctity in favour of liberated liaisons. At the same time, most of the playwrights resort to a sentimental discourse allowing them to set marriage based on love against a convenient and connived union, while, in reality, their ultimate aim may very well be to pour forth another invective against contemporary social restraints and gender discrimination.

For example, in Marshall's *Sir Harry Gaylove* Mr. Godfrey, the heroine's father, wants her to accept a marriage proposal from the wealthy Bobby Leeson, but whereas he insists on fortune and beauty as essential requirements in marriage, she believes that there could never exist any matrimonial bond without reciprocal

---

[43]   A group of rich, fashionable aristocrats with loose morals and addiction to gambling.

[44]   Eglantine Wallace, *The Ton; or the Follies of Fashion. A Comedy as it was acted at the Theatre Royal, Covent Garden* (London, 1788), p. i. The play ran for three nights. The Larpent Manuscript (nr. 801) in the Huntington Library presents numerous corrections and cancellations but just slight differences compared to the first published edition. At the end of the Preface Wallace points out that the staged version presented some alterations compared to the printed one, and that those alterations – that is, speeches deleted from the stage script – are here marked by inverted commas.

[45]   Ibid., p. ii.

affection. Ophelia's wish to find a man with more sense and honesty than wit is an image of late eighteenth-century women's claim for free choice within a gender-based (and biased) social establishment and for enfranchisement from tyrannical or simply authoritarian and unsentimental fathers, like the General in Wallace's *Diamond Cut Diamond*, who expects his daughter, Lucy, to marry a man she has never seen just because he is an affluent sea-captain. The sentimental plot, in other words, is a means for disguising their subversive engagement with important contemporary issues.[46]

Indeed Marshall's *Sir Harry Gaylove*, like her novels, is remarkably, and often unimaginatively, indebted to Richardson and the eighteenth-century sentimental tradition. However, it presents a few interesting themes in relation to women's negotiation strategies and inscribed self-performance. The central freedom/imprisonment leitmotif is not just a narrative expedient to render the intrigue more appealing and create *coups de theatre*. We know from Marshall's *A Series of Letters* (Edinburgh, 1788) and from some passing remarks in her novels (always cleverly meshed with the rather conventional romantic plot) that she espoused anti-monarchic ideas in favour of bourgeois values, and that she critiqued women's virtual enslavement in connived marriages and the false allure of safe domesticity, as well as the arrogance of patriarchal culture.

Another central theme of the play is a further example of women playwrights' use of the metatheatrical devices in order to stage their personal struggle to assert their voice in the literary world. Belfour's effort to have his comedy accepted by the theatre managers, as well as his unavoidable dealings with an influential person in the field, is clearly a ploy to stage the painful part Marshall had to perform in real life in order to convince the theatre magnates that her play was meant to be staged. When Belfour asks Sir Harry, 'Do you think I shall have interest to bring it on the stage?', and the latter replies, 'That depends on its merit … ',[47] Marshall is clearly being ironic, knowing very well from her personal experience that for a play to be staged merit was not a primary issue at all. When in Act III Belfour visits Lord Evergreen to enquire about his comedy, and he instructs his employer Lecky to tell him he has not read it yet, one immediately recalls Marshall's account of Garrick's neglect of her play in the Preface.[48]

If anonymity and pseudonymity on the stage of real life, in a sense, reinforce the paradigm of women's neglected authorship and inability to assert an independent voice, on the theatrical stage these Scottish women playwrights perform or imagine various types of female empowerment. One way of achieving this is to resort to

---

[46]   *Diamond Cut Diamond* is an adaptation of the popular French comedy by M. Antoine-Jean Dumaniant, *La Guerre ouverte; or, Ruse contre ruse*. Elizabeth Inchbald also wrote a version of the same play entitled *The Midnight Hour* (1787).

[47]   Marshall, *Sir Harry Gaylove*, Act I, p. 13.

[48]   Unfortunately the fact that the manuscript was lost does not allow us to discover whether she added the reference to a playwright's merit and moulded the character of Evergreen after her bad luck with the managers, just before publishing the comedy.

identity-related ploys or have the *dramatis personae* – both female and male – enact various forms of masquerade and cross-dressing. Effective examples are to be found in Wallace's *Diamond Cut Diamond*. One occurs when the Marquis of Dash reveals to the General his love for his niece Lucy, and the General gives him until midnight to take her out of the house successfully, even though her hand has been promised to a brave sea captain. Lucy is locked in by her uncle and her clothes are taken away, but, helped by the servants, she dresses in male attire and thus manages to escape. At the end of the play, talking to her uncle, Lucy, quite daringly, declares: 'Oh, how I love you, dear uncle, for your goodness—but you must own, that he that wishes to keep a woman against her inclination, attempts an impossibility'.[49]

In another episode the disguising stratagem is used to introduce an identity issue relating not so much to gender as to class. In order to divert the General, Slyboots, the Marquis's valet, dresses in a sea captain's uniform. When the waiting maid sees him, she exclaims: 'My own Slyboots! – Oh, delightful!—Yet I did not know him.—He talked it away, I vow, just like a man of quality.—Aye, to be sure; why he is a valet de chambre—that's next thing to it.—But how came he to pass for the Captain?'[50] This meshing of appearance and reality, fake and genuine identities runs throughout the play. It shows Wallace's consciousness, as a woman, of the performed identities all actors – and especially actresses – on the social stage must play; at the same time, she seems to present models for manipulating these social performances in order to forward women's independence and rights. A related point can be made about Dods's *Dramas*, where female empowerment is particularly personified by the rebellious and strong Semronda in *The Deluge* and by the eponymous heroine Rizpah – both images of the author's own personal endeavour to become an independent writer.

The interrelations between (self-)performativity and gender, combined with the issue of Scottishness, find a unique exemplification in the life and work of Mary Diana Dods.[51] What is still missing and worth recovering is especially an examination of her *Dramas* and of the difficulties she confronted in publishing them, not to mention her peculiar form of rebellion against gender discrimination and, at the same time, her complex negotiations with the kind of gender restrictions imposed on her female contemporaries by the masculine literary and theatrical worlds.

Dods' 'invisibility' as a woman, in fact, allowed her to establish a rich network of relationships with several eminent representatives of the publishing industry and the literary world, such as, among others, William Blackwood, John Wilson, Henry Mackenzie, William Gifford, Charles Ollier and Leigh Hunt. This is quite

---

49   Eglantine Wallace, *Diamond Cut Diamond; A Comedy in Two Acts, Translated from the French of Guerre Ouverte, ou Ruse Contre Ruse* (London, 1787), p. 58.

50   Ibid., p. 39.

51   See Betty T. Bennett, *Mary Diana Dods: A Gentleman and a Scholar* (New York, 1991).

a surprising achievement for a self-taught woman of that time, excluded, like most women of her generation, from higher education, but undoubtedly extremely knowledgeable in ancient and modern literature (she dedicates her Dramas 'to the Manes of Eschylus'), and well-versed in foreign languages, as is shown by the numerous intertextual references in her works and her laudable translations from German and French. However, one cannot overlook the fact that, by adopting a male pseudonym, Dods managed to divert the critics from the issue of gender. They would therefore publish favourable reviews of her *Dramas* and recognize her merits without ever suspecting she might be hiding behind a fictive mask, thus fuelling her literary ambition to become, as she writes, 'one of the stars of the Constellation Maga'.[52] In a letter to William Blackwood, which she signs as David Lyndsay, she compares herself to Byron and quite boastfully asserts, 'Years are before me for I am junior to my Lord Byron by several ..., but it shall be my ambition to make them [the critics] speak of me, and my future exertions rise higher than the past'.[53] One is left to wonder what those reviews would have been like if her male performance had been discovered.

Being an illegitimate daughter, Dods had no hereditary rights, but – contrary to what many women of her generation and in her position would have done – not content with earning a living by private teaching, taking in lodgers or running a school for girls, she decided instead to consecrate her life to writing. Aware of the discrimination that affected women's self-establishment in the literary market, the adoption of a masculine authorial persona was for her the only means of making her foray into that prejudicial world, and she succeeded, at least for some time. In fact, Dods's case shows that Scottishness did not necessarily hold back men in the literary and theatrical world, and that it served more as a gender tool to reinforce the literary and social subordination of women. Once she adopted a male Scottish persona, she manages to negotiate her way through the Scottish publishing world fairly well, though still with some limitations.[54]

In a letter to Blackwood dated 17 July 1826, the mysterious correspondent 'Isobel Douglas' provides a straightforward justification of her adoption of a male pseudonym in her writing: 'You are not to think it strange that I invariably assume the person of a gentleman in all I write, but in truth I do not think women gain much by being known as writers even in this age of universal charity. I have placed the signature "Lilla" to all I have written merely to distinguish them from the more and better written pieces of my husband'.[55] Considering Dods's proneness to play with her own identity, it could be that behind 'Isobel' there is once more

---

[52] *Blackwood Papers*, National Library of Scotland, MS 4007, fol. 77.

[53] Ibid., fol. 78.

[54] Even Joanna Baillie, the most acclaimed dramatist of her time, was sometimes victim of such discriminatory attitudes, as proves the following statement included in an anonymous review of her *Dramas of the Ancient World*: 'Joanna Baillie is a woman, and thence weak in many things' – *Blackwood's Magazine*, vol. 56/10 (December 1821): 731.

[55] *Blackwood Papers*, National Library of Scotland, MS 4016, fol. 253v.

Mary Diana in disguise, this time as the wife of the would-be diplomat Walter Sholto Douglas (alias herself). Evidently she felt the need to reveal to the world the reasons for a woman's cross-dressing, either literary or literal, but of course that could only be done by dissimulation in order to keep her own masquerade going. The fact that she was an excellent performer in real life, however, was not enough to secure her the right to be included among the successful writers of the time.

The correspondence between Dods and Blackwood clearly shows that he was very supportive of her work, at least as long as he hoped he would derive some profit from it, but his attitude changed when he realized the *Dramas* were not selling well either in London or Edinburgh. Dods's primary ambition, however, was not so much to see them in print as staged.[56] Evidence of this is provided, for example, by the following letter sent to Blackwood on 3 August 1823:

> I hope my tragedy will make its appearance next season, but I am by no means certain. It requires so much interest to get it played – more bowing and submission I believe than I shall ever pay to these Theatrical Monarchs. Charles Young has charge of it at present, and his opinion is very favourable to me, but though they have taken it, I shall find it hard and disagreeable work to 'butter' all the actors and actresses. They are an independent set of people, and have to be call'd on to grant favors to their betters.[57]

In addition to the impediments she underlines here – the negotiations and compromises that Dods, contrary to other women playwrights, did not want to comply with –, it cannot be denied that the *Dramas* could not satisfy the expectations of the contemporary audience, in search of entertainment either in the form of spectacular gothic theatre or in that of amusing and unchallenging pantomimes and harlequinades. It is quite indicative that most reviewers would refer to the *Dramas* as laudable poetry – not drama or, still less, theatre. In other words, Dods's plays were read as closet or mental theatre, unsuited to the stage because too sophisticated and erudite – a judgement that inevitably links us back to the generally accepted idea among the Romantics that 'high drama' is not to be performed. Byron shared this view, yet he never clearly declared that he did not want his own dramas to be staged. The reference to Byron is not 'accidental'.

---

[56]   Dods was a regular theatre-goer, as she states in a letter sent to Blackwood in June 1822 in which she offers to start a column on drama criticism: 'I am from being a passionate Lover of the Drama a constant attendant upon the theatres and am in my own person intimately acquainted with the highest rank of Performers by whom I am accounted a good judge' – *Blackwood Papers*, National Library of Scotland, MS 4009, fol. 16.

[57]   Ibid., MS 4010, fol. 234.

'Entirely accidental' is how, on the contrary, in a disclaimer preceding the plays, Dods describes the coincidence between the titles of some of her dramas and Byron's:[58]

> It may be necessary for me to say something respecting the singular coincidence of my having chosen the same subjects as LORD BYRON for two of my Dramas. I entreat permission to assert, and credit when I do assert, that it is entirely accidental: that my Dramas were written long before LORD BYRON's were announced,—before I could have had any idea that his brilliant pen was engaged upon Drama at all. The inferiority of the execution of mine may perhaps lead me to regret that I have selected the same subjects, otherwise I never can lament any coincidence with the admired Author of MANFRED and CHILDE HAROLD.[59]

Likewise, in her several letters to Blackwood she reiterates that her dramas on Sardanapalus and Cain were written long before Byron's works on the same subjects were announced. However trustworthy this may be, Dods's lyrical plays cannot escape the comparison, since Byron's dramas appeared one year earlier and inevitably obscured her success. There are obvious narrative affinities between their versions of the Assyrian King's and Cain's stories, but what is most interesting to notice here is that they are marked by similar self-performative strategies, though they are subtler in Dods's case.

Like Byron, Dods intends to produce 'high drama', as is immediately apparent in her dedication to Eschylus, 'the elder-born of the majestic muse' and 'the great lord of wild sublimity', as well as by her original idea to call the collection 'tragedies of the ancient world', and not 'dramas'.[60] Like Hannah More's *Sacred Dramas* (1782), they mostly deal with biblical themes and characters, except for the last play, *The Nereid's Love*, in which Dods exhibits her classical knowledge and taste for allegorical representation. Each drama is followed by erudite notes referring to the Bible, Greek mythology, Plutarch, rabbinical writing and various historical sources. The texts themselves are fraught with intertextual echoes, but, even more importantly, with significant examples of authorial self-inscription and performance. As in her correspondence with Blackwood, Dods, from behind the mask of 'Lyndsay', reveals a passionate and almost heroic perseverance

---

[58]   The *Dramas of the Ancient World* are eight blank verse dramas: *The Deluge*; *The Plague of Darkness*; *The Last Plague*; *Rizpah*; *Sardanapalus*; *The Destiny of Cain*; *The Death of Cain*; and *The Nereid's Love*.

[59]   David Lyndsay, 'Advertisement', *Dramas of the Ancient World* (Edinburgh, 1822), unpaged.

[60]   Lyndsay, 'Offering to the Manes of Eschylus', *Dramas of the Ancient World*, pp. v–vi. For Dods's intention to call her plays 'tragedies' in accordance with her classical taste, see *Blackwood Papers*, National Library of Scotland, MS 4007, fol. 75. She eventually accepted Blackwood's suggestion agreeing on the fact that to call them 'tragedies' might have been too pretentious.

in her struggle to have her plays published or performed, so in her dramas her masculine temper, rebelliousness and stubbornness are cleverly projected onto the heroes (less frequently, heroines), all somehow fighting for liberty from different forms of tyrannical power, and some condemned to a perpetual wandering and marginalization.

The two Cain dramas and *Sardanapalus* are exemplary in this respect. In the overture of *The Destiny of Cain*, a youth depicts the *villain* as a satanic figure, 'stranger' to all and shunned by all because of its physical deformity, the outer mark of his sin:

> Descend this mountain, for a stranger step
> Pollutes its holiness!—A giant form
> Of demon grandeur doth descend its steep,
> With threatening gestures, and with rolling eyes
> Strain'd and distorted, and his lips with foam
> Are cover'd, and his hair doth stand erect,
> Disclosing on his brow a horrid stain[61]

Although none of the other characters shows any sympathy for the outcast, by having Cain recount how his parents would not reserve the same treatment to him and Abel, Dods seems to unburden him of some responsibility for his evil, thus challenging absolute Manichaeism and turning him into another Frankenstein's Creature. As Bennett shows in her biography, Dods (alias 'Walter Sholto') was well acquainted with Mary Shelley and her work; the comparison may therefore be much more than a pure hypothesis. Like the 'monster', Cain is judged on his appearance, craving for human sympathy and understanding, and regarding woman as a reflection and counterpart of his own nature (the death of his wife Azura is a prelude to his own). Moreover, at the end of the second Cain drama, he confronts his 'creators', Adam and God, in a powerful and highly theatrical scene that calls to our mind the spectacular ending of Mary Shelley's narrative or the Alpine thunderstorms of the Swiss landscape in which she conceived it. Adam asks Heaven to have mercy on the fallen; immediately darkness falls, dramatically broken by thunder and lightning, and Cain disappears in it. Adam's last speech alludes to a final reconciliation through death and divine forgiveness:

> The Eternal hath accorded his sad prayer,
> And with the lightning is his being gone.
> He came in misery into the world,
> In darkness hath departed. Lo! a heap
> Of smoking ashes, on the mouldering bones
> Of the first sleeper lies;—it is the last

---

[61] Lyndsay, 'The Destiny of Cain', *Dramas of the Ancient World*, pp. 177–208, at pp. 181–2.

> Sad remnant of the slayer; …
> … May we to dust
> Commit those ashes? No! the winds of Heaven,
> The breath of the Almighty stirs them from
> Their resting-place, and scatters them abroad.
> Cain's atoms rise,—no more a heap of dust,
> But mingled with creation. Air, earth, water,
> Take each your several offerings![62]

The 'smoking ashes' and 'the mouldering bones' again recall the Creature's self-destruction and final speech at the end of *Frankenstein*, when, before being 'borne away by the waves, and lost in darkness and distance', he pronounces his last words: 'I shall ascend my funeral pile triumphantly, and exult in the agony of the torturing flames. The light of that conflagration will fade away; my ashes will be swept into the sea by the winds. My spirit will sleep in peace; or if it thinks, it will not surely think thus. Farewell'.[63]

If one puts the image of the plagued Cain side by side with the following portrait of the author, further considerations may follow:

> … certainly Nature, in any of its wildest vagaries, never fashioned anything more grotesque-looking than this Miss Dods. She was a woman apparently between thirty and forty years of age, with a cropped curly head of short, thick hair, more resembling that of a man than of a woman … She had … a complexion extremely pale and unhealthy, with that worn and suffering look in her face which so often and so truly—as it did, poor thing, in hers—tells of habitual pain and confirmed ill-health; her figure was short, and, instead of being in proportion, was entirely out of all proportion—the existence of some organic disease aiding this materially … My astonishment at her appearance was unbounded, and I had some difficulty to keep myself from betraying this, and to control the laughter I longed to indulge in; but the charm and fascination of her manner, the extraordinary talent which her conversation, without pedantry or pretence, displayed, soon reconciled me to all the singularities of her appearance … .[64]

Contrary to Cain, Dods deliberately chose concealment from public appearance, yet her anti-hero's abiding inner struggle to overcome guilt and to be accepted by his family and friends echoes her own existential tensions, her effort to come to

---

[62]   Lyndsay, 'The Death of Cain', *Dramas of the Ancient World*, pp. 209–56, at p. 254.

[63]   *Frankenstein or the Modern Prometheus*, in *The Novels and Selected Works of Mary Shelley*, ed. Nora Crook, 8 vols (London, 1996), vol. 1, p. 170.

[64]   Eliza Rennie, *Traits of Character; Being Twenty-Five Years Literary and Personal Recollections, by a Contemporary*, 2 vols (London, 1860), vol. 2, pp. 207–9.

terms with her multiple identity, and her stubborn resolution to be recognized by the literary and theatrical establishments.

The eponymous hero of *Sardanapalus* is another of her poetic mirrors. Like Byron, Dods probably derived the story from Seneca's tragedies and Diodorus Siculus, who in turn took it from the *Persica* by Ctesias of Cnidos, a private physician at the court of Artaxerxes Menmon (405–359 BC). In these works Sardanapalus is depicted as an effeminate *debauché*, sunk in luxury and sloth, but who eventually took up arms and preferred suicide to being captured by the enemy. In Byron he becomes a hero – still voluptuous, but also good-humoured, sarcastic and devoted to heroic chivalry. In Dods he preserves the same split personality, the effeminate bent combined with a sense of duty and an unquenchable desire to preserve his freedom. This is how Belesis describes the king:

> ... —'Tis but a year
> Since, plung'd in sloth and pleasure, wisdom was
> A jest, and valour but a shadowy dream;
> Now is he crown'd of both;—then all his days
> Were love, and mirth devoted, rioting,
> The very Phegor of the festival—
> Or in soft female garments, as the rite
> Prescribes, surrounded by his women, clad
> In warlike guise of men, low worshipping
> With song and dance, and sacrifice of doves,
> The goddess of Mount Aphac.[65]

The king's complex nature gives Dods the opportunity to address an important gender issue, which of course she had to confront constantly in her personal life and career. His sexual promiscuity and his unexpected transformation from an apathetic hedonist into a determined warrior are intended to show that no absolute and fixed label can be attached to gender because the self is unstable and malleable, that most rules established by conduct books are inapplicable since too generic and abstract, and that any society tending to discriminate individuals according to gender is flawed.[66]

---

[65] Lyndsay, 'Sardanapalus', *Dramas of the Ancient World*, pp. 127–76, at p. 134. In a note Dods clarifies that in Assyria, this goddess 'was worshipped as male and female, Mars and Venus; and her votaries were obliged, in the ceremonies of her worship, to exchange habits, the men wearing the women's dresses, and the women the men's' (p. 175n.).

[66] Geraldine Friedman makes an interesting point regarding Dods's gender performance: 'gender performance does not require the staginess of these practices, and, in fact, Dods's self-impersonation is more radical than they are precisely because it is not deliberately theatrical, but rather unintentional. Since Dods's original gender appears put on, in this case the original is itself a parody. At this point, there is no non-travestied body, and the whole idea of an original is subverted. By appearing to be in drag while wearing

The discourse of sexual difference produced positions and relations of power that Dods confuted through her own cross-dressing, which, therefore, was not only a device to secure for herself a place in the literary world but also a symbolic act to prove that the mind has no sex. Anticipating the arguments of many materialist and socialist feminist critics, her hero's cross-dressing and liminal status challenge a social system based upon established principles of hierarchy and dominion.

For Dods, negotiating her voice with the literary/theatrical establishment clearly coincided with negotiating her gender identities. The fact that her biblical plays deal mostly with catastrophes or are characterized by an apocalyptic and dark atmosphere cannot be overlooked: is she trying to suggest that women attempting those negotiations in order to enter the masculine literary and/or political spheres are doomed to fail or at least to encounter insurmountable obstacles? On the other hand, she was, like her Sardanapalus, 'faithful to the last'[67] to her cause and determined to have her voice/s recognized by the cultural establishment, despite her preoccupation of seeing her plays' worth belittled by Byron's drama.[68] Indeed she gives voice to her literary ambitions in the following speech pronounced by her hero:

> ... Now, I have
> One study farther, and that is, to die,
> And nobler than I liv'd.—Although my life
> Hath been degrading to the high reach'd fame
> Of proud Semiramis, yet shall my death
> Recover all, and add new fires unto
> The bright high soaring flame.—The startled world,
> When it shall speak of me, shall freely own,
> Although I liv'd an alien, yet I died
> True son of that world's wonder! ....[69]

This stoical attitude was equally shared by Marshall, Wallace, Carstairs and Wright, all similarly aware of the necessity to negotiate and compromise with the status quo yet also extremely able in exploiting the theatrical conventions, sexual

---

her usual clothes, Dods not only disjoins sex and gender but also makes the arbitrariness of gender coding glaringly obvious' – 'Pseudonymity, Passing, and Queer Biography: The Case of Mary Diana Dods', *Romanticism on the Net*, 23 (August 2001), at: http://users. ox.ac.uk/~scat0385/23friedman.html, accessed August 2001.

67   Lyndsay, 'Sardanapalus', p. 161.

68   Cf. the already quoted letter in which she says she will be able to compete with Byron. Talking about a performance of *Cain: A Mystery*, she admits: 'What a noble performance it is. And how delightfully the Edinburgh Reviewers will cut up little David into mince meat for his presumptuous seating himself so quietly side by side with this Goliath of Tragedy' – *Blackwood Papers*, National Library of Scotland, MS 4007, fol. 78.

69   Lyndsay, 'Sardanapalus', pp. 154–5.

politics and gendered social paradigms of their age to their advantage: in devising, that is, a variety of inventions in order to overcome gender and ethnic barriers, and to engage publicly with major social issues when the status quo prohibited them to do so. Wright and Wallace were apparently more direct in fighting for their rights to establish their literary voice than Marshall, Carstairs and Dods.

We have seen, however, how they all challenged a society that urged them to remain silent, to stay at home and be good mothers and wives, a society that conveniently discriminated the private and the public spheres, whereas their subversive performances of conventional domestic ideology actually reveals how those spheres merge into a more complex conceptual paradigm, or how public politics and ideology have an impact on the domestic space. We have also seen how the negotiations, innovations and social critiques these women playwrights were engaged in acquire further significance when inserted into the Scottish context. The problems and opportunities specifically characterizing regional theatre and peripheral cultures still deserve more critical attention and invite further inquiries into the impact of such ex-centric contexts on the development of women's engagement with the Romantic-era theatrical world.

PART III
Women Staging, Women Staged

Chapter 11

Inchbald, Holcroft and the Censorship of Jacobin Theatre

Jane Moody

The dramatist, declared Elizabeth Inchbald in 1807, exists 'under a despotic government'.[1] This pointed allusion to the conditions of theatrical performance seems somewhat unexpected in a periodical essay offering light-hearted advice to the aspiring novelist. At first glance, Inchbald's ironic contribution to the *Artist* mocks the excesses of sensibility characteristic of many contemporary novels, warning writers to avoid hackneyed signs of feeling (the blushing heroine; 'showers' and 'floods' of tears) and oft-repeated plots: too many novels, she complains, feature the destruction of innocent babies. But this is a piece of writing that conspicuously breaks the conventions of advice literature. In particular, Inchbald's argument celebrates the political freedom of the novelist whose writings subject 'kings, warriors, statesmen, churchmen' to her power. The novel, she suggests, is a cultural form whose imaginative territory and political liberties are practically unlimited: to the novelist, 'nothing is forbidden … except novels'.[2] In the theatre, by contrast, such license to range across the world 'in search of men and topics' can only be imagined. According to Inchbald, what produces this 'despotic government' is a censorial coalition between the state ('the subjection in which an author of plays is held by the Lord Chamberlain's office'), performers, and the theatrical public. Under this tyranny, national concerns may be invoked only 'in one dull round of panegyrick' and allusions to feeble ministers and ecclesiastical coxcombs are prohibited. While the novelist roams freely, eighteenth-century dramatists remain confined to 'a few particular provinces'.[3]

What lies behind this outspoken declaration? Is Inchbald writing back to herself, recalling the controversies and compromises of her playwriting career, especially during the 1790s? Or was this denunciation provoked by the damnation of several recent plays, including her friend Thomas Holcroft's comedy *The Vindictive Man*

[1] [E.I.], 'To the Artist', *The Artist*, 1/14 (13 June 1807): 10–19.

[2] Ibid., p. 18.

[3]   Ibid. Thomas Crochunis helpfully suggests that Inchbald is highlighting the particular authorial dilemmas faced by women playwrights 'under a despotic government'; see 'Authorial Performances in the Criticism and Theory of Romantic Women Playwrights' in Catherine B. Burroughs (ed.), *Women in British Romantic Theatre: Drama, Performance and Society, 1790–1840* (Cambridge, 2000), pp. 223–54, at p. 232.

(a theatrical episode that in turn provoked Charles Lamb's essay 'On the Custom of Hissing')? Or does this argument represent a less guarded version of Inchbald's remarks in *The British Theatre* about the history of stage censorship?[4]

My essay explores some of the traces and legacies of this 'despotic government' in the theatre of Elizabeth Inchbald and Thomas Holcroft. The argument begins from the conviction that the role of the Examiner of Plays has tended to dominate interpretations of theatrical censorship. As a result, critics have neglected the pervasive regulation imposed by those voluntary censors whom Inchbald explicitly identifies as participants in the 'despotic government'. This essay therefore presents censorship as a collective enterprise involving managers, audiences, and Anti-Jacobin reviewers, as well as the Examiner of Plays whose official role it was to license new plays for performance. As we shall see, the power of these voluntary censors to amend and, on occasion, to force the suppression of particular plays proved to have far-reaching effects.

Variant texts offer one important form of evidence for the presence and power of voluntary censors and confirm the difficulty of sustaining firm distinctions between 'censorship' (in its narrow sense, as carried out by the state), 'revision' (whether by the author or, for example, by actor–managers), and 'expurgation' (the voluntary removal by an author or editor of 'objectionable' material). My argument explores discrepancies between manuscripts submitted to the Examiner of Plays for licensing (usually a few weeks before the intended date of first performance) and first printed editions; in some cases, as for Inchbald's *Such Things Are*, the survival of the autograph manuscript may help to reveal another stage of censorial revision.

As Richard Bevis has observed, developing the work of Dougald MacMillan, the acting editions and printed texts of eighteenth-century theatre for the stage and the closet were destined for two distinctive cultural markets.[5] Whereas the licensing manuscript was prepared, usually by the acting manager or prompter, and submitted to the Examiner of Plays a short time before the play's first performance, the first edition of a play was not usually published until some weeks after the opening night. Changes that typically took place in the preparation of acting scripts for publication included the cutting of characters and dialogue judged to be less effective 'in the closet'; the omission of scene directions and stage business; and the expansion of sentimental speeches. Printed editions routinely used inverted commas to denote speeches omitted – for a variety of reasons, including the disapproval of the audience – in stage representation. Given these

---

[4]　See, for example, Inchbald's comments on plays such as *King Lear, Julius Caesar, Coriolanus* and *Venice Preserved* in *The British Theatre; or, A Collection of Plays which are Acted at the Theatres Royal Drury Lane, Covent Garden and Haymarket*, 25 vols (London, 1808).

[5]　See the excellent chapter 'Stage vs. Closet' in Richard Bevis, *The Laughing Tradition: Stage Comedy in Garrick's Day* (Athens, GA, 1980), and Dougald MacMillan, *Catalogue of the Larpent Plays in the Huntington Library* (San Marino, 1939).

differences, Bevis argues, publication can be a misleading lens through which to view eighteenth-century performance. My own argument seeks to demonstrate that these textual variations also offer a rich collection of evidence through which to track the censors of eighteenth-century British theatre.

The plays of Elizabeth Inchbald and Thomas Holcroft offer an intriguing dramatic field for this argument. In choosing to explore these two writers alongside each other, I wish both to acknowledge the importance and to depart from the conventions of recent scholarship, much of which has tended to study women playwrights in isolation from their male contemporaries.[6] But the time is surely ripe to reintegrate this pioneering recuperative work into broader interpretations of eighteenth-century theatrical culture. The interwoven careers of Inchbald and Holcroft – strolling actors, celebrated comic playwrights, translators, novelists, theatrical critics, members of the Godwin circle (and, for a brief period in 1793, in love) – offer illuminating evidence for such a project. Their plays are forged from conversations and debates with each other, sometimes intimate, at other times critical, hostile or even rebarbative, about politics, about the theatre as a school of morality, and about the nature and limits of comedy.[7] Yet though Inchbald and Holcroft's plays are stocked with similar characters (degenerate aristocrats, feisty servants, and disinherited women) and investigate common themes (poverty, the vice of gaming, aristocratic corruption, law), their comedies take contrasting forms and encounter very different theatrical fates. While gesturing towards this broader dialogue, the particular focus of this essay is Inchbald and Holcroft's response to the theatre's 'despotic government'.

Inchbald seems to have carried out a painstaking process of moral and political revision on her acting scripts before publication. The discrepancies between manuscripts and printed editions also suggest her suppression of political commentary or its recasting in more oblique terms. *Such Things Are* (Covent Garden, 1787) offers some intriguing insights into these censorial processes and, by extension, into Inchbald's radical dramaturgy.

Such Things Are is a deeply political drama, albeit a political drama in deep disguise.[8] In her remarks to the *British Theatre*, Inchbald presents the play as the work of an inexperienced dramatist who 'wanted experience to behold her own

---

[6]   See, for example, Ellen Donkin, *Getting into the Act: Women Playwrights in London, 1776–1829* (London, 1995), and Burroughs (ed.), *Women in British Romantic Theatre*.

[7]   Holcroft's sharply critical review of *Every One Has His Fault* in the *Monthly Review*, 91 (March 1793): 302–8 in which he objected to the 'immoral and false consequences' of Inchbald's benevolent liar, Mr Harmony, is just one example of this theatrical conversation.

[8]   For an important recent interpretation of the play, suggesting that Inchbald's play conducts an 'allegorical analysis of both George III's and Hastings' governance', see Daniel O'Quinn, *Staging Governance: Theatrical Imperialism in London, 1770–1800* (Baltimore, 2005), pp. 144–63, at p. 156 especially on the parallels between Inchbald and Montesquieu's accounts of despotism.

danger'.[9] In this comment, Inchbald seems to look back with embarrassment at her own political naïveté, rebuking herself for daring to explore the dangerous proximity of flattery and sedition. But there is also some skilful disingenuousness here, for *Such Things Are* does carefully behold the author's danger, subtly calibrating its political indirection and translucent irony.

Inchbald's tragicomedy ostensibly satirizes the corruption and hypocrisy of British colonizers and their complicity in the unjust government of the country, presided over by a surrogate Sultan. What makes possible the political restoration of this state – and the reunion of the Sultan with his long-lost wife – is the transformative agency of Haswell, a benevolent figure of British virtue, modelled upon the celebrated prison reformer John Howard. The originality of Inchbald's drama lies in a riskily comedic depiction of political corruption, but also in the way in which *Such Things Are* renders inextricable – and hence mutually complicit – the state of British prisons and the conditions of Britain's colonial administration.

Inchbald's autograph manuscript for *Such Things Are* includes a number of deleted passages – all but one made by Inchbald in her own hand – that are reinstated neither in the licensing copy nor in the first edition.[10] The manuscript is almost certainly Inchbald's working copy, incorporating a number of changes and pieces of redrafting that happened before the play went into rehearsal, and also includes a cast list, probably added at a later date, for the Covent Garden production. As the deletions reveal, Inchbald imagined the character who later emerges as Lord Flint as an intriguing French diplomat named Count Meprise. Sent from Tripoli 'to settle a treaty of Commerce with our Court', Meprise has abandoned diplomatic commerce for the thrills of sexual intrigue, namely the desire to carry on 'illicit' commerce 'with every Englishman's Wife in the Island.'[11] Meprise 'forget[s] himself so far' as to pay his addresses to a Lady 'before her own Husband'. As these speeches demonstrate, what becomes Lord Flint's political amnesia is in Inchbald's draft a manifestation of French sexual levity: 'the result of art', as Sir Luke tells his wife, not a 'Constitutional defect'. As Lady Tremor, the prime target of this levity, later comments, such behaviour is 'all very natural, to some Constitutions', to which Sir Luke tellingly replies, 'It may be natural in a Political Constitution—but never in a Civil one.' What Inchbald suppresses from *Such Things Are*, then, is the clash of colonial nations represented by the conjunction of Count Meprise's 'constitutional' and sexual ambitions.

The abandoned 'treaty of Commerce' is significant in part because it points to a neglected dimension of colonial politics in *Such Things Are*, namely Inchbald's decision to set her play not in India but on a particular island that was of major strategic importance in the East India trade. In the manuscript, Inchbald first identifies the place of the play as Borneo, only to substitute Sumatra, carefully

---

[9]   *Such Things Are*, in *The British Theatre; or, A Collection of Plays*, vol. 23, p. 2.

[10]   The autograph manuscript can be found in the British Library, Add. MSS 27, 575.

[11]   *Such Things Are*, Add. MSS 27, 575, fol. 7.

adding 'in the East Indias'. In the Preface to the first edition, Inchbald underlines this choice of Sumatra, commenting that 'the English settlement, the system of government, and every description of the manners of the people, reconcile the incidents of the Play to the strictest degree of probability'.[12] Even if this statement is partly intended as a riposte to newspaper criticisms about the implausible incidents in the play, it is nonetheless clear that the specificity of this colonial geography is important to Inchbald. The well-established settlement she depicts is probably based on Fort Marlborough, also known as Benkula, on the west coast of Sumatra, where illicit rulers, acting as agents of the English or the Dutch East India Companies, were engaged in almost continuous warfare. In the manuscript, Sir Luke laments the way in which 'this fine country' has been laid waste by Princes, Sultans, as they call themselves ~~Nabobs, Rajahs, Vice-Roys, Governors~~ (f. 12). Through this catalogue of titles, Inchbald encapsulates the internecine conflicts between and among native and colonial administrators; part of what interested her about Sumatra was the sheer volatility of this theatre of colonial power.

In this context, the character of Count Meprise, and his subsequent Anglicization as Lord Flint, is most usefully understood as a cipher of France's colonial ambitions in the East Indies. In Inchbald's original conception, Meprise seems to have been a political double agent, ostensibly working on behalf of the Sultan while illicitly gaining intelligence for France. When Inchbald abandoned her French spy, she created in his place a more sinister character who has abandoned British virtues (as exemplified by the character of Haswell) to become the Sultan's spy and 'tool of state': a figure of arbitrary power willing to inform against his own countrymen. In this transformation, the character of Flint seems to internalize Count Meprise's espionage activities, rather as if spying were a habitual practice of British colonial administration. What disappears from the play, however, is a character who evokes both the sexual subtext of colonial power and the global rivalry at stake in that power.

What we glimpse in the manuscript of *Such Things Are* is an editorial process involving a degree of shrewd self-censorship: a calculated suppression of 'nations' and 'constitutions'. It is possible that these changes reflect ideas and revisions suggested by Thomas Harris, manager of Covent Garden, and/or the advice of literary friends such as William Godwin, Thomas Holcroft and Francis Twiss.[13] Regardless of the influences involved, the fact that these changes were made sheds light on Inchbald's working methods. Whereas Betsy Bolton suggests that Inchbald's career 'depended on [her] political innocence or neutrality', my own conviction is that Inchbald succeeded in creating political drama by virtue of a

---

[12]   Ibid.

[13]   In 1792, for example, Holcroft and Godwin persuaded Inchbald to withdraw from publication her tragedy *The Massacre*. James Boaden suggests that Inchbald was also receiving anonymous letters cautioning her about her political writing during this period. See Boaden, *Memoirs of Mrs. Inchbald: Including her Familiar Correspondence with the Most Distinguished Persons of her Time*, 2 vols (London, 1833), vol. 1, p. 330.

series of astonishingly subtle but also daring calculations about the necessary balance between obliqueness and disclosure.[14]

We shall return to *Such Things Are* later, because its denouement – in which Twineall's narrow escape from the scaffold casts an uneasy shadow across the triumph of Haswell's benevolence – tells us a great deal about those equivocations or abrogations of judgement that characterize Inchbald's drama. I want to turn, now, however, to a play of 1791 that presents a slightly different conundrum in which political comments included in the licensing manuscript vanish from the first edition. In this case, the revisions were probably made between the opening night performance and the play's publication, suggesting that Inchbald's editorial practice was indeed to carry out a form of political expurgation on the acting edition. As in *Such Things Are*, the most significant variations can be found in a scene exploring the politics of 'plunder' – in other words, the aristocratic theft of female virtue.

Eleanor, the impoverished heroine of *Next Door Neighbours* (Haymarket, 1791) lives with her brother Henry in cold and decrepit lodgings owned by a corrupt lawyer named Blackman. Next door is the house of Sir George Spendorville, an indolent man whose prodigality has been financed by his father's riches, accumulated while in India. In this comedy, adapted from two French plays, Inchbald presents two attempted acts of extortion. The first takes place when Sir George imprisons Eleanor in his house in the hope of forcing her to relinquish her virtue in exchange for the sum she needs to release her father from debtors' prison; in the second, Blackman devises a plot to disinherit Sir George's long-lost sister, so that his employer becomes the sole beneficiary of his father's fortune. What connects these two acts of extortion – and crystallizes the tragic irony of Inchbald's plot – is that Sir George's long-lost sister turns out to be Eleanor herself.

Having lured Eleanor to his house, and banished his suspicious servant, Sir George prepares to carry out his plan. 'And now, my fair Lucretia', he declares, moving across the room to seize his victim. But this fantasy of sexual possession is rudely shattered when Eleanor takes up her assailant's pistol and 'presents' it, declaring, 'No, it's not *myself* I'll kill – 'Tis you'.[15] The sudden role reversal leaves Sir George almost speechless: he tries blusteringly to cajole Eleanor into giving up the weapon; she walks past him towards the door, calmly presenting the pistol as she leaves. Though the spectators can see that Bluntly is keeping watch outside the door (he appears a moment later, and the siege is broken), the sense of sexual threat is very immediate. It is a scene unprecedented in the history of comic drama: a beleaguered woman appropriating the weapon of her seducer to defend herself.

---

[14]   Betsy Bolton, *Women, Nationalism and the Romantic Stage: Theatre and Politics in Britain, 1780–1800* (Cambridge, 2001), p. 39. For Bolton's analysis of *Such Things Are*, especially her astute comments on Twineall as a satirical representation of Lord Chesterfield, see pp. 209–19.

[15]   Elizabeth Inchbald, *Next Door Neighbours* (London, 1791), II. i, p. 36.

The honest directness of Bluntly, and his frank opposition to Sir George's sexual plot, is one of Inchbald's distinctive contributions to her sources, Mercier's *L'Indigent* and Destouches's *Le Dissipateur*. So is the pistol, a violent prop whose transfer from the seducer to the victim highlights Inchbald's consummate skill in creating powerful stage effects. And whereas Mercier's steward colludes with his master in taking the heroine hostage, Inchbald's Bluntly is first a fixed moral obstacle, and later an unwitting accessory, to these acts of extortion.

In order to prove Sir George's position as the sole beneficiary of his father's fortune, Bluntly is compelled to impersonate the apothecary who attended Sir George's dying sister; his performance is so unconvincing that the lawyer becomes suspicious and the plot is uncovered. Significantly, Inchbald deploys the honest insights of one disenfranchised group (servants) to highlight the economic dependency and moral vulnerability of another (women). Before Eleanor's arrival, Bluntly had been exasperating his master by objecting to the cynicism of Sir George's strategy of trying to buy gratitude from Eleanor by giving her brother 100 guineas in order to release their father from debtors' prison. Because Sir George squanders his money in pursuit of 'treasure', Bluntly impertinently points out, his creditors struggle to survive: aristocratic decadence actually compounds urban poverty.

In the aftermath of this confrontation between Sir George and Eleanor, Bluntly is emboldened still further. 'Why did you break in upon me just now?' demands Sir George, 'Did you think I was going to murder the girl?' 'No, sir,' replies Bluntly, 'I suspected neither love nor murder', only to continue when his master presses him further, 'I was afraid the poor girl might be robbed: and of all she is worth in the world.'[16] In the printed text, Bluntly justifies his bold interruption through a densely ironic interpretation of the economics of plunder. Virtue is a currency that has become so 'scarce', and men so much 'in need' of virtue, that 'they think nothing of stopping a harmless female passenger in her road through life, and plundering her of it without remorse, though its loss embitters every hour she must afterwards pass in her journey'. Here, Bluntly ironically inverts the discourse of necessity, implicitly juxtaposing Sir George's failed act of 'plunder' against the thefts that Eleanor's brother plans to carry out merely in order to pay the rent.

This speech, however, does not appear in the licensing manuscript submitted to John Larpent, the Examiner of Plays. Here, Bluntly offers a different interpretation of the beleaguered position of women in contemporary society that suggests that the judicial system conspires to support sexual immorality by denying the truth of women's testimony. If such an act of plunder had taken place, Bluntly intimates, 'even a jury of your Countrymen, might acquit you, and the poor Girl obtain no redress'.[17] Bluntly's suggestion that juries might not credit the evidence of violated women accurately represents eighteenth-century practice: as Anna Clark has demonstrated, only three out of forty-three rape trials at the Old Bailey between

---

16 Ibid., II. i, p. 38.
17 Larpent MS 912, f. 45.

1770 and 1800 resulted in a conviction.[18] But whereas the licensing manuscript exposes judicial complicity, the printed text substitutes a more general observation about the ubiquity of 'plunder' as a form of aristocratic consumption. It is as if the manuscript for *Next Door Neighbours* points us to the political convictions underpinning Inchbald's comedy while the veiled terms of the first edition record the careful suppression of these sentiments.

Having retrieved an implicit accusation from the licensing manuscript, a significant conflict emerges between Bluntly's judicial suspicions and the Prologue's chauvinistic celebration of English juries, both legal and theatrical. Eighteenth-century prologues often drew attention to the feminine authorship of a play in order to beg the audience's kindness and condescension for a 'Female Scribbler'; the depiction of the audience as a jury was another well-established, even stale, convention. But in his Prologue for *Next Door Neighbours*, Thomas Vaughan plays a variation on this topos by encouraging Inchbald to '[t]rust to a BRITISH JURY' who will be certain to provide 'an honest Verdict'.[19] It is surely significant that Bannister, the actor who played Bluntly, speaks these lines. Moreover, the Prologue spices the invocation of a judicial audience by alluding to the controversial debate then taking place in the House of Commons surrounding the adjudication of libel.[20] Vaughan's Prologue ends with the speaker commending the female playwright to the male Court, confident that, 'as a Woman', she will be acquitted. Yet while Vaughan imagines this imaginary court/audience as a benevolent, chivalric institution, Bluntly perceives the trial room as a site of injustice where men guilty of crimes against women are acquitted. It is of course possible that Vaughan had not read Inchbald's play before writing his Prologue (such paratexts were often written hurriedly at the last minute), in which case the conflict between these two depictions of juries would be an unwitting one. In any case, the Prologue's patriotic confidence breaks with a hollow ring against the ironic, bitter structures of Inchbald's comedy, a comedy intensely concerned by the way in which such crimes go unpunished.

At the end of *Next Door Neighbours*, the embezzlement is discovered and Sir George repents of his 'folly'; in *Such Things Are*, the surrogate Sultan admits his misdeeds and undertakes to govern according to Christian principles. To a great extent, however, the power of Inchbald's satire seems to arise from the ironic inadequacy of these benevolent solutions, the provocative character of untied ends. How Eleanor responds to Sir George's declaration of his 'pure and tender affection' at the play's denouement remains thoroughly ambiguous (a source of disapprobation at the first performance and a gift to any modern director); the closeness with which the foppish Twineall escapes death on the scaffold is another

---

[18]   Anna Clark, *Women's Silence, Men's Violence: Sexual Assault in England, 1770–1845* (London, 1987), p. 58.

[19]   *Next Door Neighbours*, Prologue, written by Thomas Vaughan.

[20]   See further, Carl B. Cone, *The English Jacobins: Reformers in Late Eighteenth Century England* (New York, 1968), pp. 107–9.

notable example of the lengths to which Inchbald goes painstakingly to qualify the integrity of her sentimental resolutions.[21] The very survival of these sentimental values comes to depend, to an unprecedented degree, upon the avoidance of punishment, even for the political sponsors of tyranny and their henchmen, and on the extension of forgiveness even to men intent upon sexual assault. As Sir Luke conspicuously remarks at the end of *Such Things Are*, '[t]here does not seem to be any one sitting in judgement' (V. iv).

Audiences, by contrast, were increasingly sitting in moral and political judgement during the early 1790s. This was an age of intense theatrical surveillance in which playwrights found their dramas subjected to minute political supervision in the press, especially from Anti-Jacobin publications such as the *True Briton*. One of the newspaper's first acts of theatrical intervention, in January 1793, was to expose Inchbald's 'democratic' speeches (in part about the 'dearness of provisions in the metropolis') in *Every One Has His Fault*. The *True Briton*'s surveillance of this play, including a self-justificatory review commending its own intervention in prompting the alleged withdrawal of these speeches, exemplifies the extent of this intense conservative scrutiny.[22]

We still have much to learn about the politics of theatrical production amidst the ferment of the 1790s; by comparison with the critical attention afforded to the novels, poetry, and periodical culture of the period, drama has received little attention. The controversies in 1794/95 surrounding performances of Thomas Otway's tragedy *Venice Preserved* at Drury Lane reveal the power of a stock play as a political lightning rod: John Philip Kemble decided to withdraw the play from the repertoire rather than risk further contention.[23] To be sure, political opposition to particular plays or dramatists was not a new phenomenon in this period.[24] But the increasingly paranoid rhetoric of Anti-Jacobin reviews, especially concerning productions at Drury Lane, must have played an important role in sharpening audiences' fears and further politicizing acts of spectatorship.

---

[21] For objections to the denouement of *Next Door Neighbours*, see *Morning Herald*, 12 July 1791.

[22] See the *True Briton*, 30 January and 1 February 1793. However, the play's expurgation was firmly disputed by Inchbald in her letter to the *Diary*. Significantly, James Boaden suggests that the *True Briton*'s attack stimulated the 'immense' sales of the printed text. See Boaden (ed.), *Memoirs of Mrs. Inchbald*, vol. 1, p. 310. For a fine reading of this play, see Katherine S. Green, 'Mr. Harmony and the Events of January 1793: Elizabeth Inchbald's *Every One Has His Fault*', *Theatre Journal*, 56/1 (2004): 47–62.

[23] One accusation at the treason trials against the radical publicist, John Thelwall, was his applause for certain passages in Otway's play, notably Pierre's famous speech, 'We've neither safety, unity, nor peace', indicting the transformation of laws into 'instruments of some new tyranny, / That every day starts up t'enslave us deeper' – Thomas Otway, *Venice Preserved or, A Plot Discovered* (London, 1790), I. i, pp. 9–10.

[24] For examples of political opposition to plays in previous decades, see Allardyce Nicoll, *A History of English Drama 1660–1900*, 6 vols (Cambridge, 1955), vol. 3, p. 8.

The undisguised collisions between aristocratic corruption and lower-class virtue in Holcroft's later comedies provoked both discontent and contention both at Covent Garden and at Drury Lane. For Holcroft, plays represented 'scenic potions' designed to act as catalysts for moral and political reform;[25] unlike Inchbald, his dramatic assaults on aristocratic corruption were direct, uncompromising, and doctrinaire. In the eyes of the *True Briton*, Holcroft's plays brought 'odium upon certain classes of life, for no other *crimes* than possessing *wealth* and *titles*'.[26] Audiences certainly reacted with alarm and shock to some of the accusations leveled by Holcroft's characters. At the first performance of Holcroft's *Love's Frailties* in February 1794, for example, 'the anger of the house blazed with irresistible fury' at Craig's angry indictment of having been bred to the 'most useless, and often the most worthless of all professions: that of a gentleman'.[27]

During and after the treason trials of 1794, at which Holcroft was acquitted, audiences seem to have become more volatile in their reactions to political references in both new and old plays. Commonplace sentiments and targets of satire were now perceived as 'rancorous, dangerous, deadly effusions, adverse to government and hostile to the state'.[28] Holcroft soon resorted to having his plays announced under the names of surrogate playwrights: Inchbald assumed responsibility for *The Deserted Daughter* (Covent Garden, 1795), while both *The School for Arrogance* (Covent Garden, 1791) and *He's Much to Blame* (Covent Garden, 1798) were 'fathered' by a friend. The last part of my essay sets out to identify the censors of Holcroft's most contentious comedy in this period, *Knave or Not?* (Drury Lane, 1798).

In this play, Monrose, the son of a poor clergyman, poses as a foreign Count in order to gain the post of tutor in the house of Sir Job and Lady Ferment. There he sets out to gain the hand of Aurelia – a beautiful heiress disinherited by Sir Job and his confederates – by threatening to disclose this act of embezzlement and other instances of immorality in the household, notably the licentious liaisons of Lady Ferment. As in *Next Door Neighbours*, it is a servant – in this case, Monrose's sister, Susan – who thwarts these acts of intimidation. In the final scenes of the play, Monrose confesses his own dishonest behaviour; at the same time, he justifies his knavery as a necessary tactic for exposing both the disinheritance plot and the systemic moral decadence within the household. Holcroft's play, then, decisively departs from the comedic tradition of knavery by making Monrose the mouthpiece for a radical critique of aristocratic corruption.

'Before the comedy appeared', Holcroft explains in the Preface to the first edition, 'all parties were anxious that no sentence or word should be spoken, which

---

[25]   Thomas Holcroft, *Duplicity* (London, 1781), Epilogue.

[26]   *True Briton*, 27 January 1798, of Holcroft's *Knave or Not?*

[27]   *Times*, 6 February 1794.

[28]   John Adolphus, *Memoirs of John Bannister, Comedian*, 2 vols (London, 1839), vol. 1, p. 363.

could be liable to misrepresentation'.[29] Though Holcroft does not specify the identity of these parties, the political pruning knife was clearly applied to *Knave or Not?* before and possibly during rehearsal. Before the first performance, John Larpent, the Examiner of Plays, continued this process on behalf of the state.[30] Perhaps surprisingly, the only suppression he demanded was Monrose's ironic challenge to the aristocracy, a cynical piece of one-upmanship about his superior impersonation of their vices:

> ~~If I am not a lord, it seems I ought to have been. I find no difficulty in being as extravagant as a lord, and as impudent as a lord. I could game like a lord, be duped like a lord, run in debt like a lord, and never pay, as naturally as if I had been born a lord. Let lords look to it, then, and reform. Let them be as superior to the poor in virtue as they are in power, and I will blush for being an imposter.~~[31]

Notwithstanding these precautions, the Drury Lane audience resolutely damned Holcroft's comedy. As the *True Briton* reported, the audience 'hissed the Piece incessantly through the first four Acts, and damned it before the conclusion of the fifth.'[32] The 'judgement of the audience', stated the reviewer tersely, 'renders it unnecessary for us to enter into the particulars of the Plot. The Piece itself was "*Mitching Malecho*, and meant mischief."' Indeed, the play's 'mischief' was no doubt heightened by the glaring contrast between the 'pernicious principles' on display at Drury Lane and, by contrast, the unambiguous defeat of knavery on the Covent Garden stage in Morton's new comedy (featuring a villainous knave named Undermine), *Secrets Worth Knowing*.

In the eyes of conservative reviewers, *Knave or Not?* exemplified both the danger of a radical stage and the fortunate defeat of these 'odious' sentiments by a loyal British public. Warmly praising the play's damnation as proof of the audience's efficacy as an ideological barrier against the dramatic propagation of political disaffection, the *Anti-Jacobin* expressed its fervent hope that plays by Holcroft with similar sentiments 'will ever from Britons meet a similar reception'.[33] By contrast, the *Monthly Review* strongly objected to the play's partisan treatment by Drury Lane spectators, reinforcing Holcroft's convictions about the influence of party-spirit in the theatre on the first night and, in a pointed act of political

---

[29]   Thomas Holcroft, *Knave or Not?* (London, 1798), Preface.

[30]   Larpent MS 1192. On possible links between the Examiner's censorship of O'Keeffe's play, *She's Eloped* and his reaction to *Knave or Not?*, see further, Stewart S. Morgan, 'The Damning of Holcroft's *Knave or Not?* and O'Keeffe's *She's Eloped!*', *Huntingdon Library Quarterly* 22/1 (November 1958): 51–62.

[31]   Larpent MS 1192, Act V.

[32]   *True Briton*, 26 January 1798.

[33]   *Anti-Jacobin Review*, V (July 1798): 51–4, at p. 54.

rebuke, wishing that *Knave or Not?* 'had been allowed a fair trial, on the genuine principles of the British Constitution'.[34]

The patent houses usually chose to shelve damned plays immediately in order to prevent further disapprobation and to limit financial loss. The decision to announce *Knave or Not?* for the next evening therefore represents an exception. Possibly Holcroft had complained, as he later did in the first edition, about having been the victim of political prejudice; perhaps the manager did not have enough time or the right combination of performers to stage a new mainpiece on the next night. In the intervening period, however, the acting manager made significant cuts in the script, notably in the final prosecution scene.

The imaginary court convened by Monrose exemplifies Holcroft's attempt to create a radical dramaturgy based upon the trope of prosecution. 'Here am I a bold faced knave that appear without a summons', declares Monrose to the assembled company at the play's denouement. 'Which of you', he demands, looking at Sir Job and his lawyer Mr Taunton, 'will sit as my judge?'[35] The question, of course is never answered: both men realize that their own criminality is about to be made public. The entire scene, framed as a legal judgement, challenges the spectators (both on stage and in the theatre), to act as a jury: the trope of the juridical audience has been turned on its head. For even as he convenes a court to condemn his own knavish actions, Monrose embarks upon a form of political prosecution. The scene purports to invite the household – and the audience – to judge this imposter. But at the same time, Monrose demonstrates that the presumed judges of eighteenth-century society are in fact its greatest criminals:

> MONROSE: Proceed then! Arraign me at your bar, class me with villains, load me with opprobrium and punishment; then contrast my actions, my character, my crimes, with these honest, these magisterial men; and having so done, raise the whip, strike, and applaud the wisdom of your laws, and the justice of your decisions.
>
> SIR GUY: Is this reality?[36]

Significantly, the Drury Lane audience became the political censors of this prosecution scene. At the second performance, Monrose's conviction that ''Tis no uncommon case for the least criminal to be condemned by his accomplices' had disappeared.[37] Nor did audiences hear again the knave's ironic self-indictment, 'What is my crime? A sovereign contempt for the selfishness to which genius and virtue are the daily sacrifice; and, since honesty could procure me neither favor

---

[34]   *Monthly Review*, XXV (April 1798): 471–2.

[35]   Holcroft, *Knave or Not?*, V. viii, p. 83.

[36]   Ibid., V. viii, p. 84. This speech does not appear in the manuscript sent for licensing.

[37]   Ibid.,V. viii, p. 83.

nor fortune, a resolution to be no longer its dupe'.[38] Most significantly, Monrose's cynical challenge to his immediate auditors and the audience ('Proceed then!') was suppressed in its entirety. Such changes are not merely cosmetic; on the contrary they radically alter the nature of the knave's prosecution. In the expurgated scene, Monrose is allowed to embark upon a confession of his own guilt ('Well then, here I stand, and put myself upon my country') but not to indict his society. And although the revised script still exhibits Sir Job and Mr Taunton as criminals, Monrose's denunciation of their corrupt morality has become largely rhetorical ('Have fires like these their secret sins? Can they plunder the orphan ... and disturb the ashes of the dead until they rise and cry for vengeance?'[39]). What has vanished from this expurgated comedy is Monrose's attack on 'these magisterial men' who embody the corruption of eighteenth-century justice.

Conservative reviewers often returned to the theatre after the opening night to maintain their close surveillance of 'dangerous' plays. The *True Briton* duly attended the second performance, and acknowledged the removal of some 'offensive matter', but repeated the charge that *Knave or Not?* was 'offensive throughout in its structure and its tendency'. Moreover, in its claim that *Knave or Not?* was calculated 'to render the Theatre a scene of *political confusion*', the *True Briton* deliberately raised the political stakes, perhaps in the hope of producing some kind of state intervention. The reviewer explicitly invoked the specter of lower-class disaffection (alleging that the play's sentiments were 'merely calculated to entrap the feelings of the vulgar') as well as implicitly accusing the managers (Sheridan is clearly the chief target here) of staging *Knave or Not?* to serve their own ends ('*certain Individuals*, who would willingly sacrifice a *temporary interest* ... and possibly produce *events* by which they might expect to profit').[40]

The argument I have sketched has sought to highlight the variety of censors who shaped the production and reception of Inchbald's and Holcroft's plays. Between manuscript and print, as we have seen, Inchbald seems to have engaged in a process of self-censorship in which certain political references are modified or made more opaque. Holcroft, by contrast, chose to publicize these textual variants, ostensibly to prove his innocence of that charge of increasing 'a spirit of enmity between men of different sentiments.'[41] Significantly, although he does not acknowledge the point, the speeches restored in the first edition of *Knave or Not?* include both Monrose's challenge, censored by the Examiner of Plays, and those cut following the censure of the Drury Lane audience. The textual restoration, then, silently elides quite distinctive acts of political censorship in the play's theatrical history.

Holcroft's remarks glow with the self-righteous indignation of a man convinced that truth should always be pursued to its source 'without any reserve

---

[38]   Ibid., V. viii, p. 84.

[39]   Ibid.

[40]   *True Briton*, 27 January 1798. The reviewer has heard, but is not certain, that the play is by Holcroft.

[41]   Holcroft, *Knave or Not?*, Advertisement.

or caution of pushing the discovery too far', a conviction that Inchbald would certainly have disputed.[42] By 1799, however, he had abandoned hopes of pursuing these discoveries through the production of comedy on the London stage and went into exile on the continent, only to return several years later as a highly successful adapter of French melodrama. Significantly, Holcroft's importation of this form and its significance for nineteenth-century theatrical history have received considerably more critical attention than have his political comedies.[43] Yet such a bias needs to be addressed, not least because Holcroft's melodramas often translate themes and characters from his political dramas into new generic and ideological terms. Indeed, it seems unlikely that the history of melodrama can be written without a better understanding of what happened to political theatre, and, in particular, to Holcroft's and Inchbald's experiments on the edge of comedy, at the end of the eighteenth century.

In a longer version of this essay, I would hope to explore Holcroft's inquisitorial dramaturgy and his appropriation of stock characters and conventions to create quasi-legal indictments of aristocratic society. The motives of these individuals are various: some, like the foppish Muscadel in *Love's Frailties*, delight in unmasking the 'secret practices' of aristocratic vice; others, like Maria in *He's Much to Blame*, are virtuous characters intent upon the restoration of a broken romantic promise. Holcroft conspicuously politicizes his comic inheritance of mistaken identities and stolen objects, forging dramas that violently unmask acts of perjury, false report, and embezzlement. Audiences, however, greeted these audacious figures with open hostility; in each case, the character's bitterest indictments had to be withdrawn. It is hardly surprising that spectators took offence at Muscadel's mischievous account of his sexual escapades on the day of his father's death in *Love's Frailties* (Act I, scene vi); far more significant is the suppression of Muscadel's insinuations about the 'scandalous chronicle' of the Baronet's private life.[44] From the familiar characters of the fop and the comic servant, Holcroft had produced disconcerting figures whose refusal to be silenced seemed to be laced with an intangible kind of menace. Servants, wronged women, and a mere fop dare to present themselves in these dramas as a form of prosecution. Through these ironic characters, Holcroft mixes the distinctive 'scenic potion' through which he

---

[42]   Diary entry for 22 June 1798 in *Memoirs of the late Thomas Holcroft*, ed. William Hazlitt, reprinted as *The Complete Works of William Hazlitt*, ed. P.P. Howe, 21 vols (London, 1930–34), vol. 3, p. 169.

[43]   On Holcroft and melodrama, see *inter alia* Elaine Hadley, *Melodramatic Tactics: Theatricalized Dissent in the English Marketplace, 1800–1885* (Stanford, 1995); Jane Moody, *Illegitimate Theatre in London, 1770–1830* (Cambridge, 2000), pp. 89–91; and Jacky Bratton, 'Romantic Melodrama', in Jane Moody and Daniel O'Quinn (eds), *The Cambridge Companion to British Theatre, 1730–1830* (Cambridge, 2007), pp. 115–27, esp. pp. 119–20.

[44]   Thomas Holcroft, *Love's Frailties* (London, 1794), V. xiv, p. 77.

hopes to cure moral corruption and to bring about political reform in eighteenth-century Britain.

It has been one of the puzzles of eighteenth-century theatrical history that the number of plays banned by the Lord Chamberlain's office during the extraordinary political ferment of the 1790s was relatively small.[45] My argument, however, has questioned the assumption that we can limit the study of theatrical censorship in this period to the deletions required by the Examiner of Plays and the Lord Chamberlain. On the contrary, theatrical censorship needs to be understood as a series of practices and judgments, taking place both in private and in public, involving spectators, critics, theatre managers, and performers. Textual variations between scripts for performance and print editions offer a range of clues about these other censors, while sometimes leaving tantalizing questions behind about their identity, and the possible disputes between them. In particular, the presence of these variations gives us a new appreciation of Inchbald's watchfulness and her subtle art of political calculation.

---

[45] See further Leonard W. Conolly, *The Censorship of English Drama, 1737–1824* (San Marino, 1976).

Chapter 12

From Darkness to Light: Science and Religion on Joanna Baillie's Stage

Isabella Imperiali

A performative perspective on the plays of Joanna Baillie[1] considerably affects one's critical evaluation of their efficacy: in the light of actual performance, Baillie emerges as a brave and forthright woman prepared to take on not only the male critics, reviewers[2] and managers, but also the very tenets of contemporary popular theatre by presenting to its audience the most hidden aspects of human nature and especially by addressing the middle- and lower-class members of the public. The addressees of her plays were thus chiefly those occupying the boxes and the pit in the patent theatres.

Recent studies accord Baillie a central role in the great epistemological debate of the eighteenth and early nineteenth centuries; equally appreciated is her active part in the movement for theatre reform, considered too unfocused for theatre concerned with the poetics of mental action. The decline towards oblivion began soon after her death. In her very thorough study entitled *Closet Stages*,[3] Catherine Burroughs documents the reduced number of references to her (and most of them negative) as early as the 1860s, and the swift disappearance of any mention of the influence of her theory on naturalist drama.

The first – and for many years the only – biography, by Margaret Carhart, appeared in 1923; however, its republication in 1970,[4] soon followed by *A Series*

---

[1]   My research into English theatre has encompassed work as director in several productions, including those of plays by Joanna Baillie.

[2]   Cf. Gay Gibson Cima, 'To be Public as a Genius and Private as a Woman: The Critical Framing of Nineteenth-Century British Women Playwrights', in Tracy Davis and E. Donkin (eds), *Women and Playwriting in Nineteenth-Century Britain* (Cambridge, 1999), pp. 35–53, at p. 35.

[3]   Catherine B. Burroughs, *Closet Stages, Joanna Baillie and the Theater Theory of British Romantic Women Writers* (Philadelphia, 1997); see also Catherine B. Burroughs (ed.), *Women in British Romantic Theatre, Drama, Performance and Society, 1790–1840* (Cambridge, 2000).

[4]   Margaret S. Carhart, *The Life and Work of Joanna Baillie*, Yale Studies in English 64 (New Haven, 1923; North Haven, 1970).

of Plays, edited by Donald Reiman, in 1977,[5] contributed greatly to putting Baillie back on the critical map. The recent biography, edited by Judith Slagle,[6] has re-examined Carhart's earlier work in the light of very ample documentation, and restored prominence to Baillie's intense professional life.

In 1955 Allardyce Nicoll listed Baillie among theatre innovators, as one of the precursors of Ibsen and Maeterlinck, recognizing the seminal work achieved in placing such emphasis on the emotions,[7] although Nicoll expressed considerable reserves as concerned Baillie's contribution to tragedy as such.

In the United States, Joseph Donohue began a reconsideration of Romantic theatre in the 1970s, recognizing Baillie's importance while being unsparing in his criticism.[8] In the '80s, Jerome McGann's study *The Romantic Ideology*[9] shifted the focus to the historical and social context in which the major canonical Romantics were writing, a historicist reading that revived critical interest in the minor texts, particularly theatre scripts hitherto ignored, which were a mine of potential seams underlying the political, social and cultural dynamics of the time.[10] A number of scholars[11] began studying and publishing the lesser works, producing a critical debate so lively as to undermine the position of the lyric as the central Romantic genre; this also gave a considerable boost to the reconsideration of English drama from 1770 to 1840 that was already underway in a number of specialist publications,[12] and reopened the question of the presumed anti-theatricality of the great Romantic authors, a credo among critics until well beyond the first half of the twentieth century. Joanna Baillie was included in this re-examination, the analyses

---

[5]   Donald H. Reiman (ed.), *A Series of Plays in which it is attempted to delineate the stronger passions of the mind, 1798–1812*, 3 vols (New York and London, 1977).

[6]   Judith Bailey Slagle, *Joanna Baillie, A Literary Life* (Madison, NJ, 2002).

[7]   Allardyce Nicoll, *A History of English Drama 1660–1900*, 6 vols (Cambridge, 1955), vol. 4, p. 157.

[8]   Joseph W. Donohue, *Dramatic Character in the English Romantic Age* (Princeton, 1970), and *Theatre in the Age of Kean* (Totowa, NJ, 1975).

[9]   Jerome McGann, *The Romantic Ideology: A Critical Investigation* (Chicago and London, 1983).

[10]   George Steiner, *The Death of Tragedy* (New York, 1961); Richard Allen Cave (ed.), *The Romantic Theatre: An International Symposium* (Totowa, NJ, 1986); Janet Ruth Heller, *Coleridge, Lamb, Hazlitt and the Reader of Drama* (Columbia and London, 1990).

[11]   Jeffrey N. Cox (ed.), *Seven Gothic Dramas 1789–1825* (Athens, OH, 1992); Daniel P. Watkins, *A Materialist Critique of English Romantic Drama* (Gainesville, 1993); Marjean Purinton, *Romantic Ideology Unmasked: The Mentally Constructed Tyrannies in Dramas of William Wordsworth, Lord Byron, P.B. Shelley and Joanna Baillie* (Newark, 1994); Julie Carlson, *In the Theatre of Romanticism: Coleridge, Nationalism, Women* (Cambridge and New York, 1994).

[12]   *Studies in Romanticism, The Wordsworth Circle*; see Om Prakash Mathur, *The Closet Drama of the Romantic Revival* (Salzburg, 1978); Alan Richardson, *A Mental Theatre, Poetic Drama and Consciousness in the Romantic Age* (Philadelphia, 1988).

of a number of Anglo-American critics[13] helping her work to emerge from the general amnesia that had doomed so many other dramatists of the period, and finally recognizing the centrality of her role in the history of the English stage.

Baillie left Scotland in 1778 on the death of her father, a doctor of divinity in Glasgow, and moved with her mother and sister to England, living first in the country, then, after 1799, in Hampstead, London. Here she began to make literary connections and acquaintances in Mrs Barbauld's literary salon and in the Unitarian circle, which was to have considerable influence on her. She also took interest in the medical research of her brother Matthew, nominated 'physician extraordinary' to George III in 1810. Her two maternal uncles – William and John Hunter – were also prominent physicians whose research into anatomy and surgery undoubtedly compounded Baillie's interest in the mechanisms regulating the human mind. She was 36 when she decided to publish her analysis of 'those great disturbers of the human breast', as she describes the passions in the 'Introductory Discourse' to the first volume of *Plays on the Passions* (1798). My argument is that science and religion play a significant role in her view of a reformed stage, particularly in *De Monfort* and in some of her last plays.

In 1790 Baillie published a small volume of miscellaneous poems, again with an important Preface, which received considerable acclaim. By the end of the nineties, however, she decided that theatre was the genre with which she wished to experiment. Both the written page and the stage were to act as laboratory where the public was invited to 'inspect', as she writes in her 'Introductory Discourse', the human individual 'under the influence of the stronger [...] passions of the mind'.[14] In this 'anatomical theatre', as Karen Dwyer has defined it, she wanted to catch the moment in which the passions were self-generated, then chart their journey as they 'work their way in the heart till they become the tyrannical masters of it'.[15] Her initial project, gradually reduced in the course of writing, was to dedicate one tragedy and one comedy to each passion, using the instruments provided by the two genres, but renovating both content and form. Her aim was to penetrate into the 'secret closet' of human nature and unveil 'the human mind under the dominion of those strong and fixed passions' – an intention that, as Amanda Gilroy

---

[13]   Anne K. Mellor (ed.), *Romanticism and Feminism* (Bloomington, IN, 1988); Ellen Donkin, *Getting into the Act: Women Playwrights in London, 1776–1829* (London, 1995); Jane Moody, '"Fine Word, legitimate!": Towards a Theatrical History of Romanticism', *Texas Studies in Literature and Language*, 38.3/4 (1996): 223–44; Judith Pascoe, *Romantic Theatricality: Gender, Poetry and Consciousness in the Romantic Age* (Ithaca, NY, and London: Cornell University Press, 1997); Tracy C. Davis and Ellen Donkin, Introduction to *Women and Playwriting in Nineteenth-Century Britain* (Cambridge: Cambridge University Press, 1999).

[14]   Joanna Baillie, 'Introductory Discourse', in Peter Duthie (ed.), *Plays on the Passions* (Peterborough, ON, 2001), p. 95.

[15]   Karen Dwyer, 'Joanna Baillie's Plays on the Passions and the Spectacle of Medical Science', *Studies in Eighteenth-Century Culture*, 29 (2000): 23–46.

and Keith Hanley comment, 'is the most self-conscious elaboration of a communal Romantic programme for the drama, equally demonstrated by Wordsworth's *The Borderers*, Coleridge's *Osorio/Remorse*, and the dramatic writings of Shelley and Byron'.[16]

Although – or perhaps because – she was well aware that 'those who reflect and reason upon what human nature holds out to their observation, are comparatively but few',[17] Baillie was determined to use the most important playhouses of the period to stage the 'genuine representations of human nature'. For this she required a new dramatic form that reflected 'the ordinary forms of speech' used by her public, in sharp contrast to 'the bold hyperbolical language' of her contemporaries working in tragedy. The function of theatre was to instruct: 'the theatre is a school', she states firmly, but can only work if the characters on stage are recognized by the spectator as 'real and natural', and represented by equally natural actors.

The attentive theatre-goer, then, was offered the ultimate theatrical experience: to observe, at a distance, 'what men are in the closet', in their intimate selves, and to learn to distinguish 'the language of the agitated soul'[18]. The public would realize that, when the passions become 'tyrannic masters of the soul', the cause lies not in external circumstances but in 'our own minds', where they breed and feed off their own energy. 'It is from within that they are chiefly supplied with what they feed on', she states. By observing the way passions are shaped and emerge, the spectators would 'foresee' their own destruction and learn how to protect themselves.

Here, in my opinion, Baillie is situating herself within a tradition rooted in ancient sacred theatre, the aim of which was precisely to foster the knowledge of both the self and the laws governing human passions. It is this she is referring to, in general terms, when she writes that the theatre-goer will 'partake, in some degree, of the entertainment of the Gods, who were supposed to look down upon this world and the inhabitants of it, as we do upon a theatrical exhibition'[19] – a statement of considerable interest containing an indirect reference to St Augustine's metaphor of the *Theatrum Mundi* in the third book of the *Confessions*: the world as theatre of Divine Creation. This topos reappeared in the twelfth century in the vast world vision of St Bernard of Clairvaux[20] and was developed by his disciple John of Salisbury in the *Polycraticus*:[21] on the stage of the world, before God, all humans are of equal importance because each 'acts' the role God has assigned them.

---

[16]   Gilroy and Hanley (eds), 'General Introduction'.

[17]   Baillie, 'Introductory Discourse', in Duthie (ed.), *Plays on the Passions*, p. 75.

[18]   Ibid.

[19]   Ibid.

[20]   *The Letters of St. Bernard of Clairvaux*, trans. Bruno Scott James (London, 1953), letter 87.

[21]   John of Salisbury, *Policraticus*, ed. C.J. Webb (Oxford, 1909), p. 190.

Many contemporary experts of medieval theatre follow Johann Drumbl's conclusions[22] that it was the enacting of the *Theatrum Mundi* metaphor that allowed the emergence in twelfth-century England of a new popular religious theatre in the vernacular, independent of the liturgical tradition in Latin. This form of drama was still little known in the nineteenth century, while today's documentation has revealed it as reaching its maximum splendour from the fourteenth century onwards. I refer, of course, to the Corpus Christi Cycles (Mystery or Passion Plays), which acted out the great events of world history as presented in the Bible, from the Creation to the Last Judgement. This was undoubtedly the most wide-scale theatrical experience ever conceived in the West, encompassing a time-span that no other country witnessed, and which may well have given pause to Baillie, with her one-passion, one-plot, one-play agenda.

When watching the Cycles, the medieval spectator observed the roles acted out by humanity on the stage of the world within a macrocosmic time-span; when watching a morality play, on the other hand, they participated in a ceremony that bared the hidden laws governing the microcosm of individual human life. And while it is true, as Paul Ranger suggests, that the activities of Baillie's characters 'reflected not the actions of folk in medieval moralities and mysteries so much as the deeds of the dark characters of Jacobean and Caroline tragedy',[23] we should also remember that the purpose of these magnificent stage creations was to instruct and to reveal to their heterogeneous public how the world scene has forever been agitated by passions governed by very precise laws.

Speaking of the origins of drama in her 'Introductory Discourse', Baillie cites the *Bacchanalia* and states: 'At the beginning of its career the Drama was employed to mislead and excite'.[24] She makes no mention of Greek tragedy or of the medieval theatre tradition, rightly perceiving in the origins and successors of Roman theatre, therefore, the theatrical elements that still survived in the theatre of her day: pantomime, song, dance, melodrama and stereotype-characterization. This was a tradition she carefully distanced herself from, by proposing an ethically oriented aesthetics that aimed to stir the public's awareness through concentration on a single dominant passion. From her point of view this was a vital necessity, one that in part saved her work from the general amnesia that was the lot of Romantic women playwrights. This is also, presumably, consistent with Baillie's preoccupation to return to smaller, more intimate theatres offering the audience a closer, genuine confrontation with their inner selves.

Of her three plays published in 1798, John Philip Kemble, the actor–manager of Drury Lane theatre, decided to produce and perform the tragedy *De Monfort* in April 1800, selecting it as the one most in keeping with his own inclinations and

---

[22]   Johann Drumbl, 'Questioni metodologiche e problematica del gruppo destinatario', *Biblioteca Teatrale*, 15/16 (1976): 5–15, at pp. 15–16.

[23]   Paul Ranger, *'Terror and Pity Reign in Every Breast': Gothic Drama in the London Patent Theatres, 1750–1820* (London, 1991), p. 5.

[24]   Baillie, 'Introductory Discourse', p. 104.

those of his sister Sara Siddons. Two years earlier, Kemble had become Sheridan's partner in the stage management of Drury Lane, and was therefore responsible for choosing scripts. He was certainly aware of some of the objective limits of the play and made a number of changes during rehearsals, as well as considerable cuts during its run of eight performances, but its basic structure met his criteria for tragedy. This, Bertram Joseph explains, 'was essentially one of consistent intensity: the character must be developed undeviatingly in one straight line of progressive intensity: everything must point to the same end. This is the way in which Kemble studied, conceived and embodied a part'.[25] Moreover, Joseph continues, Kemble 'chiefly excelled where one single emotion or trait was to be clearly and strikingly developed, and failed comparatively in the parts full of the ebbs and flows of emotion, or which were influenced by external things'.[26] *De Monfort* met these requirements perfectly, since it examines how Marquis De Monfort's lifelong hatred towards Rezenvelt, a member of the bourgeoisie, increases to the point of madness when the latter buys himself the title of Marquis and 'comes out' into society, where he meets with great social success.

These were difficult years for Drury Lane, and the tragedy's failure, for all the efforts of the stage designer William Capon in foregrounding the more spectacular elements in the convent–chapel scene, created further financial problems for Kemble, who in 1802 left the theatre and moved to Covent Garden. Kemble once referred to Baillie as a 'metaphysical' dramatist, a definition pinpointing an aspect that is certainly central to her idea of theatre. 'In examining others we know ourselves', Baillie writes in her 'Introductory Discourse', echoing the words of Schiller's and Goethe's *Votive Tablets* (1797), as Peter Duthie points out.[27]

Baillie presents us with the hidden psyche of others, bringing to the surface that 'secret weakness', as De Monfort defines it (2.2.20) that nobody dares confess even to closest friends. What she aims at is the truth of the 'other': to throw light onto the shadow areas the character represses from his/her conscious mind. It is this, in my opinion, that constitutes her real contribution: perceiving the connection between passion and obsession, emotion and pathological state. Her passion-dominated characters live out an inner imbalance that gradually devours them. Marquis De Monfort, as his own landlord Jerome states at the beginning of the play, 'is not now the man he was', and 'the gloomy sternness in his eye' observed by the servant Manuel reveals all his dysfunctionality and depression. By the end it is clear that the loss of his social identity, underlined by Daniel Watkins,[28] is principally psychological – and indeed psychic. His statement 'I have no name' (4.3.26) allows him, at the end of the Act, to jettison all defences and

[25]   Bertram Leon Joseph, *The Tragic Actor* (London: Routledge and Kegan Paul, 1959), p. 187.

[26]   Ibid., p. 207.

[27]   Duthie, in Baillie, *Plays on the Passions*, p. 74

[28]   Daniel P. Watkins, 'Class, Gender and Social Motion in Joanna Baillie's *De Monfort*', *The Wordsworth Circle*, 23/2 (Spring 1992): 97–116.

throw himself into the force that now possesses him: 'Come, madness' (4.3.90), he says in a whisper; 'my mind has in a dreadful storm been tost' (5.2.46).

Baillie pulls out all the stops of a conventional Gothic scenario in representing this inner storm, albeit, as Jeffrey Cox points out, in order to subvert from within the conventional Gothic female portrait. As Cox argues in his Introduction to *Seven Gothic Dramas*, '*De Monfort* appears at first as a straight-forward Gothic psychological thriller. It uses Gothic settings (dark woods and a convent), characters (the inwardly troubled De Monfort, the villainous Conrad) and atmospherics (lightning flashes, screaming owls, tolling bells, etc.) to provide the backdrop for its close investigation of the passion of hatred'.[29] But then, as Marjean D. Purinton points out, 'Both gothic and science were discursive fields upon which anxieties about social identity and physicality could be displaced, and the gothic conventions of drama were particularly convenient for playwrights' use in negotiating the influences of science upon culture'.[30]

Psychology as we know it was still unborn in the early nineteenth century. During the previous century philosophers, doctors, scientists and writers had all striven to understand the human consciousness, and at the end a number of influential figures – Pinel in France, Chiarugi in Italy, the Tukes in England, and Reil in Germany – started to formulate the first theories on the nature of madness. Following the scientific revolution, mechanical philosophy had suggested that the body, too, was a machine. This had kick-started studies of the nervous system, freeing the field, as Duthie observes, 'from predetermined theological scripts, finding motive within the nervous system of the individual, and laying the foundations for modern psychological inquiry'.[31] Studies of the nerves and the discovery of their influence on mental conditions, moreover, had induced researchers to coin the term 'neurosis'. The psychiatric treatment invented by Philippe Pinel (1745–1826) – his so-called 'moral treatment' – represented the first attempt at individual psychotherapy, and on the basis of his work Jean-Martin Charcot, professor at the Salpetrière Hospital in Paris, was to begin his own research into traumatic hysteria, in 1885. In the same year Freud arrived in Paris, fired by Charcot's discoveries, to begin his own analyses. The rest, as it were, is history.

De Monfort's inner journey is a descent into hell that at certain points echoes that of Macbeth. His whole world gradually blackens over, and in the stage directions Baillie is at pains to point out parallel developments in the stage sets: from the many lights of the festivities in the first scenes, the action ends in a convent where the almost-total dark is suddenly interrupted when all the nuns together turn 'the light side of their lanterns', throwing into *chiaroscuro* relief De Monfort's desperate face, and his hands covered with the blood of his freshly murdered rival.

---

[29]   Cox (ed.), *Seven Gothic Dramas*, p. 74.

[30]   Marjean D. Purinton, 'Science Fiction and Techno-Gothic Drama: Romantic Playwrights Joanna Baillie and Jane Scott', *Romanticism on the Net*, 21 (February 2001), at: http://www.erudit.org/revue/ron/2001/v/n21/005968ar.html, accessed November 2009.

[31]   Duthie, in Baillie, *Plays on the Passions*, p. 29.

In reality, this rival is an inner construct. There are no antagonists in Baillie's plays, but 'the chief antagonists', she writes in her 'Introductory Discourse', 'must be the other passions and propensities of the heart, not outward circumstances'.[32] The individual dominated by a passion, she insists, can only try to free his mind from its grip through a painstaking analysis of his behaviour. In *De Monfort* this theoretical position is embodied in the protagonist's sister Jane, an extremely interesting figure based, like most of Baillie's women, on the personification of the female as celebrated by Mary Wollstonecraft and the feminist avant-garde of the end of the century. Here the character, however, is even more complex. After the death of her parents Jane, though still in her childhood, immediately had to provide the figurehead for a large family. Her inner balance and strength emit a light that other characters mention before and after her entrance, and that her brother endeavours to flee from, taking refuge in Amberg.

By the same token, De Monfort hopes likewise to escape from his enemy, but the Counts Freberg fête the dazzling Rezenvelt in a series of receptions, precisely in the place where De Monfort had hoped to find solitude. This exasperated social pressure soon begins to aggravate his depressive and obsessive state. Jane follows him to Amberg, convinced that she can and must help him. In the event, her positive attitude achieves the opposite effect, pushing him to crisis point and preventing him from experiencing the full force of his hatred towards Rezenvelt, who, to make matters worse, has just spared his life in a duel. Jane fails to recognize her brother's condition, and forbids him to express himself, i.e. to perform 'as the spoiler of social play', as Fieldman and Kelley put it, 'because she directs his social behaviour with an eye to audience approval'.[33] This has been her role for years; now it takes on something of the therapist. She invites her brother to externalize his anguish in what is virtually a session of psychoanalysis, in her closet, where, 'far from all intrusion, I will school thee' (II. ii, 210–11).

Unlike the parallel scene in *Hamlet*, here the audience is not invited to the family's psychodrama. Before withdrawing with her brother, however, we hear Jane declare her conviction that 'with the strength of heaven-endued man' it is possible to 'repel the hideous foe', a clearly biblical tone attesting to the influence of the Evangelical movement Baillie belonged to. But De Monfort's foe is made of sterner stuff, and refuses to be routed; and indeed, as she comments in the 'Introductory Discourse', '[t]o change a certain disposition of mind is almost impossible'.[34] De Monfort confirms his creator's words: 'Alas, I cannot now school my mind, / As holy men have taught, nor search it truly' (III-I, 31–2).

In the first edition of the play, the protagonist dies suddenly in a fit of remorse, and Baillie ends with Jane's words inviting us to distinguish between her brother's noble nature and his 'dark passion'. In the prefaces to further editions she had

---

[32]   Baillie, 'Introductory Discourse', p. 104.

[33]   Paula R. Feldman and Theresa M. Kelley, *Romantic Women Writers: Voices and Countervoices* (Hanover, 1995), p. 231.

[34]   Baillie, 'Introductory Discourse', p. 94.

to counter the accusation of an amoral finale. Thomas Dutton, for example, in his review of the play in the *Dramatic Censor*, accuses her, among other things, of leaving us with an ending where the main character 'is pompously lamented, instead of being execrated and despised'.[35] Baillie's justification was that her character's negative characteristics were well in evidence, Jane's words expressing merely 'the partial sentiments of an affectionate sister'.[36] This was no doubt the most direct and plausible form of defence, although in fact the ending is consonant with the author's revolutionary conception of mental pathology as a force to be isolated, an alien intrusion, a 'misfortune into which he had fallen',[37] and thus a plea to the public for tolerance towards the sufferer.

When *De Monfort* was first staged, the play was already out of print. Its earlier literary success initially assured large audiences, but the theatre-going public was less generous, and the play bombed. Nevertheless, it was staged again with success by Edmund Kean in 1815, in Edinburgh, and in 1821, at Covent Garden. On 29 April 1800, Baillie attended the Drury Lane première, which must have been somewhat bewildering. The new Drury Lane had been renovated by Sheridan in 1794 to a project by Henry Fox (Lord Holland), and seated 3,600 spectators. William Capon's famous sets were greatly appreciated in *De Monfort*. Kemble always gave great importance to the sets, and had been the first to insist on historical accuracy and on the use of practical moving sets for castles, convents, etc. – a complex stage machinery that did nothing for the concentration of an audience used to frequent set changes and to applauding at every virtuoso performance or at the entrance of the band to begin each Act. Everything conspired to banish willing suspension, including the many candles that remained alight during the performance. At a technical level, to give just one example, the frequent changes of flats was a cumbersome procedure. Each flat was divided vertically in the middle, and each scene had its own set of flats, mounted on wooden rails, or grooves, arranged in parallels at more or less regular intervals for the whole depth of the stage. When the action of a scene was over, the flats of the following one, as Hogan explains in *The London Stage 1776–1800*, 'closed upon it and often upon the actors still remaining in that scene. Or the situation might be reversed: at the end of the first scene, in which the third groove had been elected for use, the actors would make their exits, whereupon the flats would be pulled offstage, revealing the following scene, placed in the fourth groove.'[38] Baillie's stage directions often declare that the characters are 'discovered'.

The stage, then, was a busy place, and its inevitable noise only added to that coming from the house. The public would immediately fall silent, however, when Sara Siddons entered, tall, elegant, with her expressive face, intense glance,

---

[35]   Thomas Dutton, *Dramatic Censor*, quoted in Baillie, *Plays on the Passions*, ed. Duthie, p. 451.

[36]   Joanna Baillie's note, in ibid., p. 387.

[37]   Ibid.

[38]   B. Charles Hogan, *The London Stage 1776–1800* (Carbondale, 1968), p. lvii.

and contained, regal posture and gesture. Her performance as Jane De Monfort revealed all her charisma and tragic power, although, in the review mentioned above, Dutton criticized her 'exaggerated declamation'. It is possible, as a number of scholars believe today, that Baillie created the character with Siddons in mind. Her ideal interpreter, in fact – as described in the 1798 'Introductory Discourse' and the 1812 Preface[39] to the third volume of *Plays on the Passions* – would not follow Kemble's classical slant, but Siddons's style was far more vibrant and varied than her brother's rather cold and static performance style. What is certainly true is that Siddons asked Baillie to create more parts for her along Jane De Monfort lines.[40] Baillie's farsightedness consisted in her grasping that this 'false' and 'exaggerated' style, in part born of the need to offset the vastness of Drury Lane, no longer corresponded to contemporary theatrical requirements, and that the time was ripe for change. Finally, Edmund Kean, who took up the gauntlet at Byron's insistence, performed De Monfort on that very stage in 1821. Kean, however, who was clear-sighted as to the play's shortcomings, had asked Baillie to make a number of changes to the tragedy's finale. In 1869, in *The Life of Edmund Kean*, F.W. Hawkins recalled: 'He caused the fifth act to be newly arranged, the inherent gloom of the play to be relieved to some extent by the introduction of a banquet scene and a glee, a more theatrical modification of the catastrophe to be effected, and an attractive but somewhat gloomy requiem to be sang in the last scene'.[41] Baillie was only too pleased to make the changes, flattered that her play had been chosen by the greatest actor of the time: 'How proud I am', she writes in a letter to him, 'to think that any character from my pen should be represented by you, I will not attempt to express'.[42] But for all Kean's sublime interpretation, which Baillie herself enthusiastically applauded, the play was not a success, and had a run of five nights only.

The problems arising from the theatres' basic features had not, of course, changed in the meantime. Several years later, in her Preface to the second volume of her *Dramas*, published in 1836, Baillie again recalls: 'How far the smaller Theatres of later establishment, some of which are of a proper size for the production of plays that depend for success on being thoroughly understood by the audience, will in time introduce a better state of things, it would be hazardous for anyone to conjecture'.[43] The attempt to test her theories concretely, on the stage, as a number of British and American universities have done, is of considerable

---

[39]   Joanna Baillie, 'To the Reader', in *The Dramatic and Poetical Works* (1851; Hildesheim and New York, 1976), pp. 228–35.

[40]   Cf. Duthie, in Baillie, *Plays on the Passions*, p. 52.

[41]   Frederick W. Hawkins, *The Life of Edmund Kean*, 2 vols (London, 1869), vol. 2, p. 177.

[42]   *The Collected Letters of Joanna Baillie*, ed. Judith Bailey Slagle, 2 vols (Madison, NJ, 1999), vol. 2, p. 1075.

[43]   Joanna Baillie, Preface to the second volume of *Dramas*, in Baillie, *The Dramatic and Poetical Works*, p. 528.

importance, bringing out the unexpected intensity that emerges in small spaces. One of the practical applications of my own research was a reduced stage version, in Italian, of her play *De Monfort*, in which I directed a group of professional actors in 2002.[44] We found the ideal venue for this in the reading room of Rome University, the neo-Gothic ex-chapel of a neo-Classical villa. Baillie would have loved the small, cosy room, a *quasi*-closet in which the word – protagonist in all her plays – was free to exercise its dominion. The audience was for the most part composed of specialists of Romantic theatre and students, and watched with keen attention the scenes between De Monfort and his sister Jane, the core of the performance. The intense silence was more eloquent than the warm applause that followed.

In the last two decades of Baillie's life, as Judith Slagle reminds us in her perceptive biography, she 'focused on literary enterprises and religious dogma'.[45] This is particularly clear in her treatise *A View of the General Tenour of the New Testament Regarding the Nature and Dignity of Jesus Christ*, from 1831, in *The Martyr* and *The Bride*, a tragedy and a comedy published respectively in 1826 and 1828, and in her last collection of plays entitled *Dramas* (1836). These belong to a phase of her life closely influenced by Unitarianism, the branch of Protestantism that emphasizes the individual's right to an inner search and the free use of reason in the quest for truth, in parallel with a commitment to universal brother- and sisterhood. In practice, all her previous work is similarly informed by her ethical, pedagogical and religious beliefs: see, for example, her exemplary protagonists and their conviction in opposing the dominant social ethos (among others, Countess Albini, Constantine, Ethelbert and Ella, Benedict and Leonora).

As mentioned above, Baillie was from a Scottish family of famous, avant-garde doctors, and was inevitably influenced by the tenets of the Common-Sense School now known as the Scottish Enlightenment; her importance at the centre of the eighteenth-century debate on human knowledge is unquestioned. But Baillie was also a prestigious figure in the religious and philosophical debates of her age, finding herself, when she went to live in Hampstead, at the centre of the Dissenting community that had been active since 1787, led by the Aikin family and associated with the nonconformist Unitarian circle of the Warrington Academy. The earliest nonconformist academies were established following the Restoration of Charles II, as a result of the 1662 Act of Uniformity. Those who refused to conform to the Anglican religious settlement were unable to hold university or college teaching posts. During the second half of the eighteenth century, the Warrington Academy (which closed in 1782) had acquired a reputation as the greatest of the nonconformist institutions and one of the leading colleges for Dissenters, in direct

---

[44]   The reduced version, entitled *Scene da De Monfort*, was performed in February 2002; the main actors were Francesca Muzio and Andrea Peghinelli. VHS available with subtitles in English.

[45]   Slagle, *Joanna Baillie: A Literary Life*, p. 231.

opposition to the leading universities. John Aikin, Barbauld's father, taught there, as did Joseph Priestley.

Priestley was the most important exponent of eighteenth-century rational religion, and repudiated the instinctive moral sense of the Scottish philosophers.[46] Baillie thus found herself in a difficult ideological position; however, while it is true that the implicit dissent in her _Plays on the Passions_ had consolidated by the late 1820s, it is undeniable that as a Scot she was careful to adopt a measure of balance in her relations with English Dissenters. In 1820 she still proclaimed herself a member of the Church of Scotland,[47] and is nowhere recorded as a member of the Established Unitarian Church of Hampstead. This seems to me attributable more to her highly disciplined and consistent inner development than to the contradictions often discerned by critics, a development based on a concept of religion that stemmed, as Christine Colon puts it, 'from a personal theology that she crafted from her childhood education in Scottish Presbyterian Church, her adult fascination with Unitarianism, and her intense study of the Bible'.[48] The Unitarian vision of life was dynamic; Unitarians aimed at a continuous spiritual growth, which they called Self Culture.

In the Preface to the second volume of 1836, Baillie adds: 'But the cause that more, perhaps, than any other depresses the moral and rational effects of the Modern Stage, is an opinion entertained by many grave and excellent people, that dramatic exhibition is unfriendly to the principles and spirit of Christianity. This deserves to be more seriously examined'.[49] She then moves on to an extremely precise and detailed discussion in which the reader is urged to reflect on a basic commercial tenet of supply and demand: if the public evinces no desire for a more sophisticated form of drama, why should theatre managers 'provide delicate fare for those who are as well satisfied with garbage?'[50] She then depicts the types of audience in the average theatre of the time and insists that audiences are to be educated or re-educated.

'Baillie approaches her work with the fervour of a missionary', Christine Colon rightly observes, 'But rather than trying to indoctrinate others in a particular creed, she attempts to help them learn how to search for truth themselves'.[51] For all the moral and didactic zeal of her 'Introductory Discourse', of the prefaces to the other editions of her works, and, even more significantly, of her religious tract _A View of the General Tenour_, it is perfectly true that, as Colon points out, 'most scholars

---

[46]   Cf. R.K. Webb, 'Rational piety', in Knud Haakonssen (ed.), _Enlightenment and Religion_ (Cambridge, 1996), p. 298.

[47]   Cf. Slagle, _Joanna Baillie: A Literary Life_, p. 232.

[48]   Christine Colon, 'Christianity and Colonial Discourse in Joanna Baillie's _The Bride_', _Renascence_, 54 (Spring 2002): 163–76, at p. 164.

[49]   Baillie, Preface to the second volume of _Dramas_, in _The Dramatic and Poetical Works_, p. 528.

[50]   Ibid.

[51]   Ibid.

ignored her Christian framework ... Baillie's attempt to improve the moral lives of her audience is rarely discussed, and the Christian ideals behind her theories are almost never explored in depth': this, despite the fact that 'Baillie's challenges to her society conventions exist precisely because of her moral purpose'.[52]

The Romantic poets likewise believed that they were a part of an ongoing revolution in religious thought, seeing religion as a force of possible liberation rather than repression, and feeling that they were living in a time with a potential for religious change. Although it was viewed in very different terms by intellectuals outside their circle, there was in fact general agreement that, whatever the society of the future was to look like, the form and function of national religion in England needed to undergo a fundamental overhaul to achieve it. Furthermore, there was also a general belief that the time for reform was ripe. Whether such change was welcomed or feared, these views were inevitably encouraged by the recent upsurges in Europe that, despite occurring overseas, and indeed in a country often seen as basically at odds with the English way of life, was a close neighbour, and so radical in its scope as to make all kinds of social and political upsets seem possible.

There were other events, even closer to home, that made change more plausible. One was the campaign for religious freedom being carried out by the Protestant Dissenters; another was the countrywide resurgence of Christianity that we now call the Evangelical Revival. Both of these movements, in different ways, sought to bring down the barriers that the traditional church, pre- and post-Reformation, had built up between individuals and their religious experience. Inevitably, this was seen as a threat to the established Church of England.

Like the French Revolution, these forces came to a head in England in the 1790s, not least via the campaign to repeal the laws that discriminated extensively against Protestant Dissenters in the life of the country. The Dissenters were the sects officially recognized in the wake of the Act of Toleration (1689), which had allowed them to worship as they pleased, but severely limited their civil rights, not allowing them to take degrees at the leading universities, or to be married – or buried – by ministers of their own sect. So extensive were these restrictions that Dissenters were effectively relegated to the level of second-class citizens, a form of persecution continuing in both overt and other, more subtle, forms throughout the eighteenth century. The ultimate result was that the end of the century saw the different sects joining forces in a concerted national lobbying effort to get the Act repealed and to break the Anglican Church's monopoly, while at the same time advocating a parallel programme of what we would today call 'liberal' political goals.

While many of the Dissenters came from orthodox Protestant backgrounds, there were also new forces at work among them: some of the foremost speakers in favour of their cause were the so-called 'Rational Dissenters' – the name given

---

[52]   Colon, 'Christianity and Colonial Discourse in Joanna Baillie's *The Bride*', p. 164.

by Joseph Priestley to the nonconformists who denied the existence of the Holy Trinity – and in particular the newly emerged Unitarians. The Rational Dissenters held beliefs that to many seemed to verge on atheism – such as their denial of the Trinity, which left them outside even the meagre protection offered by the Act of Toleration. In particular, this central belief was anathematized by the Blasphemy Act of 1698, making it a criminal offence punishable, at least in principle, by death. This additional threat evidently acted as a spur, for despite the failure of the repeal lobbying effort, the Unitarians petitioned Parliament again in 1792 and finally saw their style of worship legalized in 1813 by the Trinity Act.

These were the lists Baillie decided to enter in 1831, offering her services to the laity who lacked the time and instruments necessary for an analysis and comparison of unabridged texts from the Gospels, the Acts of the Apostles, and the Epistles, dealing with 'The Nature and Dignity of our blessed Saviour'. The subject was controversial,[53] and, as she points out in the Introduction to her tract *A View of the General Tenour*, was at the very root of the different doctrines professed by the High Church, by the Arians and by the Socinians. Baillie collected and transcribed the relevant passages, wanting to stimulate readers to use reason in order to form their own opinions, and become 'as competent a judge of its meaning as the scholar.'[54]

In the Preface and the following pages we find all the themes Baillie cherished: the need to instruct, the defence of free thought, the importance of direct experience, the commitment to live 'with perfect rectitude', and the appeal to the imagination and understanding. Moreover, she defines the diversity of opinion within the Christian community as a positive and energizing force. These were all common goals of the Warrington Academy, where courses in theology 'involved the detailed examination of Scripture and the application of reason to test the truth.'[55]

With a slightly different emphasis, Anna Laetitia Barbauld, in her 'Thoughts on Devotional Taste, on Sects and on Establishment' (1775), published in 1792 in *Miscellaneous Pieces in Prose*, also insists that the national identity drew vigour and dynamism precisely from the opposition among the various sects. Barbauld describes three stages in the history of the sects. The first stage is that of early Christianity, in which 'the living spirit of devotion is among these little

---

[53]   Walter Scott, a great friend of Baillie's, worried about the consequences of Baillie's stand on what, in a letter of 17 May 1831, he defined the 'Socinian controversy': 'I am sorry this gifted woman is hardly doing herself justice and doing what is not required at her hands'; quoted in *The Collected Letters of Joanna Baillie*, ed. Slagle, p. 231.

[54]   Joanna Baillie, *A View of the General Tenour of the New Testament Regarding the Nature and Dignity of Jesus Christ* (London, 1831), p. 3.

[55]   David L. Wykes, 'The Contribution of the Dissenting Academy to the Emergence of Rational Dissent', in Haakonssen (ed.), *Enlightenment and Religion*, pp. 99–139, at p. 133.

communities';[56] a phase in which the early communities' 'severity of manners' corresponded, in her cyclical view of history, to the severity that characterized Puritanism under Charles II.

In her Introduction to *The Martyr*, Baillie states roundly that of all human principles 'Religion is the strongest', and that 'in the whole circle of the sciences' there exist no truths of equal importance for human happiness. She then traces the various moments in history when the early martyrs – 'when Christianity was in its simplest and most perfect state' – sacrificed their lives to defend their belief, advancing the consideration that no one had ever made the same conscious sacrifice in a pre-Christian era. It was this 'superhuman resolution', helped by the promise of the Kingdom of Heaven, that induced the pagans to look twice at a new religion that touched so profoundly 'the soul and imagination of man'.[57] This is precisely what happens to the protagonist of *The Martyr*, Cordenius Maro, 'officer of the imperial guard', who, after witnessing Nero's persecution of Nazarenes, is himself converted to Christianity by Sylvius, a centurion. It was her nostalgia for a time of such pure devotion, 'unencumbered with [the] many perplexing and contradictory doctrines which followed', Baillie writes, which caused her to write a play that, however, she considers 'too sacred .for the stage'. As such, it is the only one of her twenty-seven plays to be specifically conceived for the 'closet'. She did all she could, she states, 'to give it so much dramatic effect as to rouse [the reader's] imagination, in perusing it, to a lively representation of the characters, action and scenes', and hopes she has succeeded in 'remov[ing] from it the dryness of a mere dramatic poem'.[58] Few readers would agree: for all its moments of intensity, the play remains didactic, unconvincing, and soaked in untheatrical Unitarianism. It was not, however, without its fans: Sir Alexander Johnston, President of his Majesty's Council in Ceylon, for example, commissioned a translation into Singhalese for the moral benefit of the islanders of Sri Lanka, then Ceylon.

Johnston also asked Baillie to write a new play more appropriate to the circumstances of Ceylon. Extremely flattered, she set to work on *The Bride*, in the Preface to which she (somewhat politically incorrectly) describes the Singhalese as 'people of strong passions, emerging from a state of comparative barbarism and whose most effectual mode of receiving instruction is frequently that of dramatic representation, according to the fashion of their country': in other words, an ideal audience for Baillie, whose colonial tones are tempered by a sincere love for fellow beings of whatever nationality who have to grapple with their own overwhelming passions and learn to overcome them.[59] Slagle rightly defines *The*

---

[56]   Quoted in Daniel E. White, 'The "Joineriana": Anna Barbauld, the Aikin Family Circle, and the Dissenting Public Sphere', *Eighteenth-Century Studies*, 32/4 (1999): 511–33, at p. 527.

[57]   Joanna Baillie, *The Martyr, A Drama in Three Acts* (London, 1826), p. VII.

[58]   Ibid., p. XVI.

[59]   Christine Colon's interesting analysis of *The Bride* shows the divergence between Baillie's tone and her actual opinions: see 'Christianity and Colonial Discourse in Joanna

Martyr as a 'moral play'. It is also the only one not to be centred on a dominant passion, presenting instead the power of grace, purification, the protagonist's initiation in the catacombs of the Nazarenes, and the passage from the 'dreamy state' of his earlier existence to one of 'social love, and joy, and active bliss, a state of brotherhood': the very thing for an audience to be inspired, instructed and converted.

The Bride, on the other hand – set in Ceylon, with local characters, one of whom, Samar, was based on an actual local figure – centres on the themes of polygamy, revenge, pardon and Christian conversion. As Baillie directly and didactically informs her Singhalese audience in the Preface, her hope was that they too would undergo a similar transformation process. Baillie had always opted for such direct dialogue with her public. As Catherine Burroughs writes in expounding her 'closet theory' for Baillie's work, she 'embraced both the private closet and the public stage'.[60] looking for what we might term an 'intermediate space'. Like other middle-class Dissenters, such as the Aikins and their affiliates, Baillie too is to be included – as Daniel White points out in the essay cited above – in that 'subcategory of the classical public sphere which exerted critical pressure from within'. 'Their sphere of intervention was necessarily an intermediate space between the private realm and the state', he underlines, 'and the legal status of nonconformity thus gave added impetus to their engagement with public opinion'.[61]

Baillie's vision for the theatre was too bold and noble for the times: her attempt to go beyond the world of appearances, to show the emotions boiling within each individual needed a space that could allow a form of expression very different from the codified acting of the period, based on accepted gestures and on frozen attitude systems. This need for smaller, more intimate theatres congenial to character nuance would only be understood a century later by the theatrical avant-garde of the second half of the twentieth century.

Baillie's *The Bride*.

   [60]   Burroughs, *Closet Stages*, p. 87.
   [61]   White, 'The "Joineriana"', p. 513.

Chapter 13

Poses and Pauses: Sarah Siddons and the Romantic Theatrical Portrait

Claudia Corti

The widespread fashion for the theatrical portrait, which came to the fore in England between the eighteenth and nineteenth centuries, is a phenomenon of great aesthetic and cultural (in the broadest sense of the term) interest. It was also a wide-ranging phenomenon, the artistic representations of the best-known actresses and actors including engravings, prints, book illustrations, sculptures, ceramics (statuettes and painted tiles), and even playing cards, apart from painted portraits.[1] In this essay I will discuss the portraits of the stars of the English theatre who fascinated audiences and critics in the late eighteenth and early nineteenth centuries, with particular reference to the 'divine' Sarah Siddons.

Generally speaking, the theatrical portrait depicted the full- or half-figure of an actress/actor, preferably on stage in a historically defined role or, less commonly, in private life. In a portrait representing a performance we usually see a single figure, often standing out against a neutral background or one with few details. Whether she/he is on stage or in her/his parlour, the background tends to evoke an illusory dimension of naturalist reality rather than stage scenery.[2] Only rarely does the painting show a complete scene, with several characters interacting. Even on these rare occasions the scene reproduced only hints at period scenery. As an alternative to a single figure – which was by far the most common option chosen by artists – there were also cases of so-called 'theatre conversation pieces' (the undisputed master of which was Johann Zoffany), i.e. paintings in which the author focused on a specific moment of a play, with the (generally two) figures involved in a dialogue, posing as they really or presumably did on the real stage.

This dominant fashion for the actor's portrait, of which David Garrick had been the forerunner, with his ninety portraits of thirty of the characters he played, and hundreds of reproductions in various media, is obviously the macroscopic symptom of the widespread enthusiasm of English society in the Pre-Romantic and Romantic periods for the world of the theatre. Despite those who argued for the

---

[1]   Cf. Robert Halsband, 'Stage Drama as a Source for Pictorial and Plastic Arts', in S.S. Kenny (ed.), *British Theatre and the Other Arts* (Washington, 1984), pp. 149–70.

[2]   See my recent study 'La scena delle Muse. Mediazioni teatrali tra letteratura e arti visive', in Claudia Corti and Maria Grazia Messina (eds), *Poesia come pittura nel Romanticismo inglese* (Napoli, 2004), pp. 7–60.

'decline' or even 'degeneration' of dramatic art, irritated or, on occasion, horrified both by the dimensions of the enormous London theatres or the hybrid genres so popular among the new middle-class audiences, the theatre was an integral part of the dynamic, wide-ranging late eighteenth- and early nineteenth-century English cultural scene. This scene witnessed the triumphant march of literature, in the form of poetry and the novel; of music, which had never before been so widely composed, bought or performed; and of the visual arts under the prestigious auspices of the recently established Royal Academy. The theatre triumphed as well, albeit in the uncommon and, in the view of many, disturbing guise of an eclecticism of modes and genres that raised many an eyebrow among the custodians of the traditional idea of dramatic art as essentially a literary phenomenon.

The repertoires of the major licensed theatres, mainly Covent Garden and Drury Lane, but also, subsequently, the so-called 'minor' theatres, offered a mixed bag with the ever-present Shakespeare followed by the usual heroic tragedies and sentimental comedies, as well as novelties such as farces, pantomimes and burlettas, in addition to the obtrusive, highly popular operas imported from Italy and France.[3] So the theatre certainly changed, but did not decline; quite the opposite.

The rebuilding and extension of theatres, between 1792 and 1812, exemplified by the new Drury Lane and Covent Garden theatres (rebuilt and enlarged following new criteria), had a radical impact on the relationship between stage and audience. The distance between the stage and the boxes, pit and galleries lessened the hearing capacity of the mixed audiences. Thus actors and actresses tended to compensate for this by increasing gesture and mime, and managers (often the same person as the chief actor) demanded a more visual performance. It was now the body more than the voice that caught the attention of the audience – the latter having become more and more unruly and noisy, owing to greater distance from the performance area. So performances became a kind of *tableau vivant*, and the performers took on emphatic, rhetorical, markedly static stances leading audiences to see *pauses* in the action – with the all-too-obvious iconicism of the perceived image – as *poses* in an artist's studio. The superfluous material sumptuousness of the curtain framing the stage contributed to the creation of a pictorial illusion, visually functioning as a highly decorative period picture frame. In the words of James Boaden (the biographer of Sarah Siddons and her brother John Philip Kemble), 'when the scenes are first drawn on, or the roller descends, the work exhibited is considered a few moments as a work of art'.[4]

The close link between theatre and visual arts, which developed in part thanks to stage shapes and structures, was the subject of lively debate in reviews, essays

---

[3]   For a brief, though incisive idea of the dynamics of theatrical taste in the period, see Clifford Leech and T.W. Craik (eds), *The Revels: History of Drama in English*, 8 vols (London, 1975), vol. 6.

[4]   James Boaden, *Memoirs of Mrs. Siddons, Interspersed with Anecdotes of Authors and Actors* (Philadelphia, 1827), p. 334.

and diaries of the period, and met with a mixed reception. The review *The Artist* (1807–1809), edited by Prince Hoare (the 'artist' of the title), which aimed at being a debating forum for current discussions, not only on theatre and art, but also, more generally, on the relationship between poetry and painting, had no doubts about the fact that the theatre should belong to the group of 'sister arts' ('the Stage is very nearly related to the Arts, if not actually one of their sisters'[5]), but was about the desperate search for pictorial effect at all costs, which only foregrounded the visual surface of the text:

> The circumstances of the Drama, or the fate of the personages it represents, engage but a very small part of your interest. [...] Your all attention is taken up in admiration and pleasure in the contemplation of fine art. [...] By as much as you see the artifice obtrude or prevail, by so much it diminishes that interest which ought to be the first and predominating quality of every work which aspires to be a representation of fine nature.[6]

Even the influential critic hidden behind the pseudonym 'Dramaticus' complained that the excessive visual 'glare' of the magnificent 'Theatres Royal' enhanced rather than censured, as it should, audience taste for superficial perception of performances.[7] On the other hand, abundant pleasure for the eyes of the audience did not disturb academician Joseph Farington – better known today for his extremely long diaries providing a unique picture of the London cultural scene between 1793 and 1821 than for his landscape paintings. Farington, a friend of writers, artists, actors and other theatre people, as well as statesmen, politicians, bankers and other eminent persons, approved the layout of the new Covent Garden, which, in his view, endowed the stage with dignified solemnity, supplying 'the proper light in which to contemplate a National Theatre in a grave and moral view'.[8]

Farington was certainly under an illusion if he thought that the large, mixed audiences (socially and economically) went to the theatre in search of moral instruction; as Dramaticus was well aware, when writing that even the most cultured among 'our Lords and Ladies' filled the boxes with the sole intent 'to see some new actor or actress'.[9] This is the key to the theatre in the period: the late eighteenth and early nineteenth centuries were a golden age for the theatre, not so much for the new playwrights, who tended to be rather unoriginal and repetitive ('the new pieces exhibit the usual run of features, and the critic is only employed one month in recognizing the countenances he has seen in another', was the accusation

---

5   *The Artist*, II, XIV (1809): 142.

6   Ibid., I, XX (1807): 10.

7   Dramaticus, *An Impartial View of the Stage* (London, 1816), pp. 3, 21.

8   John Farington, *The Farington Diary*, ed. James Greig, 8 vols (London, 1922), vol. 5, p. 224.

9   Dramaticus, *An Impartial View of the Stage*, p. 3.

of John Hunt's 'The Reflector'[10]), as for the great actors and actresses, the true protagonists of the social environment. Audiences, and consequently critics, only judged productions on the basis of acting ability, and plays were subject to their interpretation by actors to the extent of encouraging the custom of printing bills with Shakespeare's name printed in smaller letters than those of Kemble or Mrs Siddons, or even entirely omitting it.

Charles Lamb was well aware of this extraordinary phenomenon of reducing a dramatic text to its appropriation by famous actors. He used this as a negative example at the service of his well-known campaign against the performance of Shakespeare's plays, which was inevitably superficial and markedly emotional as compared with their being 'read in the parlour', i.e. an intellectual reflection on them that was able to ascertain both their overt and covert aspects. This was Lamb's view of the exaggerated influence of Shakespearean actors on the minds and psychological makeup of audiences:

> It is difficult for a frequent playgoer to disembarrass the idea of Hamlet from the person and voice of Mr. K. [John Philip Kemble] We speak of Lady Macbeth, while we are in reality thinking of Mrs. S. [Sarah Siddons] Nor is this confusion incidental alone to unlettered persons, who, not possessing the advantage of reading, are necessarily dependent upon the stage-player for all the pleasure which they can receive from the drama, and to whom the very idea of *what an author is* cannot be made comprehensible without some pain and perplexity of mind: the error is one from which persons otherwise not meanly lettered, find it almost impossible to extricate themselves.[11]

Coleridge, another authoritative theatre enthusiast, nevertheless felt overwhelmed by the astonishing contemporary popular fascination for comic or tragic actors and actresses, whether professionals or charlatans, in contrast with the prestige of playwrights. Since Shakespeare was *the* playwright, Coleridge violently attacked unsophisticated audiences, who were excited by those he saw as essentially fraudulent tumblers:

> ... they went to see Mr. Kemble in Macbeth, or Mrs. Siddons's Isabel, to hear speeches usurped by fellows who owed their very elevation to dexterity in snuffing candles.[12]

---

[10]   *The Reflector*, I, XXII (1811): 232.

[11]   Charles Lamb, 'On the Tragedies of Shakespeare, Considered with Reference to their Fitness for Stage Representation', in *The Works of Charles Lamb*, ed. Thomas Hutchinson, 2 vols (London, 1924), vol. 2, p. 124 (author's italics).

[12]   Samuel Taylor Coleridge, *Shakespearean Criticism*, ed. T.M. Raysor, 2 vols (London, 1936), vol. 2, p. 68.

Even Mrs Siddons's sympathetic Victorian biographer accused her of being responsible, owing to her exceptional talent and undeniable managerial capabilities and commercial instinct, for stimulating this exaggerated audience interest in performers at the expense of play texts:

> To the example of Mrs. Siddons we owe the perpetuation of the fatal star system, by reason of which British audiences have been trained, not to go and see a great play set off by a great actor or actress, but the actor or actress alone.[13]

Despite the surly disdain shown by some traditional critics, there was actually nothing wrong with audiences wishing to see how the stars of the time performed particular moments of emotional tension in plays, in the case of well-known passages from the roles they were playing, conventionally called 'points'. A dynamic representational sequence of emotions was the yardstick by which performers' ability to satisfy audiences was judged. These audiences were as eager for surprises as well as for the usual, common interpretative models.

An example of the hostility stirred up by the exceptional social prestige of actors and actresses is a detailed, cogent critique that appeared in the celebrated review edited by the Hunt brothers, *The Examiner*, which in its regular pages devoted to the theatre ('Theatrical Examiner') was one of the most prestigious forums for debate between the various cultural trends and aesthetics of the period. On 13 August 1809, John Hunt, from an apparently objective and emotionally neutral standpoint, commented:

> Of all professions connected with the polite arts, that of a player enjoys the most immediate admiration and sympathy of the town.

But suddenly, with the aim of explaining the phenomenon, out came the hatchet. If a poet, even the most celebrated one, met with a resounding *débâcle*, the event remained within his own circle, troubling nobody except his publisher and (more so) bookseller, who had vested interests in his work. If, on the other hand, an actor – any actor – had toothache, there was not a single upper-class lady who would not reciprocate with an empathetic, splitting headache. The reason is that performers are at the centre of attention, concern and indulgence. As Hunt explained,

> … if he makes the most of a bad voice, he is applauded for charity's sake; if he has been drinking all night and has no voice at all, then he is applauded for pity's sake: to be lame in a leg is another word for going through a character to advantage; and when he recovers from a cholic and darts upon the enraptured spectators from the side-scenes, you would think he had been taking Bonaparte

---

[13]   See Percy H. Fitzgerald, *The Kembles: An Account of the Kemble Family, including the Lives of Mrs. Siddons, and Her Brother John Philip Kemble*, 2 vols (London, 1871), vol. 1, p. 175.

instead of a cold. In short, the player not only enjoys a more decided applause in one evening than some of the greatest men have obtained in their whole lives, but he even creates *aeras* in private history and becomes a kind of Olympiad in the young of both sexes.[14]

The writer's bitter irony appears not to have been directed at actors in general, but rather the paradigmatic representative of the profession at the time, John Philip Kemble. In 1809 Kemble was showing clearly visible physical and psychological signs of his addiction to alcohol and (even more) to opium, which he was taking in ever larger doses, both (in his own justification) for asthma and acute intestinal pains, before going on stage. The diary of his (and many of his associates') friend Joseph Farington is a source of detailed information on this situation. From 1807 to 1811, Farington records a great many occasions on which Kemble was taken home blind drunk, and when he rarely managed to stop drinking, he still did not stop 'taking medicines', i.e. drinking laudanum (a mix of wine and opium), as is more explicitly stated.[15] An entertaining entry tells us how he was unable to give up using strong psychic stimulants:

> Robert Smirke dined with Kemble on Sunday and sd. K. drinks no wine, & by forbearing from it has been relieved from Headaches etc. Lawrence [Thomas Lawrence the painter] remarked that K. had many times done so, but when tempted has again drank wine. He is, sd. He, like Dr. Johnson: He can abstain but nor refrain; if He drinks at all He has no limit in doing it, & it makes Him quite Childish in mind & manner.[16]

It seems clear that the caustic critic in the *Examiner* was thinking of Kemble, including the reference to his narcissistic guise as Napoleon. Farington actually tells his readers that the two 'heroes' (one on the battlefield, the other on stage) looked alike, and the actor was apparently flattered by the comparison. During a dinner in Paris, in the autumn of 1802,

> ... it was observed that Kemble was very like Buonaparte only upon a larger scale. Kemble said that the French had remarked it. West went so far in this opinion as to say that with Kemble before him and some of the imitations of Buonaparte He could make a better likeness of the Chief Consul than had yet been seen. The Hero of the Stage seemed very well pleased with the opinion.[17]

Enthusiasm, not only in London, but all over Great Britain, for the stars of the theatre was in the forefront of conversations in the best parlours, discussion

---

[14] *The Examiner*, 50 (1809): 522.
[15] Farington, *The Farington Diary*, vol. 4, pp. 140, 161, 181.
[16] Ibid., vol. 6, p. 277 (29 May 1811).
[17] Ibid., vol. 2, p. 37 (29 September 1802).

in specialized reviews, and all general critical essay writing. It was no chance that Farington's perspicacious eye and attentive ear captured many a detail, which were clearly sources of information on the social élite of the period.

The Kemble family was the constant topic of conversation in London literary and artistic circles, not only as comment on their 'grand style' manner of acting, but also discovery of their emotional personal traits. Their biographer James Boaden noted,

> I have already hinted at my impression that the powers of the truly great comedian, using the term to express an actor of either species of the drama [i.e. both a tragic and comic actor] are superior to all this aid [i.e. the emotion caused by the magnificence of the new theatres]; his commerce is with the judgment and the passions – it is vitality operating upon kindred life, man awaking the sympathies of man.[18]

Sarah the Divine is the undoubted paradigm of this enormous communicative and emotional ability, which was dominated and regulated by *passions* and owed nothing to the enormous size of the theatres:

> When we have such a being as Mrs. Siddons before us in Lady Macbeth, what signifies the order or disorder of a picture of a castle behind her, or whether the shadows lie upwards or downwards on the mouldings of a midnight apartment? It is to the terror of her eye, it is the vehement and commanding sweep of her action – it is to the perfection of her voice that I am captive, and I must pity the man who, not being the painter of the canvass, is at leisure to inquire how it is executed.
>
> ... She was in truth the organ of passion. ... The pictures of Hope, Revenge, Melancholy, Cheerfulness and Joy ... are drawn at length, and are extremely vivid.[19]

From her very debut as Lady Macbeth in 1785, Sarah's acting ability was universally acknowledged as not only being linked with her psychological knowledge of her characters, but, more fundamentally, with the pictorial and *picturesque* fascination of the passions they personified. Several sources mention the fact that Mrs Siddons studied the theory and practice of the 'passions' in the numerous treatises published in Britain in the second half of the eighteenth century (by James Parsons, Samuel Foote, William Cooke...),[20] which the best actors and actresses drew upon for stage representation of the soul's emotional states. She was the acknowledged mistress in assimilating and communicating these treatises, which were accessible both to her adoring audiences, literary experts

---

[18]   Boaden, *Memoirs of Mrs. Siddons*, p. 335.
[19]   Ibid., pp. 336–7.
[20]   See my study mentioned in note 2.

and artistic connoisseurs, making acting a work of art in itself, based on the expert use of the body and its various postures, to the extent that her main theatrical roles were regularly assigned, in theatrical reviews, to this or that specialized state of anxiety. The audiences were always ecstatic in the face of her astonishing ability to move most 'naturally' – it was actually well-rehearsed professionalism – from representation of one kind of affectivity to another, even in opposition to each other. For this reason a kind of academic erudition was created, in systematically framing her performances, mainly Shakespearean ones, which stood full comparison with the philological rigour of the recently established scholarly editing applied to the plays.

The everlasting field of the 'passions of the soul' ended up by pervading the leading actors' off-stage behaviour. Frequent reference was made, for example, to the Kembles' greed, or to the fact that Mrs Siddons behaved in society with the awareness of being a great actress, always playing a *role*:

> Rogers, the banker and poet, remarked to me a great difference in Mrs. Siddons when she is in a small familiar party from what she appears in a large company where she is reserved and cautious. Speaking of herself she says it is the effect of *timidity*.
>
> To which Farington shrewdly added: 'that is she has a character to support & is afraid of losing importance!'[21]

Their private lives were often referred to, as in the above-mentioned case of John Philip Kemble's addiction to alcohol and opium,[22] and likewise, inevitably, their real or alleged love affairs. There was a great deal of gossip about an affair between Sarah and her chosen portrait painter Sir Thomas Lawrence, something that irritated Farington: 'There is much wicked allusion about Lawrence & Her in public papers';[23] 'the calumny is shocking',[24] and so on.

It is precisely this tie – either one of love or friendship (it hardly matters nowadays) – between Mrs Siddons and the artist Thomas Lawrence that brings us back to the topic of the theatrical portrait. Various factors contributed to the widespread fashion for the theatrical portrait in Britain. The first, as we have seen, was the enormous popularity of actors and actresses. Another factor was

---

[21]   Farington, *The Farington Diary*, vol. 1, p. 182 (3 January 1797) (author's italics).

[22]   According to Farington, Kemble took opium and laudanum until he retired from the stage. His last performances were only made possible with the aid of psychic stimulants. On 1 November 1816, Farington noted: 'Kemble is going through His last Exhibition of Himself in the Characters He has been accustomed to perform. Each night before He appears He *takes Opium* which stills the Asthmatic disposition He labours under for the time while He is on stage'; cf. ibid., vol. 8, p. 96 (1 November 1816) (author's italics).

[23]   Ibid., vol. 2, p. 254 (20 June 1804).

[24]   Ibid., vol. 3, p. 26 (1 December 1804).

the general portrait boom, propelled by strong commercial interests[25] in the late eighteenth century. It is sufficient to recall that more than five thousand portraits were painted between 1750 and 1790, and that in 1757 alone Sir Joshua Reynolds was working with as many as 183 sitters. While painting was reaching the highest number of buyers to date, gallery after gallery opened, associations were started up, and countless exhibitions organized. The Royal Academy's move to its splendid new premises in Somerset House had contributed to the success of portrait painting. Ever more frequent and richer exhibitions were staged in the huge neoclassical quadrangle from the 1780s onwards, and the spot soon became extremely fashionable. This was one of the original characteristics of the late eighteenth century, which spilled over into the nineteenth- as well. People, and not only the rich, took delight in meeting at exhibitions at the Academy or in other galleries. Thus associating with art became fashionable and this fashion led people to visit artists' studios, and, for those who could afford it, have their portraits painted.

Popular actors and actresses sought a further dimension of immortality by having themselves portrayed in the poses typical of their most famous roles; theatre-goers were happy to see again, as often as pleased, the features of Kemble–Hamlet or Mrs Siddons–Lady Macbeth. Interest on the part of the Royal Academy for the theatre, starting from the presidency of Joshua Reynolds, who himself decided to paint the portraits of famous actors and actresses from Garrick to Siddons, further highlighted the link between enthusiasm for art and theatre, so much so that, at the end of the eighteenth century, regular theatre-goers also attended as many art exhibition previews as possible and visited artists' studios as well as trying to be invited by the artists to the sittings of actors and actresses.[26]

Thus the theatrical portrait became a major sub-genre of the portrait in general, which, at the turn of the eighteenth century became arguably even more prestigious than landscapes and history paintings. Regarding historical painting, it should be pointed out that theatrical portraiture could end up becoming a popular shortcut for representing historical events. The portrait of an actor performing in a history play, especially if it was glorified by the authorship of Shakespeare, took the place of historical representation *tout court*. By replacing a 'historical' scene from a Shakespearian history play with a real theatrical scene alluding to a specific performance witnessed by large audiences, a kind of equation was established, in the perception of the public visiting theatres and art galleries, between the memorized historical event by the playwright, its dramatic realization connected with this specific theatrical performance recently seen, and the definitive crystallization of

---

[25] For this socio-economic aspect see the work of Marcia R. Pointon, especially *Hanging the Head: Portraiture and Social Formation in Eighteenth-Century England* (New Haven, 1993).

[26] Cf. Shearer West, 'Performance and Display: The Actress on Stage at the Royal Academy', in Christopher Balme, Robert Erenstein and Cesare Molinari (eds), *European Theatre Iconography* (Rome, 2002), pp. 261–73.

the historical character in the painting stimulated by theatrical representation. The ever-watchful Northcote showed somewhat irritated awareness of the phenomenon in *The Artist*, where he criticized the habit of many (in his view mediocre) painters whose inspiration lay solely in the artificiality of theatrical performances, without ever turning to history, the handmaiden of nature, for the painting of historical events:

> The historical painters, instead of looking at nature as their guide, assisted themselves almost entirely from the poets and the stage, which has given to all their historical paintings of that period the exact air of a scene in an opera.[27]

And in another piece in the same review, he identified the true culprits behind the inconceivable success of these painters, i.e. art dealers, who imposed market rules and treacherously directed public taste. Shakespeare thus became an easy tool for guiding audience interest in the directions of history and painting.[28]

The theatrical portrait was a good *aide-mémoire* for critics producing instant reviews of theatrical performances for specialized periodicals. Reviewers actually betrayed the fact that they were thinking more of the painting the performance had inspired (in the case of costumes and scenery details) rather than the performance itself. The influence of paintings was so great that critical meta-language was borrowed from that of art. Acting was always, in its several aspects, a 'portrait', actors were measured by their ability (or the lack of it) to 'paint' passions, and the scenery was judged by the success of the mingling of 'light' and 'colour'. Precise references were made to paintings and artists. Boaden, for example, recalled that Mrs Siddons in the role she loved so dearly, Lady Macbeth, was 'such an impersonation as Raffael might have conceived', while Kemble's acting was compared with the 'sublimity of Michelangelo'.[29] Hazlitt also used pictorial similes in describing Kemble's acting, and not always positively. For example, he wrote about the latter's Macbeth that 'his tones had occasionally indeed a learned quaintness, like the colouring of Poussin'.[30]

In short, the stage was a painting and the actor's body its content, to be admired both as an aesthetic object and, in its tragic context, as an object of moral reflection, in the guise of a vehicle of feelings and thoughts. From Reynolds to Lawrence (i.e. from the 1770s to the 1820s), the theatrical portrait was taken up as an ethical object capable of educating members of the public in civic virtues,

---

[27]   *The Artist*, I, XX (1807): 9.

[28]   Ibid., I, IX (1807): 6.

[29]   James Boaden, *Memoirs of the Life of John Philip Kemble*, 2 vols (London, 1825), vol. 1, p. 243.

[30]   William Hazlitt, *A View of the English Stage*, in *The Selected Writings of William Hazlitt*, ed. Duncan Wu, 9 vols (London, 1998), vol. 3, p. 214.

taste and sensitivity, i.e. creating a 'gentleman'.[31] It was to be no accident then that a large number of reviews in the *Theatrical Examiner* in the period 1810–15 would highlight the fact that actors and actresses had turned their characters into gentlemen and ladies: Kemble showed 'gentlemanly air and elegant composure'; Holman always had a 'certain air of lordship'; Conway's Othello was a 'solemn gentleman'; while Mrs Edwin's Beatrice in *Much Ado About Nothing* was 'ladylike and elegant',[32] and so on.

Parallel to the progressive consolidation of the moral and social acting paradigm, the theatrical portrait tended more and more to replace the precept of the actor's physical similarity to the painted figure with that of his or her embodiment of the moral and social role of the character portrayed. The idea of Reynolds and other leading members of the Royal Academy, namely of the moral function (or 'nobler purpose') of the actor's portrait, lasted throughout the English romantic period, reaching its logical conclusion in the portraits of Thomas Lawrence. It is interesting to note how this great painter of theatrical portraits tended, paradoxically, to deny the theatrical nature of his paintings. His celebrated portrait of Kemble as Coriolanus was seen by the artist as basically a history painting ('a sort of half-history picture'[33]), foregrounding the sublimity of the literary object in respect of the pragmatic context of the sitter's pose. In the case of his painting of Kemble as Hamlet, he insisted that it is absurd to call this a theatrical portrait merely because the character of Hamlet is to be found in a play, and because the embodying of this character is taken on by an actor.[34] What appeared interesting to Lawrence was not so much the popularity and commercial success of the painting, due to the sitter's widespread fame, as his own ability in representing the psychological depths of an existential condition.

It was in this sense that Lawrence acknowledged his indebtedness to the theatrical portrait *par excellence* that offered all subsequent romantic painters their ideational and compository basics. I am referring to the portrait of Sarah Siddons as the 'Tragic Muse', painted by Joshua Reynolds in 1784 (fig. 13.1). Many contemporary observers saw it more as the representation of a tragic mood – an essential condition – than the abstract depiction of a literary genre, or portrait of a particular actress in a particular role: 'it is rather an ideal representation of despair than a copy of Mrs. Siddons's countenance when affected by that passion'.[35]

---

[31]   Cf. John Barrell, *The Political Theory of Painting from Reynolds to Hazlitt: The Body of the Public* (New Haven and London, 1986), *passim*.

[32]   *The Examiner*: 63 (1810): 41; 98 (1811): 565; 152 (1813): 652; 57 (1809): 728.

[33]   Cf. D.E. Williams, *The Life and Correspondence of Thomas Lawrence*, 2 vols (London, 1831), vol. 1, p. 197.

[34]   Ibid., vol. 1, p. 120.

[35]   Cf. William Thomas Whitley, *Artists and Their Friends in England 1700–1799*, 2 vols (London and Boston, 1928), vol. 2, p. 6.

Fig. 13.1   Joshua Reynolds, *Sarah Siddons as the Tragic Muse* (1784)

Though there is no direct evidence, it appears at least plausible that the painter, when choosing the subject and sitter, was inspired by the success of an anonymous, openly partisan poem, published a year earlier (1783) by the publisher Kearsley entitled *The Tragic Muse*, the opening lines of which are:

> Accept, fair Siddons! This spontaneous Lay,
> Which Feeling bids me, as a tribute, pay
> To that new Queen, whom every breath must own,
> Sublimely seated on the Tragic Throne.
> Yet mean I not thy Rivals to decry:
> A different grace may please a different eye.
> But partial should I seem, I just shall be
> To Nature, Reason, Sentiment, and Thee.[36]

But since this portrait is the prototype of all romantic theatrical portraits, it might be that Reynolds was thinking of another poem dedicated to Sarah the Divine, again in 1783, entitled significantly *The Theatrical Portrait*. This is how it begins:

> 'Sing heavenly Muse!' 'tis Siddons charms the Ear,
> Prompts the fond Sigh, and draws a pitying Tear.
> You that delight and glory in the Stage,
> Behold this Mirror of a polish'd Age
> Behold her charm the silent wond'ring Throng:
> With more than magic Art or Syren Song.
> Whatever Ills the tragic Muse bemoan
> The lovely SIDDONS makes each Scene her own.
> At once by her are all the Sex portray'd,
> The pious matron or the love-sick Maid –
> The female Patriot, whose avenging Deed
> To have a father, made a Tyrant bleed –
> The lowly Penitent with piercing Sighs
> Tears of Contrition bursting from her Eyes:
> So after noon-tide Tempests have I seen
> The setting Sun enamel all the Green;
> With milder Beams the closing Day adorn,
> While dropping Dews empearl the bending Corn.
> In private Life she shines as on the Stage,
> In both the Fav'rite of the Town and Age.
> Describes in each a great – a glorious Course,
> Gives Life to Language, or to Moral force.

---

[36] *The Tragic Muse: A Poem Addressed to Mrs. Siddons* (London, 1783), p. 5.

Ye Critics, say, where most does SIDDONS shine,
In Love or Virtue, or in Parts divine?[37]

The pose – taken, in the view of many, from the figure of the prophet Isaiah
in the Sistine Chapel[38] – contributes a mode of sublimity to the representation,
suggesting a parallel between the late eighteenth-century tragic acting style and
the 'Grand Manner' of academic painting, creating a kind of icon of tragedy. This
was already noted at the end of the nineteenth century, as Fitzgerald's biography
reminds us:

> To stand before this noble work – before its inspiration, grandeur, and dignity –
> makes us feel irresistibly that it is almost the finest and most satisfactory homage
> that has *ever* been paid to the stage. As he gazes, the spectator feels a sort of
> reverence, not only for the gifted woman it represents, but for the profession she
> followed. The artist, Northcote says, threw his whole soul into the work, and
> never took so much pains. Its rich brown tones are laid in the same key as those
> of Rembrandt, but its chief charm has been characterized by Mr. Taylor with
> great felicity, who describes it, justly, as the 'finest example of truly idealized
> portraiture, in which we have at once an epitome of the sitter's distinction,
> calling, or achievement, and the loftiest expression of which the real form and
> features are capable'. In short, it is earthly in the likeness, and yet spiritualized
> by the touch of poetry.[39]

The exceptional iconic strength of this portrait – between the theatrical and
historical – was greatly appreciated by Lawrence, who considered it 'a work of the
highest epic character and indisputably the finest female portrait in the world', the
portrait's unreachable quality consisting in its ability,

> To affix to passing excellence, an imperishable name; extend the justice, withheld
> by the limits of her art: and in the beauty of that unequalled countenance (fixed
> in the pale abstraction of some lofty vision, whose 'bodiless creations' are

---

[37]   *The Theatrical Portrait, a Poem on the celebrated Mrs. Siddons, in the Characters of Calista, Jane Shore, Belvidera, and Isabella* (London, 1783), pp. 1–2.

[38]   The Victorian biographer of the Kemble brothers had already correctly observed that 'the general pose was suggested by a work of Michael Angelo'; cf. Fitzgerald, *The Kembles*, vol. 1, p. 167. Surprisingly none of our modern discoverers of the source for the painting quote Fitzgerald's observation; for example, Ronald Paulson, *Emblem and Expression: Meaning in English Art of the Eighteenth Century* (London, 1975), p. 85, and Robert R. Wark, *Ten British Pictures 1740–1840* (San Marino, CA, 1971), p. 43.

[39]   Fitzgerald, *The Kembles*, vol. 1, pp. 165–6 (author's italics).

crowding on her view), leave in suspended action the majestic form, to verify the testimony of tradition.[40]

And Joseph Farington, as avid in searching out information on the cultural life of the time as he was generous in disclosing what he found, shared Lawrence's enthusiasm, providing further news regarding the great success of the painting, including its commercial success:

> We looked at the Picture of Mrs. Siddons by Sir Joshua Reynolds. – Lawrence said, 'It was His best picture'. – I said, 'It was a high refinement of Rembrandt.' – Mr. Smith said He gave £ 320 for it, – which was not half what Calonne paid.[41]

That everyone, be they artists or writers, agreed about the exceptional quality of this exemplary portrait also emerged from the unreserved appreciation of Opie (mentioned by Farington), a genre painter who was usually sparing in his praise:

> Opie thinks the Mrs. Siddons by Sir Joshua, the finest picture He knows. ... Opie thinks the picture of Mrs. Siddons much superior to any of the Titians which were brought by Day from Rome.[42]

Sarah Siddons as the Tragic Muse became a paradigm of her age, invested with historical relevance not only as a theatrical portrait but, more significantly, as the depiction of an eminent dramatic myth. Even the gossip on the origin of her unmistakeable posture shows how socially important it was. The version provided by the actress's memoirs says that the Michelangelo-style pose was an instinctive choice on her part. After so much praise, that she could not repeat, for the sake of modesty, Sir Joshua had asked her to take on a stance which she saw as most explanatory of her idea of the tragic. This version is supported by Reynolds's Victorian biographers: the painter 'had led her to the chair, and desired her to choose her own position'; the result of the sitter's choice appears to have coincided with the painter's expectations: 'she immediately placed herself in that which he has so happily adopted'.[43] Another anecdote, also in the artist's biography, based on what the actress had confided to another painter at the time, states that the pose came about by pure chance.

While Reynolds was preparing his palette, after studying how to focus on his sitter, the latter's attention strayed to a painting hanging on the studio wall.

---

[40]   Thomas Lawrence, *An Address to the Students of the Royal Academy Delivered Before the General Assembly at the Annual Distribution of Prizes* (London, 1824), p. 14.

[41]   Farington, *The Farington Diary*, vol. 5, p. 86 (4 July 1808).

[42]   Ibid., vol. 1, p. 308 (19 June 1801).

[43]   Charles Robert Leslie and Tom Taylor, *Life and Times of Sir Joshua Reynolds*, 2 vols (London, 1865), vol. 2, p. 646.

When the painter turned towards Sarah again, being struck by her new position he 'requested her not to move, and thus arose the beautiful and expressive figure we now see in the picture'.[44] Another version tends again towards the 'accidental' narrative. Mrs Siddons had arrived in a great hurry and fallen onto the sofa to get her breath back, because she was so tired, resting her head on her hand, and this is how she is supposed to have looked the painter in the eye: '"How shall I sit?", asked Sarah. "Just as you are", said Sir Joshua, and so she is painted'.[45] But the suggestion has also been made[46] that the true origin of the painting was an idea of Thomas Sheridan (the actor) or Richard Sheridan his son (the playwright), who is supposed to have invited Reynolds to produce an icon of the *new* tragic muse, i.e. Mrs Siddons, in opposition to the now defunct muse personified by Mrs Yates.

According to the editor of Farington's diaries, James Greig, it is only with this historic portrait in mind that one can understand what appeared before the eyes of Covent Garden audiences when Mrs Siddons was seen in the role of Lady Macbeth for the last time. It was 29 June 1812, and Farington went to the theatre for this farewell to the divine actress.[47] John Philip, playing the leading role, received the usual applause, but Mrs Siddons was greeted by a veritable tumult, forcing Kemble to interrupt the performance. Shortly afterwards, when silence had returned, the curtain rose again to show Lady Macbeth in the last act. Farington noted:

> Some time elapsed till at length the Curtain was drawn up and Mrs. Siddons appeared sitting at a table in her own character. She was dressed in White Sattin and had a long veil. She arose but it was sometime before she could speak the clapping and other sounds of approbation rendereing it impossible for Her to be heard. She curtsied and bowed, & at last there was silence. At 10 oClock precisely she began to speak Her farewell address which took up Eight minutes during which time there was profound silence. Having finished, the loudest claps, &c. followed, & she withdrew bowing & led off by an attendant who advanced for that purpose.[48]

So as to highlight the studied iconic and pictorial theatricality of this scene-within-a-scene, the diarist specifically invites his readers to picture Mrs Siddons's Lady

---

[44]   Ibid., vol. 2, p. 422.

[45]   Whitley, *Artists and Their Friends in England*, vol. 2, p. 5.

[46]   Maria Ines Aliverti, *La Naissance de l'acteur moderne* (Paris, 1998), pp. 162–3. Interesting reflections both on the symbolic content and technique of this famous portrait can be found in the essays making up *A Passion for Performance: Sarah Siddons and her Portraitists*, ed. Robyn Asleson (Los Angeles, 1999).

[47]   It was not actually a final farewell to the stage, because Siddons was to return sporadically to acting with her brother on several occasions, to support the theatre managed by John Philip Kemble, who was also its leading actor. She was also to act as late as 1819–20, to support the works staged by his younger brother Charles Kemble.

[48]   Farington, *The Diary of Joseph Farington*, vol. 7, pp. 88–9 (29 June 1812).

Macbeth in their minds comparing her ('face to face'[49]) with an illustration of the famous portrait *Mrs. Siddons as the Tragic Muse*.

Apart from this seminal portrait, the easiest repertoire of theatrical illustrations of Sarah the Divine to consult consists of her portraits by Thomas Lawrence, her great admirer and presumed lover. The subdued attitude of Farington (who as we have seen actually saw the gossip on the putative affair as malicious) does not prevent him from alluding to the possibility that the long (evidently too long!) night hours spent posing also involved some other demanding activity beyond the laborious work of painting the portrait:

> Lane told me that Mrs. Siddons sat to Lawrence for a *whole length last night by Lamplight*, till 2 oClock this morning, – Lawrence got up today a little before 10.[50]

Perhaps Lawrence's most famous portrait of Mrs Siddons is the one painted in 1804 (fig. 13.2), of which Farington owned an engraving given to him by the artist himself:

> Lawrence brought the fine print of Mrs. Siddons done under His direction by William Say the Engraver, and we hung it in my parlour.[51]

This painting, no less than Sir Joshua Reynolds's 'Tragic Muse', is an excellent paradigm of the romantic theatrical portrait. If the 'Tragic Muse' immediately became an icon not only of the actress but even more so of dramatic art, Lawrence's portrait immediately became the epitome of Mrs Siddons as a persona in the public eye. The artist had portrayed her in her favourite role after that of theatre actress, i.e. that of reader at Court or in other socially important venues, such as the universities of Oxford and Cambridge, of theatre texts she had been performing with ever-increasing success in British theatres. Fitzgerald's biography tells us of the great pleasure the actress found in careful reading of the texts of the plays she was going to act in, to the extent that 'she was said to prefer diligent private study to assiduous rehearsal'.[52] But it was Sarah herself, in her memoirs, who proudly noted that she had often been invited to Royal residences to delight Their Majesties with her extraordinary diction:

---

49 Ibid., vol. 7, p. 88 (29 June 1812).
50 Ibid., vol. 2, p. 198 (2 March 1804).
51 Ibid., vol. 6, p. 29 (26 March 1810).
52 Cf. Fitzgerald, *The Kembles*, vol. 1, p. 176.

Fig. 13.2   Thomas Lawrence, *Sarah Siddons* (1804)

I had very soon the honour of reading to Their Majesties at Buckingham House, an honour which now occurred frequently. ... Afterwards I had the honour of attending their Majesties at Windsor also.[53]

In her first biography, which was based on first-hand sources, we find a passage, dealing with her public readings in the Argyle Rooms, which appears to be an exact paraphrase of the portrait by Lawrence:

In front of what was the orchestra in the old Argyle Rooms, a reading-desk with lights was placed, on which lay her book, a quarto volume, printed with large letters [this refers to the fact that as she grew older Mrs Siddons had more and more problems with her sight]. A large red screen formed what painters would call a background to the person of the charming reader.[54]

There is no doubt that with the images of Mrs Siddons – and her brother John Philip Kemble – the English romantic theatrical portrait reached its apex, both from the point of view of the spread of dramatic art and from that of actresses' and actors' social self-promotion as personages in the public eye. We can thus subscribe to the words used by their Victorian biographer Percy Fitzgerald, which still maintain their interpretative perspicacity regarding what seems to me to be one of the major phenomena in the theatre in English romanticism:

The wonderful brother and sister live again on many a canvas. No two artists have been so frequently painted or engraved. Theatrical performers have always been a favourite subject with artists, for, from frequent playing, their features acquire a certain character and expression, and where there is found dramatic genius, there comes an irresistible impulse to try and preserve some records of the features which have such a magical power. ... No players have received so much of this homage as Mrs. Siddons and her brother. Much of this was owing, of course, to their noble cast of face – their grand and dignified expression.[55]

The fashion for the theatrical portrait in English romanticism regarded the typical interchange between poetry, theatre and painting characterizing British culture at the turn of the century. Actors and actresses became increasingly important sitters for portraits, one of the reasons being that theatre critics tended to apply pictorial categories to the effects of theatre performances. The painter found an easy guide to actors' portraiture, partly because their behaviour on stage could be decoded in terms of pictorial representation. And the interface between dramatic poetry and the visual arts lay in the relationship between discursive pauses

---

[53]   *The Reminiscences of Sarah Kemble Siddons* (1831), ed. William Van Lennep (Cambridge, MA, 1942), pp. 21–2.

[54]   Thomas Campbell, *Life of Mrs. Siddons* (New York, 1834), p. 243.

[55]   Fitzgerald, *The Kembles*, vol. 1, p. 400.

and the plastic poses of the actor/sitter miming the effect of reality. Reflecting the critical tenor of theatre criticism in periodical and essay literature of the period, the author of *Verses addressed to Mrs. Siddons* – an obscure playwright writing under the pseudonym of Thalia, the muse of comedy, companion to Melpomene, the muse of tragedy – issues a eulogy of the actress setting up functional and operative equivalence between the artistic technique of Sarah the Divine and that of an expert painter:

> As the fine Painter, who with choice design
> Attempts to image some rare scene of mine,
> His glowing colours blends, with nicest art,
> And gives becoming force to every part;
> *Here* graceful throws his shade, and *there* his light,
> And makes the darker tints set off the bright;
> When faithful, warm, and great the whole he sees,
> Precision joyn'd to fire, and force to ease,
> Adds numberless soft touches at the last,
> The rarest efforts of his skill and taste!
> To throw a finish'd lustre o'er the whole,
> And make it breathe my animating soul;
> So, to the Glories of her high Design,
> My SIDDONS shall those nameless graces join,
> Whose lively touches shall the whole compleat,
> And make the finish'd scene correctly great;
> That fiction, seeming banish'd from the part,
> Like truth shall strike the *well*-deluded heart.[56]

Sarah the Divine, the iconic meeting-point between the dramatic and the visual gives – more than any predecessor and indeed more than her celebrated brother – definitive meaning to the concept of the sister arts.

[56] *Verses Addressed to Mrs. Siddons, on Her Being Engaged at the Theatre-Royal, Drury Lane, in 1782, by the Reverend Mr. Whalley, author of Edwy and Edilda, Fatal Kiss, &c.&c.&c* (London, 1782), pp. 17–18. Italics appear in the text, but I subscribe to the last (*well*-deluded heart), regarding Coleridge's 'suspension of disbelief', or the illusionist pact between author and reader.

Chapter 14

When 'Poetry and Stage do Agree Together': Elizabeth Vestris's *A Midsummer Night's Dream*

Stefania Magnoni

Theatrical Life *versus* Extra-Theatrical life

A Midsummer Night's Dream occupies a high place within the iconography, the critical discourse and the literature of the romantic period. This elevated extra-theatrical position, however, coexists – paradoxically for a text written for the theatre – with a relatively 'low' theatrical life, thus creating an inversely proportional relationship between the presence of *A Midsummer Night's Dream* in the collective imagination and its presence on the stage.

Within romantic culture at large, *A Midsummer Night's Dream*, and in particular the oneiric and supernatural aspects of the comedy, represented a source of inspiration for numerous paintings by artists such as, among others, Joshua Reynolds, Johan Heinrich Fuseli and William Blake, whose works in turn inspired famous engravings.[1] At the same time the comedy, and in particular the famous lines by Theseus on the poetic imagination, exerted a powerful influence on romantic writings and discussions on the imagination:[2]

---

[1]   See, for example, Richard Rhodes's engravings after Fuseli's paintings *Oberon squeezing the Flower on Titania's Eyelids*, 1793 (*A Midsummer Night's Dream* ['*MND*'], II, ii) and *Titania, Bottom and the Fairies*, 1793 (*MND*, IV, i); James Parker's engraving after Fuseli's painting, *Robin Goodfellow-Puck*, 1787–90 (*MND*, II, i); Ryder's engraving after Fuseli's painting *Titania's Awakening*, 1786–*c*.1790 (*MND*, IV, i); Schiavonetti's engraving after Sir J. Reynolds's painting *Puck*.

[2]   When Romantic poets and critics speak about the imagination, they often refer to *A Midsummer Night's Dream* and *The Tempest*, in which the poetic imagination and the power of imagination are described. Writings on imagination cannot avoid quoting in particular Theseus's lines. In a famous passage on poetic faith from *Biographia Literaria*, Coleridge writes that 'his endeavours should be directed to persons and characters supernatural or at least romantic, yet so as to transfer from our inward nature a human interest and a semblance of truth sufficient to procure for these shadows of imagination that willing suspension of disbelief for the moment which constitutes poetic faith'; see *Collected Works*, eds James Engell and W.J. Bate, 16 vols (Princeton, 1982), vol. 7 (II), p. 6. The phrase 'shadows of imagination' recalls the lines by Theseus: 'The best in this kind

The poet's eye, in a fine frenzy rolling,
doth glance from heaven to earth, from earth to heaven,
And as imagination bodies forth
The forms of things unknown, the poet's pen
Turns them to shapes, and gives to airy nothing
A local habitation and a name. (V, i, 12–17)[3]

Furthermore, thanks to the wide circulation of Thomas Bowdler's *The Family Shakespeare*, Charles and Mary Lamb's *Tales from Shakespeare*, and other prose adaptations of the Shakespearean plays,[4] *A Midsummer Night's Dream* also became popular among young people and children.

On the stage, instead, the play received far less attention. It was produced by Frederick Reynolds in 1816 and then only twenty-four years later, in 1840, by Elizabeth Vestris. It is important to stress the difference between the two versions: the former, closely linked to the previous century, is characterized by a systematic rewriting of lines, plots and characters; the latter is particularly innovative and anticipates the nineteenth-century productions of the Shakespearean comedy. This essay will discuss Vestris's staging, with particular reference to its success in overcoming the theatrical/extra-theatrical dichotomy that conditioned the critical reception of the comedy in the period.

A Midsummer Night's Dream and its Stageability

The lack of attention to *A Midsummer Night's Dream* on stage was undoubtedly influenced by an antitheatrical prejudice against the comedy in the first half of

---

are but shadows; and the worst are no worse, if imagination amend them' (V, i, 208–9). As Jonathan Bate suggests, Coleridge's belief that Shakespeare's supernatural plays led to the imaginative principle necessary to perceive and organize nature was influenced by Richard Hurd's *Letters on Chivalry and Romance*. Cf. Jonathan Bate, *Shakespeare and the English Romantic Imagination* (Oxford, 1989), pp. 10–11. In the second edition of his *Letters* (1765), Hurd argues that poetical truth is perceived by the eye 'when rolling in a fine frenzy'. See Richard Hurd, *Hurd's Letters on Chivalry and Romance*, ed. Edith J. Morley (London, 1911), pp. 137–8. Akenside, fascinated by the imagination, its characteristics and functions, had already used this allusion to Theseus's lines in his poem *The Pleasures of Imagination* (1744). In a passage dealing with the operations of the mind in the production of imaginative works, he writes 'with loveliest frenzy caught, / From earth to heav'n he rolls his daring eye, / From heav'n to earth'; see *The Poetical Works of Mark Akenside*, ed. Robin Dix (London, 1996), book III, ll. 383–5, p. 146.

[3]   All the references to the play are from *A Midsummer Night's Dream*, ed. Harold F. Brooks (London, 1983).

[4]   See, for example, Miss Macauley, *Tales of the Drama* (London, 1822); A.S. Macfarland and Abby Sage, *Stories from Shakespeare* (London, 1882); Caroline Maxwell, *The Juvenile Edition of Shakspeare; adapted to the capacities of youth* (London, 1828).

the nineteenth century. In the romantic period the play was generally considered unsuited to the stage. William Hazlitt, reviewing Frederick Reynolds's version for *The Examiner* on 21 January 1816, writes:

> We have found to our cost, once for all, that the regions of fancy and the boards of Covent-Garden are not the same thing. All that is fine in the play, was lost in the representation. The spirit was evaporated, the genius was fled; ... Poetry and the stage do not agree together. The attempt to reconcile them fails not only of effect, but of decorum. The *ideal* has no place upon the stage, which is a picture without perspective; every thing there is in the foreground. That which is merely an airy shape, a dream, a passing thought, immediately becomes an unmanageable reality. ... Fancy cannot be represented any more than a simile can be painted; and it is as idle to attempt it as to personate Wall or Moonshine. Fairies are not incredible, but fairies six feet high are so. Monsters are not shocking, if they are seen at a proper distance. When ghosts appear in midday, when apparitions stalk along Cheapside, then may the Midsummer Night's Dream be represented at Covent-Garden or at Drury-Lane; for we hear that it is to be brought out there also, and that we have to undergo another crucifixion.[5]

Hazlitt, Coleridge and Lamb all argued that Shakespeare's plays could be better appreciated if read instead of being staged. Coleridge, who claimed never to have seen a Shakespearean play without feeling a sense of disgust and indignation, was convinced that the proper place for reading Shakespeare was the closet:

> It [*Richard II*] was a play not much acted. This was not regretted by the lecturer; for he never saw any of Shakespeare's plays performed, but with a degree of pain, disgust, and indignation. He had seen Mrs. Siddons as Lady, and Kemble as Macbeth: – these might be the Macbeths of the Kembles, but they were not the Macbeths of Shakespeare. He was therefore not grieved at the enormous size and monopoly of the theatres, which naturally produced many bad and but few good actors; and which drove Shakespeare from the stage, to find his proper place in the hearth and in the closet, where he sits with Milton, enthroned on a double-headed Parnassus; and with whom everything that was admirable, everything praiseworthy, was to be found.[6]

---

[5] William Hazlitt, "'The Midsummer Night's Dream", *A View of the English Stage*', in *The Complete Works of William Hazlitt*, ed. P.P. Howe, 21 vols (London, 1930–34), vol. 5, pp. 274–5.

[6] Samuel Taylor Coleridge, '[Lecture V]. [Historical plays. Richard II]', *Lectures of 1813–14 at Bristol, with reports by the 'Bristol Gazette' of eight lectures*, in *Coleridge's Shakespearean Criticism*, ed. Middleton Raysor, 2 vols (London, 1930), vol. 2, pp. 278–9.

Hazlitt likewise underlined how the reader of Shakespeare 'is almost always disappointed in seeing them [the plays of Shakespeare] acted; and, for our own parts, we should never go to see them acted, if we could help it'.[7]

While admitting that his opinion could seem paradoxical, Charles Lamb claimed that the Shakespearean plays were the least suited to be staged but a delight to read:

> It may seem a paradox, but I cannot help being of opinion that the plays of Shakspeare are less calculated for performance on a stage, than those of almost any other dramatist whatever. Their distinguished excellence is a reason that they should be so. There is so much in them, which comes not under the province of acting, with which eye, and tone, and gesture, have nothing to do.
>
> ...
>
> What we see upon a stage is body and bodily action; what we are conscious of in reading is almost exclusively the mind, and its movements: and this I think may sufficely account for the very different sort of delight with which the same play so often affects us in the reading and the seeing.[8]

The Romantic critics' belief that Shakespeare's plays were more suited to reading than staging resulted from their opposition to the general idolatry of actors, to the tendency to compensate for the mediocrity of plays with the spectacularity of the representation and thus satisfy the senses to the detriment of imagination. These phenomena, even if they had deep roots, were fully displayed in the contemporary theatre where the Shakespearean plays were generally 'improved' and the scenery lacked a coherent design or was too realistic.[9] It is mainly for this reason that several critics stressed the incompatibility between Shakespearean poetry and the stage.[10]

The difficulties in staging *A Midsummer Night's Dream* regarded especially the re-creation of a dreamlike atmosphere pervading the whole spectacle – as Coleridge writes, 'Shakespeare availed himself of the title of the play in his own

---

[7]   William Hazlitt, '"Mr. Kean's Richard II"', *A View of the English Stage*, in *The Complete Works of William Hazlitt*, vol. 5, p. 222.

[8]   Charles Lamb, *On the tragedies of Shakespeare, considered with reference to their fitness for stage representation*, in *The Works of Charles and Mary Lamb*, ed. E.V. Lucas, 7 vols (London, 1903–1905), vol. 1, pp. 99, 107–8.

[9]   Cf. *Charles Lamb on Shakespeare*, ed. Joan Coldwell (New York, 1978), p. 13; Janet Ruth Heller, *Coleridge, Lamb, Hazlitt and the Reader of Drama* (Columbia and London, 1990), p. 167.

[10]   On the other hand, in his letter to Richard Woodhouse (27 October 1818) in which he refers to Shakespeare's poetic genius, John Keats, an acute reader of Shakespeare's *A Midsummer Night's Dream*, describes the Poet as a chameleon, deprived of a specific identity, always 'filling some other bodies' – *The Letters of John Keats*, ed. Maurice Buxton Forman (London, 1952), p. 227.

mind as a dream throughout'[11] – and, in particular, the staging of the fairies. In *The Theatrical Inquisitor, and Monthly Mirror* we read:

> The 'Midsummer Night's Dream' is one of those dramas which should never be performed; which, indeed, *never can be* performed. The manager, 'tis true, may send on Miss A. and Mrs B., and request that the audience will imagine them to be *Puck* and *Titania*, but those 'gay creatures of the element' can never be perfectly represented by human and corporeal bodies. ... What can possibly be more dissimilar than the *Ariel* of Shakespeare and the *Ariel* of the stage? than *Titania* in the 'Midsummer Night's Dream' and *Titania* on the boards of Covent-garden theatre? It is only by the 'mind's eye' that such fantastic beings can ever be faithfully personified; the presentations of the theatre are at best but meagre and imperfect sketches, unsatisfactory alike to the eye, the ear, and the understanding.[12]

Elizabeth Vestris's version of *A Midsummer Night's Dream* belies such prejudices regarding the possibilities of staging the comedy and demonstrates that 'poetry' and 'stage' are not incompatible.

Elizabeth Vestris's *A Midsummer Night's Dream*

Like all Shakespearean plays, *A Midsummer Night's Dream* has been subjected to transformations, manipulations, rewritings, and adaptations whereby the comedy has been reconstructed and reappropriated in relation to new contexts and new intertexts.[13] During the Restoration, *A Midsummer Night's Dream* became a pre-text for new works.[14] In the eighteenth and part of the nineteenth century, the Shakespearean text continued to be transformed, altered and adapted, that is,

---

[11]   Coleridge, '"Midsummer Night's Dream", Marginalia and other notes on individual plays', in *Coleridge's Shakespearean Criticism*, vol. 1, p. 100–102, at p. 100.

[12]   *The Theatrical Inquisitor, and Monthly Mirror*, 8 (June 1816): 445.

[13]   On the appropriation of Shakespeare in the eighteenth and nineteenth centuries, see Jonathan Bate, *Shakespearean Constitutions: Politics, Theatre, Criticism, 1730–1830* (Oxford, 1989); Gary Taylor, *Reinventing Shakespeare: A Cultural History from the Restoration to the Present* (London, 1991); Jean I. Marsden (ed.), *The Appropriation of Shakespeare: Post-Renaissance Reconstruction of the Works and the Myth* (New York, 1991); Michael Dobson, *The Making of a National Poet: Shakespeare, Adaptation and Authorship, 1660–1769* (Oxford, 1992); Christy Desmet and Robert Sawyer (eds), *Shakespeare and Appropriation* (London, 1999).

[14]   Cf. The comic sketch *The Merry Conceited Humors of Bottom the Weaver* (1661), and the operatic adaptation *The Fairy Queen* (1692).

'made fit' to the taste and demands of the contemporary audience.[15] Only in 1840, thanks to Elizabeth Vestris, was Shakespeare's *A Midsummer Night's Dream* put on stage again; for the first time since Shakespeare's days it was staged almost completely, and the scenery, resulting from a coherent and organic design, was closely linked to the staged text.

The text staged by Elizabeth Vestris[16] contains neither substantial rewritings or additions of lines nor changes to the plot, but only a few omissions, transpositions of lines, and lexical changes and additions with the function of linking various passages together. The omissions affect mainly lines not strictly necessary to the development of the story, such as poetical descriptions or comments on various topics (for example, Hermia's lines on the lovers' destiny in I, i). They also affect lines characterized by a 'low' register or containing sexual references, such as the lines about Lysander's desire for Hermia (II, ii, 40–62). Likewise omitted are religious references, like the exclamation 'Oh Hell!' (III, Ii, 145) and the lines 'To vow, and swear, and superpraise my parts, / When I am sure you hate me with your hearts' (III, ii, 153–4). It is worth noting that most of the line omissions and translocations affect the plot of the lovers, while those of Theseus and Hippolyta, of the mechanicals and of the fairies are subject to few small alterations.

Elizabeth Vestris's version, despite reducing the lines concerning the lovers, breaks with what was then the usual procedure in the adaptations of the play: she offers an innovative restitution of the Shakespearean text without rewriting whole episodes or adding new passages.

The performance too, as can be inferred from the stage directions of the Pattie edition and from the theatrical reviews of the time, was particularly innovative.

---

[15]   Cf. Richard Leveridge, *The Comic Masque of Pyramus and Thisbe* (1716); J.F. Lampe, *Pyramus and Thisbe: A Mock Opera* (1745); David Garrick, *The Fairies* (1755); David Garrick and George Colman, *A Midsummer Night's Dream* (1763); George Colman, *A Fairy Tale* (1763); Frederick Reynolds, *A Midsummer Night's Dream* (1816).

[16]   'The text staged by Elizabeth Vestris' or simply 'Vestris's text' refers to Pattie's performance edition. Unlike the promptbooks of other Shakespearean productions supervised by Elizabeth Vestris, the promptbook of the production of *A Midsummer Night's Dream* is lost. However, there are two printed editions of the comedy that make reference to Vestris's version: the text, undated, included in *Lacy's Acting edition of Plays, Dramas, Farces, Extravaganzas, etc. etc. as performed at the various theatres*, ed. Thomas Hailes Lacy, vol. 28 (London, 1850); and the performance edition published in London by James Pattie, also undated – *A Midsummer-Night's Dream: a comedy, in five acts, by William Shakspere. As revived at the Theatre Royal, Covent Garden, November 16th, 1840. Correctly printed from the prompt copy, with exits, entrances etc. And, (for the First time that any Dramatic Work has possessed the same advantages in publication.) Plots of the scenery, properties, calls, copy of the original bill, incidents etc.* (London). A careful analysis of the two editions, of the reviews printed on the contemporary newspapers and magazines, and of various iconographical materials and playbills, allowed me to identify Pattie's edition as the version of the Shakespearean text staged by Elizabeth Vestris.

The spectacular and musical effects were closely linked to the Shakespearean text. As for the scenery, unlike in previous adaptations it was not a mere adjunct more or less allusive to the text, but was virtually an illustration to the text itself, for example showing a natural change symbolically parallel to a change in the situation, or making explicit an image suggested by the text: thus the third scene of the fourth act opens with the wood (*The transparent wood, as in Act 3, Scene 1. – Demetrius, Lysander, Helena, and Hermia, discovered sleeping*), and then shows the night turning into a new day through the rising of the sun, which anticipates and symbolizes the solution and the happy ending of the lovers' plot:

> *– Music – The moon sinks very gradually; the rays disappear from the water, and the sunlight begins to break through the tops of the trees; daylight continues to increase until all lights are full on.*

The spectacular final effect was similarly suggested in every detail by the Shakespearean text:

> *Scene glides away, part of it ascending, other parts descending, and going off R. 2 L. – The stage forms a flight of steps – Large flights of steps R. and L. – Platform and gallery from R. to L. – Fairies all discovered with torches of various coloured fires - stairs and gallery crowded with them – Oberon, Titania, first and second Fairies centre.*

In his *Recollections and Reflections*, James Robinson Planché, at that time 'Superintendent of the Decorative Department'[17] at Covent Garden under the management of Elizabeth Vestris, describes the achieving of the desired effect:

A Third important revival was Shakespere's 'Midsummer Night's Dream' … When this revival was first suggested, Bartley said, 'If Planché can devise a striking effect for the last scene, the play will run for sixty nights.' I pointed out that Shakespere had suggested it himself, in the words of Oberon to his attendant fairies –

'Through the house give glimmering light,
*   *   *   *   *
Every elf and fairy sprite
Hop as light as bird from brier,
And this ditty after me
Sing, and dance it trippingly.'

---

[17]   James Robinson Planché, *The Recollections and Reflections of J.R. Planché, A Professional Autobiography*, 2 vols (London, 1872), vol. 2, p. 22.

It was accordingly arranged with Grieve, the scenic artist, who is at this day still adding to his great reputation, that the back of the stage should be so constructed that at the command of Oberon it should be filled with fairies, bearing twinkling coloured lights, 'fitting through the house,' and forming groups and dancing, as indicated in the text, carrying out implicitly the directions of the author, and not sacrilegiously attempting to gild his refined gold. The result was most successful, and verified Bartley's prediction.[18]

This final effect was widely praised in the newspapers and journals of the time as one of the most beautiful and impressive fairy scenes ever seen on stage. *The Theatrical Journal* and *The Times* describe the scene as follows:

> The last scene, a hall in Theseus's house; one of those rich architectural compositions with galleries and flights of stairs, that have a most impressive effect on the stage; here assemble the entire body of fairies making merry over the triple nuptials, darting from side to side, flying round and round, now here, now there, on the ground, in the air, waving their tiny lamps till the entire place seems sparkling with the countless hues of light, and the delighted eye passing its thrill of pleasure to the tongue, one exclamation of delight springs simultaneously from the beholders as down falls the curtain.[19]

> [The] discovery of the interior of the palace, with fairies crowded in every part, gliding along galleries, ascending and descending steps, soaring in the air with blue and yellow torches, which produce a curious light, is one of the most beautiful and highly wrought fairy scenes ever introduced on the stage.[20]

What most impressed the audience and the critics was the carrying out of the implicit directions of the author, the staging of what is inscribed in Shakespeare's text. In this way, Planché recognizes in Shakespeare's play the very performability that most romantic critics denied; moreover, he emphasizes the fact that the play contains in itself all the potentialities for the performance.

Elizabeth Vestris endeavours to reconstruct ancient Athens and to create indoor spaces striking for their historical accuracy. However, it is with the bucolic scenes that she achieves her most surprising effects, allowing the audience to experience the impression of being in a supernatural or oneiric landscape:

---

[18] Ibid., vol. 2, pp. 51–2. The play was performed fifty-nine times in the 1840/41 season, and eleven times in the following one.

[19] *The Theatrical Journal*, 2/72 (1 May 1841): 139.

[20] *The Times*, 17 November (1840): 4

Between these two stately architectural realities [the opening-scene and the penultimate scene], all is sylvan and visionary: the wood-scenes change like the phases of a dream.[21]

Messrs. Grieves have surpassed themselves in several of the supernatural landscapes; and especially in one where a striking tree in the centre is illumed by a bluish light; and another where the Morning descends in pearls among the waving foliage of a forest.[22]

The scenery is beyond all praise, and the lights and shadows are so judiciously managed, as to produce occasionally a vague and dreamy indistinctness, so much allied to the fairy land of the poet that 'fancy led', we forget under the illusion, produced by what we look upon, that we still inhabit this dull, plodding and everyday world. The concluding scene is most gorgeous; yet light, airy and fantastic – but we dwell with a more pleasurable feeling on the woodland, moonlit scenery of the earlier part of the play.[23]

As far as the music is concerned, for the first time in the stage history of *A Midsummer Night's Dream* the texts of the songs are lines from the comedy. Furthermore, unlike previous adaptations of the play, the songs are much less numerous,[24] and do not have a merely decorative function intended to guarantee the success of the play; they are sung only by the fairies, serving to characterize the enchanted world as ethereal and romantic, and to distinguish it more clearly from the world of the mortals. The instrumental music again served almost exclusively as a background to the plot of the fairies, harmonizing with the Shakespearean text and helping to create a supernatural atmosphere. Furthermore, since the music was selected, arranged and directed by the same musician, Thomas Cooke, it possessed an unusual coherence and cohesion.

The reviews in the journals and newspapers of the time stressed how the costumes were strictly linked to the Classical world:

The costume for the most part rests upon authority, and is as correct as the scenery of the GRIEVES is beautiful.[25]

The dresses are splendid, and classically correct.[26]

---

[21]   *The Spectator*, 21 November (1840): 1111.
[22]   *The Literary Gazette*, 21 (November 1840): 756.
[23]   *The Theatrical Journal*, 51 (5 December 1840): 415.
[24]   In Vestris's version there are fourteen songs; in Reynold's, more than twenty; in the 1763 version, thirty-three; in Garrick's *The Fairies*, twenty-eight.
[25]   *John Bull*, 21 November (1840): 562.
[26]   *The Theatrical Journal*, 51 (5 December 1840): 415.

The costumes by Mr. Head and Miss Ireland, were classically correct.[27]

Theseus, the lovers, Egeus, Philostrate and the soldiers wore clothing and ornaments of Ancient Greece (*Grecian mantle, Greek borders, tunic, Greek armour dresses*). As for the other characters, Hippolyta was dressed like an Amazon with a tunic and a pair of trousers (*Gold tissue tunic, to fit close, crimson pantaloons, studded with gold*); the mechanicals wore simple tunics, leather belts and sandals; while the fairies, dressed in white veil gowns (*White gauze, trimmed with silver*),[28] embodied, in a sense, the lightness and the poetical quality of a romantic corps de ballet.

Vestris's production was widely praised by the press; even the critics who had some reservations about the staging of the comedy acknowledged that Madame Vestris, as far as it was possible, was able to produce a convincing theatrical version of what had until then been considered an ethereal poetic text:

> In the production of Shakespeare's *Midsummer Night's Dream* two great difficulties present themselves – the very fanciful nature of the characters, and the great want of dramatic interest. ... To the reader it is one gorgeous dream of poetry. ... With the pauses incident to theatrical production, and the necessity of fixing the attention of an audience by stronger means than those that are required to secure a reader, the representation of *Midsummer Night's Dream*, so as to charm a London public, becomes a most arduous undertaking. ... As far as theatrical representation of this ethereal drama is possible, it was achieved last night, and a gorgeous spectacle was produced. The beings of a moment could not be portrayed, little Messrs. Cobweb, Moth, and Mustardseed, with their shrill trumpet voices were but inadequate likeness of their shadowy originals; but in the conception of the whole, a fine poetical feeling was apparent, a consciousness of the difficulties with which the struggle was to be made, and a resolution to conquer them if possible. If the minute elves could not be obtained, it was still left to give a shadowy unreal character to the scenery; if the individuals could not be realized, it was still possible to give a fairy grace to the groups, and impart to the whole *tableau*, what could not be bestowed on its parts.[29]

> In the getting up of this play, nothing has been left undone that could be achieved by art, ingenuity, talent and unbounded expence, aided and controlled by the most exquisite taste. ... But alas! After all that has been, or can be, done, the adequate representation of this most wildly beautiful and poetic conception

---

[27]   Theatre Museum cutting, 22 November 1840.

[28]   List of costumes, Pattie edition, p. v. In *John Bull* there is a description of the fairies' costumes: 'The fairies are clad, according to the prescriptive usage of the stage, in virgin white, and immaculate silk stockings' (21 November 1840: 562).

[29]   *The Times*, 17 November (1840): 4.

of our divine Shakespeare, is a thing impossible. The poet here has revelled in all the boundless exuberance of his own inexhaustible fancy.

He has created a world of his own, and peopled it with beings, bright, etherial essences, who melt into the mist in the grey moonlight, or float upon the sunbeam.

The attempt to represent those creatures of the imagination by little children, with their tiny voices, is perfectly hopeless, but we can well conceive Oberon and his Queen invested with mortal lineaments, and surely Madame did well to make her Elfin King assume a knightly panoply, for he had come so chided Titania, from farthest steep of India, to the wedding of his buskined mistress and warrior love. But if Madame Vestris has not effected impossibilities, she has in this play so far exceeded all our resonable expectations, that in our admiration of the wonders of her mimic fairy land, we almost forget that anything is wanting to complete the picture that Shakespeare has drawn, and which the mind alone can contemplate in all its perfectness of beauty.[30]

In a subsequent issue, *The Theatrical Journal* praised with even more enthusiasm the result reached by Elizabeth Vestris, defining her version as the best revival of *A Midsummer Night's Dream* in the stage history of the play:

I do believe a happier revival never took place on the stage, than in the *Midsummer Night's Dream*; the spirit of poetry seems to have actuated all concerned, and right merry am I, that the public has with a profuse hand tended their thanks to Madame for so dainty a fare: I do hope it will not for some time be set aside, and that a night at least per week will still be devoted to its use, and if the public think as I think, they will visit the theatre night after night with the same thirst and veneration, as the poor Jew journeys to the Holy Land; for Shakespeare relives, and calls for the homage, nations declare to be justly his.[31]

In the version of *A Midsummer Night's Dream* staged at Covent Garden under the management of Elizabeth Vestris, the Shakespearean critic James Orchard Halliwell acknowledges the first successful attempt to reconcile the poetry of the text with the requirements of the performance and the taste of the contemporary audience:

[Vestris's management is] the only management since the days of our great dramatist that has succeeded in placing the *most* poetical and speculative play in the whole range of English drama upon the stage with advantage! When Pepys saw the 'Midsummer Night's Dream' performed, he pronounced it 'ridiculous'; Walpole called it 'one of the greatest pieces of nonsense he ever saw'; Colman and Garrick revived it without success; and when Reynolds brought it out with

---

[30]   *The Theatrical Journal and Stranger's Guide*, 51 (5 December 1840): 415.
[31]   Ibid., 2/72 (1 May 1841): 139.

alterations in 1816, it was only played a very few nights, although we have Hazlitt's authority for saying that 'the spectacle was grand'. It was left for Madame Vestris' management in 1840 to reconcile the public taste, for the first time, to genuine poetry and the stage.[32]

Being able to reconcile scenery, costumes and music with the Shakespearean text, Elizabeth Vestris succeeded in making a coherent performance that successfully evoked the fantastic world created by Shakespeare's imagination. Her version not only showed that 'poetry and stage' could 'agree together', but, thanks to a restored Shakespearean text and a simpler performance unusually faithful to the script, it also marked an important departure from preceding adaptations of *A Midsummer Night's Dream*, while at the same time becoming the cornerstone for later nineteenth- and even twentieth-century performances of the play.

---

[32]   James Orchard Halliwell, *The Management of Covent Garden Theatre vindicated from the attack of an anonymous critic, in a letter to the editor of the 'Cambridge Advertiser'* (London, 1841), pp. 8–9.

Bibliography

Adolphus, John, *Memoirs of John Bannister, Comedian*, 2 vols (London: Richard Bentley, 1839).

Aliverti, Maria Ines, *La Naissance de l'acteur moderne* (Paris: Gallimard, 1998).

Altick, Richard Daniel, *The Shows of London* (Cambridge, MA: Belknap Press, 1978).

Anon., 'The Living Poets of England' (on Wordsworth), n.s., 1 (January 1826): 17–22.

Anon., 'The Living Poets of England' (on Hemans), n.s., 3 (March 1826): 113–21.

Anon., 'Analytical Essays on the Modern English Drama', *Blackwood's Edinburgh Magazine*, 18 (July 1825): 119–36.

Anon., 'Celebrated Female Writers. No. I. Joanna Baillie', *Blackwood's Edinburgh Magazine*, 16 (August 1824): 162, 165.

Anon., [Review of Joanna Baillie's *Dramas of the Ancient World*], *Blackwood's Magazine*, vol. 56/10 (December 1821): 731.

Anon., 'Dialogue on the Drama', *The Theatrical Inquisitor* (February 1820): 74–6.

Anon., 'Review of Charles Robert Maturin's *Bertram*', *The British Lady's Magazine*, 3 (June 1816): 429.

Anon., 'Mrs. Cowley's Works', *The European Magazine*, 66 (August–September, 1814): 000.

Anon., 'Baillie's *Series of Plays*', *The Annual Review; and History of Literature*, 1 (1802): 680.

Anon., Review of *The Mysterious Marriage, or the Hermit of Roselva*, by Harriet Lee, *The Monthly Mirror*, 5 (March 1798): 166.

Anon., 'Account of Mrs. Inchbald's New Comedy [*Wives as They Were*]', *The Lady's Magazine*, 28 (1797): 120.

Anon., *The Theatrical Portrait, a Poem on the Celebrated Mrs. Siddons, in the Characters of Calista, Jane Shore, Belvidera, and Isabella* (London, 1783).

Anon., *The Tragic Muse: A Poem Addressed to Mrs. Siddons* (London: G. Kearsley, 1783).

Asleson, Robyn (ed.), *A Passion for Performance: Sarah Siddons and her Portraitists* (Los Angeles: Paul Getty Museum, 1999).

Astin, Marjorie, *Mary Russell Mitford: Her Circle and her Books* (London: Noel Douglas, 1930).

Austen, Jane, *Northanger Abbey* (Harmondsworth: Penguin, 1985).

Austin, J.L., *How to Do Things with Words* (Oxford: Clarendon, 1962).

Backsheider, Paula R. (ed.), *The Plays of Elizabeth Inchbald* (New York and London: Garland, 1980).

Baillie, Joanna, *Plays on the Passions*, ed. Peter Duthie (Peterborough, ON: Broadview Press, 2001).

Baillie, Joanna, *The Dramatic and Poetical Works of Joanna Baillie: Complete in One Volume* (London: Longman, Brown, Green, and Longmans, 1851); 2nd edn, repr., *The Dramatic and Poetical Works of Joanna Baillie* (Hildesheim and New York: Georg Olms Verlag, 1976).

Baillie, Joanna, *The Family Legend* (from *Miscellaneous Plays*), in *The Dramatic and Poetical Works of Joanna Baillie: Complete in One Volume* (London: Longman, Brown, Green, and Longmans, 1851).

Baillie, Joanna, *A View of the General Tenour of the New Testament Regarding the Nature and Dignity of Jesus Christ* (London: Longman, Rees, Orme, Brown and Greene, 1831).

Baillie, Joanna, *The Martyr, A Drama in Three Acts* (London: Longman, Rees, Orme, Brown and Greene, 1826).

Baines, Paul, and Burns, Edward (eds), *Five Romantic Plays* (Oxford: Oxford University Press, 2000).

Balme, Christopher, Erenstein, Robert and Molinari, Cesare (eds), *European Theatre Iconography* (Rome: Bulzoni, 2002).

Bann, Stephen, *Romanticism and the Rise of History* (New York and Oxford: Maxwell Macmillan International, 1995).

Barish, Jonas A., *The Antitheatrical Prejudice* (Berkeley: University of California Press, 1981).

Barrell, John, *Imagining the King's Death: Figurative Treason, Fantasies of Regicide 1793–1796* (Oxford: Oxford University Press, 2000).

Barrell, John, *The Political Theory of Painting from Reynolds to Hazlitt: The Body of the Public* (New Haven, CT, and London: Yale University Press, 1986).

Barrett Browning, Elizabeth, *The Letters of Elizabeth Barrett Browning to Mary Russell Mitford 1836–1854*, ed. Meredith B. Raymond and Mary Rose Sullivan, 3 vols (Waco: Armstrong Browning Library of Baylor University, 1983).

Bassnett, Susan, 'Still Trapped in the Labyrinth: Further Reflections on Translation and Theatre', in Bassnett and André Lefevere (eds), *Translating Cultures: Essays on Literary Translation* (Clevedon: Multilingual Matters, 1998), pp. 90–108.

Bassnett, Susan, 'When is a Translation not a Translation?', in Bassnett and André Lefevere (eds), *Constructing Cultures: Essays on Literary Translation* (Clevedon: Multilingual Matters, 1998), pp. 25–40.

Bassnett, Susan, *Translation Studies* (London and New York: Methuen, 1980).

Bassnett, Susan, and Lefevere, André, 'Introduction: Where Are We In Translation Studies?', in Bassnett and Lefevere (eds), *Constructing Cultures: Essays on Literary Translation* (Clevedon: Multilingual Matters, 1998), pp. 1–11.

Bate, Jonathan, *Shakespeare and the English Romantic Imagination* (Oxford: Clarendon Press, 1989).

Bate, Jonathan, *Shakespearean Constitutions: Politics, Theatre, Criticism, 1730–1830* (Oxford: Oxford University Press, 1989).

Beddoes, Thomas Lovell, *The Letters of Thomas Lovell Beddoes* (London: E. Mathews & J. Lane, 1894).

Behn, Aphra, *Sir Patient Fancy*, in Katharine M. Rogers (ed.), *The Meridian Anthology of Restoration and Eighteenth-Century Plays by Women* (New York: Meridian, 1994), pp. 23–130.

Bennett, Alan, *The History Boys* (London: Faber and Faber, 2004).

Bennett, Betty T., *Mary Diana Dods: A Gentleman and a Scholar* (New York: Morrow, 1991).

Berman, Antoine, 'Translation and the Trials of the Foreign', trans. Lawrence Venuti, in Venuti (ed.), *The Translation Studies Reader* (London: Routledge, 2002), pp. 276–89.

Bevis, Richard, *The Laughing Tradition: Stage Comedy in Garrick's Day* (Athens, GA: University of Georgia Press, 1980).

Blain, Virginia, Clements, Patricia and Grundy, Isobel (eds), *The Feminist Companion to Literature in English: Women Writers from the Middle Ages to the Present* (New Haven, CT: Yale University Press, 1990).

Blanchard, Laman, *Life and Literary Remains of L.E.L.*, 2 vols (London, 1841).

Bloom, Harold, *Poetry and Repression: Revisionism from Blake to Stevens* (New Haven, CT: Yale University Press, 1976).

Boaden, James, *Memoirs of Mrs. Inchbald: Including her Familiar Correspondence with the Most Distinguished Persons of her Time*, 2 vols (London: Richard Bentley, 1833).

Boaden, James, *Memoirs of Mrs. Siddons, interspersed with Anecdotes of Authors and Actors* (Philadelphia: H.C. Carey & I. Lea, 1827).

Boaden, James, *Memoirs of the Life of John Philip Kemble*, 2 vols (London: Longman, 1825).

Boehrer, Bruce, *Monarchy and Incest in Renaissance England* (Philadelphia: University of Pennsylvania Press, 1992).

Bolton, Betsy, *Women, Nationalism and the Romantic Stage: Theatre and Politics in Britain, 1780–1800* (Cambridge: Cambridge University Press, 2001).

Bolton, Betsy, 'Farce, Romance and Empire: Elizabeth Inchbald and the Colonial Discourse', *The Eighteenth Century*, 39/1 (1998): 3–24.

Booth, Michael, et al. (eds), *The Revels History of Drama in English, vol. VI: 1750–1880* (London: Methuen, 1975).

Bourdieu, Pierre, *The Rules of Art: Genesis and Structure of the Literary Field*, trans. Susan Emanuel (Stanford: Stanford University Press, 1995).

Bourdieu, Pierre, *Distinction: A Social Critique of the Judgment of Taste*, trans. Richard Nice (Cambridge, MA: Harvard University Press, 1984).

Brooke, Frances, *The Siege of Sinope* (Cambridge: Chadwyck-Healey, 1994).

Bratton, Jacky, 'Romantic Melodrama', in Jane Moody and Daniel O'Quinn (eds), *The Cambridge Companion to British Theatre, 1730–1830* (Cambridge, 2007), pp. 115–27.

Brown, Eluned (ed.), *The London Theatre 1811–1866: Selections from the Diary of Henry Crabb Robinson* (London: The Society for Theatre Research, 1966).

Burke, Edmund, *Reflections on the Revolution in France (1790)*, ed. Conor Cruise O'Brien (Harmondsworth: Penguin Books, 1969; 1983).

Burney, Fanny, *Edwy and Elgiva*, ed. Miriam J. Benkovitz (Hamden: Shoe String Press, 1957).

Burroughs, Catherine B., 'British Women Playwrights and the Staging of Female Sexual Initiation: Sophia Lee's *The Chapter of Accidents* (1780)', *Romanticism on the Net*, Special Issue: Romanticism and Sexuality, 23 (August 2001), at: http://www-sul.stanford.edu/mirrors/romnet, accessed August 2001; repr. in *European Romantic Review*, Special Issue: Romantic Drama: Origins, Permutations, and Legacies, 14/1 (2003): 7–16.

Burroughs, Catherine B. (ed.), *Women in British Romantic Theatre: Drama, Performance and Society, 1790–1840* (Cambridge: Cambridge University Press, 2000).

Burroughs, Catherine B., '"Be Good!": Acting, Reader's Theatre, and Oration in the Writing of Frances Anne Kemble', in Harriet Kramer Linkin and Stephen Behrendt (eds), *Romanticism and Women Poets: Opening the Doors of Reception* (Lexington, KY: The University Press of Kentucky, 1999), pp. 125–43.

Burroughs, Catherine B., 'Teaching the Theory and Practice of Women's Dramaturgy', *Romanticism On the Net*, 12 (November 1998), at: http://www.erudit.org/revue/ron/1998/v/n12/005823ar.html, accessed November 1998.

Burroughs, Catherine B., *Closet Stages: Joanna Baillie and the Theater Theory of British Romantic Women Writers* (Philadelphia: University of Pennsylvania Press, 1997).

Burstein, Miriam, *Narrating Women's History in Britain, 1770–1902* (Aldershot: Ashgate, 2004).

Burwick, Frederick, 'Joanna Baillie: Matthew Baillie, and the Pathology of the Passions', in Thomas C. Crochunis (ed.), *Joanna Baillie, Romantic Dramatist: Critical Essays* (London and New York: Routledge, 2004), pp. 48–68.

Burwick, Frederick, 'The Ideal Shatters: Sarah Siddons, Madness, and the Dynamics of Gesture', in Robyn Asleson (ed.), *Notorious Muse: The Actress in British Art and Culture 1776–1812* (New Haven, CT, and London: Yale University Press, 2003), pp. 129–49.

Butts, Dennis, *Mistress of Our Tears: A Literary and Bibliographical Study of Barbara Hofland* (Aldershot and Brookfield: Scolar Press, 1992).

Byron, George Gordon, *The Complete Poetical Works*, ed. Jerome McGann, 7 vols (Oxford: Oxford University Press, 1980–93).

Byron, George Gordon, *Letters and Journals*, ed. Leslie Alexis Marchand, 12 vols (London: John Murray, 1973–80).

Byron, George Gordon, 'Preface', *Marino Faliero, Doge of Venice* (1821), in *The Works of Lord Byron*, ed. E.H. Coleridge, vol. IV (London: John Murray, 1901), p. 408.

Campbell, Thomas, *Life of Mrs. Siddons* (New York: Harper; London: Effingham Wilson, 1834).

Canfield, J. Douglas, 'Introduction', in Canfield (ed.), *The Broadview Anthology of Restoration and Early Eighteenth-Century Drama* (Peterborough, ON: Broadview Press, 2001), pp. ix–xviii.

Carhart, Margaret S., *The Life and Work of Joanna Baillie*, Yale Studies in English 64 (New Haven, CT: Yale University Press, 1923; North Haven: Archon Books, 1970).

Carlson, Julie, *In the Theatre of Romanticism: Coleridge, Nationalism, Women* (Cambridge and New York: Cambridge University Press, 1994).

Carlson, Marvin, 'Introduction', in *The Heirs of Molière: Four French Comedies of the Seventeenth and Eighteenth Centuries*, trans. and ed. Carlson (New York: Martin E. Segal Theater Center, 2003), pp. i–vii.

Carlson, Marvin, 'Elizabeth Inchbald: A Woman Critic in Her Theatrical Culture', in Catherine B. Burroughs (ed.), *Women in British Romantic Theatre: Drama, Performance and Society, 1790–1840* (Cambridge: Cambridge University Press, 2000), pp. 207–22.

Carlyle, Thomas, 'Thoughts on History', *Fraser's Magazine*, II (November 1830): 413.

Carness, Patrick (with Joseph M. Moriarity), *Sexual Anorexia: Overcoming Sexual Self-Hatred* (Center City, MN: Hazelden, 1997).

Carney, Sean, 'The Passion of Joanna Baillie: Playwright as Martyr', *Theatre Journal*, 52 (2000): 227–52.

Carstairs, Christian, *The Hubble-Shue, Dedicated to the Honourable Antiquarian Society* (Edinburgh: s.n., 1780)

Cave, Richard Allen (ed.), *The Romantic Theatre: An International Symposium* (Totowa, NJ: Barnes and Noble, 1986).

Cima, Gay Gibson, 'To be Public as a Genius and Private as a Woman: The Critical Framing of Nineteenth-Century British Women Playwrights', in Tracy C. Davis and Ellen Donkin (eds), *Women and Playwriting in Nineteenth-Century Britain* (Cambridge: Cambridge University Press, 1999), pp. 35–53.

Clairvaux, St Bernard of, *The Letters of St. Bernard of Clairvaux*, trans. Bruno Scott James (London: Burns Oates, 1953).

Clark, Anna, *Women's Silence, Men's Violence: Sexual Assault in England, 1770–1845* (London and New York: Pandora, 1987).

Clarke, Norma, *Ambitious Heights: Writing, Friendship, Love, The Jewsbury Sisters, Felicia Hemans and Jane Carlyle* (London and New York: Routledge, 1990).

Clarke, Richard, *The Nabob; or, Asiatic Plunderers* (London, 1773).

Cocco, Maria Rosaria, *Arlecchino, Shakespeare e il Marinaio. Teatro Popolare e melodramma in Inghilterra, 1800–1850* (Napoli: Istituto Universitario Orientale, 1990).

Coldwell, Joan (ed.), *Charles Lamb on Shakespeare* (New York: Smythe, 1978).

Coleridge, Samuel Taylor, *Biographia Literaria*, ed. James Engell and W. Jackson Bate, 2 vols (Princeton, NJ, and London: Princeton University Press, 1983).

Coleridge, Samuel Taylor, *Shakespearean Criticism*, ed. T.M. Raysor, 2 vols (London: Constable, 1936).

Coleridge, Samuel Taylor, '[Lecture V]. [Historical plays. Richard II]', *Lectures of 1813–14 at Bristol, with reports by the 'Bristol Gazette' of eight lectures*, in *Coleridge's Shakespearean Criticism*, ed. Middleton Raysor, 2 vols (London: Constable, 1930), vol. 2, pp. 278–9.

Coleridge, Samuel Taylor, '"Midsummer Night's Dream", Marginalia and other notes on individual plays', in *Coleridge's Shakespearean Criticism*, ed. Middleton Raysor, 2 vols (London: Constable, 1930), vol. 1, p. 100–102.

Coles, William A., 'Magazine and Other Contributions by Mary Russell Mitford and Thomas Noon Talfourd', *Studies in Bibliography*, 12 (1959): 224.

Colon, Christine, 'Christianity and Colonial Discourse in Joanna Baillie's *The Bride*', *Renascence*, 54/3 (Spring 2002): 163–76.

Cone, Carl B., *The English Jacobins: Reformers in Late Eighteenth Century England* (New York: Charles Scribner's Sons, 1968).

Conolly, Leonard W., *The Censorship of English Drama, 1737–1824* (San Marino, CA: Huntington Library, 1976).

Corti, Claudia, 'La scena delle Muse. Mediazioni teatrali tra letteratura e arti visive', in Corti and Maria Grazia Messina (eds), *Poesia come pittura nel Romanticismo inglese* (Napoli: Liguori, 2004), pp. 7–60.

Cowley, Hannah, 'Preface', in *The Town Before You, a Comedy* (London, 1795), pp. ix–xi.

Cox, Jeffrey N., 'Staging Baillie', in Thomas C. Crochunis (ed.), *Joanna Baillie, Romantic Dramatist: Critical Essays* (London and New York: Routledge, 2004), pp. 146–67.

Cox, Jeffrey N., 'Baillie, Siddons, Larpent: Gender, Power, and Politics', in Catherine B. Burroughs (ed.), *Women in British Romantic Theatre: Drama, Performance and Society, 1790–1840* (Cambridge: Cambridge University Press, 2000), pp. 23–47.

Cox, Jeffrey N., 'Romantic Redefinitions of the Tragic', in Gerald Gillespie (ed.), *Romantic Drama, a Volume in A Contemporary History of Literature in European Languages* (Amsterdam and Philadelphia: John Benjamins, 1994), pp. 153–65.

Cox, Jeffrey N., 'Ideology and Genre in the British Anti-Revolutionary Drama in the 1790s', *ELH*, 58 (1992): 579–610.

Cox, Jeffrey N. (ed.), *Seven Gothic Dramas 1789–1825* (Athens, OH: Ohio University Press, 1992).

Cox, Jeffrey N., *In the Shadows of Romance: Romantic Tragic Drama in Germany, England, and France* (Athens, OH: Ohio University Press, 1987).

Cox, Jeffrey, and Gamer, Michael (eds), *The Broadview Anthology of Romantic Drama* (Peterborough, ON: Broadview Press, 2003).

Craciun, Adriana, and Lokke, Kari E., 'British Women Writers and the French Revolution', in Craciun and Lokke (eds), *Rebellious Hearts: British Women Writers and the French Revolution* (Albany, NY: State University of New York Press, 2001), pp. 3–32.

Craciun, Adriana, and Lokke, Kari E. (eds), *Rebellious Hearts: British Women Writers and the French Revolution* (Albany, NY: State University of New York Press, 2001).

Crisafulli, Lilla Maria, and Pietropoli, Cecilia (eds), *The Languages of British Romanticism* (Berne and Oxford: Peter Lang, 2008).

Crochunis, Thomas C. (ed.), *Joanna Baillie, Romantic Dramatist: Critical Essays* (London and New York: Routledge, 2004).

Crochunis, Thomas C., 'Joanna Baillie's Ambivalent Dramaturgy', in Crochunis (ed.), *Joanna Baillie, Romantic Dramatist: Critical Essays* (London and New York: Routledge, 2004), pp. 168–86.

Crochunis, Thomas C., 'Authorial Performances in the Criticism and Theory of Romantic Women Playwrights', in Catherine B. Burroughs (ed.), *Women in British Romantic Theatre: Drama, Performance and Society, 1790–1840* (Cambridge: Cambridge University Press, 2000), pp. 223–54.

Crochunis, Thomas C., 'British Women Playwrights around 1800: New Paradigms and Recoveries', Introduction to special issue of *Romanticism on the Net*, 12 (November 1998), at: http://www-sul.standford.edu/mirrors/ romnet.wp1800/

Crosby, Christina, *The Ends of History: Victorians and the 'Woman Question'* (London and New York: Routledge, 1991).

Davis, Gwenn, and Joyce, Beverly A., *Drama by Women to 1900: A Bibliography of American and British Writers* (Toronto: University of Toronto Press, 1992).

Davis, Tracy C., and Ellen Donkin (eds), *Women and Playwriting in Nineteenth-Century Britain* (Cambridge: Cambridge University Press, 1999).

Desmet, Christy, and Sawyer, Robert (eds), *Shakespeare and Appropriation* (London: Routledge, 1999).

Destouches, N., *Oeuvres Dramatiques, Précédées d'une Notion sur la Vie et les Ouvrages de Cet Auteur*, 6 vols (Paris: L. Tenré Librairie, 1832).

Destouches, Néricault Philippe, 'Deuxième Lettre a M. Le Chevalier de B****', in Destouches, *Oeuvres Dramatiques, Précédées d'une Notion sur la Vie et les Ouvrages de Cet Auteur*, 6 vols (Paris: Lefèvre, 1832), vol. 5, pp. 158–61.

Dix, Robin (ed.), *The Poetical Works of Mark Akenside* (London: Associated University Presses, 1996).

Dobrée, Bonamy (ed.), *The Letters of Philip Dormer Stanhope, 4th Earl of Chesterfield*, 6 vols (London: Eyre and Spottiswoode, 1932).

Dobson, Michael, *The Making of a National Poet: Shakespeare, Adaptation and Authorship, 1660–1769* (Oxford: Clarendon Press, 1992).

Donkin, Ellen, *Getting into the Act: Women Playwrights in London, 1776–1829* (London: Routledge, 1995).

Donohue, Joseph W., *Theatre in the Age of Kean* (Totowa, NJ: Rowman and Littlefield, 1975).

Donohue, Joseph W., *Dramatic Character in the English Romantic Age* (Princeton, NJ: Princeton University Press, 1970).

Douglass, Paul, 'Lord Byron's Feminist Canon: Notes toward Its Construction', *Romanticism on the Net*, 43 (August 2006): 1–47.

Dowd, Maureen A., 'By the Delicate Hand of a Female: Melodramatic Mania and Joanna Baillie's Spectacular Tragedies', *European Romantic Review*, 9/4 (Fall 1998): pp. 469–500.

Downer, Alan S., 'Players and the Painted Stage: Nineteenth-Century Acting', *PMLA*, 61 (1946): 522–76.

Downer, Alan S., 'Nature to Advantage Dressed: Eighteenth-Century Acting', *PMLA*, 58 (1943): 1002–37.

Drabble, Margaret (ed.), *The Oxford Companion to English Literature* (Oxford: Oxford University Press, 2006).

Dramaticus, *An Impartial View of the Stage* (London: Chapple, 1816).

Drumbl, Johann, 'Questioni metodologiche e problematica del gruppo destinatario', *Biblioteca Teatrale*, 15/16 (1976): 5–15.

Dwyer, Karen, 'Joanna Baillie's Plays on the Passions and the Spectacle of Medical Science', *Studies in Eighteenth-Century Culture*, 29 (2000): 23–46.

Elam, Keir, *Semiotics of Theatre and Drama*, 2nd edn (London: Routledge, 2001).

Elledge, Paul, *Lord Byron at Harrow School: Speaking Out, Talking Back, Acting Up, Bowing Out* (Baltimore: Johns Hopkins University Press, 2000).

Engell, James, and Bate, W.J. (eds), *Samuel Taylor Coleridge: Collected Works*, 16 vols (Princeton, NJ: Princeton University Press, 1982).

Ezell, Margaret, 'Revisioning Responding: A Second Look at Women Playwrights Around 1800', *Romanticism on the Net*, 12 (November 1998), at: http://www-sul.stanford.edu/mirrors/romnet/wp1800/essays.html

Farington, Joseph, *The Diary of Joseph Farington*, ed. Evelyn Newby, 17 vols (New Haven, CT, and London: Yale University Press, 1998).

Farington, John, *The Farington Diary*, ed. James Greig, 8 vols (London: Hutchinson, 1922).

Feldman, Paula R., and Kelley, Theresa M., *Romantic Women Writers: Voices and Countervoices* (Hanover: University Press of New England, 1995).

Felsenstein, Frank (ed.), *English Trader, Indian Maid: Representing Gender, Race and Slavery in the New World, An Inkle and Yarico Reader* (Baltimore and London: Johns Hopkins University Press, 1999).

Finberg, Melinda C. (ed.), *Eighteenth-Century Women Dramatists* (Oxford: Oxford University Press, 2001).

Findlay, Bill (ed.), *A History of Scottish Theatre* (Edinburgh: Polygon, 1998).

Fitzgerald, Percy H., *The Kembles: An Account of the Kemble Family, including the Lives of Mrs. Siddons, and Her Brother John Philip Kemble*, 2 vols (London: Tinsley Brothers, 1871).

Foucault, Michel, *Power/Knowledge: Selected Interviews and Other Writings*, ed. C. Gordon, trans. L. Marshall, J. Mepham and K. Soper (New York: Pantheon Books, 1980).

Franceschina, John (ed.), *Sisters of Gore: Seven Gothic Melodramas by British Women, 1790–1843* (New York: Garland Publishing, 1997).

Freeman, Lisa A., *Character's Theater: Genre and Identity on the Eighteenth-Century Stage* (Philadelphia: University of Pennsylvania Press, 2002).

Friedman, Geraldine, 'Pseudonymity, Passing, and Queer Biography: The Case of Mary Diana Dods', *Romanticism on the Net*, 23 (August 2001), at: http://users.ox.ac.uk/~scat0385/23friedman.html, accessed August 2001.

Friedman-Romell, Beth H., 'Staging the State: Joanna Baillie's *Constantine Paleologus*', in Tracy C. Davis and Ellen Donkin (eds), *Women and Playwriting in Nineteenth-Century Britain* (Cambridge: Cambridge University Press, 1999), pp. 151–73.

Gamer, Michael, 'National Supernaturalism: Joanna Baillie, Germany, and the Gothic Drama', in Gamer, *Romanticism and the Gothic: Genre, Reception, and Canon Formation* (Cambridge: Cambridge University Press, 2000), pp. 127–62.

Gamer, Michael, *Romanticism and the Gothic: Genre, Reception, and Canon Formation* (Cambridge: Cambridge University Press, 2000).

Garrick, David, *The Papers of David Garrick. Pt. 1. Correspondence from the John Forster Collection of the National Art Library* (London: Victoria and Albert Museum, 1998).

Gilbert, Deidre, 'Joanna Baillie, Passionate Anatomist: *Basil* and Its Masquerade', *Restoration and Eighteenth-Century Theatre Research*, 16/1 (2001): 42–54.

Gilroy, Amanda, and Hanley, Keith (eds), *Joanna Baillie: A Selection of Plays and Poems* (London: Pickering & Chatto, 2002).

Gisborne, Thomas, *An Enquiry into the Duties of the Female Sex*, in Ellen Donkin, *Getting into the Act: Women Playwrights in London, 1776–1829* (London: Routledge, 1995).

Gisborne, Thomas, *An Enquiry into the Duties of the Female Sex* (London: T. Cadell Jr. and W. Davies, 1797).

Godwin, William, 'Of History and Romance', Appendix IV, in *Caleb Williams*, ed. Maurice Hindle, (Harmondsworth: Penguin, 1988), pp. 359–74.

Green, Katherine S., 'Mr. Harmony and the Events of January 1793: Elizabeth Inchbald's *Every One Has His Fault*', *Theatre Journal*, 56/1 (2004): 47–62.

Greenblatt, Stephen, *Shakespearean Negotiations: The Circulation of Social Energy in Renaissance England* (Berkeley: University of California Press, 1988).

Gwilliam, Tassie, 'Female Fraud: Counterfeit Maidenheads in the Eighteenth Century', *Journal of the History of Sexuality*, 6/4 (1996): 518–48.

Haakonssen, Knud (ed.), *Enlightenment and Religion: Rational Dissent in Eighteenth-Century Britain* (Cambridge: Cambridge University Press, 1996).

Hadley, Elaine, *Melodramatic Tactics: Theatricalized Dissent in the English Marketplace, 1800–1885* (Stanford: Stanford University Press, 1995).

Halliwell, James Orchard, *The Management of Covent Garden Theatre vindicated from the attack of an anonymous critic, in a letter to the editor of the 'Cambridge Advertiser'* (London, 1841).

Halsband, Robert, 'Stage Drama as a Source for Pictorial and Plastic Arts', in S.S. Kenny (ed.), *British Theatre and the Other Arts* (Washington: Folger Shakespeare Library, 1984), pp. 149–70.

[Harness, William], *The Life of Mary Russell Mitford*, ed. A.G. L'Estrange, 3 vols (London: Richard Bentley, 1870).

Hawkins, Frederick W., *The Life of Edmund Kean*, 2 vols (London: Tinsley Brothers, 1869).

Hays, Mary, *Female Biography; or Memoirs of Illustrious and Celebrated Women of All Ages and Countries. Alphabetically Arranged, in Six Volumes*, printed for Richard Phillips, 6 vols (London: St Paul's Church Yard; Philadelphia: Birch and Small, 1803).

Hazlitt, William, *A View of the English Stage*, in *The Selected Writings of William Hazlitt*, ed. Duncan Wu, 9 vols (London: Pickering and Chatto, 1998).

Hazlitt, William, 'On the Living Poets', in *The Selected Writings of William Hazlitt*, ed. Duncan Wu, 9 vols (London: Pickering and Chatto, 1998), vol. 2, pp. 298–320.

Hazlitt, William, '"Mr. Kean's Richard II"', *A View of the English Stage*, in *The Complete Works of William Hazlitt*, ed. P.P Howe, 21 vols (London and Toronto: J.M. Dent, 1930–34), vol. 5, p. 222.

Hazlitt, William, '"The Midsummer Night's Dream", *A View of the English Stage*', in *The Complete Works of William Hazlitt*, ed. P.P. Howe, 21 vols (London and Toronto: J.M. Dent, 1930–34), vol. 5, pp. 274–5.

Hazlitt, William, *Lectures on the Living Poets: The Spirit of the Age* (London: J.M. Dent and Sons, 1910).

Hazlitt, William, 'The Drama. No.1', *The London Magazine*, 1 (January–June 1820): 64–70.

Hazlitt, William, *A View of the English Stage; or a Series of Dramatic Criticisms* (London: Robert Stodart, Anderson & Chase, 1818).

Hazlitt, William, *Memoirs of the late Thomas Holcroft*, 3 vols (London: Longman, 1816).

Heller, Janet Ruth, *Coleridge, Lamb, Hazlitt and the Reader of Drama* (Columbia and London: University of Missouri Press, 1990).

Hemans, Felicia, *The Siege of Valencia. A Parallel Text Edition. The Manuscript and the Publication of 1823*, eds Susan J. Wolfson and Elizabeth Fay (Peterborough, ON: Broadview Press, 2002).

Hemans, Felicia, 'German Studies, By Mrs. Hemans', *New Monthly Magazine*, 40 (January 1834): 1–8.

Highfill, Philip H. Jr., Burnim, Kalman A., and Langhans, Edward A. (eds), *A Biographical Dictionary of Actors, Actresses, Musicians, Dancers, Managers*

& Other Stage Personnel in London, 1660–1800 (Carbondale: Southern Illinois University Press, 1973–93).

Hoagwood, Terence, 'Elizabeth Inchbald, Joanna Baillie, and Revolutionary Representation in the "Romantic" Period', in Adriana Craciun and Kari E. Lokke (eds), *Rebellious Hearts: British Women Writers and the French Revolution* (Albany, NY: State University of New York Press, 2001), pp. 293–316.

Hoagwood, Terence Allen, 'Romantic Drama and Historical Hermeneutics', in Hoagwood and Daniel P. Watkins (eds), *British Romantic Drama: Historical and Critical Essays* (London: Associated University Presses, 1998), pp. 22–55.

Hoagwood, Terence Allan, and Watkins, Daniel P. (eds), *British Romantic Drama: Historical and Critical Essays* (London: Associated University Presses, 1998).

Hogan, B. Charles, *The London Stage 1776–1800* (Carbondale: Southern Illinois University Press, 1968).

Holcroft, Thomas, *Duplicity*, in *The Plays of Thomas Holcroft*, ed. Joseph Rosenblum, 2 vols (New York: Garland, 1980).

Holcroft, Thomas, *He's Much to Blame* (1798b), Larpent MS 1195.

Holcroft, Thomas, *Knave or Not?* (1798a), Larpent MS 1192.

Holcroft, Thomas, *Love's Frailties* (1794), Larpent MS 1008.

Holcroft, Thomas, 'Review of Inchbald *Every One Has His Fault*', *Monthly Review*, X (March 1793): 302–8.

Holcroft, Thomas, *Duplicity* (London: G. Robinson, 1781).

Howarth, W.D., 'Assimilation and Adaptation of Existing Forms in Drama of the Romantic Period', in Gerald Gillespie (ed.), *Romantic Drama, a Volume in A Contemporary History of Literature in European Languages* (Amsterdam and Philadelphia: John Benjamins, 1994), pp. 81–97.

Hughes, Alan, 'Art and Eighteenth-Century Acting Style, III: Passions', *Theatre Notebook*, 41 (1987): 128–39.

Hughes-Hallett, Penelope, *The Immortal Dinner: A Famous Evening of Genius and Laughter in Literary London, 1817* (London: Viking, 2000).

Hunt, Leigh, *Leigh Hunt's Dramatic Criticism*, eds Lawrence Huston Houtchens and Carolyn Washburn Houtchens (New York: Columbia University Press, 1949).

Hunt, Lynn, 'Introduction: Obscenity and the Origins of Modernity, 1500–1800', in Hunt (ed.), *The Invention of Pornography: Obscenity and the Origins of Modernity, 1500–1800* (New York: Zone Books, 1993), pp. 9–45.

Hurd, Richard, *Hurd's Letters on Chivalry and Romance*, ed. Edith J. Morley (London: Henry Frowde, 1911).

Imperiali, Isabella, *Le passioni della mente nel teatro di Joanna Baillie* (Rome: Editoria e Spettacolo, 2007).

Imperiali, Isabella, 'Joanna Baillie's Last Phase', unpublished essay.

Imperiali, Isabella, 'The Active Language of Closet Drama: Joanna Baillie and *De Monfort*', unpublished essay.

Inchbald, Elizabeth, *Remarks for the British Theatre 1806–09*, with an introduction by Cecilia Macheski (Delmar, NY: Scholars' Facsimiles & Reprints, 1990).

Inchbald, Elizabeth, *The Plays of Elizabeth Inchbald*, ed. Paula R. Backscheider, 2 vols (New York: Garland, 1980).

Inchbald, Elizabeth, 'Remarks on *Lover's Vows* by Elizabeth Inchbald', in *The British Theatre, or, a Collection of Plays which are Acted at the Theatres Royal Drury Lane, Covent Garden and Haymarket*, vol. 23 (London: Longman, 1808), pp. 7–9.

Inchbald, Elizabeth, 'Remarks on *The Distress't Mother* by Ambrose Phillips', in *The British Theatre, or, a Collection of Plays which are Acted at the Theatres Royal Drury Lane, Covent Garden and Haymarket*, 25 vols (London: Longman, 1808), vol. VII, pp. 3–5.

Inchbald, Elizabeth, 'To The Artist', *The Artist*, 1/14 (13 June 1807): p. 14.

Inchbald, Elizabeth, *Remarks* for *The British Theatre*, 25 vols (London: Longman, Hurst and Rees, 1806–1809).

Inchbald, Elizabeth, *Next Door Neighbours* (1791), Larpent MS 912.

Inchbald, Elizabeth, *Such Things Are* (1787), British Library, Add. MSS 27, 575.

Inglis, Ralston, *The Dramatic Writers of Scotland* (Glasgow: G.D. Mackellar, 1868).

Jameson, Anna, *Characteristics of Women: Moral, Political, and Historical*, 2 vols (London: Saunders & Otley, 1832).

Jeffrey, Francis, 'Miss Baillie's Miscellaneous Plays', *The Edinburgh Review*, 5 (1805): 421.

Jeffrey, Francis, 'Miss Baillie's *Plays on the Passions*', *The Edinburgh Review*, 2 (July 1803): 277, 280.

Jenkins, Annabel, *I'll Tell You What: The Life of Elizabeth Inchbald* (Lexington, KY: University Press of Kentucky, 2003).

Jewett, William, *Fatal Autonomy: Romantic Drama and the Rhetoric of Agency* (New York: Cornell University Press, 1997).

John of Salisbury, *Policraticus*, ed. C.J. Webb (Oxford: Oxford University Press, 1909).

Jones, Caroline M. Duncan, *Miss Mitford and Mr Harness: Records of a Friendship* (London: S.P.C.K., 1955).

Joseph, Bertram Leon, *The Tragic Actor* (London: Routledge and Kegan Paul, 1959).

Karr, David, '"Thoughts that Flash like Lightning": Thomas Holcroft, Radical Theatre, and the Production of Meaning in 1790s London', *Journal of British Studies*, 40 (2001): pp. 324–56.

Keane, Angela, *Women Writers and the English Nation* (Cambridge: Cambridge University Press, 2000).

Keats, John, *The Poems of John Keats*, ed. Jack Stillinger (London: Heinemann, 1978).

Keats, John, *The Letters of John Keats*, ed. Hyder Edward Rollins, 2 vols (Cambridge, MA: Harvard University Press, 1958).

Keats, John, *The Letters of John Keats*, ed. Maurice Buxton Forman (London: Oxford University Press, 1952).

Kelly, Gary, 'Feminine Romanticism, Masculine History, and the Founding of the Modern Liberal State', in Anne Janowitz (ed.), *Romanticism and Gender* (Woodbridge: Brewer, 1998), pp. 1–18.

Kelly, Gary, 'Last Men: Hemans and Mary Shelley in the 1820s', *Romanticism*, 3/2 (1997): 198–208.

Kemble, Frances Anne, *Records of a Girlhood* (New York: Henry Holt and Company, 1879).

Kemble, Frances Anne, *An English Tragedy. Plays* (London: Longman, Green, Longman, Roberts, and Green, 1863).

Kraakman, Dorelies, 'Reading Pornography Anew: A Critical History of Sexual Knowledge for Girls in French Erotic Fiction, 1750–1840', *Journal of the History of Sexuality*, 4/4 (1994): 517–48.

Kucich, Greg, 'Joanna Baillie and the Re-Staging of History and Gender', in Thomas C. Crochunis (ed.), *Joanna Baillie, Romantic Dramatist: Critical Essays* (London and New York: Routledge, 2004), pp. 108–29.

Kucich, Greg, 'Mary Shelley: Biographer', in Esther Schor (ed.), *The Cambridge Companion to Mary Shelley* (Cambridge: Cambridge University Press, 2003), pp. 226–41.

Kucich, Greg, 'Women's Historiography and the (dis)Embodiment of Law: Ann Yearseley, Mary Hays, Elizabeth Benger', *Wordsworth Circle*, 33/1 (2002): 3–7.

Kucich, Greg. 'Reviewing Women in British Romantic Theatre', in Catherine B. Burroughs (ed.), *Women in British Romantic Theatre: Drama, Performance and Society, 1790–1840* (Cambridge: Cambridge University Press, 2000), pp. 56–83.

Kucich, Greg, 'A Haunted Ruin: Romantic Drama, Renaissance Tradition, and the Critical Establishment', in Terence A. Hoagwood and Daniel P. Watkins (eds), *British Romantic Drama: Historical and Critical Essays* (London: Associated University Presses, 1998), pp. 56–83.

L'estrange, A.G. (ed.), *The Friendships of Mary Russell Mitford as recorded in letters from her literary correspondents*, 2 vols (London: Hurst and Blackett, 1882).

Lacy, Thomas Hailes (ed.), *Lacy's Acting edition of Plays, Dramas, Farces, Extravaganzas, etc. etc. as performed at the various theatres*, vol. 28 (London: Samuel French & Son, 1850).

Lamb, Charles, *The Works of Charles Lamb*, ed. Thomas Hutchinson, 2 vols (London: Oxford University Press, 1924).

Lamb, Charles, *On the tragedies of Shakespeare, considered with reference to their fitness for stage representation*, in *The Works of Charles and Mary Lamb*, ed. E.V. Lucas, 7 vols (London: Methuen & Co., 1903–1905), vol. 1, pp. 97–111.

Lamb, Charles, 'On the Tragedies of Shakespeare, Considered with Reference to their Fitness for Stage Representation', *The Reflector*, IV, ix (1811).

Landon, Letitia Elizabeth, 'The Female Picture Gallery', in Laman Blanchard, *Life and Literary Remains of L.E.L.*, 2 vols (London: Henry Colburn, 1841), vol. 2, pp. 81–194.

Lansdown, Richard, *Byron's Historical Drama* (Oxford: Oxford University Press, 1992).

Lawrence, Thomas, *An Address to the Students of the Royal Academy Delivered Before the General Assembly at the Annual Distribution of Prizes* (London: Clowes, 1824).

Lawson, Robb, *The Story of The Scots Stage* (Paisley: A. Gardner, 1917).

Leech, Clifford, and Craik, T.W. (eds), *The Revels: History of Drama in English*, 8 vols (London: Methuen, 1975).

Lefevere, André, 'Mother Courage's Cucumbers: Text, System and Refraction in a Theory of Literature', in Lawrence Venuti (ed.), *The Translation Studies Reader* (London: Routledge, 2002), pp. 239–55.

Lefevere, André, *Translation, Rewriting and the Manipulation of Literary Fame* (London and New York: Routledge, 1992).

Leslie, Charles Robert, and Taylor, Tom, *Life and Times of Sir Joshua Reynolds*, 2 vols (London: John Murray, 1865).

Löfgren, Hans, 'Romanticism, History, and the Individual Subject', in David Robertson (ed.), *English Studies and History* (Tampere: University of Tampere Press, 1994), pp. 89–101.

Looser, Devoney, *British Women Writers and the Writing of History: 1670–1820* (Baltimore: Johns Hopkins University Press, 2000).

Lyndsay, David, *Dramas of the Ancient World* (Edinburgh: Blackwood, 1822).

Lyndsay, David, 'Sardanapalus', in *Dramas of the Ancient World* (Edinburgh: Blackwood, 1822), pp. 127–76.

Lyndsay, David, 'The Death of Cain', in *Dramas of the Ancient World* (Edinburgh: Blackwood, 1822), pp. 209–56.

Lyndsay, David, 'The Destiny of Cain', in *Dramas of the Ancient World* (Edinburgh: Blackwood, 1822), pp. 177–208

Lyster, Gertrude (ed.), *A Family Chronicle Derived from Notes and Letters Selected by Barbarina, the Hon. Lady Grey* (London: John Murray, 1908).

Macaulay, Catharine, *The History of England, from the Accession of James I to that of the Brunswick Line*, 8 vols ([Dublin]; London: printed for J. Nourse, 1763–83).

Macauley, Elizabeth, *Mary Stuart* (London, 1823).

Macauley, Miss, *Tales of the Drama* (London: Chiswick, 1822).

Macfarland, A.S., and Sage, Abby, *Stories from Shakespeare* (London: Blackie, 1882).

Mackenzie, Henry, *Letters to Elizabeth Rose of Kilravock, on Literature, Events and People 1768–1815*, ed. Horst W. Drescher (Edinburgh and London: Oliver & Boyd, 1967).

MacMillan, Dougald, *Catalogue of the Larpent Plays in the Huntington Library* (San Marino: Huntington Library, 1939).

Macready, William Charles, *The Diaries of William Charles Macready 1833–1851*, ed. William Toynbee, 2 vols (London: Chapman & Hall, 1912).

Mahoney, Charles, 'Upstaging the Fall: *Coriolanus* and the Spectacle of Romantic Apostasy', *Studies in Romanticism*, 38 (Spring 1999): 29–50.

Maillard, Michel, 'L'antinomie du référent: Walter Scott et la poétique du roman historique', *Fabula*, 2 (1983): 65–76.

Mann, David D., and Mann, Susan Garland, with Garnier, Camille (eds), *Women Playwrights in England, Ireland and Scotland, 1660–1823* (Bloomington and Indianapolis: Indiana University Press, 1996).

Manvell, Roger, *Elizabeth Inchbald* (New York and London: University Press of America, 1987).

Marsden, Jean I. (ed.), *The Appropriation of Shakespeare: Post-Renaissance Reconstruction of the Works and the Myth* (New York: St Martin's Press, 1991).

Marshall, Jean, *Sir Harry Gaylove; or, Comedy in Embryo. In Five Acts* (Edinburgh: A. Kincaid and W. Creech, 1772).

Mathur, Om Prakash, *The Closet Drama of the Romantic Revival* (Salzburg: Institut für Anglistik und Amerikanistik, Universität Salzburg, 1978).

Maxwell, Caroline, *The Juvenile Edition of Shakespeare; adapted to the capacities of youth* (London, 1828).

McGann, Jerome, *The Romantic Ideology: A Critical Investigation* (Chicago and London: University of Chicago Press, 1983).

McMillan, Dorothy, '"Dr." Baillie', in Richard Cronin (ed.), *1798: The Year of the Lyrical Ballads* (Houndmills and London: Macmillan Press, 1998), pp. 68–92.

Mee, Jon, 'Examples of Safe Printing: Censorship and Radical Literature in the 1790s', in Nigel Smith (ed.), *Literature and Censorship* (Cambridge: DS Brewer, 1993), pp. 81–95.

Mellor, Anne K., *Mothers of the Nation: Women's Political Writing in England, 1780–1830* (Bloomington: Indiana University Press, 2000).

Mellor, Anne K., 'Joanna Baillie and the Counter-Public Sphere', *Studies in Romanticism*, 33 (1994): 560–67.

Mellor, Anne K., *Romanticism & Gender* (New York and London: Routledge, 1993).

Mellor, Anne K. (ed.), *Romanticism and Feminism* (Bloomington: Indiana University Press, 1988).

Mitford, Mary Rusell, *Letters of Mary Russell Mitford: Second Series*, ed. Henry Chorley, 2 vols (London: Richard Bentley & Son, 1872).

Mitford, Mary Russell, *Recollections of a Literary Life; or, Books, Places, and People*, 3 vols (London: Richard Bentley, 1852).

Mitford, Mary Russell, *Foscari: A Tragedy* (London: G.B. Whittaker, 1826).

Mitford, Mary Russell, *Rienzi: A Tragedy* (London: Cumberland, 1828).

Moody, Jane, *Illegitimate Theatre in London, 1770–1830* (Cambridge: Cambridge University Press, 2000).

Moody, Jane, '"Fine Word, legitimate!"': Towards a Theatrical History of Romanticism', in *Texas Studies in Literature and Language*, 38.3/4 (1996): 223–44.

Moore, Thomas, *Life of Lord Byron: With his Letters and Journals. In Six Volumes*, vol. V (London, John Murray, 1854).

More, Hannah, *Percy, a Tragedy as it is acted at the Theatre Royal in Covent Garden* (London: T. Cadell, 1778).

Moreux, F., *Elizabeth Inchbald et la Révendication Féminine au Dix-Huitième Siècle* (Lille: Universitè de Lille III, 1974).

Morgan, Edwin, 'Scottish Drama: An Overview', *ScotLit*, 20 (Spring 1999), at: http://www.arts.gla.ac.uk/ScotLit/ASLS/Scottishdrama.html, accessed October 2009.

Morgan, Lady (Sydney), *Woman and Her Master*, 2 vols (Westport, CT, 1976).

Morgan, Stewart S., 'The Damning of Holcroft's *Knave or Not?* and O'Keeffe's *She's Eloped*', *Huntingdon Library Quarterly* 22/1 (November 1958): 51–62.

Moulton, Ian Frederick, *Before Pornography: Erotic Writing in Early Modern England* (Oxford: Oxford University Press, 2000).

Mudge, Bradford K., 'Romanticism, Materialism, and the Origins of Pornography', *Romanticism on the Net*, 23 (August 2001), at: http://users.ox.ac.uk-scat0385/23mudge.html, accessed August 2004.

Neville-Sington, Pamela, *Fanny Trollope: The Life and Adventures of a Clever Woman* (London: Viking, 1997).

Newey, Katherine, 'Women and History on the Romantic Stage: More, Yearsley, Burney Mitford', in Catherine B. Burroughs (ed.), *Women in British Romantic Theatre: Drama, Performance and Society, 1790–1840* (Cambridge: Cambridge University Press, 2000), pp. 79–101.

Nicoll, Allardyce, *A History of English Drama 1660–1900*, 6 vols (Cambridge: Cambridge University Press, 1955).

Novy, Marianne (ed.), *Women's Revisions of Shakespeare* (Urbana and Chicago: University of Illinois Press, 1990).

O'Brien, Karen, *Narratives of Enlightenment: Cosmopolitan History from Voltaire to Gibbon* (Cambridge: Cambridge University Press, 1997).

O'Quinn, Daniel, *Staging Governance: Theatrical Imperialism in London, 1770–1800* (Baltimore: Johns Hopkins University Press, 2005).

O'Quinn, Daniel, 'Scissors and Needles: Inchbald's *Wives as They Were, Maids as They Are* and the Governance of Sexual Exchange', *Theatre Journal*, 51 (Summer 1999): 105–25.

Otway, Thomas, *Venice Preserv'd or, A Plot Discovered*, in *The Works of Thomas Otway*, ed. J.C. Ghosh, 2 vols (Oxford: Clarendon Press, 1932), vol. 1, pp. 197–289.

Otway, Thomas, *Venice Preserved or, A Plot Discovered* (London: W. Lowndes, 1790).

Pascoe, J., *Romantic Theatricality: Gender, Poetry and Consciousness in the Romantic Age* (Ithaca, NY, and London: Cornell University Press, 1997).

Paulson, Ronald, *Emblem and Expression: Meaning in English Art of the Eighteenth Century* (London: Thames & Hudson, 1975).

Peake, Richard Brinsley, *Memoirs of the Colman Family*, 2 vols (London: R. Bentley, 1841).

Peakman, Julie, 'Initiation, Defloration, and Flagellation: Sexual Propensities in *Memoirs of a Woman of Pleasure*', in Patsy S. Fowler and Alan Jackson (eds), *Launching Fanny Hill: Essays on the Novel and Its Influences* (New York: AMS Press, 2003), pp. 153–72.

Peakman, Julie, *Mighty Lewd Books: The Development of Pornography in Eighteenth-Century England* (Basingstoke and New York: Palgrave Macmillan, 2003).

Pearson, Jacqueline, 'Crushing the Convent and the Dread Bastille: The Anglo-Saxons, Revolution and Gender in Women's Plays of the 1790s', in Donald Scragg and Carole Weinberg (eds), *Literary Appropriations of the Anglo-Saxons from the Thirteenth to the Twentieth Century* (Cambridge: Cambridge University Press, 2000), pp. 122–37.

Pearson, Jacqueline, *Women's Reading in Britain, 1750–1835* (Cambridge: Cambridge University Press, 1999).

Perry, Ruth, 'Colonizing the Breast: Sexuality and Maternity in Eighteenth-Century England', in John C. Fout (ed.), *Forbidden History: The State, Society, and the Regulation of Sexuality in Modern Europe* (Chicago and London: University of Chicago Press, 1992), pp. 107–37.

Phillips, Mark Salber, *Society and Sentiment: Genres of Historical Writing in Britain, 1740–1820* (Princeton, NJ: Princeton University Press, 2000).

Philp, Mark, *Godwin's Political Justice* (London: Duckworth, 1986).

Pietropoli, Cecilia, 'The Story of the Foscaris, a Drama for Two Playwrights: Mary Mitford and Lord Byron', in Lilla Maria Crisafulli and Pietropoli (eds), *The Languages of British Romanticism* (Berne and Oxford: Peter Lang, 2008), pp. 115–26.

Pietropoli, Cecilia, 'Il Medioevo nel romanzo storico europeo', in Piero Boitani, Mario Mancini and Alberto Varvaro (eds), *Lo spazio letterario del Medioevo, L'attualizzazione del testo*, 5 vols (Rome: Salerno editore, 2004), vol. 4, pp. 39–65.

Pix, Mary, *The Spanish Wives*, in Katharine M. Rogers (ed.), *The Meridian Anthology of Restoration and Eighteenth-Century Plays by Women* (New York: Penguin Books, 1994), pp. 131–84.

Planché, James Robinson, *The Recollections and Reflections of J.R. Planché, A Professional Autobiography*, 2 vols (London, 1872).

Plumptre, A., 'Translator's Preface to *The Natural Son*', at: http://www.etang.umontreal.ca/bwp/1800/essays/plumptre_natural_preface.html, accessed October 2009.

Pointon, Marcia R., *Hanging the Head: Portraiture and Social Formation in Eighteenth-Century England* (New Haven, CT: Yale University Press, 1993).

Porter, Roy, 'A Touch of Danger: The Man-Midwife as Sexual Predator', in G.S. Rousseau and Porter (eds), *Sexual Underworlds of the Enlightenment* (Chapel Hill: University of North Carolina Press, 1988), pp. 206–32.

Purinton, Marjean D., 'Science Fiction and Techno-Gothic Drama: Romantic Playwrights Joanna Baillie and Jane Scott', *Romanticism on the Net*, 21 (February 2001), at: http://www.erudit.org/revue/ron/2001/v/n21/005968ar.html, accessed November 2009.

Purinton, Marjean D., 'Revising Romanticism by Inscripting Women Playwrights', *Romanticism On the Net*, 12 (November 1998), at: http://www.erudit.org/revue/ron/1998/v/n12/005822ar.html, accessed November 1998.

Purinton, Marjean D., *Romantic Ideology Unmasked: The Mentally Constructed Tyrannies in Dramas of William Wordsworth, Lord Byron, P.B. Shelley and Joanna Baillie* (Newark: University of Delaware Press, 1994).

Puschmann-Nalenz, Barbara, 'Using Shakespeare? The Appropriation of *Coriolanus* and *Henry V* in John Philip Kemble's 1789 Productions', *Shakespeare Yearbook*, 5 (1995): 219–32.

Ramsay, Thomas, *The Life and Literary Remains of Barbara Hofland* (London: W.J. Cleaver, 1849).

Rand, Erica, 'Diderot and Girl-Group Erotics', *18th-Century Studies*, 25/4 (1992): 495–516.

Ranger, Paul, *'Terror and Pity Reign in Every Breast': Gothic Drama in the London Patent Theatres, 1750–1820* (London: The Society for Theatre Research, 1991).

Rannie, David Watson, *Wordsworth and his Circle* (London: Methuen & Co., 1907).

Reiman, Donald H. (ed.), *A Series of Plays in which it is attempted to delineate the stronger passions of the mind, 1798–1812*, 3 vols (New York and London: Garland, 1977).

Rennie, Eliza, *Traits of Character; Being Twenty-Five Years Literary and Personal Recollections, by a Contemporary*, 2 vols (London: Hurst & Blackett, 1860).

Richardson, Alan, *A Mental Theatre, Poetic Drama and Consciousness in the Romantic Age* (Philadelphia: Pennsylvania University Press, 1988).

Riley, Denise, 'Does a Sex have a History?', in Joan Wallach Scott (ed.), *Feminism and History* (Oxford: Oxford University Press, 1996), pp. 7–33.

Ripley, John, *Coriolanus on Stage in England and America, 1609–1994* (Madison, NJ: Fairleigh Dickinson University Press, 1998).

Robinson, Henry Crabb, *Henry Crabb Robinson on Books and their Writers*, ed. Edith J. Morley, 2 vols (London: J.M. Dent & Sons, 1938).

Rogers, Katharine M. (ed.), *The Meridian Anthology of Restoration and Eighteenth-Century Plays by Women* (New York: Meridian, 1994).

Rogers, Katharine M., 'Britain's First Woman Drama Critic: Elizabeth Inchbald', in A.M. Schofield and C. Macheski (eds), *Curtain Calls: British and American*

Women and the Theater (Athens, OH: Ohio University Press, 1991), pp. 277–90.

Rogers, Katharine, 'Introduction', in Rogers (ed.), *The Meridian Anthology of Restoration and Eighteenth-Century Plays by Women* (New York: Meridian, 1994), pp. vii–xviii.

Ross, Marlon B., *The Contours of Masculine Desire: Romanticism and the Rise of Women's Poetry* (New York and Oxford: Oxford University Press, 1989).

Rostron, David, 'Contemporary Political Comment in Four of J.P. Kemble's Shakespearean Productions', *Theatre Research/Researches Theatrales*, 12 (1972): 113–19.

Rousseau, G.S., and Porter, Roy (eds), *Sexual Underworlds of the Enlightenment* (Chapel Hill: University of North Carolina Press, 1988).

Rubik, Margarete, *Early Women Dramatists 1550–1800* (Basingstoke: Macmillan, 1998).

Russell, Gillian, and Tuite, Clara, 'Introducing Romantic Sociability', in Russell and Tuite (eds), *Romantic Sociability: Social Networks and Literary Culture in Britain, 1770–1840* (Cambridge: Cambridge University Press, 2002), pp. 108–29.

Saglia, Diego, '"The Talking Demon": Liberty and Liberal Ideologies on the 1820s British Stage', *Nineteenth-Century Contexts*, 28/4 (December 2006): 347–77.

Saglia, Diego, 'Public and Private in Women's Romantic Poetry: Spaces, Gender, Genre in Mary Russell Mitford's *Blanch*', *Women's Writing*, 5 (1998): 405–19.

Schoch, Richard W., '"We Do Nothing but Enact History": Thomas Carlyle Stages the Past', *Nineteenth-Century Literature*, 54/1 (June 1999): 27–52.

Schofield, Mary Anne, and Macheski, Cecilia (eds), *Curtain Calls: British and American Women and the Theater, 1660–1820* (Athens, OH: Ohio University Press, 1991).

Scolnicov, Hanna, *Woman's Theatrical Space* (Cambridge: Cambridge University Press, 1994).

Scott, Joan Wallach (ed.), *Feminism and History* (Oxford: Oxford University Press, 1996).

Scott, Walter, *Essays on the Drama: Essays in Chivalry, Romance, and the Drama* (London: Chandos, 1868).

Scott, Walter, *Familiar Letters*, ed. David Douglas (Edinburgh: Douglas, 1894).

Scott, Walter, *Ivanhoe*, ed. A.N. Wilson (Harmondsworth: Penguin, 1984).

Scullion, Adrienne, 'Some Women of the Nineteenth-Century Scottish Theatre: Joanna Baillie, Frances Wright and Helen MacGregor', in Douglas Gifford and Dorothy McMillan (eds), *A History of Scottish Women's Writing* (Edinburgh: Edinburgh University Press, 1997), pp. 158–78.

Scullion, Adrienne (ed.), *Female Playwrights of the Nineteenth Century* (London: Dent, 1996).

Seward, Anna, *Letters of Anna Seward: Written between the Years 1784 and 1807*, 6 vols (Edinburgh and London: Archibald Constable, 1811).

Shakespeare, William, *Twelfth Night*, ed. Keir Elam (London: Arden Shakespeare, 2008).

Shakespeare, William, *A Midsummer Night's Dream*, ed. Harold F. Brooks (London: Methuen, 1983).

Shakespeare, William, *The Tragedy of Coriolanus*, ed. Reuben Brower (New York: New American Library, 1966).

Shakespeare William, *The Winter's Tale*, ed. J.H.P. Pafford (London: Methuen, 1963).

Shapiro, Ann-Louise, *Feminists Revision History* (New Brunswick: Rutgers University Press, 1994).

Sharpe, Lesley, *Friedrich Schiller: Drama, Thought and Politics* (Cambridge: Cambridge University Press, 1991).

Shelley, Mary, *Frankenstein or the Modern Prometheus*, in *The Novels and Selected Works of Mary Shelley*, ed. Nora Crook, 8 vols (London: William Pickering, 1996), vol. 1.

Shelley, P.B., *Shelley's Poetry and Prose*, eds Donald H. Reiman and Neil Fraistat (New York: W.W. Norton, 2002).

Shinagel, Michael, '*Memoirs of a Woman of Pleasure*: Pornography and the Mid-Eighteenth-Century English Novel', in Paul J. Korshin (ed.), *Studies in Change and Revolution: Aspects of English Intellectual History, 1640–1800* (Menston: Scolar Press, 1972), pp. 10–36.

Sichel, Walter, *Sheridan*, 2 vols (London: Constable & Co., 1909).

Siddons, Sarah Kemble, *The Reminiscences of Sarah Kemble Siddons* (1831), ed. William Van Lennep (Cambridge, MA: Widener Library, 1942).

Slagle, Judith Bailey, *Joanna Baillie: A Literary Life* (Cranbury, NJ: Fairleigh Dickinson University Press; London: Associated University Presses, 2002).

Slagle, Judith Bailey (ed.), *The Collected Letters of Joanna Baillie*, 2 vols (Madison, NJ: Fairleigh Dickinson University Press; London: Associated University Presses, 1999).

Smith, Bonnie, *The Gender of History: Men, Women, and Historical Practice* (Cambridge, MA: Harvard University Press, 1998).

Stallbaumer, Virgil R., 'Thomas Holcroft: A Satirist in the Stream of Sentimentalism', *English Literary History*, 3 (1936): pp. 31–62.

Steiner, George, *After Babel: Aspects of Language and Translation* (Oxford: Oxford University Press, 1975).

Steiner, George, *The Death of Tragedy* (New York: Knopf, 1961).

Stephen, Leslie, and Lee, Sidney (eds), *Dictionary of National Biography*, 22 vols (London: Smith, Elder, & Co., 1908–1909).

Sulloway, Alison, *Jane Austen and the Province of Womanhood* (Philadelphia: University of Pennsylvania Press, 1989).

Taylor, Gary, *Reinventing Shakespeare: A Cultural History from the Restoration to the Present* (London: Vintage, 1991).

Taylor, George, *The French Revolution and the London Stage, 1789–1805* (Cambridge: Cambridge University Press, 2000).

Teltscher, Kate, *India Inscribed: European and British Writing on India 1600–1800* (Delhi: Oxford University Press, 1995).

Thirlwal, T., *Against the Revival of Scenic Exibitions and Interludes at the Royality: Containing Remarks on Pizarro, the Stranger and John Bull* (London, 1803).

Thomson, A., *Sermons on Theatrical Amusements* (London, 1817).

Thompson, Sharon, *Going All the Way: Teenage Girls' Tales of Sex, Romance and Pregnancy* (New York: Hill and Wang, 1995).

Tobin, Terence, *Plays by Scots, 1660–1800* (Iowa City: University of Iowa Press, 1974).

Toepfer, Karl, *Theatre, Aristocracy, and Pornocracy: The Orgy Calculus* (New York: PAJ Publications, 1991).

Trumbach, Randolph, 'Modern Prostitution and Gender in Fanny Hill: Libertine and Domesticated Fantasy', in G.S. Rousseau and Roy Porter (eds), *Sexual Underworlds of the Enlightenment* (Chapel Hill: University of North Carolina Press, 1988), pp. 69–85.

Venuti, Lawrence, 'Translation, Community, Utopia', in Venuti (ed.), *The Translation Studies Reader* (New York: Routledge, 2004).

Vermeer, Hans J., 'Skopos and Commission in Translational Action', trans. Andrew Chesterman, in Lawrence Venuti (ed.), *The Translation Studies Reader* (London: Routledge, 2002), pp. 227–32.

Vickery, Amanda, *The Gentleman's Daughter: Women's Lives in Georgian England* (New Haven, CT, and London: Yale University Press, 1998).

Wake, Ann M. Frank, 'Women in the Active Voice: Recovering Female History in Mary Shelley's *Valperga* and *Perkin Warbeck*', in Syndy M. Conger, Frederick S. Frank, Gregory O'Dea and Jennifer Yocum (eds), *Iconoclastic Departures. Mary Shelley after Frankenstein: Essays in Honor of the Bicentenary of Mary Shelley's Birth* (Cranbury, NJ, London and Mississauga, ON: Associated University Presses, 1997), pp. 235–59.

Wallace, Eglantine, *The Whim* (Margate: W. Epps, 1795).

Wallace, Eglantine, *The Ton; or the Follies of Fashion. A Comedy as it was acted at the Theatre Royal, Covent Garden* (London, 1788).

Wallace, Eglantine, *Diamond Cut Diamond; A Comedy in Two Acts, Translated from the French of Guerre Ouverte, ou Ruse Contre Ruse* (London: J. Debrett, 1787).

Wark, Robert R., *Ten British Pictures 1740–1840* (San Marino, CA: The Huntington Library, 1971).

Warrack, Alexander, *A Scots Dialect Dictionary, Comprising the Words in Use from the Latter Part of the Seventeenth Century to the Present Day* (London: W. & R. Chambers, 1911).

Waters, Mary A., *British Women Writers and the Profession of Literary Criticism, 1789–1832* (Houndmills and Basingstoke: Palgrave Macmillan, 2004).

Watkins, Daniel P., *A Materialist Critique of English Romantic Drama* (Gainesville: University Press of Florida, 1993).

Watkins, Daniel P., 'Class, Gender and Social Motion in Joanna Baillie's *De Monfort*', *The Wordsworth Circle*, 23/2 (Spring 1992): 97–116.

Watson, Vera, *Mary Russell Mitford* (London: Evans Brothers, 1949).

Webb, R.K., 'Rational Piety', in Knud Haakonssen (ed.), *Enlightenment and Religion: Rational Dissent in Eighteenth-Century Britain* (Cambridge: Cambridge University Press, 1996).

West, Mrs. (Jane), *Poems and Plays*, 4 vols (London: Longman, 1799).

West, Shearer, 'Performance and Display: The Actress on Stage at the Royal Academy', in Christopher Balme, Robert Erenstein and Cesare Molinari (eds), *European Theatre Iconography* (Rome: Bulzoni, 2002), pp. 261–73.

West, Shearer, *The Image of the Actor: Verbal and Visual Representation in the Age of Garrick and Kemble* (London: Pinter, 1991).

White, Daniel E., '"The Joineriana": Anna Barbauld, the Aikin Family Circle, and the Dissenting Public Sphere', *Eighteenth-Century Studies*, 32/4 (1999): 511–33.

Whitley, William Thomas, *Artists and Their Friends in England 1700–1799*, 2 vols (London and Boston: Medici Society, 1928).

Williams, D.E., *The Life and Correspondence of Thomas Lawrence*, 2 vols (London: Colburn and Bentley, 1831).

Williams, Linda (ed.), *Porn Studies* (Durham, NC, and London: Duke University Press, 2004).

Wilson, Carol Shiner, and Haefner, Joel (eds), *Re-visioning Romanticism: British Women Writers 1776–1837* (Philadelphia: University of Pennsylvania Press, 1994).

Wilson, Michael S., '*Ut Pictura Tragoedia*: An Extrinsic Approach to British NeoClassic and Romantic Theatre', *Theatre Research International*, 12 (1987): pp. 201–20.

Wolf, Naomi, *Promiscuities: The Secret Struggle for Womanhood* (New York: The Ballantine Publishing Group, 1997).

Wollstonecraft, Mary, *Maria, or the Wrongs of Woman*, ed. Gary Kelly (Oxford: Oxford University Press, 1980).

Woolf, Virginia, *A Room of One's Own* and *Three Guineas* (London: Chatto and Windus, 1984).

Wordsworth, William, *The White Doe of Rylstone; or The Fate of the Nortons*, ed. Kristine Dugas (Ithaca, NY, and London: Cornell University Press, 1988).

Wright, Frances, 'Advertisement', *Altorf* (London, 1822).

Wright, Frances, 'Preface', *Altorf* (Philadelphia: M. Carey & Son, 1819).

Wykes, David L., 'The Contribution of the Dissenting Academy to the Emergence of Rational Dissent', in Knud Haakonssen (ed.), *Enlightenment and Religion: Rational Dissent in Eighteenth-Century Britain* (Cambridge: Cambridge University Press, 1996), pp. 99–139.

Yearsley, Ann, *Earl Goodwin, an Historical Play* (London: G.G.J. and J. Robinson, 1791).

Z., 'Cockney School of Poetry. No IV', *Blackwood's Edinburgh Magazine*, 3 (August 1818): 519–20.

Z., 'Plays, by Joanna Baillie', *The Imperial Review; or London and Dublin Literary Journal*, 1 (1804): 338.

Index

www.ingramcontent.com/pod-product-compliance
Ingram Content Group UK Ltd.
Pitfield, Milton Keynes, MK11 3LW, UK
UKHW020359010325
455677UK00021B/535